NEWTON FORSTER

OR

THE MERCHANT SERVICE

BY

CAPTAIN FREDERICK MARRYAT

With Introduction by

W. L. COURTNEY, M. A., LL. D.

WILDSIDE PRESS

INTRODUCTION

AT the time when Captain Marryat wrote "Newton Forster" he was in the midst of literary and journalistic engage-
ments in London. From 1830 onwards he was writing in
the *Metropolitan Magazine,* and had besides received an offer
from Bentley to become an editor on his own account. The
terms which he proposed proved that he already knew something of the value of his services. In the case of this new
venture, a nautical magazine, which was to be framed on the
lines of the *United Service Journal,* Captain Marryat declared
that he must be despotic as the sole condition of ultimate
success, that he was to have a sub-editor who was a nautical
man, and that his remuneration was to be £400 per annum
until the end of the first year, afterwards rising, if the work
were successful, to £600 per annum. Moreover, he added
that he had reason to expect a rather better offer from
another quarter, which he would certainly accept if it seemed
profitable. The second proposal was the editorship of the
Metropolitan Magazine itself, which he took in 1832, the very
year which saw the publication of "Newton Forster," three
volumes, post octavo. So far as the sub-editorship was concerned he obtained his wish, for the gentleman who helped
him with the *Metropolitan* was Mr. E. Howard, the real author
of "Rattlin the Reefer," which was only edited by Captain
Marryat. Inasmuch as in some senses he was responsible for
the issue, it is often included amongst Marryat's works; but
the real facts will be laid bare, with the help of information
supplied by some of Mr. Howard's relatives, when "Rattlin
the Reefer" is published in this edition.

Whether through inexperience of the conditions of the
writing trade, or through a congenital intolerance of all
adverse comment, Captain Marryat is still smarting under the
treatment of his critics. The opening pages of "Newton
Forster; or, the Merchant Service," bear testimony to the

fact. In the very first chapter we come across the following passage: "Gracious Heaven, what a revengeful feeling is there in the exclamation, 'Oh that mine adversary had written a book!' To be snarled at and bow-wowed at by those who find fault because their intellect is not sufficient to enable them to appreciate! Authors, take my resolution, which is, never to show your face until your work has passed through the ordeal of the reviews. Keep your room for a month after your literary labour. Reviews are like .Jesuit father-confessors, guiding the opinions of the multitude, who blindly follow the suggestions of those to whom they may have entrusted their literary consciences. If your work is denounced and damned, still you will be the gainer; for is it not better to be released at once from your sufferings by one blow from the paw of a tiger, than to be worried piecemeal by creatures who have all the will but not the power to inflict a *coup de grace?*" Probably when he wrote this passage, Captain Marryat was more than ordinarily troubled by the letters of correspondents. Apparently he found the conduct of the *Metropolitan Magazine* no very easy task. Thomas Moore once wrote to him, insisting, with a fervent declaration of proprietorial rights, that he must see the proofs of his work, and must make final arrangements as to his financial recompense. It is also clear that many people had objected to the termination of "The King's Own," published in 1830, which had defrauded its readers of the customary sound of marriage bells. When Marryat had brought the story of "Newton Forster" to a conclusion with a double marriage, he writes almost petulantly this brief epilogue: "And now, most arbitrary public, I consider that I have made the *amende honorable,* and that we are quits; for if you were minus a happy marriage in the last work, you have a couple to indemnify you in the present." There are one or two other personal references in "Newton Forster" which are interesting. Evidently some one had told him that he was not very methodical in the treatment of his stories. Here is his answer in the first chapter: "That such preparation ought to be made I will not deny; but were I to attempt an adherence to these rules, the public would never be troubled with any production of mine. It would be too tedious a journey in prospective for my wayward intellect; and if I calculated stages before I ordered my horses, I should abandon the attempt and remain quietly at home. . . . I never have made any arrangement of plot when I commenced a work of fiction, and often finish a chapter without having the slightest idea of what materials the ensuing one is to be constructed. . . . So now, reader, you may understand that I continue to write, as Tony Lumpkin says, not to please my good-natured friends, but 'because I can't bear to disappoint myself;' for that which I commenced as an amusement and continued as a drudgery, has ended in becoming a confirmed habit." Perhaps another candid friend had told him that his was not a soaring and ambitious genius. Here is his comment in Chapter xl. : "Thank Heaven, I have not been entrusted with one of those thorough-bred, snorting, champion, foaming sort of intellects which run away with Common Sense, who is jerked from his saddle at the beginning of its wild career. Mine is a good, steady, useful hack, who trots along the high-road of life, keeping on his own side, and only stumbling a little now and then when I happen to be careless—ambitious only to arrive safely at the end of his journey, not to pass by others." Marryat's daughter tells us that his family were often asked whether he was bright and amusing at home. This is what he says of himself : "I am a grave, heavy man, with my finger continually laid along my temple, seldom speaking unless spoken to ; and when ladies talk I never open my mouth. The consequence is that sometimes, when there is a succession of company, I do not speak for a week. Moreover, I am married, with five small children, and now all I look forward to, and all I covet, is to live in peace and die in my bed." Despite these and other passages of self-criticism, "Newton Forster," at its first appearance in 1832, was very well received. A complimentary notice was published in the *Westminster Review* (xvi. 390–4); the *Athenæum* said of the book that "those who read for amusement will be instructed, and those who wish to be instructed will be amused. We have been both ;" while the *London Literary Gazette* declared that the writer of this novel was "one of the most original, striking, and powerful authors of the day."

"Newton Forster," to those who read it with some knowledge of Marryat's best work, will certainly not be placed in the first rank. The characterisation is by no means as firm as we shall find it later, and none perhaps of the personages

of the tale live in our memory. Newton Forster, himself,
is a very different hero from Frank Mildmay ; a most exem-
plary youth, who supports his father, is kind to his sharp-
tongued mother, rises steadily through the branches of his
profession, and ends by marrying the girl of his choice.
There is some humour about the subordinate members of the
dramatis personæ, but not nearly so much as we shall encounter
in subsequent novels.   Perhaps Captain Marryat has not yet
discovered for himself the capital material which can be found
among the mates, midshipmen, and captains of the navy.
There is more construction in the book than in " Frank
Mildmay " ; and the story begins excellently with the washing
ashore of an apparently fatherless and motherless babe, whose
identity is only revealed in the concluding pages.   Unfortunately, however, she is not, as we are led to expect, the
heroine, nor does she marry the hero.   It takes some time,
in fact, before the story is well on its legs, although it must
certainly be added that the interest is well sustained to the
end.   Oddly enough, there are few pages of spirited description until we reach Chapters xlvii. and xlix.   There the
combat between the East Indiaman, the *Windsor Castle*, and
the French corvette commanded by Surcœuf, supplemented
by the later struggle with the pirates, is described with all
Marryat's customary fire and naturalness.

The fact is, perhaps, that the author is at the stage in
which he thinks he has a mission to fulfil.   His head is full
of certain topics on which he believes that the ordinary
public opinion is wrong.   Thus he introduces a long account
of some of the happier conditions of slavery in the West
Indies, in Chapters xiv. and xv.   He discusses duelling in
Chapter xxxv. ; he interposes a few remarks on the real value
of Madeira as compared with sherry ; above all, he is wroth
with those merchants who obtained possession of India and
called themselves the East India Company.   All the earlier
paragraphs in Chapter xl. are occupied with a denunciation
of old " John Company," conceived and written in much the
same spirit as that in which some of the more furious of its
critics at present denounce the Chartered Company in South
Africa.

W. L. C.

April 1896.

NEWTON FORSTER

CHAPTER I

"And what is this new book the whole world makes such a rout about?—Oh! 'tis out of all plumb, my lord—quite an irregular thing; not one of the angles at the four corners was a right angle. I had my rule and compasses, my lord, in my pocket.—Excellent critic!

"Grant me patience, just Heaven! Of all the cants which are canted in this canting world—though the cant of hypocrites may be the worst, the cant of criticism is the most tormenting."
—STERNE.

WHAT authors in general may feel upon the subject I know not, but I have discovered, since I so rashly took up my pen, that there are three portions of a novel which are extremely difficult to arrange to the satisfaction of a fastidious public.

The first is the beginning, the second the middle, and the third is the end.

The painter who, in times of yore, exposed his canvas to universal criticism, and found, to his mortification, that there was not a particle of his composition which had not been pronounced defective by one pseudo-critic or another, did not receive severer castigation than I have experienced from the unsolicited remarks of "d—d good-natured friends."

"I like your first and second volume," said a tall, long-chinned, short-sighted blue, dressed in yellow, peering into my face as if her eyes were magnifying glasses, and she was obtaining the true focus of vision; "but you fall off in your last, which is all about that nasty line-of-battle ship."

1.   A

"I don't like your plot, sir," bawls out, in a stentorian voice, an elderly gentleman; "I don't like your plot, sir," repeated he, with an air of authority, which he had long assumed from supposing, because people would not be at the trouble of contradicting his opinions, that they were incontrovertible— "there is nothing but death."

"Death, my dear sir," replied I, as if I was hailing the look-out man at the mast-head, and hoping to soften him with my intentional bull; "is not death, sir, a true picture of human life?"

"Ay, ay," growled he, either not hearing or not taking; "it's all very well, but—there's too much killing in it."

"In a novel, sir, killing's no murder, you surely will admit; and you must also allow something for professional feeling—''tis my occupation;' and after five-and-twenty years of constant practice, whether I wield the sword or the pen, the force of habit——"

"It won't do, sir," interrupted he; "the public don't like it. Otherwise," continued this hypercritic, softening a little, "some of the chapters are amusing, and, on the whole, it may be said to be rather—that is—not unpleasantly written."

"I like your first and third volumes, but not your second," squeaked out something intended to have been a woman, with shoulder-blades and collar-bones, as De Ville would say, most strongly developed.

"Well, now, I don't exactly agree with you, my dear Miss Pegoo; I think the second and third volumes are by far the most readable," exclaimed another thing, perched upon a chair, with her feet dangling half-way between her seat and the carpet.

"If I might presume upon my long standing in the service, Captain ——," said a pompous general officer, whose back appeared to have been *fished* with the kitchen poker—"if I might venture to offer you advice," continued he, leading me paternally by the arm a little on one side, "it would be, not again to attempt a defence of smuggling: I consider, sir, that as an officer in his Majesty's service, you have strangely committed yourself."

"It is not my defence, sir: they are the arguments of a smuggler."

"You wrote the book, sir," replied he sharply; "I can assure you that I should not be surprised if the Admiralty took notice of it."

"Indeed, sir," replied I, with assumed alarm.

I received no answer, except a most significant nod of the head, as he walked away.

But I have not yet arrived at the climax, which made me inclined to exclaim, with the expiring Lion in the fable——

A midshipman —yes, reader, a midshipman — who had formerly belonged to my ship, and had trembled at my frown, ranged up alongside of me, and with a supercilious air, observed—

"I have read your book, and—there are one or two good things in it."

Hear this, admirals and captains on half-pay! hear this, port-admirals and captains afloat! I have often heard that the service was deteriorating, going to the devil, but I never became a convert to the opinion before.

Gracious Heaven! what a revengeful feeling is there in the exclamation, "O that mine adversary had written a book!" To be snarled at, and bow-wowed at, in this manner, by those who find fault because their intellect is not sufficient to enable them to appreciate! Authors, take my resolution, which is, never to show your face until your work has passed through the ordeal of the Reviews. Keep your room for a month after your literary labour. Reviews are like Jesuit father-confessors, guiding the opinions of the multitude, who blindly follow the suggestions of those to whom they may have entrusted their literary consciences. If your work is denounced and damned, still you will be the gainer; for is it not better to be released at once from your sufferings by one blow from the paw of a tiger, than to be worried piecemeal by creatures who have all the will, but not the power, to inflict a *coup de grâce*?

The author of "Cloudesley," enumerating the qualifications necessary to a writer of fiction, observes, "When he introduces his ideal personage to the public, he enters upon his task with a preconception of the qualities that belong to this being, the principle of his actions, and its necessary concomitants," &c., &c. That such preparation ought to be made, I will not deny;

3

but were I to attempt an adherence to these rules, the public would never be troubled with any production of mine. It would be too tedious a journey in prospective for my wayward intellect; and if I calculated stages before I ordered my horses, I should abandon the attempt, and remain quietly at home. Mine is not a journey of that methodical description; on the contrary, it is a ramble hand-in-hand with Fancy, with a light heart and a lighter baggage; for my whole wallet, when I set off, contains but one single idea—but ideas are hermaphrodite, and these creatures of the brain are most prolific. To speak more intelligibly, I never have made any arrangement of plot when I commenced a work of fiction, and often finish a chapter without having the slightest idea of what materials the ensuing one is to be constructed. At times I feel so tired that I throw down the pen in despair; but it is soon taken up again. Like a pigmy Antæus, it seems to have imbibed fresh vigour from its prostration.

I remember when the "King's Own" was finished, I was as happy as a pedestrian who had accomplished his thousand miles in a thousand hours. My voluntary slavery was over, and I was emancipated. Where was I then? I recollect; within two days' sail of the Lizard, returning home, after a six weeks' cruise to discover a rock in the Atlantic, which never existed except in the terrified or intoxicated noddle of some master of a merchant vessel. It was about half-past five in the evening, and I was alone in my after-cabin, quite alone, as the captain of a man-of-war must be, even when in presence of his ship's company. If being sent to sea has been pronounced by the officers and men to be *transportation*, being the captain of the ship may truly be designated as *solitary confinement*.

I could not send for any one to whom I could impart the intelligence — there was no one whom I could expect to sympathise with me, or to whom I could pour out the abundance of my joy; for that the service prohibited. What could I do? Why, I could dance; so I sprang from my chair, and singing the tune, commenced a quadrille movement—"Tal de ral la, tal de ral la, lity, lity, lity liddle-um, tal de ral la tal——"

"Three bells, sir," cried the first lieutenant, who had opened my door unperceived by me, and showed evident

4

surprise at my motions. "Shall we beat to quarters?"—
"Certainly, Mr. B——," replied I, and he disappeared. But
this interruption produced only a temporary cessation: I was
in the height of "Cavalier seul," when his head popped into
the cabin—

"All present and sober, sir," reported he, with a demure
smile.

"Except the captain, I presume you are thinking," replied I.

"Oh! no, indeed, sir; I observed that you were very
merry."

"I am, Mr. B——, but not with wine; mine is a sort of
intellectual intoxication not provided for in the Articles of
War."

"A what! sir?"

"Oh! something that you'll never get drunk upon, as you
never look into a book—beat a retreat."

"Ay, ay, sir," replied the first lieutenant; and he disappeared.

And I also beat a retreat to my sofa; and as I threw myself upon it, mentally vowed that, for two months at the
least, I never would take up a pen. But we seldom make
a vow which we do not eventually break; and the reason
is obvious. We vow only when hurried into excesses;
we are alarmed at the dominion which has been acquired
over us by our feelings, or by our habits. Checked for
a time by an adherence to our resolution, they gradually recover their former strength, until they again break
forth, and we yield to their overpowering influence. A
few days after I had made the resolution, I found myself,
like the sailor, *rewarding* it by writing more indefatigably
than ever.

So now, reader, you may understand that I continue to
write, as Tony Lumpkin says, not to please my good-natured
friends, "but because I can't bear to disappoint myself;" for
that which I commenced as an amusement, and continued as
a drudgery, has ended in becoming a confirmed habit.

So much for the overture. Now let us draw up the curtain,
and our actors shall appear upon the stage.

5

CHAPTER II

" Boldly I venture on a naval scene,
  Nor fear the critic's frown, the pedant's spleen :
  Sons of the ocean, we their rules disdain."

" Hark !—a shock
Tears her strong bottom on a marble rock.
Down on the vale of death, with dismal cries,
The fated victims, shuddering, roll their eyes
In wild despair—while yet another stroke
With deep convulsion rends the solid oak,
Till like the mine in whose infernal cell
The lurking demons of destruction dwell,
At length, asunder torn, her frame divides,
And crashing, spreads in ruin o'er the tides."

—FALCONER.

IT was in the dreary month of fog, misanthropy, and suicide—the month during which Heaven receives a scantier tribute of gratitude from discontented man—during which the sun rises, but shines not—gives forth an unwilling light, but glads us not with his cheerful rays—during which large tallow candles assist the merchant to calculate his gains, or to philosophise over his losses—in short, it was one evening in the month of November of the year 17—, that Edward Forster, who had served many years in his Majesty's navy, was seated in a snug arm-chair, in a snug parlour, in a snug cottage to which he had retired upon his half pay, in consequence of a severe wound which had, for many years, healed but to break out again each succeeding spring.

The locality of the cottage was not exactly so snug as it has been described in itself and its interior; for it was situated on a hill which terminated at a short distance in a precipitous cliff, beetling over that portion of the Atlantic which lashes the shores of Cumberland under the sub-denomination of the Irish Sea. But Forster had been all his early life a sailor, and still felt the same pleasure in listening to the moaning and whistling of the wind as it rattled the shutters of his cottage (like some importunate who would

6

gain admittance), as he used to experience when, lying in his hammock, he was awakened by the howling of the blast, and shrouding himself in his blankets to resume his nap, rejoiced that he was not exposed to its fury.

His finances did not allow him to indulge in luxuries, and the distillation of the country was substituted for wine. With his feet upon the fender, and his glass of whisky-toddy at his side, he had been led into a train of thought by the book which he had been reading, some passage of which had recalled to his memory scenes that had long passed away—the scenes of youth and hope—the happy castle-building of the fresh in heart, invariably overthrown by time and disappointment. The night was tempestuous; the rain now pattered loud, then ceased as if it had fed the wind, which renewed its violence, and forced its way through every crevice. The carpet of his little room occasionally rose from the floor, swelled up by the insidious entrance of the searching blast; the solitary candle, which from neglect had not only elongated its wick to an unusual extent, but had formed a sort of mushroom top, was every moment in danger of extinction, while the chintz curtains of the window waved solemnly to and fro. But the deep reverie of Edward Forster was suddenly disturbed by the report of a gun, swept to leeward by the impetuosity of the gale, which hurled it with violence against the door and front windows of his cottage, for some moments causing them to vibrate with the concussion. Forster started up, dropping his book upon the hearth, and jerking the table with his elbow, so as to dash out the larger proportion of the contents of his tumbler. The sooty coronal of the wick also fell with the shock, and the candle, relieved from its burden, poured forth a brighter gleam.

"Lord ha' mercy, Mr. Forster; did you hear that noise?" cried the old housekeeper (the only inhabitant of the cottage except himself), as she bolted into the room, holding her apron in both hands.

"I did indeed, Mrs. Beazely," replied Forster; "it's the signal of a vessel in distress, and she must be on a dead lee-shore. Give me my hat!" and draining off the remainder in his tumbler, while the old lady reached his hat off a peg in the passage, he darted out from the door of his tenement.

7

The door, which faced to seaward, flew open with violence, as Forster disappeared in the darkness of the night.

The old housekeeper, on whom had devolved the task of securing it, found it no easy matter; and the rain, blown in by the sweeping gale, proved an effectual and unwelcome shower-bath to one who complained bitterly of the rheumatics. At last her object was accomplished, and she repaired to the parlour to re-light the candle which had been extinguished, and await the return of her master. After sundry ejaculations and sundry wonders, she took possession of his arm-chair, poked the fire, and helped herself to a glass of whisky-toddy. As soon as her clothes and her tumbler were again dry, she announced by loud snores that she was in a happy state of oblivion; in which we shall leave her, to follow the motions of Edward Forster.

It was about seven o'clock in the evening when Forster thus exposed himself to the inclemency of the weather. But a few weeks before how beautiful were the evenings at this hour; the sun disappearing beyond the distant wave, and leaving a portion of his glory behind him, until the stars, in obedience to the divine fiat, were lighted up to "shine by night"; the sea rippling on the sand, or pouring into the crevices of the rocks, changing its hue, as daylight slowly disappeared, to the more sombre colours it reflected, from azure to each deeper tint of grey, until darkness closed in, and its extent was scarcely to be defined by the horizontal line.

Now all was changed. The roaring of the wind and the hoarse beating of the waves upon the streaming rocks deafened the ears of Edward Forster. The rain and spray were hurled in his face, as, with both hands, he secured his hat upon his head; and the night was so intensely dark that but occasionally he could distinguish the broad belt of foam with which the coast was lined. Still Forster forced his way towards the beach, which it is now requisite that we should more particularly describe.

As we before observed, the cottage was built upon a high land, which terminated in a precipitous cliff about two hundred yards distant, and running in a direct line to the westward. To the northward the coast for miles was one continued line of rocky cliffs, affording no chance of life to those who might be dashed upon them; but to the southward of the cliff which formed the promontory opposite to Forster's cottage, and which terminated the range, there was a deep indent in the line of coast, forming a sandy and nearly land-locked bay, small indeed, but so sheltered that any vessel which could run in might remain there in safety until the gale was spent. Its only occupant was a fisherman, who, with his family, lived in a small cottage on the beach. He was an ally of Forster, who had entrusted to his charge a skiff, in which, during the summer months, he often whiled away his time. It was to this cottage that Forster bent his way, and loudly knocked when he arrived.

"Robertson—I say, Robertson," called Forster, at the full compass of his voice.

"He is not here, Mr. Forster," answered Jane, the wife of the fisherman; "he is out looking for the vessel."

"Which way did he go?"

Before an answer could be returned, Robertson himself appeared. "I'm here, Mr. Forster," said he, taking off his fur cap, and squeezing out with both hands the water with which it was loaded; "but I can't see the vessel."

"Still, by the report of the gun, she must be close to the shore. Get some faggots out from the shed, and light as large a fire as you can: don't spare them, my good fellow; I will pay you."

"That'll I'll do, sir, and without pay; I only hope that they'll understand the signal, and lay her on shore in the cove. There's another gun!"

This second report, so much louder than the former, indicated that the vessel had rapidly neared the land; and the direction from which the report came proved that she must be close to the promontory of rocks.

"Be smart, my dear fellow, be smart," cried Forster. "I will go up to the cliff, and try if I can make her out;" and the parties separated upon their mutual work of sympathy and good-will.

It was not without danger, as well as difficulty, that Forster succeeded in his attempt; and when he arrived at the summit, a violent gust of wind would have thrown him off his legs, had he not sunk down upon his knees and clung to the herbage, losing his hat, which was borne far away to leeward. In this position, drenched with the rain and shivering with the cold, he remained some minutes, attempting in vain, with straining eyes, to pierce through the gloom of the night, when a flash of lightning, which darted from the zenith, and continuéd its eccentric career until it was lost behind the horizon, discovered to him the object of his research. But a few moments did he behold it, and then, from the sudden contrast, a film appeared to swim over his aching eyes, and all was more intensely, more horribly dark than before; but to the eye of a seafaring man this short view was sufficient. He perceived that it was a large ship, within a quarter of a mile of the land, pressed gunnel under with her reefed courses, chopping through the heavy seas—now pointing her bowsprit to the heavens, as she rose over the impeding swell; now plunging deep into the trough encircled by the foam raised by her own exertions, like some huge monster of the deep, struggling in her toils, and lashing the seas around in her violent efforts to escape.

The fire burnt up fiercely in the cove, in defiance of the rain and wind, which, after in vain attempting to destroy it in its birth, now seemed to assist it with their violence.

"She may yet be saved," thought Forster, "if she will only carry on. Two cables' length more, and she will be clear of the point."

Again and again was the vessel momentarily presented to his view, as the forked lightning darted in every quarter of the firmament, while the astounding claps of thunder bursting upon his ears before the lightning had ceased to gleam, announced to him that he was kneeling in the very centre of the war of the elements. The vessel neared the cliff in about the same proportion that she forged ahead. Forster was breathless with anxiety, for the last flash of electricity revealed to him that two moments more would decide her fate.

The gale now redoubled its fury, and Forster was obliged to cling for his existence as he sank, from his kneeling posture, flat upon the wet herbage. Still he had approached so near to the edge of the cliff that his view below was not interrupted by his change of posture. Another flash of lightning. It was enough! "God have mercy on their souls!" cried he, dropping his face upon the ground as if to shut out the horrid vision from his sight.

He had beheld the vessel within the surf, but a few yards

10

distant from the outer rocks, thrown on her beam-ends, with both foresail and mainsail blown clean out of their bolt-ropes. The cry for succour was raised in vain; the wail of despair was not heard; the struggles for life were not beheld, as the elements in their wrath roared and howled over their victim.

As if satiated with its devastation, from that moment the storm gradually abated, and Forster, taking advantage of a lull, slowly descended to the cove, where he found Robertson still heaping fuel on the fire.

"Save your wood, my good fellow; it's all over with her; and those who were on board are in eternity at this moment," said Forster, in a melancholy tone.

"Is she gone then, sir?"

"Right on the outer ledge; there's not a living soul to see your beacon."

"God's will be done!" replied the fisherman; "then their time was come—but He who destroys can save if He pleases; I'll not put out the fire while there's a faggot left, for you know, Mr. Forster, that if any one should by a miracle be thrown into the smooth water on this side of the point, he might be saved; that is, if he swam well;"—and Robertson threw on more faggots, which soon flared up with a brilliant light. The fisherman returned to the cottage, to procure for Forster a red woollen cap in lieu of the hat which he had lost, and they both sat down close to the fire to warm themselves and to dry their streaming clothes.

Robertson had once more replenished the fuel, and the vivid blaze glared along the water in the cove, when the eye of Forster was attracted by the appearance of something floating on the wave, and evidently nearing to the shore. He pointed it out to the fisherman, and they descended to the water's edge, awaiting its approach with intense anxiety.

"It's not a man, sir, is it?" observed Robertson, after a minute's pause.

"I cannot make it out," replied Forster; "but I rather think that it is an animal—something living, most assuredly."

In another minute or two the point was decided; they distinguished a large dog bearing something white in its mouth, and making for the shore where they were standing. Calling to the poor beast, to cheer him, for he evidently was much exhausted and approached but slowly, they soon had the satisfaction of seeing him pass though the surf, which, even at this time, was not heavy in the cove, and with the water pouring from his shaggy coat, stagger towards them, bearing in his mouth his burden, which he laid down at Forster's feet, and then shook off the accumulation of moisture from his skin. Forster took up the object of the animal's solicitude—it was the body of an infant, apparently a few months old.

"Poor thing!" cried Forster mournfully.

"It's quite dead, sir," observed the fisherman.

"I am afraid so," replied Forster, "but it cannot have been so long; the dog evidently bore it up clear of the water, until it came into the surf. Who knows but we could restore it?"

"If anything will restore it, sir, it will be the warmth of a woman's breast, to which it hitherto hath clung. Jane shall take it in her bed, between her and the little ones;" and the fisherman entered the hut with the child, which was undressed, and received by his wife with all the sympathy which maternal feelings create, even towards the offspring of others. To the delight of Forster, in a quarter of an hour Robertson came out of the cottage, with the intelligence that the child had moved and cried a little, and that there was every chance of its recovery.

"It's a beautiful little girl, sir, Jane says; and if it lives, she will halve her milk between it and our little Tommy."

Forster remained another half-hour, until he had ascertained that the child had taken the breast and had fallen asleep. Congratulating himself at having been the means of saving even one little life out of the many which, in all probability, had been swallowed up, he called to the dog, who had remained passive by the fire, and rose up to return home; but the dog retreated to the door of the cottage, into which he had seen the infant carried, and all attempts to coax him away were fruitless.

Forster summoned Robertson, to whom he gave some further directions, and then returned to his home, where, on his arrival, his old housekeeper, who had never been awakened from her sound nap until roused by his knocking at the door, scolded him not a little for being out in such tempestuous weather, and a great deal more for having obliged her to sit up and watch all night until his return.

CHAPTER III

" Creaticn smiles around ; on every spray
The warbling birds exalt their evening lay ;
Blithe skipping o'er yon hill, the fleecy train
Join the deep chorus of the lowing plain :
The glassy ocean, hushed, forgets to roar,
But trembling, murmurs on the sandy shore."
—FALCONER.

FORSTER was soon fast asleep after his night of exertion : his dreams were confused and wild; but I seldom trouble people about dreams, which are as nought. When Reason descends from her throne, and seeks a transitory respite from her labour, Fancy usurps the vacant seat, and, in pretended majesty, would fain exert her sister's various powers. These she enacts to the best of her ability, and with about the same success as attends a monkey when he attempts the several operations connected with the mystery of shaving—and thus ends a very short and conclusive dissertation upon dreams.

But to use a nautical phrase, we must " heave-to " in our narrative awhile, as it is necessary that we should enter a little more into the previous history of Edward Forster; which we can now do without interruption, as the parties we have introduced to the reader are all asleep.

The father of Edward Forster was a clergyman, who, notwithstanding he could reckon up some twenty or thirty first, second, and third cousins with high-sounding titles, officiated as curate in a district not far from that part of the country where Forster at present was located. He was one of the bees of the Church, who are constantly toiling, while the drones are eating up the honey. He preached three sermons, and read three services, at three different stations, every Sunday throughout the year ; while he christened, married, and buried a population extending over some thousands of square acres, for the scanty stipend of one hundred per annum. Soon after he was in possession of his curacy, he married a young woman, who brought him beauty and modesty as her dower, and subsequently pledges of mutual love *ad lib.* But He that giveth,

13

taketh away; and out of nearly a score of these interesting but expensive presents to her husband, only three, all of the masculine gender, arrived at years of maturity. John (or Jock as he usually was called), who was the eldest, was despatched to London, where he studied the law under a relation, who, perceiving that Mrs. Forster's annual presentation *of* the living was not followed up by any presentation *to* the living, kindly took charge of and received him into his own house.

Jock was a hard-headed fellow, studied with great diligence, and retained what he read, although he did not read fast; but that which he lost in speed he made up by perseverance, and had now, entirely by his own exertions, risen to considerable eminence in his profession; but he had been severed from his family in early days, and had never been able to return to them. He heard, indeed, of the birth of sundry brothers and sisters; of their deaths, and lastly, of the demise of his parents—the only communication which affected him; for he loved his father and mother, and was anticipating the period when he might possess the means of rendering them more comfortable. But all this had long passed away. He was now a bachelor past fifty, bearish and uncouth in his appearance, and ungracious in his deportment. Secluded in his chambers, poring over the dry technicalities of his profession, he had divided the moral world into two parts—honest and dishonest, lawful and unlawful. All other feelings and affections, if he had them, were buried, and had never been raised to the surface. At the time we speak of, he continued his laborious yet lucrative profession, toiling in his harness like a horse in a mill, heaping up riches, knowing not who should gather them; not from avarice, but from long habit, which rendered his profession not only his pleasure, but essential to his very existence. Edward Forster had not seen him for nearly twenty years; the last time was when he passed through London on his retirement from the service. Indeed, as they never corresponded (for there was nothing in common between them), it is a matter of doubt whether Jock was exactly aware which of his brothers remained alive; and had it been a subject of interest, he would, in all probability, have referred to the former letters of his father and mother as legal documents, to ascertain who was remaining of his kin.

14

The next surviving son was *yclept* (there's something very *consonant* in that word) Nicholas. The Reverend Mr. Forster, who had no inheritance to bequeath to his family except a good name, which, although better than riches, will not always procure for a man one penny loaf, naturally watched for any peculiar symptoms of genius in his children which might designate one of the various paths to wealth and fame by which it would be most easy for the individual to ascend. Now, it did occur that when Nicholas was yet in womanish attire, he showed a great partiality to a burning-glass, with which he contrived to do much mischief. He would burn the dog's nose as he slept in the sun before the door. His mother's gown showed proofs of his genius by sundry little round holes, which were considerably increased each time that it returned from the wash. Nay, heretical and damnable as is the fact, his father's surplice was as a moth-eaten garment from the repeated and insidious attacks of this young philosopher. The burning-glass decided his fate. He was bound apprentice to an optical and mathematical instrument maker; from which situation he was, if possible, to emerge into the highest grade of the profession; but somehow or another, a want of ambition or of talent did not permit him to ascend the scale, and he now kept a shop in the small seaport town of Overton, where he repaired damaged articles of science—a watch one day, a quadrant or a compass another; but his chief employment and his chief forte lay in telescopes; and accordingly, a large board with "Nicholas Forster, Optician," surmounted the small shop window at which he was invariably to be seen at his employment. He was an eccentric person, one of those who had narrowly escaped being clever; but there was an obliquity in his mind which would not admit of lucid order and arrangement. In the small town where he resided, he continued to pick up a decent sustenance; for he had no competitor, and was looked upon as a man of considerable ability. He was the only one of the three brothers who had ventured upon wedlock. But of this part of our history we shall at present say no more than that he had an only child, and had married his wife, to use his own expression, because she "suited his focus."

Edward Forster, the youngest, whom we have already introduced to the reader, showed strong nautical propensities; he swam nut-shells in a puddle, and sent pieces of lath with paper sails floating down the brook which gurgled by the parsonage. This was circumstantial evidence : he was convicted, and ordered off to sea, to return a Nelson. For his conduct during the time he served her, Edward Forster certainly deserved well of his country; and had he been enabled to continue in his profession, would in all probability have risen by his merit to its highest grades; but having served his time as midshipman, he received a desperate wound in "cutting out," and shortly after obtained his promotion to the rank of lieutenant for his gallant conduct. His wound was of that severe description that he was obliged to quit the service, and for a time retire upon his half-pay. For many years he looked forward to the period when he could resume his career—but in vain; the wound broke out again and again, fresh splinters of the bone continually worked out, and he was doomed to constant disappointment. At last it healed; but years of suffering had quenched the ardour of youth, and when he did apply for employment, his services had been forgotten. He received a cool negative, almost consonant to his wishes ; and returned, without feeling mortified, to the cottage we have described, where he lived a secluded yet not an unhappy life. His wants were few, and his half-pay more than adequate to supply them. A happy contemplative indolence, arising from a well-cultivated mind, feeding rather upon its previous acquirements than adding to its store—an equanimity of disposition and a habit of rigid self-command—were the characteristics of Edward Forster; whom I shall now awaken, that we may proceed with our narrative.

"Well, I do declare, Mr. Forster, you have had a famous nap," cried Mrs. Beazely, in a tone of voice so loud as to put an immediate end to his slumber, as she entered his room with some hot water to assist him in that masculine operation, the diurnal painful return of which has been considered to be more than tantamount in suffering to the occasional "pleasing punishment which women bear." Although this cannot be proved until ladies are endowed with beards (which Heaven forfend !), or some modern Tiresias shall appear to decide the point, the assertion appears to be borne out, if we reason by analogy from human life ; where we find that it is not the heavy blow of sudden misfortune tripping the ladder of our ambition and laying us prostrate, which constitutes life's intermittent "fitful fever," but the thousand petty vexations of hourly occurrence.——We return to Mrs. Beazely, who continued, "Why, it's nine o'clock, Mr. Forster, and a nice fresh morning it is too, after last night's tempest. And, pray, what did you hear and see, sir?" continued the old woman, opening the shutters and admitting a blaze of sunshine, as if determined that at all events he should now both hear and see.

"I'll tell you all, Mrs. Beazely, when I am dressed. Let me have my breakfast as soon as you can, for I must be off again to the cove. I did not intend to have slept so late."

"Why, what's in the wind now, Mr. Forster?" said the old lady, borrowing one of his nautical phrases.

"If you wish to know, Mrs. Beazely, the sooner you allow me to get out of bed, the sooner I shall be able to give you the information you require."

"But what made you stay out so late, Mr. Forster?" continued the housekeeper, who seemed determined, if possible, to have a little information *en attendant*, to stay her appetite until her curiosity could obtain a more substantial repast.

"I am sorry to say there was a vessel wrecked."

"O dear! O dear! Any lives lost?"

"All, I am afraid, except one, and even that is doubtful."

"O Lord! O Lord! Do, pray, Mr. Forster, tell me all about it."

"As soon as I am dressed, Mrs. Beazely," replied Mr. Forster, making a movement indicative that he was about to "turn out," whether or no, and which occasioned Mrs. Beazely to make a hasty retreat.

In a few minutes Forster made his appearance in the parlour, where he found both the kettle and the housekeeper boiling with impatience. He commenced eating and narrating until the respective appetites of Mrs. Beazely and himself were equally appeased, and then set off for the abode of Robertson, to ascertain the fate of the infant.

How different was the scene from that of the night before! The sea was still in commotion, and as the bright sun shone upon its agitated surface, gilding the summits of the waves, although there was majesty and beauty in the appearance, there was naught to excite terror. The atmosphere, purified by the warfare of elements, was fresh and bracing. The short verdure which covered the promontory and hills adjacent was of a more brilliant green, and seemed as if to bask in the sun after the cleansing it had received from the heavy rain; while the sheep (for the coast was one extended sheep-walk) studded the sides of the hills, their white fleeces in strong yet beautiful contrast with the deep verdure of nature. The smooth water of the cove, in opposition to the vexed billows of the unsheltered ocean; the murmuring of the light waves, running in long and gently curved lines to their repose upon the yellow sand; their surface occasionally rippled by the eddying breeze as it swept along; his own little skiff safe at her moorings, undulating with the swell; the seagulls, who but a few hours ago were screaming with dismay as they buffeted against the fury of the gale, now skimming on the waves or balanced on the wing near to their inaccessible retreats; the carolling of the smaller birds on every side of him, produced a lightness of heart and quickened pulse to which Edward Forster had latterly been a stranger.

He soon arrived at the cottage, where the sound of his footsteps brought out the fisherman and his wife, the latter bearing in her arms the little object of his solicitude.

"See, Mr. Forster," said Jane, holding out the infant, "it's quite well and hearty, and does nothing but smile. What a lovely babe it is!"

Forster looked at the child, who smiled as if in gratitude; but his attention was called away by the Newfoundland dog, who fawned upon him, and after having received his caresses, squatted down upon the sand, which he beat with his tail as he looked wistfully in Forster's face.

Forster took the child from the arms of its new mother. "Thou hast had a narrow escape, poor thing," said he, and his countenance assumed a melancholy cast as the idea floated in his mind. "Who knows how many more perils may await thee? Who can say whether thou art to be restored to the arms of thy relatives, or to be left an orphan to a sailor's care. Whether it had not been better that the waves should have swallowed thee in thy purity, than thou shouldst be exposed to a heartless world of sorrow and of crime? But He who willed thee to be saved knows best for us who are in darkness;" and Forster kissed its brow and returned it to the arms of Jane.

18

THE MERCHANT SERVICE

Having made a few arrangements with Robertson and his wife, in whose care he resolved at present to leave the child, Forster bent his steps towards the promontory, that he might ascertain if any part of the vessel remained. Stretching over the summit of the cliff, he perceived that several of the lower futtocks and timbers still hung together, and showed themselves above water. Anxious to obtain some clue to her identity, he prepared to descend by a winding and hazardous path which he had before surmounted. In a quarter of an hour he had gained a position close to the wreck, but, with the exception of the shattered remnant which was firmly wedged between the rocks, there was nothing to be seen; not a fragment of her masts and spars, or sails, not a relic of what was once life remained. The tide, which ran furiously round the promontory, had swept them all away, or the undertow of the deep water had buried every detached particle, to be delivered up again "far, far at sea." All that Forster could ascertain was, that the vessel was foreign built and of large tonnage; but who were its unfortunate tenants, or what the cargo of which she had been despoiled by the devouring waves, was not even to be surmised. The linen on the child was marked J. de F., and this was the only clue which remained for its identity. For more than an hour did Forster remain fixed as a statue upon the rock, where he had taken his station with arms folded, while he contemplated the hoarse waves dashing against the bends, or dividing as they poured themselves between the timbers of the vessel, and he sunk into deep and melancholy thought.

And where is the object exciting more serious reflection than a *wreck*?

The pride and ingenuity of man humbled and overcome; the elements of the Lord occupying the fabric which had set them at defiance; tossing, tumbling, and dancing, as if in mockery at their success! The structure, but a few hours past as perfect as human intellect could devise, towering with its proud canvas over space, and bearing man to greet his fellow-man over the *surface of death !*—dashing the billow from her stem as if in scorn, while she pursued her trackless way—bearing tidings of peace and security, of war and devastation—tidings of joy or grief, affecting whole kingdoms and empires, as if they were but individuals!

Now, the waters delight in their revenge, and sparkle with joy as the sun shines upon their victory. That keel, which with the sharpness of a scythe has so often mowed its course through the reluctant wave, is now buried—buried deep in the sand, which the angry surge accumulates each minute, as if determined that it never will be subject to its weight again.

How many seasons had rolled away, how many millions had returned to the dust from which they sprung, before the kernels were swelled into the forest giants levelled for that structure; what labour had been undergone to complete the task; how many of the existent race found employment and subsistence, as they slowly raised that monument of human skill; how often had the weary miner laid aside his tool to wipe his sweating brow, before the metal required for its completion had been brought from darkness; what thousands had been employed before it was prepared and ready for its destined use ! Yon copper bolt, twisted with a force not human, and raised above the waters, as if in evidence of their dreadful power, may contain a history in itself.

How many of her own structure must have been employed bringing from the north, the south, the east, and the west, her masts, her spars, her *" hempen tackle,"* and her canvas wings; her equipment in all its variety; her stores for the support of life; her magazines of *quiescent death.*[1]   And they who so fearlessly trod her decks, conscious of their own powers and confident in their own skill; they who expanded her thousands of yards of canvas to the pursuing breeze, or reduced them like magic at the approaching storm—where are they now ?   How many sighs have been lavished at their absence ! how many hearths would have been gladdened by their return !   Where are the hopes, the fears, the ambition, and the pride; the courage and the enterprise; the love and the yearnings after their kin; the speculations of the present, and the calculations of the future, which occupied their minds or were cherished in their bosoms ?   All—all wrecked !

Days, weeks, and months rolled away; yet every step that could be taken to find out the name of the vessel proved unavailing.   Although the conjectures of Forster, that she

---

[1] We presume the gentleman means gunpowder.—ED.

was one of the many foreign West Indiamen which had met with a similar fate during that tempestuous winter, was probably correct; still no clue could be gathered by which the parentage of the little girl could be ascertained. The linen was indeed marked with initials; but this circumstance offered but a faint prospect of discovery. Either her relations, convinced of her loss, made no inquiries, or the name of the vessel in which she had been a passenger was not known to them. The child had been weaned, and removed to the cottage, where it occupied much of the attention of the old housekeeper and Forster, who, despairing of its ever being reclaimed, determined to bring it up as his own.

Mrs. Beazely, the housekeeper, was a good-tempered woman, long past the grand climacteric, and strongly attached to Forster, with whom she had resided many years. But, like all women, whether married or single, who have the responsibility of a household, she would have her own way; and scolded her master with as little ceremony as if she had been united to him by matrimonial bonds.

To this Forster quietly submitted; he had lived long enough to be aware that people are not the happiest who are not under control, and was philosopher sufficient to submit to the penal code of matrimony without tasting its enjoyments. The arrival of the infant made him more than ever feel as if he were a married man; for he had all the delights of the nursery in addition to his previous discipline. But, although bound by no ties, he found himself happier. He soon played with the infant, and submitted to his housekeeper with all the docility of a well-trained married man.

The Newfoundland dog, who, although (like some of his betters) he did not change his name for a fortune, did, in all probability, change it with his fortune, soon answered to the deserved epithet of "Faithful," and slept at the foot of the crib of his little mistress, who also was to be re-christened "She is a treasure which has been thrown up by the ocean," said Forster, kissing the lovely infant. "Let her name be *Amber.*"

But we must leave her to bud forth in her innocence and purity, while we direct the attention of the reader to other scenes, which are contemporary with those we have described.

CHAPTER IV

" A woman moved is like a fountain troubled,
  Muddy, ill-seeming, thick, bereft of beauty;
  And while 'tis so, none so dry or thirsty
  Will deign to sip or touch one drop of it."
                                        —SHAKSPEARE

A MAN may purchase an estate, a tenement, or a horse,
because they have pleased his fancy, and eventually find out
that he has not exactly suited himself; and it sometimes
will occur that a man is placed in a similar situation relative
to his choice of a wife—a more serious evil, as, although
the prime cost may be nothing, there is no chance of getting
rid of this latter speculation by re-vending, as you may the
former. Now it happened that Nicholas Forster, of whom
we have already made slight mention, although he considered at the time of his marriage that the person he had
selected would " exactly suit his focus," did eventually discover
that he was more short-sighted in his choice than an optician
ought to have been.

Whatever may have been the personal charms of Mrs.
Nicholas Forster at the time of their union, she had, at the
period of our narrative, but few to boast of, being a thin,
sharp-nosed, ferret-eyed little woman, teeming with suspicion,
jealousy, and bad humours of every description; her whole
employment (we may say her whole delight) was in finding
fault; her shrill voice was to be heard from the other side
of the street from morning until night. The one servant
which their finances enabled them with difficulty to retain,
and whom they engaged as a maid-of-all-work (and certainly
she was not permitted by Mrs. Forster to be idle in her multi-
farious duty), seldom remained above her month; and nothing
but the prospect of immediate starvation could induce any one
to offer herself in that capacity.

Mr. Nicholas Forster, fortunately for his own happiness, was
of that peculiar temperament that nothing could completely
rouse his anger: he was absent to an excess, and if any
language or behaviour on the part of his wife induced his

choler to rise, other ideas would efface the cause from his memory; and this hydra of the human bosom, missing the object of its intended attack, again laid down to rest.

The violence and vituperation of his spouse were, therefore, lost upon Nicholas Forster, and the impossibility of disturbing the equanimity of his temper increased the irritability of her own. Still Mr. Nicholas Forster, when he did reflect upon the subject, which was but during momentary fits of recollection, could not help acknowledging that he should be much more quiet and happy when it pleased Heaven to summon Mrs. Forster to a better world; and this idea ultimately took possession of his imagination. Her constant turbulence interfered so much with the prosecution of his plans, that, finding it impossible to carry them into execution, everything that he considered of moment was mentally put off until *Mrs. Forster was dead* !

"Well, Mr. Forster, how long is the dinner to wait before you think proper to come? Everything will be cold, as usual. (N.B.—The dinner consisted of the remains of a cold shoulder of mutton.) Or do you mean to have any dinner at all? Betty, clear away the table; I have my work to do, and won't wait any longer."

"I'm coming, my dear, I'm coming; only this balance-spring is a job that I cannot well leave," replied Nicholas, continuing his vocation in the shop with a magnifying-glass attached to his eye.

"Coming ! yes, and Christmas is coming, Mr. Forster. Well, the dinner's going, I can tell you."

Nicholas, who did not want appetite, and who was conscious that if the mutton returned to the cupboard there would be some difficulty in reproducing it, laid down the watch and came into the back-parlour.

"Well, my dear, here I am; sorry to have kept you waiting so long, but business must be attended to. Dear me ! why, the mutton is really quite cold," continued Nicholas, thrusting a large piece into his mouth, quite forgetting that he had already dined twice off the identical joint. "That's a fine watch of Mr. Tobin's; but I think that my improvement upon the duplex when I have finished it——"

"When you have finished it indeed !" retorted the lady;

23

"why, when did you ever finish anything, Mr. Forster?
Finish indeed!"

"Well, my dear," replied the husband, with an absent air,
"I do mean to finish it, when—*you are dead!*"

"When I am dead!" screamed the lady, in a rage;
"when I am dead!" continued she, placing her arms akimbo,
as she started from the chair. "I can tell you, Mr. Forster,
that I'll live long enough to plague you. It's not the first
time that you've said so; but depend upon it, I'll dance upon
your grave yet, Mr. Forster."

"I did not exactly mean to say that; not exactly that, my
dear," replied Nicholas, confused. "The fact is, that I was
not exactly aware of what I was saying—I had not precisely
the——"

"Precisely the fiddlestick, Mr. Forster! you did mean it,
and you do mean it, and this is all the return that I am to
expect for my kindness and anxiety for your welfare—slaving
and toiling all day as I do; but you're incorrigible, Mr. Forster:
look at you, helping yourself out of your snuff-box instead
of the salt-cellar. What man in his senses would eat a cold
shoulder of mutton with tobacco?"

"Dear me! so I have," replied Forster, removing the snuff
taken from the box, which as usual lay open before him, not
into the box again, but into the salt-cellar.

"And who's to eat that salt now, you nasty beast?"

"I am not a beast, Mrs. Forster," replied her husband,
whose choler was roused; "I made a mistake, I do perceive
—now I recollect it, did you send Betty with the 'day and
night glass' to Captain Simkins?"

"Yes, I did, Mr. Forster; if I did not look after your
business, I should like to know what would become of us;
and I can tell you, Mr. Forster, that if you do not contrive to
get more business, there will soon be nothing to eat; seventeen and sixpence is all that I have received this last week;
and how rent and fire, meat and drink, are to be paid for
with that, you must explain, for I can't."

"How can I help it, my dear? I never refuse a job."

"Never refuse a job? no; but you must contrive to make
more business."

"I can mend a watch and make a telescope, but I can't
make business, my dear," replied Nicholas.

24

"Yes, you can, and you must, Mr. Forster," continued the lady, sweeping off the remains of the mutton, just as her husband had fixed his eye upon the next cut, and locking it up in the cupboard ; "if you do not, you will have nothing to eat, Mr. Forster."

"So it appears, my dear," replied the meek Nicholas, taking a pinch of snuff; "but I really don't——"

"Why, Mr. Forster, if you were not one of the greatest——"

"No, no, my dear," interrupted Nicholas, from extreme modesty. "I am not one of the greatest opticians of the present day ; although, when I've made my improve——"

"Greatest opticians!" interrupted the lady. "One of the greatest fools, I meant!"

"That's quite another thing, my dear; but——"

"No buts, Mr. Forster; please to listen, and not interrupt me in that bearish manner. Why do you repair in the way you do? Who ever brings you a watch or a glass that you have handled a second time?"

"But why should they, my dear, when I have put them in good order?"

"Put them in order! but why do you put them in order?"

"Why do I put them in order, my dear?" replied Forster, with astonishment.

"Yes; why don't you leave a screw loose somewhere? then they must come again. That's the proper way to do business."

"The proper way to do my business, my dear, is to see that all the screws are tight."

"And starve," continued the lady.

"If it please God," replied the honest Nicholas.

But this matrimonial duet was interrupted by the appearance of their son, whom we must introduce to the reader, as he will play a conspicuous part in our narrative.

Newton Forster (for thus had he been christened by his father, out of respect for the great Sir Isaac) was now about seventeen years old—athletic and well-proportioned in person, handsome in features, and equally gifted in mind. There was a frankness and sincerity in his open brow, an honesty in his smile, which immediately won upon the beholder, and his countenance was but an index to his mind. His father had bestowed all his own leisure, and some expense, which he

25

could ill afford, upon his education, trusting one day that he would rival the genius after whom he had been christened; but Newton was not of a disposition to sit down either at a desk or a work-bench. Whenever he could escape from home or from school, he was to be found either on the beach or at the pier, under the shelter of which the coasting vessels discharged or received their cargoes, and he had for some years declared his intention to follow the profession of a sailor. To this his father had reluctantly consented, with the proviso that he would first finish his education; and the mutual compact had been strictly adhered to by each party.

At the age of fifteen, Newton had acquired all that could be imparted to him by the pedagogue of the vicinity, and had then, until something better should turn up, shipped himself on board of a coasting vessel, in which, during the last two years, he made several trips, being usually absent about six weeks, and remaining in port about the same time, until another cargo could be procured.

Young as he was, the superiority of his education had obtained him the situation of mate of the vessel, and his pay enabled him to assist his father, whose business, as Mrs. Forster declared, was not sufficient to "make both ends meet." Upon his return, his love of knowledge and active habits induced him to glean as much as he could of his father's profession, and he could repair most articles that were sent in. Although Newton amused himself with the peculiarities and eccentricity of his father, he still had a high respect for him, as he knew him to be a worthy, honest man. For his mother he certainly had none: he was indignant at her treatment of his father, and could find no redeeming quality to make amends for her catalogue of imperfections. Still he had a peculiar tact, by which he avoided any serious altercation. Never losing his own temper, yet quietly and firmly resisting all control, he assumed a dominion over her, from which her feelings towards him, whatever they may have been in his early years, were now changed into those of positive hatred. His absence this morning had been occasioned by his assistance being required in the fitting of a new mainstay for the sloop to which he belonged. "Please God what, father?" said Newton, as he came in, catching his father's last words.

26

"Why, your mother says that we must starve or be dishonest."

"Then we'll starve, father, with a clear conscience; but I hope things are not so bad yet, for I am devilish hungry," continued Newton, looking at the dinner-table, which offered to his view nothing but a table-cloth, with the salt-cellar and the snuff-box. "Why, mother, is it dead low water, or have you stowed all away in the locker?" and Newton repaired to the cupboard, which was locked.

Now Mrs. Forster was violent with others, but with Newton she was always sulky.

"There's nothing in the cupboard," growled the lady.

"Then why lock up nothing?" rejoined Newton, who was aware that veracity was not among Mrs. Forster's catalogue of virtues. "Come, mother, hand me the key, and I'll ferret out something, I'll answer for it."

Mrs. Forster replied that the cupboard was her own, and she was mistress of the house.

"Just as you please, mother. But, before I take the trouble, tell me, father, is there anything in the cupboard?"

"Why, yes, Newton, there's some mutton. At least, if I recollect right, I did not eat it all—did I, my dear?"

Mrs. Forster did not condescend to answer. Newton went into the shop, and returned with a chisel and hammer. Taking a chair to stand upon, he very coolly began to force the lock.

"I am very sorry, mother, but I must have something to eat; and since you won't give me the key, why——" observed Newton, giving the handle of the chisel a smart blow with the hammer.

"Here's the key, sir," cried Mrs. Forster, with indignation, throwing it on the table, and bouncing out of the room.

A smile was exchanged between the father and son, as she went backwards, screaming, "Betty—I say, Betty, you idle slut, where are you?" as if determined to vent her spleen upon somebody.

"Have you dined, father?" inquired Newton, who had now placed the contents of the cupboard upon the table.

"Why, I really don't quite recollect; but I feel very

hungry," replied the optician, putting in his plate to receive
two large slices; and father and son sat down to a hearty
meal, proving the truth of the wise man's observation,
that " Better is a dinner of herbs where love is, than the
stalled ox and hatred therewith."

CHAPTER V

" Whate'er it be,
'Tis wondrous heavy. Wrench it open straight.
If the sea's stomach be o'ercharged with gold,
It is a good constraint to fortune, that
It belches on us."

—SHAKSPEARE.

ABOUT three weeks after the events narrated in the preceding chapter, Newton Forster sailed in his vessel with a
cargo to be delivered at the seaport of Waterford. The
master of her was immoderately addicted to liquor, and
during the time that he remained in port, seldom was to be
found in a state of perfect sobriety, even on a Sunday. But
to do him justice, when his vessel was declared ready for sea,
he abstained from his usual indulgence, that he might be
enabled to take charge of the property committed to his
care, and find his way to his destined port. It was a point
on which his interest overcame, for a time, his darling propensity; and his rigid adherence to sobriety when afloat
was so well ascertained, that his character as a trustworthy
seaman was not injured by his continual intemperance when
in harbour. Latterly, however, since Newton had sailed
with him, he had not acted up to his important resolution.
He found that the vessel was as safe under the charge of
Forster as under his own; and having taken great pains to
instruct him in seamanship, and make him well acquainted
with the dangers of the coast, he thought that, as Newton
was fully equal to the charge of the vessel, he might as well
indulge himself with an occasional glass or two, to while away
the tedium of embarkation. A stone pitcher of liquor was
now his constant attendant when he pulled on board to weigh

28

his anchor; which said pitcher, for fear of accidents, he carried down into the cabin himself. As soon as sail was on the vessel, and her course shaped, he followed his darling companion down into the cabin, and until the contents were exhausted was never sufficiently sober to make his appearance on deck; so that Newton Forster was, in fact, the responsible master of the vessel.

The wind, which had been favourable at the time of heaving up the anchor, changed, and blew directly in their teeth before they were well out of sight of the port of Overton. On the third day they were stretching off the land, to meet the first of the tide, under a light breeze and smooth water, when Newton perceived various objects floating in the offing. A small thing is a good prize to a coaster; even an empty beaker is not to be despised; and Newton kept away a point or two, that he might close and discover what the objects were. He soon distinguished one or two casks, swimming deeply, broken spars, and a variety of other articles. When the sloop was in the midst of them, Newton hove-to, tossed out the little skiff, and in the course of an hour, unknown to his captain, who was in bed sleeping off the effect of his last potations, brought alongside and contrived to parbuckle in the casks, and as many others of the floating articles as he could conveniently stow upon her decks. The boat was again hoisted in by the united exertions of himself and his crew, consisting of one man and one boy, and the sloop, wearing round, reached in for the land.

It was evident to Newton that some large vessel had lately been wrecked, for the spars were fresh in the fracture and clean—not like those long in the water, covered with seaweed and encircled by a shoal of fish, who finding sustenance from the animalculæ collected, follow the floating pieces of wood up and down, as their adopted parent, wherever they may be swept by the inconstant winds and tides.

Newton examined the heels of the spars, but they were not marked with the name of the vessel to which they had belonged. The two casks had only initials branded upon their heads, but nothing could be found which would designate the owners of the property. A large trunk riveted his attention, but he would not open it till the master of the vessel came upon deck. Having ascertained by spilling that

29

the contents of the casks were *real Jamaica,* he went down into the cabin to announce what he knew would be most grateful intelligence.

It was some time before Newton could rouse his stupefied senior.

" Spars—wrecked ! "

" What spars ?   D—n the wreck ! " growled old Thompson (for such was his name), as he turned his back in no very ceremonious manner, and recommenced his snore.

" There's a trunk besides, sir, a large trunk : but I did not open it, as you were not on deck.   A large trunk, and rather heavy."

" Trunk !—well, what then ?   Trunk !—oh, d—n the trunk ! —let me go to sleep," muttered the master.

" There's two large casks, too, sir ; I've spilled them, and they prove to be puncheons of rum," bawled Newton, who pertinaciously continued.

" Eh, what ?—casks ! what casks ? "

" Two puncheons of rum."

" Rum !—did you say rum ? " cried old Thompson, lifting his head off the pillow, and staring stupidly at Newton; " where ? "

" On deck.   Two casks : we picked them up as we were standing off the land."

" Picked them up ?—are they on board ? " inquired the master, sitting upright in his bed and rubbing his eyes.

" Yes, they're on board.   Won't you come on deck ? "

" To be sure I will.   Two puncheons of rum, you said ? " and old Thompson gained his feet, and reeled to the companion ladder, holding on by all fours as he climbed up without his shoes.

When the master of the sloop had satisfied himself as to the contents of the casks, which he did by taking about half a tumbler of each, Newton proposed that the trunk should be opened.   " Yes," replied Thompson, who had drawn off a mug of the spirits, with which he was about to descend to the cabin, " open if you like, my boy.   You have made a *bon prize* to-day, and your share shall be the trunk ; so you may keep it, and the things that are stowed away in it, for your trouble ; but don't forget to secure the casks till we can stow them away below.   We can't break bulk now, but the sooner they

30

are down the better; or we shall have some quill-driving rascal on board, with his *flotsam* and *jetsam*, for the Lord knows who;" and Thompson, to use his own expression, went down again " to lay his soul in soak."

Reader, do you know the meaning of *flotsam* and *jetsam*? None but a lawyer can, for it is old law language. Now, there is a slight difference between language in general and law language. The first was invented to enable us to explain our own meaning and comprehend the ideas of others; whereas the second was invented with the view that we should not be able to understand a word about it. In former times, when all law, except *club* law, was in its infancy, and practitioners not so erudite or so thriving as at present, it was thought advisable to render it unintelligible by inventing a sort of lingo, compounded of bad French grafted upon worse Latin, forming a mongrel and incomprehensible race of words, with French heads and Latin tails, which answered the purpose intended—that of mystification. *Flotsam* and *jetsam* are of this breed. *Flot*, derived from the French *flottant*, floating; and *jet* from the verb *jeter*, to throw up; both used in seignorial rights granted by kings to favourites, empowering them to take possession of the property of any man who might happen to be unfortunate, which was in those times tantamount to being guilty. I daresay, if one could see the deed thus empowering them to confiscate the goods and chattels of others for their own use, according to the wording of the learned clerks in those days, it would run thus: "Omnium quod flotsam et jetsam, et everything else-um, quod findetes;" in plain English, "Everything floating or thrown up, and everything else you may pick up." Now, the admiral of the coast had this piratical privilege; and as, in former days, sextants and chronometers were unknown, seafaring men incurred more risk than they do at present, and the wrecks which strewed the coast were of very great value. I had a proof the other day that this right is still exacted—that is, as far as regards property unclaimed. I had arrived at Plymouth from the Western Islands. When we hove up our anchor at St. Michael's we found another anchor and cable hooked most lovingly to our own, to the great joy of the first lieutenant, who proposed buying silk

31

handkerchiefs for every man in the ship, and expending the residue in paint. But we had not been at anchor in Plymouth Sound more than twenty-four hours, and he hardly had time to communicate with the gentlemen-dealers in marine stores, when I received a notification from some lynx-eyed agent of the present admiral of the coast (who is a lawyer, I believe), requesting the immediate delivery of the anchor and cable, upon the plea of his seignorial rights of *flotsam* and *jetsam*. Now, the idea was as preposterous as the demand was impudent. We had picked up the anchor in the roadstead of a foreign power, about fifteen hundred miles distant from the English coast.

We are all lawyers now, on board ship; so I gave him one of my legal answers, "That, in the first place, *flotsam* meant floating, and anchors did not float; in the second place, that *jetsam* meant thrown up, and anchors never were thrown up; in the third and last place, *I'd see him d—d first!*"

My arguments were unanswerable. Counsel for the plaintiff (I presume) threw up his brief, for we heard no more of "*Mr. Flotsam and Jetsam.*"

But to proceed. The man and boy, who, with Newton, composed the whole crew, seemed perfectly to acquiesce in the distribution made by the master of the sloop, taking it for granted that their silence, as to the liquor being on board, would be purchased by a share of it as long as it lasted.

They repaired forward with a panikin from the cask, with which they regaled themselves, while Newton stood at the helm. In half-an-hour Newton called the boy aft to steer the vessel, and lifted the trunk into the cabin below, where he found that Thompson had finished the major part of the contents of the mug, and was lying in a state of drunken stupefaction.

The hasp of the lock was soon removed by a claw-hammer, and the contents of the trunk exposed to Newton's view. They consisted chiefly of female wearing-apparel and child's linen; but with these articles there was a large packet of letters, addressed to Madame Louise de Montmorenci, the contents of which were a mystery to Newton, who did not understand French. There were also a red morocco case, containing a few diamond ornaments, and three or four crosses of different orders of knighthood. All the wearing-apparel of the lady was marked with the initials L. M., while those appertaining to the infant were marked with the letters J. F.

After a careful examination, Newton spread out the clothes to dry, over the cabin lockers and table ; and depositing the articles of value in a safe place, he returned on deck. Although Thompson had presented him with the trunk and its contents, he felt that they could not be considered as his property, and he determined to replace everything, and, upon his return, consult his father as to the proper measures which should be taken to discover who were the lawful owners.

The sloop, under the direction of Newton, had continued her course for two days against the adverse yet light breeze, when the weather changed. The wind still held to the same quarter, but the sky became loaded with clouds, and the sun set with a dull red glare, which prognosticated a gale from the N.W. ; and before morning the vessel was pitching through a short chopping sea. By noon the gale was at its height, and Newton, perceiving that the sloop did not "hold her own," went down to rouse the master, to inquire what steps should be taken, as he considered it advisable to bear up, and the only port under their lee for many miles was one with the navigation of which he was himself unacquainted.

The vessel was under close-reefed mainsail and storm foresail, almost buried in the heavy sea, which washed over the deck from forward to the companion hatch, when Newton went down to rouse the besotted Thompson, who having slept through the night without having had recourse to additional stimulus, was more easy to awaken than before.

"Eh ! what ?—blows hard—whew !—so it does. How's the wind ?" said the master, throwing his feet outside the standing bedplace as he sat up.

"N.W., veering to N.N.W. in the squalls. We have lost good ten miles since yesterday evening, and are close to Dudden Sands," replied Newton. "I think we must bear up, for the gale shows no signs of breaking."

"Well, I'll be on deck in a moment, my boy," rejoined Thompson, who was now quite himself again, and was busy putting on his shoes, the only articles which had been removed when he turned in. "Go you up, and see that they keep her clean, full and bye—and those casks well secured. Dudden Sands—awkward place, too—but I've not been forty years a-boxing about this coast for nothing."

In a minute Thompson made his appearance on deck, and steadying himself by the weather topmast backstay, fixed his leaden eyes upon the land on the quarter. "All right, younker, that's the head, sure enough;" then turning his face to the wind, which lifted up his grey curling locks and bore them out horizontally from his fur cap, "and it's a devil of a gale, sure enough. It may last a month of Sundays, for all I know. Up with the helm, Tom. Ease off the main sheet, handsomely, my lad—not too much. Now, take in the slack afore she jibes;" and the master ducked under the main boom, and took his station on the other side of the deck. "Steady as you go, now.—Newton, take the helm. D'ye see that bluff?—keep her right for it. Tom, you and the boy rouse the cable up—get about ten fathoms on deck, and bend it. You'll find a bit of seizing and a marline-spike in the locker abaft." The sloop scudded before the gale, and in less than two hours was close to the headland pointed out by the master. "Now, Newton, we must hug the point or we shall not fetch—clap on the main sheet here, all of us. Luff you may handsomely. That's all right; we are past the Sand-head, and shall be in smooth water in a jiffy. Steady, so-o. Now for a drop of swizzle," cried Thompson, who considered that he had kept sober quite long enough, and proceeded to the cask of rum lashed to leeward. As he knelt down to pull out the spile, the sloop, which had been brought to the wind, was struck on her broadside by a heavy sea, which careened her to her gunnel: the lashings of the weather cask gave way, and it flew across the deck, jamming the unfortunate Thompson, who knelt against the one to leeward, and then bounding overboard. The old man gave a heavy groan, and fell upon his back; the man and boy ran to his assistance, and by the directions of Newton, who could not quit the helm, carried him below, and placed him on his bed. In a few minutes the sloop was safe at anchor in smooth water, and Newton ran down into the cabin. Thompson's head had been crushed against the chime of the cask; for an hour or two he breathed heavily, and then—he was no more!

CHAPTER VI

" The Indian weed, unknown to ancient times,
Nature's choice gift, whose acrimonious fume
Extracts superfluous juices and refines
The blood distempered from its noxious salts ;
Friend to the spirit, which with vapours bland
It gently mitigates—companion fit
Of 'a good pot of porter.'"

—PHILLIPS.

" There's a pot of good double beer, neighbour.
Drink——"

—SHAKSPEARE.

THE next day the remains of old Thompson were carried on shore in the long-boat, and buried in the churchyard of the small fishing-town that was within a mile of the port where the sloop had anchored. Newton shipped another man ; and when the gale was over, continued his voyage, which was accomplished without further adventure.

Finding no cargo ready for him, and anxious to deliver up the vessel to the owner, who resided at Overton, he returned in ballast, and communicated the intelligence of Thompson's death ; which, in so small a town, was long the theme of conversation and the food of gossips.

Newton consulted with his father relative to the disposal of the trunk ; but Nicholas could assist him but little with his advice. After many *pros* and *cons*, like all other difficult matters, it was postponed. " Really, Newton, I can't say. The property certainly is not yours, but still we are not likely to find out the lawful owner. Bring the trunk on shore ; we'll nail it up, and perhaps we may hear something about it by-and-by. We'll make some inquiries—by-and-by—when your mother——"

" I think," interrupted Newton, " it would not be advisable to acquaint my mother with the circumstances ; but how to satisfy her curiosity on that point, I must leave to you."

" To me, boy ! no ; I think that you had better manage that, for you know you are only *occasionally* at home."

35

"Well, father, be it so," replied Newton, laughing; "but here comes Mr. Dragwell and Mr. Hilton, to consult with us what ought to be done relative to the effects of poor old Thompson. He has neither kith nor kin, to the ninety-ninth degree, that we can find out."

Mr. Dragwell was the curate of the parish; a little fat man with bow-legs, who always sat upon the edge of the chair leaning against the back, and twiddling his thumbs before him. He was facetious and good-tempered, but was very dilatory in everything. His greatest peculiarity was, that although he had a hearty laugh for every joke, he did not take the jokes of others at the time that they were made. His ideas seemed to have the slow and silent flow ascribed to the stream of lava (without its fire); and the consequence was, that although he eventually laughed at a good thing, it was never at the same time with other people; but in about a quarter or half a minute afterwards (according to the difficulty of the analysis), when the cause had been dismissed for other topics, he would burst out in a hearty " Ha, ha, ha!"

Mr. Hilton was the owner of the sloop. he was a tall, corpulent man, who for many years had charge of a similar vessel, until, by "doing a little contraband," he had pocketed a sufficient sum to enable him to purchase one for himself. But the profits being more than sufficient for his wants, he had for some time remained on shore, old Thompson having · charge of the vessel. He was a good-tempered, jolly fellow, very fond of his pipe and his pot, and much more fond of his sloop, by the employment of which he was supplied with all his comforts. He passed most of the day sitting at the door of his house, which looked upon the anchorage, exchanging a few words with every one that passed by, but invariably upon one and the same topic—his sloop. If she was at anchor, "There she is," he would say, pointing to her with the stem of his pipe. If she was away, she had sailed on such a day; he expected her back at such a time. It was a fair wind—it was a foul wind for his sloop. All his ideas were engrossed by this one darling object, and it was no easy task to divert him from it.

I ought to have mentioned that Mr. Dragwell, the curate, was invariably accompanied by Mr. Spinney, the clerk of the parish, a little spare man, with a few white hairs straggling on each side of a bald pate. He always took his tune, whether in or out of church, from his superior, ejecting a small treble " He, he, he ! " in response to the loud " Ha, ha, ha ! " of the curate.

" Peace be unto this house ! " observed the curate, as he crossed the threshold, for Mrs. Forster's character was notorious; then laughing at his own wit with a " Ha, ha, ha ! "

" He, he, he ! "

" Good morning, Mr. Forster; how is your good lady ? "

" She's safe moored at last," interrupted Mr. Hilton.

" Who ? " demanded the curate, with surprise.

" Why, the sloop, to be sure."

" Oh ! I thought you meant the lady—Ha, ha, ha ! "

" He, he, he ! "

" Won't you sit down, gentlemen ? " said Nicholas, showing the way from the shop into the parlour, where they found Mrs. Forster, who had just come in from the back premises.

" Hope you're well, Mr. Curate," sharply observed the lady, who could not be persuaded, even from respect for the cloth, to be commonly civil; " take a chair; it's all covered with dust; but that Betsy is such an idle slut ! "

" Newton handles her as well as any man going," observed Hilton.

" Newton ! " screamed the lady, turning to her son, with an angry inquiring look; " Newton handles Betsy ! " continued she, turning round to Hilton.

" Betsy ! no; the sloop I meant, ma'am."

Newton burst out into a laugh, in which he was joined by Hilton and his father.

" Sad business—sad indeed ! " said Hilton, after the merriment had subsided. " Such an awful death ! "

" Ha, ha, ha ! " roared the curate, who had but just then taken the joke about Betsy.

" He, he, he ! "

" Nothing to laugh at, that I can see," observed Mrs. Forster snappishly.

" Capital joke, ma'am, I assure you ! " rejoined the curate. " But, Mr. Forster, we had better proceed to business. Spinney, where are the papers ? " The clerk produced an inventory of the effects of the late Mr. Thompson, and laid them on the table. " Melancholy thing, this, ma'am,"

37

continued the curate, "very melancholy, indeed! But we must all die."

"Yes, thank Heaven!" muttered Nicholas, in an absent manner.

"Thank Heaven, Mr. Forster!" cried the lady; "why, do you wish to die?"

"I was not exactly thinking about myself, my dear," replied Nicholas; "I——"

"Depend upon it she'll last a long while yet," interrupted Mr. Hilton.

"Do you think so?" replied Nicholas mournfully.

"Oh! sure of it; I stripped her the other day and examined her all over; she's as sound as ever."

Nicholas started, and stared Hilton in the face; while Newton, who perceived their separate train of thought, tittered with delight.

"What are you talking of?" at last observed Nicholas.

"Of the sloop, to be sure," replied Hilton.

"I rather imagine you were come to consult about Mr. Thompson's effects," observed Mrs. Forster angrily—"rather a solemn subject, instead of——"

"Ha, ha, ha!" ejaculated the curate, who had just *taken* the equivoque which had occasioned Newton's mirth.

"He, he, he!"

This last merriment of Mr. Dragwell appeared to the lady to be such a pointed insult to her, that she bounded out of the room, exclaiming, "That an alehouse would have been a more suitable rendezvous."

The curate twiddled his thumbs, as the eyes of all the party followed the exit of Mrs. Forster; and there were a few moments of silence.

"Don't you find her a pleasant little craft, Forster?" said Hilton, addressing Newton.

Nicholas Forster, who was in a brown study about his wife, shook his head without lifting up his eyes, while Newton nodded assent.

"Plenty of accommodation in her," continued Hilton. Another negative shake from Nicholas, and assented nod from Newton.

"If I thought you could manage her, Forster," continued Hilton, "tell me, what do you think yourself?"

"Oh, quite impossible!" replied Nicholas.

"Quite impossible, Mr. Forster! Well, now, I've a better opinion of Newton—I think he can."

"Why, yes," replied Nicholas, "certainly better than I can; but till she's——"

"She's a beauty, Mr. Forster."

"Mrs. Forster's a beauty!" cried Nicholas, looking at Hilton with astonishment.

Newton and Hilton burst into a laugh. "No, no," said the latter, "I was talking about the sloop; but we had better proceed to business. Suppose we have pipes, Mr. Forster. Mr. Dragwell, what did you say?"

"Ha, ha, ha!" roared the curate, who had just taken the last joke.

"He, he, he!"

"Why, yes," continued the curate, "I think it is a most excellent proposition; this melancholy affair requires a great deal of consideration. I never compose so well as I do with a pipe in my mouth. Mrs. Dragwell says that she knows all my best sermons by the smell of them; d'ye take?—Ha, ha, ha!"

"He, he, he!"

The pipes, with the addition of a couple of pots of porter, were soon procured from the neighbouring alehouse; and while the parties are filling them, and pushing the paper of tobacco from one to the other, I shall digress, notwithstanding the contrary opinion of the other sex, in praise of this most potent and delightful weed.

I love thee, whether thou appearest in the shape of a cigar, or diest away in sweet perfume enshrined in the meerschaum bowl; I love thee with more than woman's love! Thou art a companion to me in solitude. I can talk and reason with thee, avoiding loud and obstreperous argument. Thou art a friend to me when in trouble, for thou advisest in silence, and consolest with thy calm influence over the perturbed spirit.

I know not how thy power has been bestowed upon thee; yet, if to harmonise the feelings, to allow the thoughts to spring without control, rising like the white vapour from the cottage hearth on a morning that is sunny and serene; if to impart that sober sadness over the spirit which inclines us to forgive our enemy, that calm philosophy which reconciles us to the ingratitude and knavery of the world, that heavenly contemplation whispering to us as we look around, that "all is good;"—if these be merits, they are thine, most potent weed.

What a quiet world this would be if every one would smoke! I suspect that the reason why the fairer sex decry thee is, that thou art the cause of silence. The ancients knew thee not, or the lips of Harpocrates would have been closed with a cigar, and his forefinger removed from the mouth unto the temple.

Half-an-hour has passed without any observation from our party, as the room gradually filled with the volumes of smoke, which wreathed and curled in graceful lines, as they ascended in obedience to the unchangeable laws of nature.

Hilton's pipe was first exhausted; he shook the ashes on the table. "A very melancholy business, indeed!" observed he, as he refilled. The rest nodded a grand assent; the pipe was relighted; and all were silent as before.

Another pipe is empty. "Looking at this inventory," said the curate, "I should imagine the articles to be of no great value. One fur cap, one round hat, one pair of plush breeches——; they are not worth a couple of pounds altogether," continued he, stuffing the tobacco into his pipe which he re-lighted, and no more was said. Nicholas was the third in, or rather out. "It appears to me," observed he; but what appeared is lost, as some new idea flitted across his imagination, and he commenced his second pipe without further remark.

Some ten minutes after this, Mr. Spinney handed the pot of porter to the curate, and subsequently to the rest of the party. They all took largely, then puffed away as before.

How long this cabinet council might have continued, it is impossible to say; but Silence, who was in "the chair," was soon afterwards driven from his post of honour by the most implacable of his enemies, a "woman's tongue."

"Well, Mr. Forster! well, gentlemen! do you mean to poison me? Have you made smell and dirt enough? How long is this to last, I should like to know?" cried Mrs. Forster, entering the room. "I tell you what, Mr. Forster, you had better hang up a sign at once, and keep an ale-house. Let the sign be a Fool's Head, like your own. I wonder you are not ashamed of yourself, Mr. Curate; you that ought to set an example to your parishioners!"

But Mr. Dragwell did not admire such remonstrance; so taking his pipe out of his mouth, he retorted: "If your husband does put up a sign, I recommend him to stick you up as the 'Good Woman;' that would be without your head —Ha, ha, ha!"

"He, he, he!"

"He, he, he! you pitiful 'natomy," cried Mrs. Forster in a rage, turning to the clerk, as she dared not revenge herself upon the curate. "Take that for your He, he, he!" and she swung round the empty pewter pot, which she snatched from the table, upon the bald pericranium of Mr. Spinney, who tumbled off his chair and rolled upon the sanded floor.

The remainder of the party were on their legs in an instant. Newton jerked the weapon out of his mother's hands, and threw it in a corner of the room. Nicholas was aghast; he surmised that his turn would come next, and so it proved. "An't you ashamed of yourself, Mr. Forster, to see me treated in this way—bringing a parcel of drunken men into the house to insult me? Will you order them out or not, sir? Are we to have quiet or not?"

"Yes, my love," replied Nicholas, confused, "yes, my dear, by-and-by, as soon as you're——"

Mrs. Forster darted towards her husband with the ferocity of a mad cat. Hilton, perceiving the danger of his host, put out his leg so as to trip her up in her career, and she fell flat upon her face on the floor. The violence of the fall was so great that she was stunned. Newton raised her up, and, with the assistance of his father (who approached with as much reluctance as a horse spurred towards a dead tiger), carried her upstairs and laid her on her bed.

Poor Mr. Spinney was now raised from the floor. He still remained stupefied with the blow, although gradually recovering. Betsy came in to render assistance. "O dear, Mr. Curate, do you think that he'll die?"

"No, no; bring some water, Betsy, and throw it in his face."

"Better take him home as he is," replied Betsy, "and say that he is killed; when Missus hears it, she'll be frightened out of her life. It will keep her quiet for some time at least."

"An excellent idea, Betty; we will punish her, for her conduct," replied Hilton. The curate was delighted at the plan. Mr. Spinney was placed in an arm-chair, covered over with a tablecloth, and carried away to the parsonage by two men, who were provided by Betsy before Nicholas or Newton had quitted the room where Mrs. Forster lay in a deplorable condition; her sharp nose broken and twisted on one side; her eyebrow cut open to the bone, and a violent contusion on her forehead. In less than half-an-hour it was spread through the whole town that Spinney had been murdered by Mrs. Forster, and that his brains were bespattered all over the shop windows!

CHAPTER VII

" That she is mad, 'tis true : 'tis true, 'tis pity ;
And pity 'tis, 'tis true : a foolish figure ;
But farewell it, for I will use no art.
Mad let us grant her then ; and now remains
That we find out the cause of this effect,
Or rather say, the cause of this defect."
—SHAKSPEARE.

MR. DRAGWELL has already made honourable mention of his wife; it will therefore only be necessary to add that he had one daughter, a handsome, lively girl, engaged to a Mr. Ramsden, the new surgeon of the place, who had stepped into the shoes and the good-will of one who had retired from forty years' practice upon the good people of Overton. Fanny Dragwell had many good qualities, and many others which were rather doubtful. One of the latter had procured her more enemies than at her age she had any right to expect. It was what the French term "malice," which bears a very different signification from the same word in our own language. She delighted in all practical jokes, and would carry them to an excess, at the very idea of which others would be startled; but it must be acknowledged that she generally selected as her victims those who from their conduct towards others richly deserved retaliation.

The various tricks which she had played upon certain cross old spinsters, tattlers, scandalmongers, and backbiters, often were the thème of conversation and of mirth; but this description of *espièglerie* contains a most serious objection; which is, that to carry on a successful and well-arranged plot, there must be a total disregard of truth. Latterly, Miss Fanny had had no one to practise upon except Mr. Ramsden, during the period of his courtship—a period at which women never appear to so much advantage, nor men appear so silly. But even for this the time was past, as latterly she had become so much attached to him that distress on his part was a source of annoyance to herself. When, therefore, her father came home, narrating the circumstances which had occurred, and the plan which had been meditated, Fanny entered gaily into the scheme. Mrs. Forster had long been her abhorrence; and an insult to Mr. Ramsden, who had latterly been designated by Mrs. Forster as a "pill-gilding puppy," was not to be forgotten. Her active and inventive mind immediately conceived a plan which would enable her to carry the joke much further than the original projectors had intended. Ramsden, who had been summoned to attend poor Mr. Spinney, was her sole confidant, and readily entered into a scheme which was pleasing to his mistress, and promised revenge for the treatment he had received; and which, as Miss Dragwell declared, would be nothing but retributive justice upon Mrs. Forster.

Late in the evening a message was received from Newton Forster, requesting that Mr. Ramsden would attend his mother. He had just visited the old clerk, who was now sensible, and had nothing to complain of except a deep cut on his temple from the rim of the pewter-pot. After receiving a few parting injunctions from Miss Dragwell, Mr. Ramsden quitted the parsonage.

"I am afraid it's a very bad business, Mr. Forster," replied the surgeon to Newton, who had been interrogating him relative to the injury received by Mr. Spinney. "Evident concussion of the brain; he may live, or he may not; a few days will decide the point: he is a poor feeble old man."

Newton sighed as he reflected upon the disaster and disgrace which might ensue from his mother's violence of temper.

"Eh! what, Mr. Ramsden?" said Nicholas, who had been

for some time contemplating the battered visage of his spouse.
"Did you say she'll die?"

"No, no, Mr. Forster, there's no fear of Mrs. Forster; she'll
do well enough. She'll be up and about again in a day or
two, as lively as ever."

"God forbid!" muttered the absent Nicholas.

"Mr. Forster, see if I don't pay you off for that, as soon as
I'm up again," muttered the recumbent lady, as well as the
bandages passed under her chin would permit her.

"Pray call early to-morrow, Mr. Ramsden, and let us know
how Mr. Spinney is going on," said Newton, extending his
hand as the surgeon rose to depart. Mr. Ramsden shook it
warmly, and quitted the house he had left them about half-
an-hour when Betsy made her appearance with some fomen-
tations which had been prepared in the kitchen. Out of
revenge for sundry blows daily received, and sundry epithets
hourly bestowed upon her by her mistress, the moment she
entered she exclaimed, in a half-crying tone, "O dear, Mr.
Newton! there's such shocking news just come from the
parsonage! Mr. Spinney is just dead—and my Missis will
be hanged!"

Mrs. Forster said not a word; she quailed under dread of
the report being correct. Newton and his father looked at
each other; their mute anguish was expressed by covering up
their faces with their hands.

When Hilton and the curate arranged their plans for the
mortification of Mrs. Forster, it was considered advisable that
Newton (who was not so easily to be imposed upon) should be
removed out of the way. Hilton had already stated his intention to give him charge of the vessel; and he now proposed
sending him for a cargo of shingle, which was lying ready for
her, about fifty miles down the coast, and which was to be
delivered at Waterford. At an early hour on the ensuing
morning he called at Forster's house. Newton, who had not
taken off his clothes, came out to meet him.

"Well, Newton, how is your mother?" said Hilton. "I
hope you are not angry with me: I certainly was the occasion
of the accident, but I could not bear to see your worthy
father treated in that manner."

"I blush to acknowledge, Mr. Hilton, that she deserved
it all," replied Newton; "but I am very much alarmed
44

about the condition of Mr. Spinney. Have you heard this morning?"

"No; but between ourselves, Newton, doctors always make the worst of their case. I never heard of a pewter pot killing a man; he'll do well enough, never fear. I came to tell you that I've a letter last night from Repton, who says that the shingle must be delivered before the tenth of next month, or the contract will be void. He desires that I will send the sloop directly, or he must employ another craft. Now, I think you had better start at once; there's a nice fair wind for you, and you'll be down afore night."

"Why, really, Mr. Hilton, I do not exactly like to leave home just now," replied Newton thoughtfully.

"Well, as you please, Mr. Forster," rejoined Hilton, with apparent displeasure. "I have offered you the command of the vessel, and now you object to serve my interests on the very first occasion, merely because there are a couple of broken heads!"

"I am wrong, most certainly," replied Newton; "I beg your pardon—I will just speak a word or two to my father, and be on board in less than half-an-hour."

"I will meet you there," said Hilton, "and bring your papers. Be as quick as you can, or you'll lose the first of the tide."

Newton returned to the house; his father made no objection to his departure; and, in fulfilment of his promise, Newton was ready to start, when he encountered Ramsden at the door.

"Mr. Ramsden," said Newton, "I am requested by the owner of my vessel to sail immediately; but if you think that the life of Mr. Spinney is seriously in danger, I will throw up the command of the vessel, rather than leave my mother under such an accumulation of disasters. I beg as a favour that you will not disguise the truth."

"You may sail this minute, if you please, Mr Forster; I am happy to be able to relieve your mind. Mr. Spinney is doing very well, and you'll see him at his desk on the first Sunday of your return."

"Then I'm off good-bye, Mr. Ramsden; many thanks."

With a lightened heart, Newton leapt into the skiff which was to carry him on board of the sloop, and in less than half-an-hour was standing away to the southward before a fine wind, to execute the orders which he had received.

Ramsden remained a few minutes at the door, until he saw Newton ascend the side of the vessel; then he entered, and was received by Betsy.

"Well, Betsy, you agreed to make Mrs. Forster believe that Mr. Spinney was dead, but we little thought that such would really be the case."

"Lord love you, sir! why, you don't say so?"

"I do, indeed, Betsy; but mind, we must keep it a secret for the present, until we can get Mrs. Forster out of the way. How is she this morning?"

"Oh, very stiff, and very cross, sir."

"I'll go up to her," replied Ramsden; "but recollect, Betsy, that you do not mention it to a soul;" and Ramsden ascended the stairs.

"Well, Mrs. Forster, how do you feel this morning? do you think you could get up?"

"Get up, Mr. Ramsden! not to save my soul—I can't even turn on my side."

"Very sorry to hear it, indeed," replied the surgeon; "I was in hopes that you might have been able to bear a journey?"

"Bear a journey, Mr. Ramsden! why bear a journey?"

"I am sorry to inform you that Mr. Spinney's gone, poor old man! There must be a coroner's inquest. Now, it would be as well if you were not to be found, for the verdict will be 'Wilful Murder.'"

"O dear! O dear!" exclaimed Mrs. Forster, jumping out of her bed with fright, and wringing her hands. "What can I do?—what can I do?"

"At present it is a secret, Mrs. Forster, but it cannot be so long. Miss Dragwell, who feels for you very much, begged me not to say a word about it. She will call and consult with you, if you would like to see her. Sad thing, indeed, Mrs. Forster, to be placed in such a situation by a foolish husband."

"You may well say that, Mr. Ramsden," replied the lady, with asperity; "he is the greatest fool that ever God made! Every one knows what a sweet temper I was before I married; but flesh and blood cannot bear what I am subjected to."

"Would you like to see Miss Dragwell?"

"Yes, very much; I always thought her a very nice girl—a little wild—a little forward indeed, and apt to be impertinent; but still, rather a nice girl."

"Well, then, I will tell her to call, and the sooner the better, for when it is known, the whole town will be in an uproar. I should not be surprised if they attacked the house—the people will be so indignant."

"I don't wonder at it," replied Mrs. Forster; "nothing can excuse such provocation as I receive from my husband, stupid wretch!"

"Good morning, Mrs. Forster; do you think, then, that you could bear moving?"

"O yes! O yes! But where am I to go?"

"That I really cannot form an idea of—you had better consult with Miss Dragwell. Depend upon it, Mrs. Forster, that I will be most happy to render you all my assistance in this unfortunate dilemma."

"You're very good," snarled Mrs. Forster; and Ramsden quitted the room.

I have one or two acquaintances, to whom, if I wish a report to be circulated, I immediately impart the substance as a profound secret; and I find that by these means it obtains a much more extensive circulation than if I sent it to the newspapers.

Ramsden was aware of Betsy's cackling propensities; and long before he quitted Mrs. Forster, it was generally believed throughout the good town of Overton that Mr. Spinney, although he had not been killed outright, as reported in the first instance, had subsequently died of the injuries received from this modern Xantippe.

Mrs. Forster had half-an-hour to reflect upon her supposed awkward situation; and, to drive away thought, had sent for Nicholas, whom she loaded with the bitterest invectives, when Miss Dragwell was announced.

"See, sir," continued Mrs. Forster, "the condition to which you have reduced a fond and faithful wife—one that has so studied your interests; one——"

"Yes, indeed," added Miss Dragwell, who heard the attack as she ascended the stairs, and took up the cause of Mrs. Forster to obtain her confidence,—"yes, indeed, Mr. Forster,

47

see the consequences of your folly, your smoking, and your drinking. Pray leave the room, sir; I wonder how Mrs. Forster can bear the sight of you."

Nicholas stared, and was about to throw in a detached word or two by way of vindication, when a furious "Begone!" from his wife occasioned a precipitate retreat.

"We have all been consulting about this sad business, my dear Mrs. Forster," commenced Miss Dragwell, "and, after much consideration, have hit upon the only plan by which you may escape the penalty of the law. Yes, my dear ma'am," continued Miss Dragwell, in the most bland and affectionate voice, "it is unwise to conceal the truth from you; the depositions of my father and Mr. Hilton, when they are called upon, will be such that 'Wilful Murder' must be returned, and you—(the young lady faltered and put up her handkerchief)—you must inevitably be hanged!"

"Hanged!" screamed Mrs. Forster.

"Yes, hanged—'hanged by the neck until you are dead, and the Lord have mercy upon your soul!' that will be your sentence," replied the young lady, sobbing; "such an awful, such a disgraceful death for a woman too!"

"O Lord, O Lord!" cried Mrs. Forster, who was now really frightened. "What will become of me?"

"You will go to another and a better world, as my papa says in his sermons; I believe that the pain is not very great, but the disgrace——"

Mrs. Forster burst into tears. "Save me! save me, Miss Dragwell!—Oh! Oh! that stupid Nicholas, Oh! Oh!"

"My dear Mrs. Forster, we have all agreed at the parsonage that there is but one method."

"Name it, my dear Miss Dragwell, name it!" cried Mrs. Forster imploringly.

"You must pretend to be mad, and then there will be a verdict of insanity; but you must carry it through everything, or it will be thought you are shamming. Mr. Ramsden is acquainted with Dr. B——, who has charge of the asylum at D——. It is only nine miles off : he will take you there, and when the coroner's inquest is over you can return. It will be supposed then to have been only temporary derangement. Do you like the proposal?"

"Why, I have been mad for a long time," replied Mrs.

Forster ; " the conduct of my husband and my son has been too much for my nerves ; but I don't like the idea of actually going to a madhouse. Could not——"

" Oh ! dear, marm," cried Betsy, running into the room, " there's a whole posse of people about the house ; they want to take you to the town-jail for murdering Mr. Spinney. What shall I say to them ? I'm feared they'll break in."

" Go and tell them that Mrs. Forster is too ill to be taken out of bed, and that she is out of her senses—d'ye hear, Betsy, tell them all she is stark staring mad ! "

" Yes, I will, marm," replied Betsy, wiping her eyes as she left the room.

Miss Dragwell walked to the window. Although the report spread by Betsy had collected a crowd opposite the house, still there was no attempt at violence.

" I'm afraid that it's too late," said the young lady, turning from the window. " What a crowd ! and how angry they seem to be ! You must be hanged now ! "

" Oh ! no : I'll be mad—I'll be anything, my dear Miss Drag-well."

. " Well, then, we must be quick. Don't put your gown on —petticoats are better—I'll dress you up." Miss Dragwell rummaged the drawers, and collecting a variety of feathers and coloured ribbons, pinned them over the bandages which encircled Mrs. Forster's head ; then pulling out a long-tailed black coat of her husband's, which had been condemned, forced her arms through it, and buttoned it in front. " That will do for the present," cried Miss Dragwell ; " now here's the cat, take it in your arms, go to the window, and nurse it like a baby. I'll throw it open—you come forward and make them a curtsey ; that will spread the report through the town that you are mad, and the rest will then be easy."

" Oh ! I can't—I can't go to the window, I can't, indeed."

" I'll open the window and speak to the people," said Miss Dragwell ; and she threw up the sash, informing the gaping multitude that Mrs. Forster was quite out of her senses, but perfectly harmless.

" Perfectly harmless after killing a man ! " observed one of the party below.

" They won't believe me, Mrs. Forster ; come, you must, or you will certainly be hanged."

D

Urged by her fears, Mrs. Forster approached the window and showed herself to the astonished crowd. "Curtsey to them," said Miss Dragwell, holding her handkerchief before her mouth.

Mrs. Forster curtsied.

"Smile upon them," continued the malicious young lady.

Mrs. Forster grinned horribly.

"Now dance your cat."

Mrs. Forster obeyed the injunction.

"Now give a loud shriek, and toss the cat out of the window."

Mrs. Forster uttered a hideous yell, and threw the animal at the heads of the spectators, who retreated with alarm in every direction.

"Now burst into a fit of laughter, curtsey to them, and wave your hand, and that will be sufficient."

Mrs. Forster obeyed the last order, and Miss Dragwell shut the window. In a few minutes the report spread that Mrs. Forster had gone out of her senses; and the murder of Mr. Spinney—a topic which was nearly exhausted—was dismissed for the time to dwell and comment upon the second catastrophe.

CHAPTER VIII

"Mad as the sea and wind, when both contend which is the mightier."

—SHAKSPEARE.

So far we have succeeded, my dear Mrs. Forster," said Miss Dragwell; "I will now return home, and come back as soon as I can with the post-chaise. Mr. Ramsden's servant shall come with me to conduct you to the asylum; and I trust in a quarter of an hour to see you clear of these foolish people of Overton, who think that you are the party in fault. You had better remain in your room, and not appear again at the window; the crowd will disperse when they are tired of watching—good-bye, my dear Mrs. Forster, good-bye."

Mrs. Forster was in too sulky a humour to vouchsafe an

answer, and Miss Dragwell quitted the house. Betsy had taken advantage of the turmoil and the supposed lunacy of her mistress to gossip in the neighbourhood. Nicholas Forster was in the shop, but took no notice of Miss Dragwell as she passed through. He appeared to have forgotten all that had occurred, and was very busy filing at his bench. There we must leave him, and follow the motions of the mischief-loving Miss Dragwell.

Upon her return, the party collected at the parsonage considered that they had proceeded far enough; but Miss Dragwell thought otherwise; she had made up her mind that Mrs. Forster should pass a day or two in the Lunatic Asylum; and she felt assured that Mr. Ramsden, through whose assistance her intention must be accomplished, would not venture to dispute her wishes.

Her father, with a loud " Ha, ha, ha!" proposed that Mr. Spinney should appear as a ghost by the bedside of Mrs. Forster, wrapped up in a sheet, with a " He, he, he!" and that thus the diversion should end; but this project was overruled by Mr. Spinney, who protested that nothing should induce him again to trust himself, with a " He, he, he!" in the presence of Mrs. Forster.

Ramsden, although well acquainted with Dr. Beddington, who had charge of the asylum, was not sure that he would be pleased with their freak, and earnestly dissuaded his intended from proceeding any further.

" It is useless to argue, my dear George, I am Quixote enough to revenge the injuries of those who have been forced to submit to her temper; and moreover, I hope to effect a cure. Desperate diseases, you must be aware as a medical man, require desperate remedies. I consider that a termagant and a lunatic are during their paroxysms on a par, as rational behaviour in either party may be considered as a lucid interval. Let her, if it be only for once hour, witness herself reflected in the various distorted mirrors of perverted mind; and if she has any conscience whatever, good will spring from evil. I joined this plot from a love of mischief; but I carry it on from a feeling that favourable results will be produced."

" But, my dear Fanny——"

" I will have it so, Ramsden, so don't attempt to dissuade

me; we are not married yet, and I must not be thwarted in my short supremacy. Surely you ought not to be displeased at my desire to 'tame a shrew.' I give a fair promise not to fall into an error which I so ardently detest; now, send for the chaise, write a letter to Dr. Beddington, and leave me to arrange with Mrs. Forster."

Ramsden, like many others, when teased by a pretty woman, consented against his will; he wrote a letter to Dr. Beddington, explaining circumstances, and requesting his pardon for the liberty which he had been persuaded to take.

Miss Dragwell, as soon as the letter was sealed, put on her bonnet, and taking Mr. Ramsden's servant with her, stepped into the chaise, and drove to the house of Mr. Nicholas Forster. She found Mrs. Forster squatted on the bed in her ludicrous attire, awaiting her return with impatience.

"Oh! Mrs. Forster, I have had such trouble, such difficulty; but Mr. Ramsden has been persuaded at last. There is a letter to Dr. Beddington, and Mr. Ramsden's servant is in the chaise at the door: the sooner you are off the better; the people are so outrageous, and call you such shocking names."

"Do they?" replied Mrs. Forster, whose wrath kindled at the information.

"Yes, indeed; and that wretch Betsy declares that she'll put the rope over your neck with her own hands."

"Does she?" cried Mrs. Forster, her eyes twinkling with rage.

"Yes; and your husband, your foolish husband, says that he'll be able to make his improvement in the duplex, now that you'll be hanged."

"He does, does he?" replied Mrs. Forster, catching her breath, and grinding her teeth as she jumped off the bed.

"Now, my dear Mrs. Forster, it's no use minding what they say, all you have to do is to escape as soon as possible; the magistrate's warrant may arrive this minute, and then it will be too late; so come down at once. How lucky that you have escaped! it must be a dreadful thing to be hanged!"

This last remark, always brought forward by Miss Dragwell when she had a point to carry, induced Mrs. Forster to hasten downstairs to the post-chaise, which she found already occupied by Mr. Ramsden's servant. As soon as she entered, it was driven off with speed in the direction already communicated to the post-boy.

We shall leave the town of Overton to recover its quiet— for such a bustle had not occurred for many years—and Miss Dragwell to exult in the success of her plot, while we follow Mrs. Forster to her new quarters.

The chaise rattled on—Mr. Ramsden's servant crouching in a corner, as far as possible from Mrs. Forster, evidently about as well pleased with his company as one would be in a pitfall with a tiger. At last it stopped at the door of the Lunatic Asylum, and the post-boy, dismounting from his reeking horses, pulled violently at a large bell, which answered with a most lugubrious tolling, and struck awe into the breast of Mrs. Forster.

When the door was opened, Mr. Ramsden's servant alighted, and went in to deliver his letter to the doctor. The doctor was not at home; he had obtained his furlough of three weeks, and was very busy with his fishing-rod some thirty miles distant; but the keepers were in attendance, and, as Mr. Ramsden's servant stated the insanity of Mrs. Forster, and that she had been sent there by his master, they raised no objections to her reception. In a few minutes the servant reappeared with two keepers, who handed Mrs. Forster out of the chaise, and conducted her to a receiving-room, where Mrs. Forster waited some minutes in expectation of the appearance of Dr. Beddington. In the meantime, Mr. Ramsden's servant, having no further communication to make, left the letter for Dr. Beddington, and returned in the chaise to Overton.

After a quarter of an hour had elapsed, Mrs. Forster inquired of one of the keepers, who had, much to her annoyance, taken a chair close to her, whether the doctor intended to come.

"He'll come by-and-by, good woman. How do you feel yourself now?"

"Very cold—very cold, indeed," replied Mrs. Forster, shivering.

"That's what the poor brutes always complain of—aren't it, Jim?" observed another keeper, who had just entered. "Where be we to stow her?"

"I sent Tom to get No. 14 ready."

"Why, you don't think that I'm mad!" cried Mrs. Forster, with terror.

"So, softly—so—so," said the keeper next to her, patting her as he would soothe a fractious child.

The violence of Mrs. Forster, when she discovered that she was considered as a lunatic, fully corroborated to the keepers the assertion of Mr. Ramsden's servant; but we must not dwell upon the scene which followed. After an ineffectual struggle, Mrs. Forster found herself locked up in No. 14, and left to her own reflections. The previous scenes which had occurred, added to the treatment which she received in the asylum, caused such excitement, that before the next morning she was seized with a brain fever, and raved as loudly in her delirium as any of the other unfortunate inmates there incarcerated.

CHAPTER IX

" Who by repentance is not satisfied,
  Is not of heaven, nor earth ; for these are pleased ;
By penitence the Eternal's wrath's appeased."
—SHAKSPEARE.

MR. RAMSDEN'S servant returned to Overton, stating that the doctor was not at home, but that he had left Mrs. Forster and the letter. The time that Dr. Beddington was to be absent had not been mentioned by the keepers; and Mr. Ramsden imagining that the doctor had probably gone out for the evening, made no further inquiries, as he intended, in a day or two, to call and bring Mrs. Forster back to her own house. On the third day of her removal he set off for the asylum; and when he discovered the situation of Mrs. Forster, he bitterly repented that he had been persuaded to a step which threatened such serious results. To remove her was impossible; to assert to the keepers that she was of sound mind, would have been to commit himself; he therefore withdrew his letter to Dr. Beddington, who was not expected home for a fortnight,

54

and with a heavy heart returned to Overton. Miss Drag-well was as much shocked when she was informed of the unfortunate issue of her plot, and made a resolution, to which she adhered, never to be guilty of another practical joke.

In the meantime Newton Forster had made every despatch, and returned to Overton with the cargo of shingle a few days after his mother's incarceration. He had not been ten minutes on shore before he was made acquainted with the melancholy history of her (supposed) madness and removal to the asylum. He hastened home, where he found his father in a profound melancholy; he received Newton with a flood of tears, and appeared to be quite lost in his state of widowhood. The next morning Newton set off to the asylum, to ascertain the condition of his mother. He was admitted; found her stretched upon a bed in a state of delirium, raving in her fever, and unconscious of his presence. The frenzy of his mother being substantiated by what he had witnessed, and by the assurances of the keepers, to whom he made a present of half his small finances to induce them to treat her with kindness, Newton returned to Overton, where he remained at home shut up with his father. In a few days notice was given by the town-crier that the remaining stock of Mr. Nicholas Forster, optician, was to be disposed of by public auction.

The fact was, that Nicholas Forster, like many other husbands, although his wife had been a source of constant annoyance, had become so habituated to her, that he was miserable now that she was gone. Habit is more powerful than even love, and many a married couple continue to live comfortably together long after love has departed, from this most binding of all human sensations. Nicholas determined to quit Overton, and Newton, who perceived that his father's happiness was at stake, immediately acquiesced in his wish. When Nicholas Forster resolved to leave the town where he had so long resided, he had no settled plans for the future; the present idea to remove from the scene connected with such painful associations was all which occupied his thoughts. Newton, who presumed that his father had some arranged plan, did not attempt to awaken him from his profound melancholy, to inquire into his intentions; and Nicholas

55

had never given the subject one moment of his thought. When all was ready, Newton inquired of his father in what manner he intended they should travel? "Why, outside the coach will be the cheapest, Newton, and we have no money to spare. You had better take our places to-night."

"To what place, father?" inquired Newton.

"I'm sure I don't know, Newton," replied Nicholas, as if just awoke.

This answer produced a consultation; and after many pros and cons, it was resolved that Nicholas should proceed to Liverpool, and settle in that town. The sloop commanded by Newton was found defective in the stern port; and as it would take some little time to repair her, Newton had obtained leave for a few days to accompany his father on his journey. The trunk picked up at sea, being too cumbrous, was deposited with the articles of least value in the charge of Mr. Dragwell; the remainder was taken away by Newton, until he could find a more secure place for their deposit. On their arrival at Liverpool, with little money and no friends, Nicholas rented a small shop; and Newton having extended his leave of absence to the farthest, that he might contribute to his father's comfort, returned to Overton to resume the command of the sloop. The first object was to call at the asylum, where he was informed that his mother was much less violent, but in so weak a state that he could not be admitted. Dr. Beddington had not returned, but a medical gentleman, who had been called in during his absence, stated to Newton that he had no doubt, if his mother should recover from her present state of exhaustion, that her reason would be restored. Newton returned to Overton with a lightened heart, and the next day sailed in the sloop for Bristol. Contrary winds detained him more than a fortnight on his passage. On his arrival, his cargo was not ready, and Newton amused himself by walking about the town and its environs. At last his cargo was on board, and Newton, who was most anxious to ascertain the fate of his mother, made all haste to obtain his clearance and other papers from the Custom-house. It was late in the evening before he had settled with the house to which the sloop had been consigned, but, as the wind and tide served, and there was a bright moon, he resolved to weigh that night. With his papers carefully buttoned in his coat, he was proceeding to the boat at the jetty, when he was seized by two men, who rushed upon him from behind. He hardly had time to look round to ascertain the cause, when a blow on the head stretched him senseless on the ground.

Now, my readers may probably feel some little distress at the misfortune of Newton, and have some slight degree of curiosity to know the grounds of this severe treatment. I, on the contrary, am never more pleased than when I find my principal character in a state of abeyance, and leave him so with the greatest indifference, because it suits my convenience. I have now an opportunity of returning to Mrs. Forster, or any other of the parties who act a subordinate part in my narrative; and as Newton is down on the ground and *hors de combat*, why, there let him lie until I want him again.

Dr. Beddington returned home long before the recovery of Mrs. Forster from her severe attack. As it may be presumed, he found her perfectly rational; but still he had no doubt of the assertions of his keepers, that she was insane at the time that she was sent to the asylum by Mr. Ramsden. The latter gentleman kept aloof until the issue of Mrs. Forster's malady should be ascertained: if she recovered, it was his intention to call upon Dr. Beddington and explain the circumstances; if she died, he had determined to say nothing about it. Mrs. Forster's recovery was tedious; her mind was loaded with anxiety, and what was infinitely more important, with deep remorse. The supposed death of Mr. Spinney had been occasioned by her violence, and she looked forward with alarm, as great as the regret with which she looked back upon her former behaviour. When she called to mind her unfeeling conduct towards her husband—the many years of bitterness she had created for him—her infraction of the marriage vow—the solemn promise before God to love, honour, and obey, daily and hourly violated—her unjust hatred of her only son—her want of charity towards others—all her duties neglected—swayed only by selfish and malignant passions—with bitter tears of contrition and self-abasement, she acknowledged that her punishment was just. With streaming eyes, with supplicating hands and bended knees, she implored mercy and forgiveness of Him to whom appeal is never made in vain. Passion's infuriate reign was over—her heart was changed!

To Dr. Beddington she made neither complaint nor explanation. All she wished was to quit the asylum as soon as she was restored to health, and prove to her husband, by her future conduct, the sincerity of her reformation. When she became convalescent, by the advice of Dr. Beddington, she walked in a garden appropriated for the exercise of the more harmless inmates of the asylum. The first day that she went out she sat down upon a bench near to the keepers who were watching those who were permitted to take the air and exercise, and overheard their discourse, which referred to herself.

" Why, what was it as made her mad, d'ye know, Tom ? "

" They say she's been no better all her life," replied the other ; " a rat would not live in the house with her. At last, in one of her tantrums, she nearly murdered old Spinney, the clerk at Overton. The report went out that he was dead ; and conscience, I suppose, or summat of that kind, run away with her senses."

" Oh ! he warn't killed then ? "

" No, no : I seed him and heard him too, Sunday 'fore last, when I went to call upon old father ; I was obligated to go to church, the old gemman's so remarkable particular."

" And what's become of her husband, and that handsome young chap, her son ? "

" I don't know, nor nobody else either. The old man, who was as worthy an old soul as ever breathed (more shame to the old faggot for the life she led him !), grew very unhappy and melancholy, and would not stay in the place : they disposed of everything, and both went away together ; but nobody knows-where the old man is gone to."

" And the young 'un ? "

" Oh ! he came back and took command of the sloop. He was here twice, to see how his mother was. Poor lad ! it was quite pitiful to see how unhappy he was about the old cata-maran. He give me and Bill a guinea apiece to be kind to her ; but, about three days back, the sloop came into the harbour without him. They suppose that he fell off the jetty at Bristol and was drowned, for he was seen coming down to the boat ; and a'ter that they never heard no more about him."

"Well, but, Tom, the old woman's all right now?"

"Yes, she's right enough; but where be her husband, and where be her son? She'll never plague them any more, that's pretty sartain."

The feelings of Mrs. Forster at the finale of this discourse are not easy to be portrayed. One heavy load was off her mind—Mr. Spinney was not dead; but how much had she also to lament? She perceived that she had been treacherously kidnapped by those who detested her conduct, but had no right to inflict the punishment. The kind and feeling conduct of her husband and of her son—the departure of the one, and supposed death of the other, were blows which nearly overwhelmed her. She tottered back to her cell in a state of such extreme agitation as to occasion a return of fever, and for many days she was unable to quit her bed.

CHAPTER X

" When Britain first at Heaven's command
Arose from out the azure main,
This was the charter, the charter of the land,
And guardian angels sung the strain,—
Rule Britannia, Britannia rules the waves,
For Britons never shall be slaves."

WE left Newton Forster senseless on the pavement leading to the quay at Bristol, floored by a rap on the head from a certain person or persons unknown; he did not, however, remain there long, being hoisted on the shoulders of two stout fellows, dressed in blue jackets and trousers, with heavy clubs in their hands, and a pistol lying *perdu* between their waistcoats and shirts. These nautical personages tumbled him into the stern-sheets of a boat, as if not at all sorry to rid themselves of his weight; and in a continued state of insensibility, Newton was hoisted up the side of a cutter which lay at anchor about one hundred yards from the shore.

When Newton recovered his senses, his swimming eyes could just enable him to perceive that something flashed

upon them, and in their weak state created a painful sensation. As he became more collected, he discovered that a
man was holding a small candle close to them, to ascertain
whether the vein which had been opened in his arm had
produced the desired effect of restoring him to animation.
Newton tried to recollect where he was, and what had
occurred; but the attempted exercise of his mental powers
was too much, and again threw him into a state of stupor.
At last he awoke as if from a dream of death, and looking
round, found himself lying on the deck attended by a female,
who bathed his forehead.

"Where am I?" exclaimed Newton.

"Is it where you are that you'd want for to know? A'nt ye
on board of the *Lively* cutter, sure? and a'nt you between
decks in her, and I looking a'ter ye, honey?"

"And who are you?"

"And who am I? Then, if I'm not somebody else, I'm
Judy Malony, the wife of the boatswain's mate, and a lawful
married woman."

"How did I come here?" continued Newton, raising himself on his elbow.

"You didn't come at all, honey; you were brought."

"Who brought me?"

"Who brought ye! it was either the gig or the jolly-boat;
but I wasn't on deck at the time, so I can't upon my oath
say exactly which."

"Then, pray can you tell me why I was brought here?"
replied Newton.

"Sure I can guess, bating you don't know already. It
was to sarve your king and your country, like a brave volunteer as you are."

"Then I'm impressed?"

"You may take your Bible oath of it, my jewel, and commit no perjury. It's a hard rap that ye got, anyhow, just
a hint that ye were wanted; but plase God, if ye live and do
well, 'twill be nothing at all to what ye'll have by-and-by, all
for the honour and glory of Ould England."

Newton, who during these remarks was thinking of his
father's situation, and the distress he would suffer without his
assistance, and then of the state in which he had left his
mother, again sank on the deck.

THE MERCHANT SERVICE

"Why, he's off again!" muttered Judy Malony; "he's no countryman of mine, that's clear as the mud in the Shannon, or he'd never fuss about a rap with a shillelah;" and Judy, lifting up her petticoats first, gained her feet, and walked away forward.

Newton remained in a state of uneasy slumber until daylight, when he was awakened by the noise of boats coming alongside and loud talking on deck. All that had passed did not immediately rush into his mind; but his arm tied up with the bandage, and his hair matted, and his face stiff with the coagulated blood, soon brought to his recollection the communication of Judy Malony, that he had been impressed. The 'tween decks of the cutter appeared deserted, unless indeed there were people in the hammocks slung over his head; and Newton, anxious to obtain further information, crawled under the hammocks to the ladder, and went up on deck.

About twenty sailors, well armed, were busy handing out of the boats several men whom they had brought on board, who were ordered aft by the officer in command. Newton perceived that most of them had not received much better treatment than he had on the preceding evening; some were shockingly disfigured, and were still bleeding profusely.

"How many have you altogether, Mr. Vincent?" said the lieutenant to a stout master's mate with a tremendous pair of whiskers, which his loose handkerchief discovered to join together at his throat.

"Seventeen, sir."

"And how many had we before—twenty-six, I think."

"Twenty-seven, sir, with the young chap I sent on board last night."

"Well, that will do; it's quite as many as we can stow away or take care of: pass them all down below forward; take up the ladder, and put on the grating till we are out of the harbour. As soon as the jolly-boat comes on board we'll up anchor."

"She'll be off directly, sir; I ordered her to wait for Johnson and Merton, who did not come down with us."

"Do you think they have given you the slip?"

"I should think not, sir. Here is the jolly-boat coming off."

"Well, pass the men forward and secure them," replied

64

the lieutenant. "Overhaul the boat's falls and bring to with the windlass."

Newton thought this a good opportunity to state that he was the master of a vessel, and, as such, protected from the impress ; · he therefore walked over to the lieutenant, and addressing him, "I beg your pardon, sir——"

"Who are you?" interrupted the lieutenant gruffly.

"I was impressed last night, sir; may I speak to you?"

"No, sir, you may not."

"It might save you some trouble, sir——"

"It will save me more to send you down below. Mr. Vincent, shove this man down forward; why is he at large?"

"He was under the doctor's hands, I believe, sir. Come this way, my hearty—stir your stumps."

Newton would have expostulated, but he was collared by two of the press-gang, and very unceremoniously handed forward to the hatchway; the grating was taken off, and he was lowered down to the deck below, where he found himself cooped up with more than forty others, almost suffocated for the want of air and space. The conversation (if conversation it could be called) was nothing but one continued string of curses and execrations, and vows of deep revenge.

The jolly-boat returned, pulling only two oars; the remainder of her crew, with Thompson and Merton, having taken this opportunity of deserting from their forced servitude. With some hearty execrations upon the heads of the offending parties, and swearing that by G—d there was no such thing as *gratitude* in a sailor, the commander of the cutter weighed his anchor and proceeded to sea.

The orders received by the lieutenant of the cutter, although not precisely specifying, still implying that he was to bring back his cargo alive, as soon as his Majesty's cutter *Lively* was fairly out at sea, the hatches were taken off, and the impressed men allowed to go on deck in the proportion of about one half at a time, two sailors, with drawn cutlasses, still remaining sentry at the coombings of the hatchway, in case of any discontented fellow presuming to dispute such lawful authority.

Newton Forster was happy to be once more on deck; so much had he suffered during his few hours of confinement, that he really felt grateful for the indulgence. The sky was bright, and the cutter was dashing along the coast with the wind two points free, at the rate of seven or eight miles an hour. She was what sailors term rather *a wet one,* and as she plunged through the short waves the sea broke continually over her bows and chesstree, so that there was no occasion to draw water for purification. Newton washed his face and head and felt quite revived as he inhaled the fresh breeze, and watched the coast as the vessel rapidly passed each head-land in her course. All around him were strangers, and no one appeared inclined to be communicative; even the most indifferent, the most stoical, expressed their ideas in disjointed sentences; they could not but feel that their projects and speculations had been overthrown by a captivity so anomalous with their boasted birthright.

"Where are we going?" inquired Newton of a man who stood next him, silently watching the passing foam created by the rapid course of the vessel.

"To hell, I hope, with those who brought us here!" replied the man, grinding his teeth with a scowl of deep revenge.

At this moment Judy Malony came pattering along the wet deck with a kid of potato-peelings to throw over the bows. Newton recognised her, and thanked her for her kindness.

"It's a nice boy that you are, sure enough, now that you're swate and clean," replied Judy. "Bad luck to the rapparee who gave you the blow! I axed my husband if it was he; but he swears upon his salvation that it was no one if it wasn't Tim O'Connor, the baste!"

"Where are we going?" inquired Newton.

"A'nt we going to dinner in a minute or two?"

"I mean where is the cutter bound to?"

"Oh! the cutter you mane! If she can only find her way, it's to Plymouth, sure; they're waiting for ye."

"Who is waiting for us?"

"Why, three fine frigates as can't go to sea without hands. You never heard of a ship going to sea without hands; the poor dumb craturs can't do nothing by themselves."

"Do you know where the frigates are going?"

"Going to *say,* I lay my life on't," replied Judy, who then walked forward, and broke up the conversation.

The next morning the cutter ran into Hamoaze, and boats were sent on board to remove the impressed men to the guard-ship. There, much to his annoyance and mortification, Newton found that, with the others, he was treated as a close prisoner. The afternoon of the same day another vessel arrived from the eastward with a collection of offenders, who for a variety of crimes and misdemeanours had been sentenced to serve on board of a man-of-war. No distinction was made ; all were huddled together and treated alike, until summoned on the quarter-deck, when their names were called out for distribution to the several men-of-war. Each ship having a quota of seamen and pickpockets allotted to her in due proportion, the men were ordered down into the boats ; and in less than an hour Newton found himself on board of a fine frigate lying in the Sound, with her foretop-sail loose as a signal of her immediate departure.

CHAPTER XI

" 'Tis man's bold task the gen'rous strife to try,
But in the hands of God is victory."
—*Iliad.*

NEWTON, and the other men who had been selected for the frigate on board of which they had been despatched (victualled the day discharged), were mustered on the quarter-deck by the first lieutenant, who asked them the questions whether they were bred to the sea, and could take the helm and lead. Having noted down their answers, he stationed them accordingly, and they were dismissed. Newton would again have appealed, but on reflection thought it advisable to await the arrival of the captain. Beds and blankets were not supplied that evening: the boats were hoisted up, sentries on the gangways supplied with ball-cartridges to prevent desertion, and permission granted to the impressed men to " prick for the softest plank " which they could find for their night's repose.

At daylight the hands were turned up, the capstern manned, the frigate unmoored, and hove " short stay a peak " on her anchor remaining down. The gig was sent on shore with two midshipmen, one to watch the men and prevent their desertion, while the other went up to the captain's lodgings to report her arrival, the topsails were loosed, sheeted home, and hoisted, the yards braced by, and Newton to his sorrow perceived that the captain's arrival would be the signal for immediate departure. The signal-man, on the look-out with his glass, reported the gig coming off with the captain; and in obedience to the orders he had received, the first lieutenant immediately hove up, and the anchor having been "catted and fished," the frigate lay-to in the Sound. As soon as the boat came alongside, and the captain had been received with the customary honours, he desired sail to be made on her as soon as the boat was hoisted up, and then descended to his cabin. In three minutes Newton perceived that all chance of release for the present was over; the courses and top-gallant sails were set, and the frigate darted past the Ram Head at the rate of ten miles per hour.

In about twenty minutes, after the messenger had been stowed away, the cables coiled in the tiers, and the ropes flemished down on deck, the captain made his appearance, and directed the first lieutenant to send aft the newly-impressed men. In few words he pointed out to them the necessity of their servitude, and concluded by recommending them to enter his Majesty's service, and receive the bounty to which they would become entitled; observing, that the men who did so would raise themselves in his good opinion, and, as far as he had the power, would not be forgotten by him, provided that their general good conduct merited his favour. Some few accepted the terms, but the most of them positively refused. When Newton was addressed, he stated to the captain that he was master of a vessel, and exempted by law from the impress.

"It is easy to assert that," observed the captain; "but where are your proofs? Your youth almost denies what you affirm."

"There are my papers, sir, my clearance from the Custom-house, and my bill of lading, which I had in my pocket, intending to sail a few minutes after the time that I was impressed."

"I observe," replied the captain, examining the papers, "they appear to be all correct. What is your name?"

"Newton Forster."

"Then this is your signature?"

"It is, sir."

"Mr. Pittson, desire the clerk to bring up a pen and ink."
The clerk made his appearance. "Now, sign your name."
Newton obeyed, and his signature was compared with that
on the bill of lading, by the captain and first lieutenant.

"Why did you not mention this before?" continued the
captain.

"I attempted several times, but was not permitted to speak."
Newton then stated how he had been treated when impressed,
and afterwards by the officer commanding the cutter.

"You certainly were exempted from the impress, if what
you state is true; and I believe it so to be," replied the
captain. "It is a hard case, but what can I do? Here we
are at sea, and likely to remain on a cruise of several months.
You cannot expect to eat the bread of idleness on board of
a man-of-war. You will do your duty wherever you are
stationed. There is no disgrace in serving his Majesty in
any capacity. I tell you candidly, that although I would
not have impressed you myself, I am very glad that I have
you on board; I wish I had fifty more of the same sort,
instead of the sweepings of the gaols, which I am obliged
to mix up with prime seamen."

"Perhaps, sir, you will have the kindness to send me
back by the first homeward-bound vessel?"

"No, that I cannot do; you are on the ship's books, and
the case must be referred to the Admiralty on our return;
that it will be my duty to attend to, upon your application; but I hope before that you will have entered into his
Majesty's service."

"And in the meantime my poor father may starve," said
Newton, with a sigh, not addressing those around him, but
giving utterance to his thoughts.

The captain turned away, and paced the quarter-deck
with the first lieutenant. At last he was overheard to say,
"It's a very hard case, certainly. Forster, can you navigate?" continued the captain, addressing Newton.

"Yes, sir, I can work up a dead reckoning and take the
sun's altitude."

"Very well, that will do. Mr. Pittson, you may dismiss
them. Are they put into messes?"

THE MERCHANT SERVICE

" All, sir."

" It's twelve o'clock, sir," said the master, touching his hat, with his quadrant in his hand.

" Make it so, and pipe to dinner."

Newton was stationed in the foretop. In a few days the awkwardness arising from the novelty of the scene, and from the superior dimensions of every variety of equipment on board of the frigate, compared to the small craft to which he had been accustomed, passed away. The order which was exacted to preserve discipline, the precision with which the time was regulated, the knowledge of the duty allotted to him, soon made him feel that no more was exacted than what could easily be performed, and that there was no hardship in serving on board of a man-of-war; the only hardship was, the manner in which he had been brought there. Although he often sighed as he thought of his father and mother, he did his duty cheerfully, and was soon distinguished as a most promising young sailor.

Captain Northfleet was a humane and good officer, and his first lieutenant followed in his steps, and equally deserved the character. Before the ship's company had been six weeks together, they were in a tolerable state of discipline, and proved such to be the case by acknowledging that they were happy. This, added to the constant excitement of chasing and capturing the vessels of the enemy, with the anticipation of prize-money, soon made most of those who had been impressed forget what had occurred, or cease to lament it as a hardship. The continual exercise of the guns was invariably followed up by a general wish that they might fall in with an enemy of equal force, to ascertain whether such constant drilling had been thrown away upon them. The *Terpsichore* received supplies of provisions and water from other ships, and for nine months continued a successful cruise.

Several prizes had already been captured and sent home to England. The complement of the frigate was materially reduced by so many absentees, although some of her men had been brought out to her by other vessels, when a strange sail was discovered from the mast-head. A few hours sufficed, to bring the swift *Terpsichore* alongside of the stranger, who first hoisted, and then immediately hauled down the tricoloured flag in token of submission. She proved to be a French brig, bound to the Cape of Good Hope with ammunition and Government stores. The third lieutenant, and all the midshipmen who could navigate, were already away; and this prize proving valuable, Captain Northfleet resolved to send her in. The difficulty relative to a prize master was removed by the first lieutenant, who recommended Newton Forster. To this suggestion the captain acceded; and Newton, with five men, and two French prisoners to assist, was put on board of the *Estelle*, with written instructions to repair to Plymouth, and, upon his arrival there, deliver up the prize to the agent, and report himself to the admiral.

Captain Northfleet also returned to Newton the papers of his sloop, and gave him a letter to the admiral, stating the hardship of his case. At the same time that he informed him of the contents of his letter, he recommended Newton to continue in the service, promising that, if he took the vessel safe into port, he would put him on the quarter-deck, as one of the mates of the frigate. Newton thanked Captain Northfleet for his good intentions; and requesting permission to reflect upon his proposal, took his leave, and in a few minutes was on board of the *Estelle*.

There was a buoyancy of spirits in Newton when he once more found himself clear of the frigate. He acknowledged that he had been well treated, and that he had not been unhappy; but still it was emancipation from forced servitude. It is hard to please where there are so many masters; and petty tyranny will exist, and cause much discontent before it is discovered, even where the best discipline prevails. The imperious behaviour of the young midshipmen, who assume the same despotic sway which is exercised over themselves, as soon as their superiors are out of sight and hearing, was often extremely galling to Newton Forster, and it frequently required much forbearance not to retort. However in strict justice this might be warranted, discipline would not permit it, and it would have been attended with severe punishment. It was therefore with a feeling of delight that Newton found himself his own master, and watched the hull and canvas of the *Terpsichore* as they gradually sunk below the horizon.

THE MERCHANT SERVICE

The *Estelle* was a fine vessel, and her cargo not being all composed of heavy materials, was sufficiently light on the water to sail well. At the time of her capture, they were, by the reckoning of the frigate, about fourteen hundred miles from the Lizard. In a fortnight, therefore, with the wind at all propitious, Newton hoped to set his foot upon his native land. He crowded all the sail which prudence would allow, and, with the wind upon his quarter, steered his course for England.

The men sent with him in the brig consisted of two able seamen, and three of the gang which had been collected from the gaols and brought round from the eastward. Captain Northfleet spared the former, as it was necessary that a part of the crew should be able to steer and navigate the vessel; the latter, with the sincere hope of never seeing them again, taking it for granted that they would run away as soon as they arrived at Plymouth. With the two prisoners, they were sufficient to work the vessel.

During the first ten days the wind was generally in their favour, and the brig was not far off from the chops of the Channel when a low raking vessel was perceived bearing down upon them from the N.W. Newton had no glass; but as they neared to within three miles, the vessel wore the appearance of a privateer schooner; but whether an enemy or not, it was impossible to decide. The *Estelle* had two small brass guns on her forecastle; and Newton, to ascertain the nation to which the privateer belonged, hoisted the French ensign and fired a gun. In a minute the privateer hoisted English colours; but as she continued to bear down upon them, Newton, not feeling secure, rove his studding-sail gear, and made all preparation for running before the wind, which he knew to be the brig's best point of sailing. The privateer had approached to within two miles, when Roberts, one of the seamen, gave his decided opinion that she was a French vessel, pointing out the slight varieties in the rigging and build of the vessel, which would not have been apparent to any one but a thorough-bred seaman.

"We'd better up helm, and get the sail upon her. If she be French, she'll soon show herself by firing at us."

Newton was of the same opinion. The brig was put before the wind, and gradually all her canvas was spread. The privateer immediately shook out all her reefs, set her lofty sails, hoisted French colours, and in a few minutes a shot whizzed through the rigging of the *Estelle* and pitched into the water ahead of them.

"I thought so," cried Roberts. "It's a Johnny Crapeau. A starn chase is a long chase, anyhow. The brig sails well, and there aren't more than two hours daylight; so Monsieur must be quick, or we'll give him the slip yet."

The privateer was now within a mile of them; both vessels had "got their way," and their respective powers of sailing were to be ascertained. In half-an-hour the privateer had neared to three-quarters of a mile.

"I think our little guns will soon reach her," observed Newton. "Williams, give me the helm. Go forward with Roberts and the men, and rouse them aft. Be smart, my lads, for she has the heels of us."

"Come along," said Roberts. "You, Collins, why don't you stir?—do you wish to see the inside of a French prison?"

"No," replied Collins, sauntering forward, "not particularly."

"Only by way of a change, I suppose," observed Thompson, another of the convicts. "You have been in every gaol in England, to my knowledge—haven't you, Ben?"

"Mayhap I have," replied Collins; "but one gentleman should never interfere with the consarns of another. I warn't whipped at the cart-tail, as you were, last Lancaster 'sizes."

"No; but you had a taste of it on board of the *Terpsichore*. Ben, you arn't forgot that?" retorted Hillson, the other of the three characters who had been sent with Newton.

In a few minutes the guns were run aft and the ammunition brought on deck. Newton then gave the helm to Williams and served one gun, while Roberts took charge of the other. The privateer had continued to near them, and was now within their range. A smart fire was kept up on her, which she returned with her superior metal.

After the firing had commenced, the approach of the privateer was in some degree checked. The guns fired from the stern of the *Estelle* assisted her velocity through the water; while, on the contrary, the privateer being obliged

70

to yaw from her course that her guns might bear, and firing from the bow, her impetus was checked. Still the privateer had the advantage in sailing, and slowly neared the brig.

"There's no need of your coming aft so close upon us," said Roberts to the two Frenchmen who had been sent on board; "go forward, and keep out of the way. That 'ere chap is after mischief; he had his eye upon the amminition," continued the sailor to Newton. "Go forward, d'ye hear? or I'll split your d—d French skull with the handspike."

"Don't touch him, Roberts," said Newton.

"No, I won't touch him if he keeps out of my way. Do you hear?—go forward!" cried Roberts to the Frenchman, waving his hand.

The Frenchman answered with a sneer and a smile, and was turning to obey the order, when a shot from the privateer cut him nearly in two. The other Frenchman, who was close to him, made a rapid descent into the cabin.

"That was well meant, anyhow," observed Roberts, looking at the dead body; "but it wasn't meant for him. Shall I toss him overboard?"

"No, no—let him lie. If they capture us, they will perceive it was their own doing."

"Well, then, I'll only haul him into the lee-scuppers, out of the way."

Another shot from the privateer passed through the cabin windows, and went forward into the hold. The French prisoner ran on deck with as much haste as before he had run below.

"Ay, it will be your turn next, my cock," cried Roberts, who had been removing the body to the gunnel. "Now, let me try my luck again," and he hastened to his gun. Newton fired before Roberts was ready. The topsail-sheet of the schooner was divided by the shot, and the sail flew out before the yard.

"That's a good two cables' length in our favour," cried Roberts. "Now for me." Roberts fired his gun, and was more fortunate; his shot struck away the fore-top gallant mast, while the royal and top-gallant-sail fell before the topsail.

"Well done, my little piece of brass!" said Roberts,

71

slapping the gun familiarly on the breech; "only get us out of our scrape, and I'll polish you as bright as silver."

Whether the gun understood him or not, or what is more probable, the short distance between the brig and the privateer made it more effective, more mischief took place in the sails and rigging of the schooner. Her topsail-sheet was, however, soon re-bent, the sail reset, and her other casualties made good. She ceased firing her long gun, and at dusk had crept up to within a quarter of a mile, and commenced a heavy fire of musketry upon the brig.

"This is rather warm work," observed Williams at the helm, pointing to a bullet-hole through his jacket.

"Rather too warm," observed Collins, the convict. "I don't see why we are to risk our lives for our paltry share of prize-money. I vote for hauling down the colours."

"Not yet," said Newton, "not yet, my lads. Let us try a few shots more."

"Try!—to be sure," rejoined Roberts; "didn't I say before that a starn chase was a long one."

"That only makes the matter worse," replied Collins; "for while we are to be peppered in this way, I think the shorter the chase the better. However, you may do as you please, but I'm not so fond of it; so here's down below to the fore-peak!"

"Ben, you're a sensible chap, and gives good advice; we'll just follow you," said Hillson.

"Birds of a feather always flock together; so, Ben, I'm of your party," added Thompson.

The convicts then descended forward out of the fire of the musketry, while Newton and Roberts continued to load and fire, and Williams steered the brig. The Frenchman had already found his way below again, before the convicts.

The schooner was within two cables' length, and the fire of the musketry was most galling; each of the English seamen had received slight wounds, when, just as it was dark, one of the shots from the brig proved more effective. The main-boom of the schooner was either cut in two, or so much injured as to oblige them to lower her mainsail. The brig now increased her distance fast, and in a few minutes they lost sight of the schooner in the darkness of the night.

" Huzza !" cried Roberts, "didn't I tell you that a starn chase was a long one ? "

Not a star was to be seen, the darkness was intense, and Newton consulted with Williams and Roberts as to what was their best plan of proceeding. It was agreed to haul up for a quarter of an hour, then furl all, and allow the privateer to pass them. This was put in execution ; the convicts, now that there was no more firing, coming to their assistance.. The next morning the weather proved hazy, and the schooner, who had evidently crowded sail in pursuit of them, was nowhere to be seen.

Newton and his crew congratulated themselves upon their escape, and again shaped their course for the Channel. The wind would not allow them to keep clear of Ushant, and two days afterwards they made the French coast near to that island. The next morning they had a slant of wind, which enabled them to lay her head up for Plymouth, and anticipated that in another twenty-four hours they would be in safety. Such, however, was not their good fortune ; about noon a schooner hove in sight to leeward, and it was soon ascertained to be the same vessel from which they had, previously escaped. Before dusk she was close to them, and Newton, aware of the impossibility of resistance, hove-to as a signal of surrender.

CHAPTER XII

" Misery acquaints a man with strange bedfellows."
—SHAKSPEARE.

As the reader may have before now occasionally heard comments upon the uncertainty of the moon and the sea, and also perhaps of human life, I shall not venture any further remarks upon the subject; for were they even new, I should never have the credit of them. This is certain, that instead of finding themselves, as they anticipated to be in the next twenty-four hours, safely moored in the port of Plymouth, Newton and his comrades found themselves, before that time had elapsed, safely locked up in the prison of Morlaix. But we must not proceed so fast.

73

Although the *Estelle* had squared her mainyard as a signal of submission, the privateer's men, as they ranged their vessel alongside, thought it advisable to pour in a volley of musketry; this might have proved serious, had it not been that Newton and his crew were all down below, hoping to secure a few changes of linen, which in a prison might prove very useful. As it was, their volley only killed the remaining French prisoner, who remained on deck, overjoyed at the recapture, and anticipating an immediate return to his own country; by which it would appear that the *L'homme propose, mais Dieu dispose* of France, is quite as sure a proverb as the more homely "Many a slip between the cup and lip" of our own country.

The boat of the privateer was sent on board. A dozen men, with their cutlasses flourishing over their heads, leapt on the deck of the *Estelle*, and found nobody to exercise their valour upon, except the body of their departed comrade; upon which they shouted for the "Sacré's God dams" to "monter." Newton and the rest obeyed the summons, with their bundles in their hands; the latter they were soon relieved of by their conquerors, who, to prove that it was not out of *politesse* that they carried their effects, at the same time saluted them with various blows with their cutlasses upon their backs and shoulders. Newton, who felt that resistance would only be an excuse for further aggression, bore with philosophy what he could not prevent, and hastened into the boat. The convicts also took their share with patience—they had been accustomed to "many stripes." Roberts and Williams, in spite of the remonstrances of Newton, with all the reckless spirit of English sailors, would not submit so quietly. The first object which attracted Roberts' attention, as he came up the ladder, was the body of the remaining French prisoner.

"What, Johnny! so you're gone! Didn't I tell you that your turn would come next? I say, my hearties, you keep all your bullets for your friends," continued Roberts, addressing the privateer's men.

A few "sacrés" and "f——s" was the reply, as one of them attempted to twitch his bundle out of his hand. "Hold fast there, old chap; don't take what you never paid for."

A scuffle now ensued, which ended in Roberts, who found that he could not retain possession, shying his bundle at the

74

foremost man, with such force as to lay him on the deck. "Well, if you will have it, take it," cried Roberts.

"The beggars have chopped my fingers," growled Williams. "I say, Mounseer, don't make quite so free with that iron of yours, or I'll smash your top-lights."

"I wish I had three on 'em on Point Beach, one up and one down. I'd sarve you out, you d——d frog-eating sea-cooks!" said Roberts, squaring at the privateer's men with clenched fists.

This obstreperous conduct produced a shower of blows with the backs of the cutlasses. Williams, in a rage, wrenched a cutlass from one of the Frenchmen, and laid about him; while Roberts, with his fists, rushed within their guards, and laid two of them at his feet. At last they were overpowered and thrown into the boat, bleeding profusely from various cuts which they had received in the unequal scuffle. The privateer's people then shoved off and rowed on board of the schooner.

As soon as Newton and the other Englishmen were up the side, they were pushed aft; their persons were then searched, and every part of their apparel which appeared to be of good materials or little worn was taken from them. Collins, the convict, was a good prize; he had put on shirt over shirt, stocking over stocking, and trousers over trousers, so that the Frenchmen began to wonder if ever they should arrive at the "inner man." At last he was uncased, an old pair of trousers thrown to him, and he was left without any other garment, shivering in the cold. Newton, who still retained his waistcoat and shirt, took off the former, and gave it to the convict, who whispered as he thanked him, "I don't care a fig; they have left me my old hat." As soon as the recapture was manned, the privateer bore up for the French coast, and before morning anchored in the rocky harbour of Morlaix. At daylight, the prisoners, who had received no refreshment, were handed into a boat, and on their landing, conducted by a party of gendarmes to the prison. During their progress to their place of confinement, Collins excited the amusement of the bystanders, and the surprise of his fellow-prisoners, by walking with his hands and arms raised in a certain position. After they had been locked up, he went to the barred window, and continued the same gestures to the people who were crowded about the prison, most of whom continued their mockery. Newton, who came forward to the window to request a little water for Roberts and Williams, who wished to quench their thirst and wash their wounds, which had not been dressed, inquired of Collins his reasons for so doing. "It is for your benefit as well as mine," replied Collins. "At least I hope so. There are Freemasons in all countries."

A few minutes afterwards, one of the people outside came forward and pointed out to the sentry that the prisoners were making signs for water. The gendarme, who paid no attention to Newton, listened to the appeal of his country-man, who, upon the grounds of common humanity, persuaded him to allow them such a necessary boon. The water was brought, and as the man walked away, a sign, unperceived by all but Collins, gave him to understand that his appeal had been understood.

"All's right," said Collins to Newton, as he quitted the grating. "We have friends without, and we have *friends* within." In about an hour some bread was brought in, and among those who brought it Collins perceived the person who had answered his signal; but no further recognition took place. At noon the door of the prison was again unbarred, and a surgeon came to dress the wounded men. He was accompanied by two or three others, deputed by the governor of the town to obtain intelligence, and the new acquaintance of Collins appeared as interpreter. While the surgeon dressed the wounds of Roberts and Williams, which, although numerous, were none of any importance, many ques-tions were asked, and taken down when interpreted. Each prisoner was separately interrogated; Collins was one of the first examined. The questions put and answers given were carefully intermixed with more important matter. The person who acted as interpreter spoke English too well for a Frenchman; apparently he was a Dane or Russian, who was domiciliated there. He commenced with—

"No one understands English but me, but they are sus-picious; be careful. What is your name?"

"John Collins."

"Comment?" said the French amanuensis, "John Co—lin. C'est bien; continuez."

"What is your rank—*and in your Lodge?*"

"Common seaman—*master*," answered Collins adroitly.

"Comment?" said the party with his pen.

"Matelot," replied the interpreter.

"Demandez-lui le nom du bâtiment."

"What is the name of your ship?—*how can we assist you?*"

"*Terpsichore—a boat, with provisions.*"

"Comment?"

"Frégate croiseur *Terpsichore.*"

"Does she sail well?—*at what time?*"

"*To-night, with a guide.*"

"Que dit-il?"

"Elle marche bien avec le vent large."

"Demandez-lui la force."

"What number of guns?—*how can you get out?*"

"Thirty-six—*I have the means.*"

"Trente-six canons."

"Trente-six canons," repeated the Frenchman, writing, "c'est bien—alors, l'équipage."

"How many men?—*I will be here at dark.*"

"Two hundred and seventy men; but many away in prizes."

"Deux cents soixante-dix hommes d'équipage; mais il y a beaucoup dans les bâtimens pris."

Newton and the others were also interrogated, the names taken down, and the party then quitted the prison.

"Now, if we make a push for it, I think we may get off," said Collins to Newton and the rest, after the door had closed. "I never saw the prison in England which could hold me when I felt inclined to walk out of it; and as for their bars, I reckon them at about an hour's work. I never travel without my little friends;" and Collins, taking off his old hat, removed the lining and produced a variety of small saws made from watch-springs, files, and other instruments. "Then," continued he, "with these, and this piece of tallow stuck outside my hat, I will be through those bars in no time. French iron arn't worth a d—n, and the sentry sha'n't hear me if he lolls against them; although it may be just as well if Thompson tips a stave, as then we may work the faster."

"I say, Bill," observed Hillson, "who is your friend?"

"I don't know—he may be the governor; but this I do

know, for the honour of Freemasonry, we may trust him and all like him; so just mind your own business, Tom."

"He said he would be here at dark," observed Newton.

"Yes, I must prepare. Go to the grating some of you, that they may not look in upon me."

This unexpected prospect of deliverance created an anxious joy in the prisoners; the day appeared interminable. At last the shades of night set in, and a clouded sky with mizzling rain raised their hopes. The square in front of the prison was deserted, and the sentinel crouched close against the door, which partially protected him from the weather. In a few minutes a person was heard in conversation with the sentinel. "He must be coming now," observed Collins, in a low tone; "that must be one of his assistants who is taking off the attention of the gendarme."

"Make no noise," said a voice in a whisper at the outside of the bars.

"I am here," replied Collins softly.

"How can you get out of the prison?"

"Get the sentry out of the way when we leave off singing; the bars will then be removed."

"Everything is prepared outside. When you get out, keep close under the wall to the right. I shall be at the corner, if I am not here."

The Freemason then retired from the grating.

"Now, Thompson, not too loud, there's no occasion for it; two of us can work."

Thompson commenced his song; Newton took a small saw from Collins, who directed him how to use it. The iron bars of the prison yielded like wood to the fine-tempered instruments which Collins employed. In an hour and a half three of the bars were removed without noise, and the aperture was wide enough for their escape. The singing of Thompson, whose voice was tolerably good and ear very correct, had not only the effect of preventing their working being heard, but amused the sentinel, who remained with his back to the wall listening to the melody.

Their work was so far accomplished. Thompson ceased, and all was silence and anxiety; in a few minutes the sentinel was again heard in conversation, and the voices receded, as if he had removed to a greater distance.

78

"Now, brother," said the low voice under the aperture.

In a minute the whole of the prisoners were clear of the walls, and followed their guide in silence, until they reached the landing-place.

"There is the boat, and provisions sufficient," said the Freemason, in a low tone ; "you will have to pass the sentries on the rocks, but we can do no more for you. Farewell, brother; and may you and your companions be fortunate !" So saying, their friendly assistant disappeared.

The night was so dark, that although close to the boat, it was with difficulty that its outline could be discerned. Newton, recommending the strictest care in entering, stepped into it, and was followed by the rest. Roberts, whose eye-sight was a little affected from the wounds in his head, stumbled over one of the oars.

"*Qui vive ?*" cried out one of the sentries on the rock.

No answer was made ; they all remained motionless in their seats. The sentry walked to the edge of the rock and looked down; but not distinguishing anything, and hearing no further noise, returned to his post.

For some little time Newton would not allow them to move. The oars were then carefully lifted over the gunnel, and their clothes laid in the rowlocks, to muffle the sound ; the boat was pushed from the landing-place into the middle of the narrow inlet. The tide was ebbing, and with their oars raised out of the water, ready to give way if perceived, they allowed the boat to drift out of one of the narrow channels which formed the entrance of the harbour.

The rain now beat down fast; and anxious to be well clear of the coast before daylight, Newton thought they might venture to pull. The oars were taken by him and Collins, but before they had laid them three times in the water, one of the sentries, hearing the noise, discharged his musket in the direction.

"Give way, now, as hard as we can," cried Newton; "it's our only chance."

Another and another musket was fired. They heard the guard turned out, lights passing on the batteries close to them, and row-boats manning. They double-banked their oars, and, with the assistance of the ebb tide and obscurity, they were soon out of gunshot. They then laid in their oars, shipped their mast, and sailed away from the coast.

79

It was nine o'clock in the evening when they started, and at daylight the French coast was not to be seen. Overjoyed at their escape, they commenced an attack upon the provisions and a small keg of wine; and perhaps a more joyful breakfast never was made. The sun rose in vapour, the sky threatened, but they were free and happy. The wind freshened, and the boat flew before the gale; the running seas topping over her stern, and forcing them continually to bale her out; but all was joy, and freedom turned their "danger to delight." They passed several vessels at a distance, who did not observe them, and before sunset the English coast was in sight. At ten o'clock the double lights on the Lizard were on their starboard bow. They hauled up upon the larboard tack with the ebb tide, and having passed the Lizard, kept away for Mount's Bay, to avoid the chance of falling in with any of the king's vessels, and being again impressed. At daylight they ran in under St. Michael's Mount, and once more stepped upon English ground.

Here, as by previous agreement, they divided the provisions, and took farewell of each other.

"Good-bye, gentlemen," said Collins; "allow me to observe that, for once, you may think yourselves fortunate in having been placed in my very respectable company!"

CHAPTER XIII

"Once more upon the waters."—BYRON.

As Newton had lost his credentials from Captain Northfleet, as well as the vessel confided to his charge, he did not consider it necessary to pay his respects to the port-admiral at Plymouth. On the contrary, he set off, as fast as his legs could carry him, to Liverpool, to ascertain the condition of his father. We shall pass over the difficulties he experienced on his journey. There is no country where travelling is more easy or more rapid than in England, provided that you have plenty of money; but when you travel *in formâ pauperis,* there is no country in which you get on so badly. Parish rates and poor laws have dried up the sources of benevolence; and as Newton did not apply to the overseers for his three-halfpence a mile, he got on how he could, which was badly enough. When at last he did arrive at Liverpool, he found himself a stone or two the lighter, and would have been pronounced by Captain Barclay to have been in excellent training.

Newton had written to his father, acquainting him with his impressment, but was doubtful whether the letter had ever been received, as it had been confided to the care of one of the women who left the frigate the evening previous to her sailing. When he arrived at the house, he perceived his father at his bench as usual, but doing nothing, and the shop windows were bare.

Newton entered, and his father looked up.

"Why, Newton, my dear boy, is it you?" cried Nicholas; "what a long while you have been away! Well, how is Mr. Hilton?—and how is your poor mother?"

"My dear father," replied Newton, taking his hand, "did not you receive my letter?"

"No, I received no letter What a time you have been away; I declare it must be two or three months, or more."

"It is nearly twelve months, my dear father. I was pressed at Bristol, have been on board of a man-of-war, and have just escaped from a French prison."

Newton then entered into a narrative of his adventures, to the astonishment of Nicholas, who heard him with open mouth.

"Dear me! so you've been in a man-of-war, and in France; then you don't know how your poor mother is?"

"Have you not inquired, my dear father?"

"No, I thought you would come home and tell me all about it," replied Nicholas, with a sigh.

"How have you got on here?" said Newton, to change the conversation.

"Very bad indeed, Newton—very bad indeed; I have not had six jobs since you left me."

"I am sorry to hear it, father; have you anything to eat in the house, for I am very hungry?"

"I am afraid not much," replied Nicholas, going to the

81   F

cupboard, and producing some bread and cheese. "Can you eat bread and cheese, my dear boy?"

"I could eat a horse, my dear father," replied Newton, who had walked the last twelve hours without sustenance.

Newton attacked the provender, which soon disappeared.

"I have been obliged to sell most of the shop furniture," said Nicholas, observing Newton to cast his eyes at the empty window. "I could not help it. I believe nobody wears spectacles in Liverpool."

"It can't be helped, father; we must hope for better times."

"Yes, we must trust in God, Newton. I sold my watch yesterday, and that will feed us for some time. A sailor came into the shop, and asked if I had any watches to sell. I told him that I only repaired them at present, but that when my improvement in the duplex——" Here Nicholas forgot the thread of his narrative, and was commencing a calculation upon his intended improvement, when Newton interrupted him—

"Well, sir, what did the sailor reply?"

"Oh! I forgot; I told him that I had a watch of my own, that I would part with it, which went very well, and that it would be cheaper to him than a new one. That it cost fifteen pounds; but I was in want of money, and would take five pounds for it. He saw how sorry I was to part with it—and so I was." Here Nicholas thought of his watch, and forgot his story.

"Well, my dear father," said Newton, "what did he give you for it?"

"Oh! why, he was a kind, good creature, and said that he was not the man to take advantage of a poor devil in distress, and that I should have the full value of it. He put the watch into his fob and counted out fifteen pounds on the counter. I wanted to return part; but he walked out of the shop, and before I could get round the counter, he had got round the corner of the street."

"'Twas a godsend, my dear father," replied Newton, "for I have not a halfpenny. Do you know what became of my chest, that I left on board of the sloop?"

"Dear me! now I think of it, it came here by the waggon. I put it upstairs. I wondered why you sent it."

THE MERCHANT SERVICE

Newton having appeased his hunger, went upstairs, and found all his wearing apparel had been forwarded by Mr. Hilton, who supposed him dead ; and thus he was enabled to make a more respectable appearance than what the privateer's people had hitherto permitted him. In a few days he felt quite recovered from his fatigue, and sallied forth in search of employment. On the day after his arrival at Liverpool he had written to the asylum to inquire the fate of his mother. The answer which he received was, that Mrs. Forster had recovered, and remained many months in the establishment as nurse ; but that ten days back she had quitted the asylum, and that her address was not known.

Newton, who had no means of prosecuting further inquiry, was obliged to be satisfied with the intelligence that his mother was alive and well. He communicated the information to Nicholas, who observed—

" Poor thing ! she's looking for us, depend upon it, Newton, and will be here very soon ; " and this expectation was revived whenever Nicholas thought of his wife; and he continued satisfied.

We must allow many months to pass away in one paragraph —months of ineffectual struggle against poverty and want of employment, which Newton made every exertion to obtain as mate of a merchant vessel. The way in which he had been impressed had caused a dread of the king's service, which he could not overcome ; and although he had but to choose his ship as a sailor before the mast, he could not prevail upon himself to accept a berth which was not protected from the impress. Without recommendation he could not obtain the situation of mate, and he continued to work as a rigger in the docks, until his hand was unfortunately severely jammed by the heel of a topmast, and he was laid up for many weeks. Each day their fare became scantier, and they were reduced to their last shilling, when Newton was again able to go out and seek employment.

It was a rough day, blowing hard from the S.E., when Newton, who had tried his fortune on board of every vessel (crowded as they were in the docks) without success, walked in a melancholy and disappointed mood along the splendid pier which lines the river-side. Few people were out, for the gusts of wind were accompanied by smart driving showers

of rain. Here and there was to be seen a boat pulling up
in-shore to fetch the shipping in the stream, which with a
heavy strain on their cables were riding to the S.E. gale and
a strong ebb tide. Newton had made up his mind to enter
on board of one of these vessels about to sail, provided they
would advance him a part of his wages for his father's support;
when, as a heavy squall cleared away, he perceived that
a boat had broken adrift from the outermost vessel (a large
brig), with only one man in it, who was carried away by the
rapid current, assisted by the gale blowing down the river, so as
to place him in considerable risk. The man in the boat tossed
out his oar, and pulling first on one side, and then on the other,
tried to make for the shore; but in vain. He was swept away
with a rapidity which threatened in less than an hour to carry
him out to sea, unless assistance were afforded him.

Another heavy squall again hid the boat from the sight of
Newton, who had been anxiously watching to ascertain if any
relief was sent from the shipping, and who was now convinced that the disaster had not been perceived. He therefore ran down the bank of the river, waiting until the squall
should blow over and enable him to discover the boat.

In about ten minutes the squall passed over, and the boat
was again presented to his sight; she was still in the centre
of the stream, about three hundred yards from the shore.
The man who was in her, finding all his attempts futile, had
lain on his oar and was kneeling in the stern-sheets, apparently in supplication. Newton could not resist the appeal;
it appeared to point out to him that he was summoned to
answer the call made upon Providence. The boat was now
a quarter of a mile farther down the river than where he
stood, and about three miles from the town and shipping,
both of which were no longer discernible from the thickness
of the weather. Newton threw off his coat, and plunging
into the agitated water, the cold of which nearly checked
his respiration, swam off into the stream in a direction so as
to allow himself to fetch to windward of the boat. He was
soon carried down to it by the rapidity of the tide, and as
he approached he shouted to announce his presence. The
man in the boat started up at the sound of a human voice,
and perceiving Newton close to the bows, leant over and
extended his hand towards him. Newton seized hold of it,

84

and then was whirled round by the tide fore and aft with
the side of the boat, with such violence as nearly to drag
the other man out, and half fill the boat with water. It was
with great difficulty, although assisted by the occupant, that
Newton contrived at last to get in, when, exhausted with
the efforts he had made, he remained a few seconds without
motion, the man, whom he had just risked his life to save,
perceiving his condition, and not speaking to him.

"We have no time to lose," said Newton at last; "take an
oar, and let us pull in for the shore. If once we are swept
down to the narrows there will be little chance for us."

The other complied without speaking; and after a few
minutes' exertion, the boat was safely landed on the Liverpool side of the river.

"The Lord be praised!" ejaculated Newton's companion,
as he laid on his oar. "I did not call upon Him in vain;
your accident has been the means of my preservation."

"How do you mean?" inquired Newton.

"Why, did you not fall overboard?" replied the other.

Newton then explained to his companion what we have
already related to the reader, ending his narrative with the
observation, that when he perceived him praying for assistance in his peril, he could not resist the appeal.

"God will reward you, young man," continued he; "and
now I will explain to you how it was that I was adrift, like
a bear in a washing-tub. My first mate was below. I had
just relieved the deck, for in this blowing weather we must
keep watch in harbour. The men were all at their dinner,
when I heard the boat thumping under the main channels.
I got into her to ease off a fathom or two of the painter;
but as I hauled her ahead to get at the bend, it appears
that the monkey of a boy who made her fast, and has been
but a few months at sea, had made a slippery hitch, so away
we went, and I was adrift. I hailed them on board, but
they did not hear me, although the first mate might have,
for he was in the cabin, and the stern-window was up; but
hailing to windward is hard work, such weather as this—the
words are blown back again down your own throat. And
now, let me know a little about you, my lad, and see whether
I cannot in return be of some use to you."

Newton's history was soon told; and at the conclusion he

85

had the satisfaction of finding that he had obtained the very situation which he had been in search of.

"I have no second mate on board," observed the captain of the brig; "but I intended to have shipped one to-morrow. I was only divided between which to take of two who have offered themselves, with equally good recommendations. Fortunately, I would promise neither; and as I think your own recommendation stronger than theirs, the berth is at your service. I only wish, for your sake, that it was that of first mate. I am sure you would prove yourself fit for the situation; and I cannot say that I am very partial to the one that I have at present, but he is a relation of the owner."

The arrangements were soon made. Mr. Berecroft, the master of the vessel, advanced Newton a sum to fit himself out, and agreed with the owner at Liverpool that one-half of Newton's wages should be allotted monthly to his father. The next morning (as the vessel had a pilot on board and the weather had moderated) Newton took leave of his father, and with a light heart accompanied his new acquaintance on board of the vessel.

It was early in the morning when they embarked in a hired boat—the one belonging to the brig still remaining down the river, where they had landed. The first mate, as it appeared, was in the cabin shaving himself, previous to his going on shore to report the supposed loss of his superior. The sailors were either busy or down below, so that no notice was taken of the boat coming alongside; and Newton, with the master, were both on deck before the circumstance was known to the first mate. It so happened, that at the very same moment that they came on board, the first mate was ascending the companion hatch to order a boat to be lowered down and manned. When he perceived Mr. Berecroft he fell back with astonishment and turned pale.

"I thought you were gone," said he. "Why, what could have saved you? Did you not drift out to sea?"

"It appears then, Mr. Jackson, that you knew that I was adrift," replied the master seriously, looking him steadfastly in the face.

"That is," replied the mate, confused, "I thought—of course, seeing the boat was not alongside—that you had drifted away in her. How it happened—of course, I know not."

86

"I should trust, for your conscience' sake, Mr. Jackson, that you did not; however, here I am again, as you see, by the blessing of Providence and the exertions of this young man, whom I must introduce to you as our second mate."

Jackson cast an angry glance at Newton upon the conclusion of this speech. The master had truly observed that it was strange the first mate did not hear him when he had hailed the brig for assistance. The fact was, that Jackson had both heard him and seen him; but he was a wretch devoid of all feeling, who consulted nothing except his own interest. He had made sure that the master would be carried out to sea, there to perish by a most miserable death, and that he would succeed in command of the vessel. He was then going on shore to report the supposed "falling overboard" of the master, which, as the brig was to sail as the weather moderated, would have secured to him the command, and at the same time have put an end to the search which (should he have reported the truth) would immediately have taken place for the boat in which the master had been adrift. Foiled in his hopes by the courage of Newton, Jackson had already formed towards him a deadly hatred and determination of revenge.

That evening the wind abated and the vessel sailed. The ensuing morning she was clear of the sands, and a pilot-vessel off Holyhead having received the pilot, she steered down the Irish Channel to join a convoy for the West Indies collecting at Falmouth.

Mr. Berecroft, the master of the vessel, who has not hitherto been described, was a spare, light-built person, of about sixty years of age, still active and a thorough seaman. He had crossed the ocean for forty-five years, and his occasional narratives, as he walked the deck, or sat over his evening glass of grog, proved that his life must have been one of no ordinary variety and interest. He was serious and rationally devout. He checked all swearing from the men under his command, and rebuked it, although he could not prevent it in the first mate, who, to annoy him, seldom made his appearance on deck without making use of some execration or another. It was Mr. Berecroft's custom to call down the seamen into his cabin every evening, and read to them a short prayer; and although this unusual ceremony often caused a leer in some of the newly-entered men, and was not only unattended but ridiculed by Jackson, still the whole conduct of Berecroft was so completely in unison, that even the most idle and thoughtless acknowledged that he was a good man, and quitted the ship with regret. Such was Mr. Berecroft; and we have little further to add, except that he was very superior to the generality of masters of merchant vessels. His family, it was reported, were strict Quakers.

Jackson, the first mate, was a bull-headed, sandy-haired Northumbrian; as we before stated, a relation of the owner, or he never would have been permitted to remain in the ship. The reader has already had some insight into his diabolical character. It will be sufficient to add, that he was coarse and blustering in his manners; that he never forgot and never forgave an injury; gratitude was not in his composition; and to gratify his revenge he would stop at nothing.

On the third day, the brig, which was named the *Eliza and Jane*, after the two daughters of the owner, arrived at Falmouth, where she anchored in the outer roads, in company with thirty or forty more, who had assembled at the appointed rendezvous. On the second day after their arrival, a fifty-gun ship, frigate, and two corvettes, made their appearance off the mouth of the harbour; and after a due proportion of guns, some shotted and some not, the whole convoy were under weigh, and hove-to round their protectors. The first step taken by the latter was to disembarrass their *protégés* of one-third of their crews, leaving them as defenceless as possible, that they might not confide in their own strength, but put their whole trust in the men-of-war, and keep as close to them as possible. Having taken out every unprotected man, they distributed convoy signals in lieu, and half-a-dozen more guns announced that they were to make sail— an order immediately complied with; the merchant vessels, loaded with canvas below and aloft, while the men-of-war, with their topsails on the caps, sailed round and round them, firing shot at every unfortunate vessel which was not able to sail as well as the rest.

The convoy left Falmouth, seventy-five in number, but in a few days there were but forty in sight. Those who remained behind either made their voyage how they could, or were taken by the enemy's privateers, who followed in the

88

wake of the convoy. Some few were carried into the French ports; and the underwriters of the policy ate but little dinner on the day which brought the intelligence of their capture. Others were retaken by the English blockading squadrons, who received then one-eighth for salvage. At last the men-of-war were fairly running down the trades, with about twenty-five of the best sailers in company; and the commodore deemed it advisable to take particular care of the few which remained, lest he should be "hauled over the coals" by the Admiralty. Nothing worth comment occurred during the remainder of the passage. They all arrived safe at Barbados, when the commodore brought in his returns to the admiral, and complained bitterly of the obstinacy of the masters of merchant vessels, who would part company with him, in defiance of all his injunctions, and in spite of all the powder which he fired away to enforce his signals. There certainly was a fault somewhere.

During the passage, which lasted seven weeks, Newton had ample opportunity of ascertaining his situation. The master invariably treated him with kindness and consideration, and before the voyage was completed, he treated him as if he were his own son. Jackson lost no opportunity of annoying or insulting him; but the support of his patron indemnified Newton for the conduct of the first mate, and he resolved to take no notice of that which could not well be prevented. On their arrival at Barbados, Mr. Berecroft went on shore to the house of the consignee, and then it was that the malignity of Jackson broke out in all its violence.

The brig had discharged her cargo, and was lying in Carlisle Bay, waiting for the sugars which were to be shipped for Liverpool. One morning, when Newton, who for some time had submitted to the tyranny of Jackson without complaint, was standing at the main hatchway, giving directions to the men below, who were arranging the dunnage at the bottom of the vessel, the first mate came on deck, and, watching his opportunity, staggered, with a rope in his hand, against Newton, as if by accident, so as to throw him over the coombings. Newton, who would have immediately fallen to the bottom of the hold upon the ballast, at the risk of his life, suddenly seized hold of the first mate, not in sufficient time to recover his own balance, but so firmly as to drag Jackson with him; and down they were both precipitated together. The first mate, having hold of one of the ropes leading down the main-mast, clung fast to save himself, and in so doing also broke the fall of Newton; but the weight of their bodies dragged the rope through Jackson's hands, which were lacerated to the bone. Neither party was much hurt by the fall, so that the treachery of Jackson recoiled upon himself.

After this specimen of animosity, which was duly reported to Mr. Berecroft, on his return on board, by the seamen, who detested Jackson, and anything like foul play, his protector determined that Newton should no longer be subjected to further violence. At the request of Mr. Berecroft, Newton was invited to stay at the house of Mr. Kingston, the gentleman to whom the vessel had been consigned—an offer which was gladly accepted.

Newton had not been many days on shore, when Mr. Kingston, who had taken a strong interest in him, proposed, in answer to many of his questions relative to the slave-trade, that they should make a party to visit a plantation, the proprietor of which had been a resident since his youth, and judge for himself as to the truth of the reports so industriously circulated by those who were so inimical to the employment of a slave population.

CHAPTER XIV

> "*Aboan.* The innocent!
> *Oronoko.* These men are so whom you would rise against.
> If we are slaves, they did not make us slaves,
> But bought us in the honest way of trade,
> As we have done before 'em, bought and sold
> Many a wretch, and never thought it wrong.
> They paid our price for us, and we are now
> Their property, a part of their estate,
> To manage as they please."

At an early hour the party, consisting of Mr. Kingston, the master of the brig, and Newton, set off upon mules for the habitation of the planter. The sun had illumined the sky, but had not yet made his appearance, although the golden fringes upon the clouds, which floated in broad belts in the horizon, indicated his glorious yet withering approach. The dew moistened each leaf, or hung in glittering pendent drops upon the thorn of the prickly pears which lined the roads. The web of the silver-banded spider was extended between the bushes, and, saturated with moisture, reflected the beams of the rising orb, as the animals danced in the centre to dazzle their expected prey. The mist still hovered on the valleys, and concealed a part of the land-scape from their view; and the occasional sound of the fall of water was mingled with the twittering and chirping of the birds, as they flew from spray to spray. The air was fresh, even to keenness, and any one suddenly wafted to the scene would little have imagined that he was under the torrid zone.

"How different this is from the ideas generally formed of the climate in the West Indies!" observed Newton. "In England, we couple it with insufferable heat and the yellow fever."

"Your reports are from those who seldom leave the harbours or towns, where such indeed prevail," replied Kingston. "There is no island in the Caribbean Sea where the early riser may not enjoy this delightful, bracing atmosphere: at Jamaica, in particular, where they collect as much snow as they please in the mountains; yet at the same time there is not a more fatal and unhealthy spot than Port Royal harbour in the same island."

"Is the plantation we are going to situated as high above the level of the sea as we are now?"

"No; most plantations are in the ravines, between the hills. The sugar-cane requires heat. As soon as we are on the summit of this next hill we shall descend to it."

In half-an-hour they arrived at the end of their journey, when they stopped at an extensive range of low buildings, situated at the head of the valley, which descended to the sea—now for the first time presented to their view since they had quitted Bridgetown. The owner of the estate was at the door to receive them. He was a tall, spare man, dressed in nankeen jacket and trousers, with a large-brimmed straw hat upon his head.

"Welcome, gentlemen, welcome. Kingston, how are you?" said he, as they stopped. "Now dismount, gentlemen; the boys will take the mules. Boy Jack, where are you? Where's Baby, and where's Bulky? Come here, you lazy rascals, and take the mules. Now then, gentlemen, I'll show you the way. I ordered breakfast on the table, as I saw you coming down the hill."

So saying, the old gentleman led the way through a portico. At the sight of strangers, the windows underneath were crowded with faces of various degrees of colour—eyes and mouths wide open, the latter displaying rows of teeth, so even and so brilliantly white, that they might cause a sensation of envy to many an English belle.

The party were ushered into a spacious and cool apartment on the ground-floor, where a table was covered with all the varieties of a tropical breakfast, consisting of fried fish, curries, devilled poultry, salt meats, and everything which could tend to stimulate an enfeebled appetite.

"Now, gentlemen, let me recommmend you to take a white jacket; you'll be more at your ease, and there is no ceremony here. Boy Jack, where's the sangoree? This is a fine climate, Captain Berecroft; all you have to attend to is —to be temperate, and not to check the perspiration."

Boy Jack, who, *par parenthèse*, was a stout, well-looking negro of about forty years of age, now made his appearance with the sangoree. This was a beverage composed of half a bottle of brandy and two bottles of Madeira, to which were added a proportion of sugar, lime-juice, and nutmeg, with water *ad lib*. It was contained in a glass bowl, capable of holding two gallons, standing upon a single stalk, and bearing the appearance of a Brobdingnag rummer. Boy Jack brought it with both hands, and placed it before his master.

"Now sir, will you drink?" said the planter, addressing Mr. Berecroft.

"Thank you," replied Mr. Berecroft, "I never drink so early in the morning."

"Drink! why, this is nothing but *swizzle*. Here's your health, sir, I'll show you the way."

The large goblet was fixed to his lips for upwards of a minute. At last they unwillingly separated, and the old planter recovered his respiration with a deep sigh. "Now then, gentlemen, do you take a little; don't be afraid; there's nothing you mayn't do in this climate, only be temperate and don't check the perspiration." At this moment Newton was startled, and looked under the table.

"I thought it was a dog, but it's a little black child."

"Oh! there's one out, is there? Why, Boy Jack, did I not tell you to shut them all in?"

"Yes, sar, so I did," said the black man, looking under the table. "Eh!—it's that d—d little nigger—two-year-old Sambo—no possible keeping him in, sar. Come out, Sambo."

The child crawled out to his master, and climbed up by his knee. The old planter patted his woolly head, and gave him a piece of grilled turkey, with which he immediately dived again under the table.

"The fact is, captain, they are accustomed to come in at breakfast-time; they are only shut out to-day because I have company. That door behind me leads into the nursery yard."

"The nursery yard!"

"Yes, I ll show it you by-and-by; there's plenty of them there."

"Oh! pray let us have them in. I wish to see them, and should be sorry to be the cause of their being disappointed."

"Open the door, Boy Jack." As soon as it was open, about twenty black children, from seven to three years old, most of them naked, with their ivory skins like a polished table, and quite pot-bellied from good living, tumbled into the room, to the great amusement of Newton and the party. They were followed by seven or eight more, who were not yet old enough to walk; but they crawled upon all-fours almost as fast as the others who could walk erect after the image of their Maker.

The company amused themselves with distributing to the children the contents of the dishes on the table—the elder ones nestling alongside of the planter and his friends with great familiarity, while the youngest sat upright on the floor, laughing as they devoured their respective portions.

"Of course, these are all slaves?" observed Mr. Berecroft.

"Yes, bred them all myself," replied the planter; "indeed, out of two hundred and fifteen which I have on the estate, I think that there are not more than twelve who were not born on this property, during my father's time or mine. Perhaps, as breakfast is over, you will like to inspect my nursery."

The planter led the way into the yard from which the children had entered. It was a square, of about two roods of ground, three sides of which were enclosed by rows of small houses, of two rooms each; and most of them were occupied by female slaves, either nursing children at the breast, or expecting very soon to have that duty to perform. They received their master with a smiling face, as he addressed a question to each of them when he entered their abode.

"Now these are all my *breeding* women; they do no work, only take care of the children, who remain here until they are eight or nine years old. We have a surgeon on the estate, who attends them as well as the other slaves when they are sick. Now, if you feel inclined, we will go round the works."

The old planter, in a few minutes' walk, brought them to an extensive row of detached cottages, each centred in a piece of garden-ground, well stocked with yams, sweet potatoes, bananas, and other tropical productions. Poultry of all descriptions were scattered in profusion about the place, and pigs appeared to be abundant.

"Now, captain, these are the cottages of the working slaves. The garden-gound is allowed to them; and whatever they can make by its produce, or by their pigs and their poultry, is all their own."

"But how are they subsisted?"

"By rations, as regularly served out as yours are on board of your vessel, and they have as much as they can consume."

"Are they all single men?"

"No, mostly married to slave girls on the estate. Their wives live with them, unless they breed, and then they are removed up to the nurseries."

"And what work do you exact from them?"

"Eight hours a day, except in crop-time, and then we are very busy; so that they have plenty of leisure to look after their own interests if they choose."

"Do they ever lay up much money?"

"Very often enough to purchase their freedom, if they wished it."

"If they wished it!" replied Mr. Berecroft, with surprise.

"Yes; without explanation, that may appear strange to you, and still more strange the fact, that freedom offered has often been refused. A man who is a clever workman as a carpenter, or any other trade, will purchase his freedom if he can, because artisans can obtain very high wages here; but a slave who, if I may use the term, is only a common labourer, would hardly support himself, and lay by nothing for his old age. They are aware of it. I have offered emancipation to one or two who have grown old, and they have refused it, and now remain as heir-looms on the estate, provided with everything, and doing little or no work, if they please. You saw that old man sweeping under the portico? Well, he does that every day; and it is all he has done for these five years. Now, if you please, we will go through the plantations and visit the sugar-mills."

They passed the slaves, who were at work hoeing between the canes; and certainly, if an estimate of their condition was to be taken by the noise and laughter with which they beguiled their labour, they were far from demanding pity.

"But I must confess that there is something in that cart-whip which I do not like," observed Newton.

"I grant it; but custom is not easily broken through, nor do we know any substitute. It is the badge of authority, and the noise of it is requisite to summon them to their labour. With me it is seldom used, for it is not required; and if you were captain of a man-of-war, I should answer you as I did Captain C——; to wit—I question much whether my noisy whip is half so mischievous as your silent cat."

The sugar mills, stables of mules, boilers, coolers, &c. were all examined, and the parties returned to the plantation-house.

"Well, captain, now you have witnessed what is termed slavery, what is your opinion? Are your philanthropists justified in their invectives against us?"

"First assure me that all other plantations are as well regulated as your own," replied Mr. Berecroft.

"If not, they soon will be—it is to the interest of all the planters that they should; and by that, like all the rest of the world, they will be guided."

95

"But still there have been great acts of cruelty committed; quite enough to prepossess us against you as a body."

"I grant that such has been the case, and may occasionally be so now; but do not the newspapers of England teem with acts of barbarity? Men are the same everywhere. But, sir, it is the misfortune of this world that we never know when to stop. The abolition of the slave-trade was an act of humanity, worthy of a country acting upon an extended scale like England; but your philanthropists, not content with relieving the blacks, look forward to the extermination of their own countrymen, the whites, who, upon the faith and promise of the nation, were induced to embark their capital in these islands."

"Doubtless they wish to abolish slavery altogether," replied Berecroft.

"They must be content with having abolished the horrors of it, sir," continued the planter. "At a time when the mart was open, and you could purchase another slave to replace the one that had died from ill-treatment or disease, the life of a slave was not of such importance to his proprietor as it is now. Moreover, the slaves imported were adults, who had been once free; and, torn as they were from their natural soil and homes, where they slept in idleness throughout the day, they were naturally morose and obstinate, sulky, and unwilling to work. This occasioned severe punishment; and the hearts of their masters being indurated by habit, it often led to acts of barbarity. But slavery, since the abolition, has assumed a milder form—it is a species of bond-slavery. There are few slaves in existence who have not been born upon the estates, and we consider that they are more lawfully ours."

"Will you explain what you mean by *more lawfully?*"

"I mean, captain (for instance), that the father of that boy" (pointing to one of the negro lads who waited at breakfast) "was my slave; that he worked for me until he was an old man, and then I supported him for many years until he died. I mean, that I took care of this boy's mother, who, as she bore children, never did any work after her marriage, and has since been only an expense to me, and probably will continue to be so for some years. I mean, that that boy

96

was taken care of, and fed by me until he was ten years old, without my receiving any return for the expense which I incurred; and I therefore consider that he is indebted to me as a bond-slave, and that I am entitled to his services; and he, in like manner, when he grows too old to work, will become a pensioner, as his father was before him."

"I perceive the drift of your argument; you do not defend slavery generally."

"No; I consider a man born free and made a slave is justified in resorting to any means to deliver himself; but a slave that I have reared is lawfully a slave, and bound to remain so, unless he can repay me the expense I have incurred. But dinner is ready, captain; if you wish to argue the matter further, it must be over a bottle of claret."

The dinner was well dressed, and the Madeira and claret (the only wines produced) of the best quality. Their host did the honours of his table with true West Indian hospitality, circulating the bottle after dinner with a rapidity which would soon have produced an effect upon less prudent visitors; and when Mr. Berecroft refused to take any more wine, he ordered the ingredients for arrack-punch.

"Now, Mr. Forster, you must take a tumbler of this, and I think that you'll pronounce it excellent."

"Indeed!" replied Newton.

"Nay, I will take no denial; don't be afraid; you may do anything you please in this climate, only be temperate, and don't check the perspiration."

"Well, but," observed Newton, who placed the tumbler of punch before him, "you promised to renew your argument after dinner; and I should like to hear what you have to urge in defence of a system which I never have heard defended before."

"Well," replied his host, upon whom the wine and punch had begun to take effect, "just let me fill my tumbler again to keep my lips moist, and then I'll prove to you that slavery has existed from the earliest times, and is not at variance with the religion we profess. That it has existed from the earliest times, you need only refer to the book of Genesis; and that it is not at variance with our religion, I must refer to the Fourth Commandment. How can that part of the commandment be construed, 'and the stranger
97   G

that is within thy gates'? To whom can this possibly apply but to the slave? After directing that the labour of all the household, 'man-servant and maid-servant,' should cease, it then proceeds to the ox and the ass, and the stranger that is within thy gates. Now, gentlemen, this cannot be applied to the stranger in the literal sense of the word, the hospitality of the age forbidding that labour should be required of him. At that time slaves were brought from foreign lands, and were a source of traffic, as may be inferred by the readiness with which the Ishmaelites purchased Joseph of his brethren, and resold him in Egypt.

"Nay, that slavery was permitted by the Almighty is fully proved by the state of the Jewish nation, until He thought proper to bring them out of the house of bondage.

"If, then, the laws of God provided against the ill-treatment of the slave, slavery is virtually acknowledged as not being contrary to His Divine will. We have a further proof, subsequent to the mission of our Saviour, that the apostles considered slavery as lawful."

"I remember it: you refer to Paul sending back the runaway slave Onesimus. Well, I'll admit all this," replied Mr. Berecroft, who had a great dislike to points of Scripture being canvassed after dinner; "and I wish to know what inference you would draw from it."

"That I was just coming to. I assert that my property in slaves is therefore as legally mine as my property in land or money; and that any attempt to deprive me of either is equally a robbery, whether it be made by the nation or by an individual. But now, sir, allow me to ask you a question, show me where liberty is? Run over all the classes of society, and point out one man who is free?"

Mr. Berecroft, who perceived the effect of the arrack-punch, could not refrain from laughing, as he replied, "Well, your friend Mr. Kingston, is he not free?"

"Free! Not half so free as that slave boy who stands behind your chair. Why, he is a merchant; and whether he lives upon a scale of princely expenditure, whether wholesale or retail, banker, or proprietor of a chandler's shop, he is a speculator. Anxious days and sleepless nights await upon speculation. A man with his capital embarked, who may be a beggar on the ensuing day, cannot lie down upon roses; he is the slave of Mammon. Who are greater slaves than sailors? So are soldiers, and all who hold employ under Government. So are politicians: they are slaves to their tongues; for opinions once expressed, and parties once joined, at an age when reason is borne down by enthusiasm, and they are fixed for life against their conscience, and are unable to follow its dictates without blasting their characters. Courtiers are slaves, you must acknowledge."

"I beg your pardon," interrupted Kingston, "but I perceive that you make no distinction between those enthralled by their own consent, and against it."

"It is a distinction without a difference," replied the planter; "even if it were so, which it is not, but in particular cases. The fact is, society enthrals us all. We are forced to obey laws, to regard customs, to follow the fashion of the day, to support the worthless by poor-rates, to pay taxes, and the interest of a debt which others have contracted, or we must go to prison."

"And the princes and rulers of the land—do you include them?" inquired Newton.

"They are the greatest of all; for the meanest peasant has an advantage over the prince in the point on which we most desire to be free—that of the choice in his partner in life. He has none, but must submit to the wishes of his people, and, trammelled by custom, must take to his bed one whom he cannot take to his heart."

"Well, by your account, there is nobody free, unless it be *Liberty* herself."

"Why, sir," rejoined the planter, "to prove to you that I was correct when I asserted that there was no such thing in this world as liberty, paradoxical as it may appear, Liberty is but Liberty when in bondage. Release her, and she ceases to exist; she has changed her nature and character; for Liberty unrestrained becomes Licentiousness."

"Well," said Mr. Kingston, laughing with the rest at this curious remark, "as you have now arrived at your climax, with your leave we will go to bed."

"Have I convinced you?" demanded the planter, taking the tumbler from his lips.

"At least you have silenced us. Now, if you please, we will put on our coats and retire to our apartments."

99

"Yes—do," replied the other, who was not very steady; "do—or you may check the perspiration. Boy Jack, where are the lights? Good-night, gentlemen."

The negro led the way to a large room with two beds in it, for Newton and the master of the brig. Having first pointed out to them that there was a jug of sangoree, "Suppose gentlemen thirsty," he wished them good-night and left the room.

"Well, Newton," said Mr. Berecroft, as soon as they were alone, "what do you think of the planter?"

"I think that, considering his constant advice to be temperate, he swallowed a very large quantity of arrack-punch."

"He did indeed; but what think you of his arguments?"

"I hardly can say, except that none of them were sufficiently convincing to induce me to be a slave proprietor. We may perhaps, as he asserts, have contented ourselves with the shadow instead of the substance; but even the shadow of liberty is to be venerated by an Englishman."

"I agree with you, my boy. His discourse did, however, bring one idea into my head, which is, that there is a remarkable connection between religion and slavery. It was in a state of bondage that the Jews were prepared to receive the promised land, and whenever they fell off from the true worship, they were punished by captivity. It was through the means of slavery that the light of the true faith was first brought to our island, where it has burnt with a purer flame than elsewhere; for, if you recollect, the beauty of some English children exposed for sale at Rome, assisted by a Latin pun, caused the introduction of Christianity into Great Britain; and who knows but that this traffic, so offensive to humanity, has been permitted by an All-wise Power with the intent that some day it shall be the means of introducing Christianity into the vast regions of African idolatry?"

"True," observed Newton; "and the time may not be far distant."

"That it is impossible to calculate upon. *He* worketh by His own means, which are inscrutable. It was not the cause of virtue, but a desire that vice might be less trammelled, which introduced the Reformation in England. The more we attempt to interfere with the arrangements of the Almighty, the more we shall make evident our own folly and blindness and His unsearchable and immutable wisdom. Good-night, my boy."

CHAPTER XV

" *Lucy.* Are all these wretches slaves ?
Stanley. All sold, they and their posterity all slaves.
Lucy. O miserable fortune !
Bland. Most of them know no better, but were
   Born so, and only change their masters."
                                        —*Oroonoko.*

THE party were up at an early hour on the ensuing morning, that they might enjoy the delightful freshness of the air,
which so soon evaporates before the scorching rays of the
tropical sun. They were joined at breakfast by the doctor
who attended the estate, and who had called in to announce
the birth of a little negro boy in the early part of the night.

"Who did you say, doctor ? " answered the planter, " Mattee Sally ? Why, I thought Jane Ascension was in advance
of her."

"They were running it neck and neck, sir," replied the
surgeon.

" How is she—quite hearty ? "

" Quite, sir ; but very anxious about the child's name, and
requests to speak with you as soon as you have breakfasted."

"We will go to her. You have no idea," observed the
planter to Mr. Berecroft and Newton, " what importance
these people attach to the naming of their children. Nothing
but a fine long name will satisfy them. I really believe that
if I refused her, or called the boy Tom, she would eat dirt.
I believe we have all done. Boy Jack, bring the sangoree.
Doctor, I daresay that your clay wants moistening, so take
the first pull."

This important commencement and finale to the repast
having been duly administered, they proceeded to the
range of buildings before mentioned, in one of which they
found the lady *in the straw*, sitting up, and showing her white
teeth at her master's approach, as if nothing very particular
had occurred.

" Well, Mattee, how are you ? " said the planter. " Where's
the piccaninny ? "

101

"Ab um here, sar—keep im warm," replied the woman, pointing to a roll of blanket, in which the little creature was enveloped.

"Let us see him, Mattee."

"No, sar, too cold yet—bye bye, massa see um; make very fine sleep now. Suppose white piccaninny, suppose black piccaninny—all same—like plenty sleep. Um know very well, hab plenty work to do by-and-by—sleep all dey can, when lilly."

"But you'll smother him," observed Newton.

"Smoder him ?—what dat—eh ? I know now : massa mean stop um breath. No : suppose him no smoder before, no smoder now, sar. Massa," continued the woman, turning to the planter, "no ab name for piccaninny ?"

"Well, Mattee, we must find one ; these gentlemen will give him a name. Come, captain, what name do you propose ? "

"Suppose we christen him *Snub*," replied Berecroft, winking at the rest.

"Snob ! What sort a name you call dat, sar ? " replied the woman, tossing up her head. "Snob ! no, sar, you 'front me very much. Snob not proper name."

"Well then, Mr. Forster," said the planter, "try if you can be more fortunate."

"What do you think of Chrononhotonthologus ? " said Newton to the woman.

"Eh ! what dat ?—say dat again, sar," replied the woman.

"Chrononhotonthologus."

"Eh ! dat real fine name for piccaninny," cried the woman, with delight in her countenance. "Many tanky, sar. Chrotonpolygarse.

"No, no," replied Newton, laughing ; "Chrononhotonthologus."

"Es, hab um now—Hoton—tolyglass."

"No, that's only part. Chronon—hoton—thologus."

"I see—very fine name—Proton—choton—pollyglass."

"Yes, that's nearer to it," replied Newton.

"Well then, that point's settled," said the planter to the woman. "Is it all right, Mattee ?"

"Es, massa ; many tanks to gentleman—very fine name, do very well, sar."

102

"Doctor, put the name down opposite the register of the birth. Now, Mattee, all's right, good-bye," said the planter, leaving the room, followed by the others.

"Do you really intend to call the child by that name?" inquired Mr. Berecroft.

"Why not? it pleases the woman, and is as good as any other; it is of no consequence. They almost all have names, certainly not quite so long as the present; but as they grow longer, their names grow shorter. This name will first be abbreviated to Chrony; if we find that too long, it will be reduced again to Crow, which, by-the-bye, is not a bad name for a negro," said the planter, laughing at the coincidence.

Reader, did you ever, perchance, when in a farmyard, observe a hen or other domestic fowl, who having pounced upon half a potato, or something of the same description, too large to be bolted down at once, tries to escape with her prize, followed by all the rest, until she either drops it or eludes their vigilance? If so, you form some idea of a negro woman with a hard word in her mouth, which, although she does not know the meaning of, she considers as an equal treasure.

Newton had turned round to the courtyard, in the centre of which several women were sitting down at various employments, when one who had been busied in some little offices for the woman whom they had just visited, and had in consequence been present at the choice of the name, took her seat with the party in question. To several queries put to her she replied with extreme hauteur, as if she considered them as impertinent, and frowned upon her companions most majestically.

After a short time she rose, and turning round with the look of an empress, said, "Now, I shall go look after my Hoton-poton-bollyhass."

"Eh," cried one, opening her eyes with wonder.

"What dat?" screamed another.

"How you call dat long ting?" demanded a third.

"Eh! you tupid black tings," replied the proud possessor of the new word, with a look of ineffable scorn, "you no know what um call Poton-hoton-poll-fuss. Me no tell you," continued she, as she walked away, leaving the others almost white with envy and astonishment.

Shortly after this Mr. Kingston with his party took their leave of the hospitable old planter, and commenced their return to Bridgetown. They had not proceeded farther than a quarter of a mile, when, ascending a little hill, Newton discovered that a negro was assisting his own ascent by hanging on to the tail of his mule.

"How do you do this morning, sar?" said the man, grinning, as Newton looked round.

"I'm very well, sir, I thank you; but I'm afraid I shall not be able to keep up with the rest if my mule has to pull you up hill as well as carry me."

"Es, sar, mule go faster. Massa not understand; mule very obstinate, sar. Suppose you want go one way, he go anoder—suppose you pull him back by tail, he go on more."

"Well, if that's the case, you may hold on. Do you belong to the plantation?"

"No, sar, me free man. Me work there—carpenter, sar."

"A carpenter! How did you learn your trade and obtain your freedom?"

"Larn trade board of man-of-war, sar—man-of-war make me free."

Mr. Berecroft, who had been listening to the colloquy, took up the discourse.

"Were you born in this country?"

"No, sar, me Ashantee man."

"Then how did you come here?"

"Why, sar, ab very fine battle in Ashantee country. Take me and send me down to coast; sell me for slave. Go on board French schooner—English frigate take schooner, send me to Sarra Leon."

"Well, what did you do there?"

"Bind 'pentice, sar, to Massa Cawley, for farteen years—all de same as slave; work very hard; yam bad; plenty fever in that country—much better here."

"Then how did you get away from Sierra Leone?"

"Go to sleep one day in de bush—tieves come steal me, take me down to coast, sell me again."

"Well, where did you go then?"

"Bard schooner again, sar. Another man-of-war take schooner in West Indies; send her in prize. Keep me and some on board becase want hands; keep me, becase speak little English."

"How did you like a man-of-war?" inquired Newton.

"Man-of-war very fine place; but all slaves there—captain steal men every ship he come to. But sailor no tink so; ebery night we all sing Britong nebber, nebber, nebber, will be slave. Make me laugh, sar," continued the man, showing his teeth with a broad grin.

"What was the frigate's name?"

"Very fine name, sar—call her *Daddy Wise.*"[1]

"How long were you on board of her?"

"Far year, sar; larn carpenter trade—go to England – pay off—get plenty money—come out here in marchant vessel; England very fine place, but too much cold," said the negro, shuddering at the bare recollection.

"Now, tell me," said Kingston, "of course you recollect being in your own country? Which do you like best—that or this?"

"Ashantee very good country—Barbados very good country. Ashantee nebber work, hab no money—here plenty work, plenty money."

"Well, but where would you rather be—here or there?"

"Don't know, sar. Like to find country where no work, plenty money."

"Not singular in his opinion," observed Newton.

"Men do all work here, sar; women only talk," continued the negro. "My country, men nebber work at all—women do all work, and feed men."

"Then what does the man do?" inquired Berecroft.

"Man, sar," replied the negro proudly, "man go fight—go kill."

"Is that all?"

"Yes, sar, that all."

"So, you then mean to say, that if you could go back to Ashantee now you would remain there?"

"Yes, sar, stay there—do no work—sleep all day—make women feed me."

"How inveterate is early habit!" observed Mr. Berecroft. "This man, although free in a civilised country,

[1] *Dedaigneuse,* we suppose.

would return to his idleness, and resume his former ignorance."

"And so would every slave not born in the country. It
requires one or two generations to destroy this savage
nature," replied Kingston. "I believe idleness, like gout,
to be a hereditary disease either in black or white; I have
often observed it in the latter. Now, until man labours
there is no chance of civilisation; and improved as the race
of Africa have been in these islands, I still think that if
manumitted, they would all starve. In their own country
nature is so bountiful that little or no labour is required for
the support of life; but in these islands the soil, although
luxuriant, must be nurtured."

"You do then look forward to their ultimate freedom?"
inquired Newton.

"Most assuredly. Already much has been done, and if not
persecuted, we should be able and willing to do much more."

"The public mind in England is certainly much inflamed
against you," said Berecroft.

"It is; or rather, I should say, the more numerous public
composed of those persons unable to think for themselves,
and in consequence led by others, styling themselves philanthropists, but appearing to have very jesuitical ideas with
regard to truth. This I have no hesitation in asserting, that
if philanthropy had not been found to have been so very
profitable it never would have had so many votaries: true
philanthropy, like charity, begins at home. Observe how
the papers teem with the misery of the lower classes in
England, yet this affects not the West India philanthropist.
You perceive not their voices raised in behalf of their
suffering countrymen. They pass the beggar in the street;
they heed not the cry of starvation at home; but everywhere
raise petitions for emancipation; or, in fact, for the destruction of the property of others. That it is an invidious property I grant, and I wish I could dispose of mine; but that
is not so easy. My ancestors embarked their capital in these
islands upon the faith and promises of the country, when
opinions were very different from what they are now, and I
cannot help myself. However, the time will come when
England will bitterly rue the having listened to the suggestions and outcries of these interested people."

106

"I do not understand you. How do you mean?"

"I said before that it was on the faith of the country that we embarked our property in these islands. You are not perhaps aware that when, in the reign of Queen Anne, the Assiento treaty was made, by which we obtained the privilege of supplying all the islands with slaves, it was considered as one of the most important acquisitions that could be obtained. Public opinion has now changed; but if a nation changes her opinion, she must at the same time be just. Let the country take our estates and negroes at a fair valuation, and we shall be most happy to surrender them. If she frees the slaves without so doing, she is guilty of robbery and injustice, and infringes on the constitution of the country, which protects all property, and will of course allow us to decide upon our own measures."

"May I inquire what those would be?"

"Throwing off the yoke, declaring ourselves independent, and putting ourselves under the protection of America, who will gladly receive us, aware that we shall be a source not only of wealth but of security."

"Would America risk a war to obtain these islands?"

"She would be foolish not to do so, and England would be more than foolish to engage in one. It is true that, if not immediately supported by America, England might create a scene of confusion and bloodshed in the colonies; but the world has too often had the severe lesson that colonies once detaching themselves are never to be regained. England would therefore be only entailing a useless expense, however gratifying it might be to her feelings of revenge."

"But do you think that this is likely to occur?"

"I do, most certainly, if those who govern continue to listen to the insidious advice of the party denominated 'Saints'; and I am afraid that it will not be until these islands are separated from the mother-country that she will appreciate their value. Our resolution once formed, we white slaves (for slaves we are) will not flinch; and the islands of the Caribbean Sea will be enrolled as another star, and add another stripe to the independent flag which is their natural protector."

"I trust that will never come to pass."

"And so do I, Mr. Berecroft; for I am an Englishman,

and love my country, and the loss of these colonies would be a blow from which England would never recover."

"You forget her extensive colonies in the East."

"I do not; but the West Indies add to her wealth and her commercial prosperity, to her nursery of seamen and her exhausted revenue. They, on the contrary, add only to her grandeur, for they cost the country three millions a year; and I doubt whether at that expense it is worth while to retain any colony, however vast and extensive it may be. I consider that if the East India ports were open to all the world, and the territory governed by its former princes, England, with all the competition which would take place, would yet be a gainer; and on the other hand, I know that by the loss of these islands she would find a decrease of millions in her revenue."

"Then the philanthropists must pay the national debt?" observed Newton, laughing.

"They be d—d!" replied Kingston, who was warm with argument; "they would not pay a farthing."

CHAPTER XVI

" The sea-breached vessel can no longer bear
The floods that o'er her burst in dread career.
The labouring hull already seems half filled
With water, through an hundred leaks distilled :
Thus drenched by every wave, her riven deck,
Stript and defenceless, floats a naked wreck."

—FALCONER.

NEWTON remained at Bridgetown, under the roof of Mr. Kingston, for more than three weeks, by which time the brig was laden and waiting for convoy to proceed to England.

Mr. Berecroft had made every preparation for his voyage, when an unexpected circumstance occurred, which eventually proved the occasion of great hardship and danger to Newton. This was, the master of a large ship belonging to the same owners, and then lying in Carlisle Bay to proceed homeward by the same convoy, had so ingratiated himself with a wealthy widow residing upon the island, that rather than he should again trust himself to the fickle element, she had been induced to surrender up to him her plantation, her negroes, and her fair self—all equally bound to honour and obey through their future lives.

Mr. Berecroft, in consequence of this resignation of his brother captain, was appointed to the command of the larger vessel; and Jackson, the first mate, ordered to take the command of the *Eliza and Jane.* This was a sad blow to Newton, and one which he could not avoid, as Mr. Berecroft could not take him in his new ship—all the subordinate situations being already filled up.

At first he was inclined to quit the brig; but by the advice of Mr. Berecroft and Kingston he was persuaded to go the passage home, as he was now first mate of the vessel, and would incur forfeiture of all wages if he broke the articles which he had signed at Liverpool. Unpleasant as the prospect was, he was further induced by Berecroft's assurance, that now Jackson was provided for, he would arrange with the owners that Newton should be appointed the first mate of his own ship as soon as they arrived in England.

In a few days the men-of-war made their appearance. Newton, who had remained on shore until the last moment, shook hands with his friendly patron, and thanking Mr. Kingston for his kindness, went on board of the vessel with a sorrowful and foreboding heart.

Nor was he at all inclined to cheer up as he stepped on the deck of the brig, and beheld Jackson, with a handspike still brandishing over his head, standing across the body of one of the seamen, whom he had just dashed to the deck with the implement in his hand. At the sight of Newton, the wrath of the new captain appeared to be increased. He eyed him malevolently, and then observed, with a sneer, " That's what all skulkers may expect on board of my vessel."

Newton made no answer, and Jackson went forward, where the remainder of the crew were heaving up the anchor with the windlass. Newton walked up to the seaman, who appeared still insensible, and examined him. The iron plate at the end of the handspike had cut deep into the skull, and there was every appearance of a contusion of the brain.

Calling the boy who attended the cabin, Newton, with his assistance, carried the man below and laid him in his berth. He then repaired on deck and took the helm, the anchor of the brig being atrip. In a quarter of an hour the sail was on her, and she followed the course steered by the men-of-war, who were about to run through the other islands, and pick up several vessels, who were waiting for their protection.

" If you expect an easy berth as first mate you are mistaken, my joker," said Jackson to Newton, as he steered the vessel ; " you've skulked long enough, and shall now work double tides, or take the consequence. If you don't, I'll be d—d !"

" I shall do my duty, Mr. Jackson," replied Newton, "and fear no consequences."

" Indeed ! You saw how I settled a skulk just now ; beware of his fate !"

" I neither anticipate it nor fear it, Mr. Jackson. If it comes to handspikes, two can play at that game. I rather think that before many hours are over you will be sorry for your violence, for I believe that man to be in considerable danger. Even now, I should recommend you to demand surgical assistance from the frigate."

" Demand it, if you dare ! I am captain of this ship, sir. The rascal may die and be d—d !"

To this disgusting speech Newton made no reply. He had made up his mind to put up with everything short of down-right aggression, and for three days more he obeyed all orders, however arbitrary and however annoying. During this period the man who had been injured became gradually worse, his illness increased rapidly ; and on the fifth day he became delirious, and in a state of high fever, when Newton again pointed out the propriety of asking surgical aid from one of the men-of-war. This suggestion was answered by Jackson, who was now really alarmed, with a volley of oaths and execrations, ending with a flat refusal. The crew of the brig murmured, and collected together forward, looking occasionally at the men-of-war as they spoke in whispers to each other ; but they were afraid of Jackson's violence, and none ventured to speak out. Jackson paced the deck in a state of irritation and excitement, as he listened to the ravings of his victim, which were loud enough to be heard all over the vessel.

THE MERCHANT SERVICE

As the evening closed, the men, taking the opportunity of Jackson's going below, went up to Newton, who was walking aft, and stated their determination that the next morning, whether the master consented to it or not, they would hail the frigate and demand surgical assistance for their shipmate. In the midst of the colloquy, Jackson, who, hearing the noise overhead of the people coming aft, had a suspicion of the cause, and had been listening at the bottom of the ladder to what was said, came up the hatchway, and accusing Newton of attempting to raise a mutiny, ordered him immediately to his cabin, stating his intention of sending him on board of the frigate the next morning to be placed in confinement.

"I shall obey your order," replied Newton, "as you are in command of this vessel. I only hope that you will adhere to your resolution in communicating with the frigate." So saying, he descended the companion hatch.

But Jackson, who, both from the information of the cabin boy, and the fact that the incoherent ravings of his victim became hourly more feeble, thought himself in jeopardy, had no such intention. As the night closed in he remained on deck, gradually taking off first one sail and then another, until the brig was left far astern of the rest of the convoy, and the next morning there was no other vessel in sight; then, on pretence of rejoining them, he made all sail, at the same time changing his course, so as to pass between two of the islands. Newton was the only one on board who understood navigation besides Jackson, and therefore the only one who could prove that he was escaping from the convoy. He was in confinement below; and the men, whatever may have been their suspicions, could not prove that they were not steering as they ought.

About twelve o'clock on that day the poor sailor breathed his last. Jackson, who was prepared for the event, had already made up his mind how to proceed. The men murmured, and proposed securing Jackson as a prisoner, and offering the command to Newton. They went below and made the proposal to him, but he refused; observing that until it was proved by the laws of the land that Jackson had murdered their shipmate, he was not guilty, and therefore they had no right to dispossess him of his command; and until their evidence could be taken by some of the authorities, he must remain; further pointing out to them, that as he could be seized immediately upon his arrival at an English port, or falling in with a man-of-war during their passage, the ends of justice would be equally answered as if they committed themselves by taking the law into their own hands.

The men, although not satisfied, acquiesced and returned to their duty on deck. Jackson's conduct towards them was now quite altered; he not only treated them with lenity, but supplied them with extra liquor and other indulgences, which as a captain he could command. Newton, however, he still detained under an arrest, watching him most carefully each time that he was necessitated to come on deck. The fact was, Jackson, aware that his life would be forfeited to the laws of his country, had resolved to wreck the brig upon one of the reefs to the northward, then take to his boats and escape to one of the French islands. At his instigation, the body of the man had been thrown overboard by some of the crew, when they were in a state of half intoxication.

Newton, who had been below four days, had retired as usual to his hammock, when a sudden shock, accompanied by the fall of the masts by the board, woke him from a sound sleep to all the horrors of shipwreck. The water pouring rapidly through the sides of the vessel, proved to him that there was no chance of escape except by the boats. The shriek, so awful when raised in the gloom of night by seamen anticipating immediate death, the hurried footsteps above him, the confusion of many voices, with the heavy blows from the waves against the side of the vessel, told him that danger was imminent, even if escape were possible. He drew on his trousers, and rushed to the door of his cabin. Merciful Heaven! what was his surprise, his horror, to find that it was fastened outside! A moment's thought at the malignity of the wretch (for it was indeed Jackson, who during the night had taken such steps for his destruction) was followed by exertions to escape. Placing his shoulders against his sea-chest, and his feet against the door, his body in nearly a horizontal position, he made a violent effort to break open the door. The lock gave way, but the door did not open more than one or two inches; for Jackson, to make sure, had coiled down against it a hawser which lay a few yards farther forward in the steerage, the weight of which the strength of no five men could remove. Maddened with the idea of perishing by such treachery, Newton exerted his frantic efforts again and again without success. Between each pause, the voices of the seamen asking for the oars and other articles belonging to the long-boat, proved to him that every moment of delay was a nail in his coffin. Again and again were his efforts repeated with almost superhuman strength; but the door remained fixed as ever. At last, it occurred to him that the hawser, which he had previously ascertained by passing his hand through the small aperture which he had made, might only lay against the lower part of the door, and that the upper part might be free. He applied his strength above, and found the door to yield. By repeated attempts he at last succeeded in kicking the upper panel to pieces, and having forced his body through the aperture, Newton rushed on deck with the little strength he had remaining.

The men—the boat—were not there! He hailed, but they heard him not; he strained his eyes—but they had disappeared in the gloom of the night; and Newton, overcome with exhaustion and disappointment, fell down senseless on the deck.

CHAPTER XVII

" *Paladore.* I have heard,
Have read bold fables of enormity,
Devised to make men wonder, and confirm
The abhorrence of our nature ; but this hardness
Transcends all fiction."

—Law of Lombardy.

WE must now relate what had occurred on deck during the struggle of Newton to escape from his prison. At one o'clock Jackson had calculated that in an hour or less the brig would strike on the reef. He took the helm from the man who was steering, and told him that he might go below. Previous to this, he had been silently occupied in coiling the hawser before the door of Newton's cabin, it being his intention to desert the brig with the seamen in the long-boat, and leave Newton to perish. When the brig dashed upon the reef, which she did with great violence, and the crew hurried upon deck, Jackson, who was calm, immediately proceeded to give the orders which he had already arranged in his mind; and the coolness with which they were given quieted the alarm of the seamen, and allowed them time to recall their scattered senses. This, however, proved unfortunate to Jackson. Had they all hurried in the boat at once and shoved off, he would in all probability have been permitted to go with them, and Newton, in the hurry of their self-preservation, would have been forgotten; but his cool behaviour restored their confidence, and, unhappily for him, gave the seamen time to reflect. Every one was in the boat; for Jackson had quietly prepared and put into her what he considered requisite, when one of the men called out for Newton.

" D—n Newton now !—save your own lives, my lads. Quick in the boat, all of you."

" Not without Mr. Newton !" cried the men unanimously. " Jump down, Tom Williams, and see where he is; he must sleep devilish sound."

The sailor sprung down the companion-hatch, where he found the hawser coiled against the door, and heard Newton struggling inside. It was enough. He hastened on deck, and told his companions, adding that "it would take half-an-hour to get the poor fellow out, and that's longer than we dare stay, for in ten minutes the brig will be to pieces."

" It is you, you murdering rascal, who did it !" cried the man to Jackson. " I tell you what, my lads, if poor Mr. Newton is to die, let this scoundrel keep him company."

A general shout proclaimed the acquiescence of the other seamen in this act of retributive justice. Jackson, with a loud oath, attempted to spring into the boat, but was repelled by the seamen; again he made the attempt, with dreadful imprecations. He was on the plane-sheer of the brig, and about to make a spring, when a blow from a handspike (the same handspike with which he had murdered the unfortunate seaman) struck him senseless, and he fell back into the lee-scuppers. The boat then shoved off, and had not gained more than two cables' lengths from the vessel when Newton

114

effected his escape and ran on deck, as narrated in our last chapter.

The brig had now beat up so high on the reef that she remained firmly fixed upon it, and the tide having ebbed considerably, she was less exposed to the beating of the waves. The sun was also about to make his appearance, and it was broad daylight when Jackson first came to his recollection. His brain whirled, his ideas were confused, and he had but a faint reminiscence of what had occurred. He felt that the water washed his feet, and with a sort of instinct he rose and staggered up to windward. In so doing, without perceiving him, he stumbled over the body of Newton, who also was roused up by the shock. A few moments passed before either could regain his scattered senses, and at the same time, both sitting up on the deck at about a yard distant, they discovered and recognised each other.

Newton was the more collected of the two, for Jackson's insensibility had been occasioned by bodily—his, by mental concussion. The effect of the blow was still felt by Jackson, and although recovered from the stupor, a dull, heavy sensation affected his eyesight and confused his ideas.

The sight of Newton went far to recover Jackson, who started up as if to grapple with the object of his hatred. Newton was on his legs at the same moment, and retreating, seized upon the handspike, which lay on the deck close to where Jackson had been struck down, and placed himself in an attitude of defence. Not a word was exchanged between them. They remained a few minutes in this position, when Jackson, whose brain was affected by the violence of his feelings, dropped down upon the deck in a renewed state of insensibility.

Newton had now time to look about him, and the prospect was anything but cheering. It was almost low water, and in every direction he perceived reefs of coral rock and large banks of sand, with deep channels between them, through which the tide flowed rapidly. The reef upon which the brig had been grounded was of sharp coral, and in the deeper parts the trees could be discerned, extending a submarine forest of boughs; but it was evident that the reef upon which the vessel lay was, as well as most of the others, covered at high water. As a means of escape, a small boat was still hanging over the stern, which Newton was able to manage either with her sails or her oars, as might be required.

As there was no time to be lost, and the only chance of escape remained with the boat, Newton commenced his arrangements. The mast and sails were found and the latter bent; a keg was filled with water, a compass taken out of the binnacle, a few pieces of beef and some bread collected in a bag and thrown in. He also procured some bottles of wine and cider from the cabin; these he stowed away carefully in the little locker which was fitted under the stern-sheets of the boat. In an hour everything was ready: and throwing into her some pieces of spare rope, and a small grapnel to anchor with, there being still sufficient water alongside to float her, Newton gradually lowered one tackle, and then another, until the boat was safe in the water. He then hauled her up alongside, made her fast by the painter, and stepped her mast.

All was now ready. But to leave Jackson to be washed away by the returning tide, when the brig would unquestionably go to pieces !—Newton could not do it. True, he had sought his life, and still displayed the most inveterate rancour towards him ; and Newton felt convinced that no future opportunity would occur that his enemy would not profit by to ensure his destruction. Yet to leave him—a murderer !—with all his sins upon his soul, to be launched so unprepared into the presence of an offended Creator !—it was impossible—it was contrary to his nature, and to the religion which he professed. How could he hope for the Divine assistance in his perilous undertaking, wh _n he embarked on it regardless of the precept to forgive his enemy ?

Newton ascended to that part of the deck where Jackson lay, and roused him. Jackson awoke, as from a deep sleep, and then stared at Newton, who as a precaution held the handspike in his hand.

"Mr. Jackson," said Newton, "I have roused you to let you know that the boat is now ready, and that I am going to shove off."

Jackson, who recollected the scene of the previous night, and perceived Newton standing over him with the handspike, appeared wholly unnerved. In point of muscular

116

power Newton was his superior, independent of the weapon in his possession.

"Not without me!—not without me!" cried Jackson, raising himself upon his knees. "For mercy's sake, Mr. Newton, do not leave me to this horrid death!"

"You would have left me to one even more dreadful," replied Newton.

"I beg your pardon! Pardon me, Mr. Newton; I was drunk at the time—indeed I was. I don't know what I do when I'm in liquor. Don't leave me! I'll obey your orders, and do anything you wish! I'll wait upon you as your servant! I will, indeed, Mr. Newton!"

"I neither ask that you will obey my orders nor wait upon me," replied Newton. "All I request is, that you will lay aside your wanton animosity, and exert yourself to save your life. For what you have already attempted against me, may God forgive you, as I do! For what you may hereafter attempt, you will find me prepared. Now, follow into the boat."

Without further exchange of words, Newton, followed by Jackson, went into the boat and shoved off. The weather was moderate and the wind light. There were two islets which Newton had marked, which apparently were not covered at high water, one about ten miles distant in the supposed direction of the land—for Newton had shrewdly guessed the locality of the reef—and the other about two miles from the first, farther out, with trees growing to the water's edge. To this latter Newton proposed pulling, and waiting there until the next morning. When they were both in the boat, Newton finding that the wind was contrary, unshipped the mast, and taking the foremost oar, that Jackson might not sit behind him, desired him to take the other. The tide, which was now flood, and swept out to the southward, obliged them to pull at an angle to reach their intended destination. It was not until sunset that, with great exertion, they fetched the island nearest to the land, not the one that was covered with trees, as they had intended. As soon as the boat was secured, exhausted with fatigue they both threw themselves down on the sand, where they remained for some time. Having recovered a little, Newton procured from the boat some of the supplies which they required, and after satisfying their hunger in silence, they both lay down to repose. Newton, who was still afraid of Jackson's diabolical enmity, which his silence implied to be again at work, closed his eyes and pretended for some time to be asleep. As soon as it was dark he rose, and first listening to the breathing of his comrade, who appeared to be in a sound slumber, he walked away from him about one hundred yards, so that it would be difficult to find him; he placed the handspike under his head for a pillow, and, worn out with mental and bodily fatigue, was soon in a state of oblivion.

His sleep, although profound for three or four hours, was subsequently restless. The mind when agitated watches for the body, and wakes it at the time when it should be on the alert. Newton woke up: it was not yet daylight, and all was hushed. He turned round, intending to get up immediately; yet yielding to the impulse of wearied nature, he again slumbered. Once he thought that he heard a footstep, roused himself and listened; but all was quiet and still, except the light wave rippling on the sand. Again he was roused by a sort of grating noise; he listened, and all was quiet. A third time he was roused by a sound like the flapping of a sail; he listened—he was sure of it, and he sprang upon his feet. It was dawn of day, and as he turned his eyes towards the beach, he perceived to his horror that the boat was indeed under sail, Jackson, who was in it, then just hauling aft the main-sheet and steering away from the island. Newton ran to the beach, plunged into the sea, and attempted to regain the boat; but he was soon out of his depth, and the boat running away fast through the water. He shouted to Jackson as a last attempt. The scoundrel waved his hand in ironical adieu and continued his course.

"Treacherous villain!" mentally exclaimed Newton, as his eyes followed the boat. "Was it for this that I preserved your life, in return for your attempts on mine? Here, then, must I die of starvation! God's will be done!" exclaimed he aloud, as he sat down on the beach and covered his face with his hands.

" The scoundrel waved his hand in ironical adieu and continued his course."

CHAPTER XVIII

" For now I stand as one upon a rock,
    Environed with a wilderness of sea,
    Who marks the waxing tide grow wave by wave,
    Expecting ever when some envious surge
    Will in his brinish bowels swallow him."
                                        —SHAKSPEARE.

THE tide was on the ebb when Newton was left in this
desolate situation. After some minutes passed in bitterness
of spirit, his natural courage returned; and although the
chance of preservation was next to hopeless, Newton rose
up, resolved that he would use his best efforts, and trust to
Providence for their success. His first idea was to examine
the beach, and see if Jackson had left him any portion of the
provisions which he had put into the boat; but there was
nothing. He then walked along the beach, following the re-
ceding tide, with the hope of collecting any shell-fish which
might be left upon the sands; but here again he was disappointed. It was evident, therefore, that to stay on this
islet was to starve; his only chance appeared to remain in his
capability of reaching the islet next to it, which, as we have
before mentioned, was covered with trees. There, at least,
he might find some means of sustenance, and be able with
the wood to make a raft, if nothing better should turn up in
his favour.

The tide swept down towards the islet, but it ran so strong
that there was a chance of his being carried past it; he
therefore determined to wait for an hour or two, until the
strength of the current was diminished, and then make the
attempt. This interval was passed in strengthening his mind
against the horror of the almost positive death which stared
him in the face.

It was about an hour before low water that Newton walked
into the sea, and commending himself to Providence, struck
out for the islet, keeping his course well to windward to
allow for the tide sweeping him down. To use a nautical
phrase, he "held his own" extremely well, until he reached

119

the centre of the channel, where the water ran with great velocity, and bore him down rapidly with the stream. Newton struggled hard, for he was aware that the strength of the current once passed, his labour would be comparatively easy; and so it proved. As he neared the shore of the islet, he made good way; but he had been carried down so far when in the centre of the stream that it became a nice point, even to the calculation of hope, whether he would fetch the extreme point of the islet. Newton redoubled his exertions; when within thirty yards of the shore an eddy assisted him, and he made sure of success; but when within ten yards a counter current again caught him, and swept him down. He was now abreast of the very extreme point of the islet; a bush that hung over the water was his only hope; with three or four desperate strokes he exhausted his remaining strength, at the same time that he seized hold of a small bough. It was decayed—snapped asunder, and Newton was whirled away by the current into the broad ocean.

How constantly do we find people running into real danger to avoid imaginary evil! A mother will not permit her child to go to sea lest it should be drowned, and a few days afterwards it is kicked to death by a horse. Had the child been permitted to go afloat, he might have lived and run through the usual term of existence. Wherever we are, or wherever we may go, there is death awaiting us in some shape or another, sooner or later; and there is as much danger in walking through the streets of London as in ploughing the foaming ocean. Every tile over our heads contains a death within it as certain, if it were to fall upon us, as that occasioned by the angry surge which swallows us up in its wrath. I believe, after all, that as many sailors in proportion run out their allotted span as the rest of the world that are engaged in other apparently less dangerous professions; although it must be acknowledged that occasionally we do become food for fishes. "There is a tide in the affairs of men," says Shakspeare; but certainly, of all the tides that ever interfered in a man's prospects, that which swept away Newton Forster appeared to be the least likely to "lead to fortune." Such, however, was the case. Had Newton gained the islet which he coveted, he would have perished miserably; whereas

120

it will soon appear that, although his sufferings are not yet ended, his being carried away was the most fortunate circumstance which could have occurred, and proved the means of his ultimate preservation.

Newton had resigned himself to his fate. He ceased from further exertion, except such as was necessary to keep him above water a little longer. Throwing himself on his back, he appealed to Heaven for pardon as he floated away with the stream. That Newton had as few errors and follies to answer for as most people is most certain; yet even the most perfect soon run up a long account. During our lives our sins are forgotten, as is the time at which they are committed; but when death is certain, or appears to be so, it is then that the memory becomes most horribly perfect, and each item of our monstrous bill requires but a few seconds to be read, and to be acknowledged as too correct. This is the horror of death; this it is which makes the body struggle to retain the soul, already pluming herself and rustling her wings impatient for her flight. This it is which constitutes the pang of separation, as the enfeebled body gradually relaxes its hold, and—all is over, at least on this side of the grave.

Newton's strength was exhausted; his eyes were fixed on the clear blue sky, as if to bid it farewell; and resigned to his fate, he was about to give over the last few painful efforts, which he was aware could only prolong, not save his life, when he received a blow on his shoulder under the water. Imagining that it proceeded from the tail of a shark, or of some other of the ravenous monsters of the deep which abound among these islands, and that the next moment his body would be severed in half, he uttered a faint cry at the accumulated horror of his death; but the next moment his legs were swung round by the current, and he perceived to his astonishment that he was aground upon one of the sandbanks which abounded on the reef, and over which the tide was running with the velocity of a sluice. He floundered, then rose, and found himself in about one foot of water. The ebb-tide was nearly finished; and this was one of the banks which never showed itself above water except during the full and change of the moon. It was now about nine o'clock in the morning, and the sun shone with great power

Newton, faint from want of sustenance, hardly knew whether to consider this temporary respite as an advantage. He knew that the tide would soon flow again, and he felt that his strength was too much spent to enable him to swim back to the islet which he had missed when he had attempted to reach it, and which was more than two miles from the bank upon which he then stood. What chance had he, then, but to be swept away by the return of the tide? He almost regretted that it had not been a shark instead of the sandbank which had struck him; he would then have been spared a few hours of protracted misery.

As Newton had foreseen, the ebb-tide was soon over; a short pause of "slack water" ensued, and there was an evident and rapid increase of the water around him. The wind, too, freshened, and the surface of the ocean was in strong ripples. As the water deepened, so did the waves increase in size; every moment added to his despair. He had now remained about four hours on the bank; the water had risen to underneath his arms, the waves nearly lifted him off his feet, and it was with difficulty that he could retain his position. Hope deserted him, and his senses became confused. He thought that he saw green fields, and cities, and inhabitants. His reason was departing; he saw his father coming down to him with the tide, and called to him for help, when the actual sight of something recalled him from his temporary aberration. There was a dark object upon the water, evidently approaching. His respiration was almost suspended as he watched its coming. At last he distinguished that it must either be a whale asleep, or a boat bottom up. Fortunately for Newton, it proved to be the latter. At last it was brought down by the tide to within a few yards of him, and appeared to be checked. Newton dashed out towards the boat, and in a minute was safely astride upon it. As soon as he had recovered a little from his agitation, he perceived that it was the very boat belonging to the brig, in which Jackson had so treacherously deserted and left him on the island!

At three o'clock it was high water, and at five the water had again retreated, so that Newton could quit his station on the bottom of the boat and walk round her. He then righted her, and discovered that the mast had been carried away close to the step, but with the sail still remained fast to the boat by the main-sheet, which had jammed on the belaying pin, so that it still was serviceable. Everything else had been lost out of the boat, except the grapnel, which had been bent, and which, hanging down in the water from the boat being capsized, had brought it up when it was floated on the sandbank. Newton, who had neither eaten nor drunk since the night before, was again in despair, tormented as he was by insufferable thirst; when he observed that the locker under the stern-sheets was closed. He hastened to pull it open, and found that the bottles of wine and cider that he had deposited there were remaining. A bottle of the latter was soon poured down his throat, and Newton felt as if restored to his former vigour.

At seven o'clock in the evening the boat was nearly high and dry. Newton baled her out, and fixing the grapnel firmly in the sand, lay down to sleep in the stern-sheets covered over with the sail. His sleep was so sound that he did not wake until six o'clock the next morning, when the boat was again aground. He refreshed himself with some wine and meditated upon his prospects. Thanking Heaven for a renewed chance of escape, and lamenting over the fate of the unprepared Jackson, who had evidently been upset, from the main-sheet having been jammed, Newton resolved to make for one of the English isles, which he knew to be about two hundred miles distant.

The oars had been lost, but the rudder of the boat was fortunately made fast by a pennant. In the afternoon he drew up his grapnel, and made sail in the direction, as well as he could judge from the position of the sun, of the English isles. As the night closed in he watched the stars, and steered his course by them.

The next day came, and although the boat sailed well and went fast before a free wind, no land was in sight. Newton had again recourse to the cider and the wine.

The second night he could hardly keep his eyes open; yet, wearied as he was, he still continued his course, and never quitted his helm. The day again dawned, and Newton's strength was gone, from constant watching ; still he bore up against it until tne sun had set.

No land was yet to be seen, and sleep overpowered him. He took a hitch of the main-sheet round his finger, that should the breeze freshen he might be roused, in case he should go to sleep; and having taken this precaution, in a few minutes the boat was steering herself.

CHAPTER XIX

" But man, proud man,
Dressed in a little brief authority,
Most ignorant of what he's most assured,
His glassy essence, like an angry ape,
Plays such fantastic tricks before high Heaven."

—SHAKSPEARE.

THE reef upon which the brig had been wrecked was one of those extending along the southward of the Virgin Isles. Newton had intended to steer well to the eastward, with the view of reaching one of the northernmost English colonies; but not having a compass, he naturally was not very equal in his course. The fact was that he steered well to the southward of it; and after he fell asleep the boat ran away still farther off her course, for she was on the larboard tack ; and having no weight in her except Newton, who was aft in the stern sheets, she did not feel inclined to keep her wind. Newton's sleep was so profound that neither the pulling of the main-sheet, which he held with a round turn round his hand, nor the dancing of the boat, which during the night had run fast before an increasing breeze, roused him from his lethargy. On sailed the boat, left to the steerage of Providence ; on slept Newton, as if putting firm reliance on the same. It was not until the break of day that his repose was very abruptly broken by a shock, which threw him from the stern-sheets of the boat, right over the aftermost thwart. Newton recovered his legs and his senses, and found himself alongside of a vessel. He had run stem on to a small schooner which was lying at

124

anchor. As the boat was drifting fast by, Newton made a spring, and gained the deck of the vessel.

" Ah ! mon Dieu !—les Anglais—les Anglais ; nous-sommes prisonniers !" cried out the only man on deck, jumping on his feet and making a precipitate dive below.

The vessel of which Newton had thus taken possession was one employed in carrying the sugars from the plantations round to Basseterre (the port of Guadaloupe), there to be shipped for Europe—Newton's boat having run away so far to the southward as to make this island. She was lying at anchor off the mouth of a small river waiting for a cargo.

It happened that the crew of the schooner, who were all slaves, were exactly in the same situation as Newton when their vessels came in contact—viz., fast asleep. The shock had awakened them, but they were all below except the one who had kept such a remarkably good watch.

Exhausted as Newton was, he could not but smile at his uninterrupted possession of the vessel's decks. Anxious to have communication with the people on board, he sat down awaiting their coming up from below. In a minute or two, a black head was seen to rise slowly and fearfully out of the fore-scuttle; then it disappeared. Another rose up and went down again as before; and thus it went on until Newton reckoned ten different faces. Having individually ascertained that there was but one man, and that one not provided with any weapons, the negroes assumed a degree of courage. The first head that had made its appearance, the woolly hair of which was of a grizzly grey from age, was again popped up the fore-scuttle, with an interrogatory to Newton in French, who he was and what he wanted? Newton, who did not understand a word of the language, shook his head, and opening his hands and extending his arms to show that he had no means of defence, he beckoned to them to come up. The man's head had again disappeared, and after a little demur nine or ten negroes crawled up out of the fore-scuttle one after another, each with some weapon or another by way of security. They remained on the forecastle of the vessel until the last was up ; and then at a nod given by their grizzle-headed leader, they advanced aft in a body towards Newton. Newton rose and pointed to the boat, which had now drifted about a quarter of a mile astern. He then made signs, to give them to understand that he had been wrecked.

"Apparemment c'est un pauvre misérable, qui a fait naufrage," observed the old negro, who appeared to have the charge of the vessel. "Gustave Adolphe, tu parles bien l'Anglais; demandez-lui les nouvelles," continued the old man, folding his arms across and looking very big indeed, as he reclined against the mainmast of the vessel.

Gustave Adolphe stood forward from the rest of the negroes. He was a short, fat, shiny-faced fellow, with his hair plaited into about fifty little tails. He first bowed to his old commander, then placing his arms akimbo, walked up to Newton, and looking him full in the face, commenced his duty of interpreter as follows—

"I say—God dam——"

Newton smiled.

"Oui, monsieur, c'est un Anglais."

"Continuez, Gustave Adolphe," replied the old negro, with a majestic air.

Gustave Adolphe, with another bow, resumed—

"I say—where com ?"

"Barbados," replied Newton.

"Monsieur, il vient de Barbados."

"Continuez, Gustave Adolphe," replied his superior, with a wave of his hand.

"I say—where go ?"

"Where go ?" replied Newton, "go to the bottom."

"Monsieur, il allait au port de Bo—tom."

"Bo — tom," repeated the old negro. "Où, diable, est ça ?"

Here a general consultation was held, by which it appeared that such a port had never been heard of in the West Indies.

"Gustave Adolphe, demandez-lui si c'est un port Anglais."

"I say—Bo—tom—English port ?"

"No," replied Newton, amused with the mistake; "I should rather call it neutral."

"C'est un port neutral, monsieur."

"Gustave Adolphe, demandez-lui de quelle ile."

"I say, what ile—Bo—tom ?"

Newton, who was faint with hunger and thirst, was not inclined at the moment to continue the conversation, which otherwise would have been a source of amusement. He replied by making signs that he wished to eat and drink.

"Monsieur," said Gustave Adolphe to the old negro, "le prisonnier refuse de faire réponse, et demande à manger et à boire."

"Va l'en chercher, Gustave Adolphe," replied the old man. "Allons, messieurs," continued he, addressing the other negroes. "Il faut lever l'ancre de suite, et amener notre prisonnier aux autorités; Charles Philippe, va chercher mon porte voix."

The negro captain walked up and down the deck of the schooner, a vessel about thirty feet long, until Charles Philippe made his appearance with the speaking-trumpet. He then proceeded to get the vessel under weigh, with more noise and fuss than is to be heard when the proudest three-decker in the English navy expands her lofty canvas to the gale.

Gustave Adolphe, in obedience to the commands he had received, brought up to Newton a bunch of bananas, a large piece of salt fish, and a calabash of water. The latter was immediately applied to his lips, and never removed while a drop remained, much to the astonishment of the negro, who again sported his English.

"I say—very good—ab more?"

"If you please," replied Newton.

"Monsieur," said Gustave Adolphe to his commander, "le prisonnier a soif, et demande encore de l'eau."

"Va l'en chercher donc," replied the old negro, with a wave of his speaking-trumpet "Charles Philippe, attention à la barre,[1] sans venir au vent, s'il vous plaît. Matelots [2] du gaillard d'avant !" continued he, roaring through his speaking-trumpet; "bordez le grand foc."

In the space of two hours, the schooner was brought to an anchor, with as much noise and importance as she had been got under weigh. A boat, capable of holding three people —one rower and two sitters—was shoved off the vessel's deck, and the negro captain, having first descended to his cabin for a few minutes, returned on deck dressed in the extremity of their fashion, and ordered the boat to be manned.

Gustave Adolphe accordingly manned the boat with his

---

[1] Mind your weather-helm.

[2] Forecastlemen, haul aft the jib-sheet.

own person, and the negro captain politely waved his hand for Newton to enter; and then, following himself, Gustave Adolphe rowed to a landing-place, about twenty yards from the schooner.

"Gustave Adolphe, suivez en arrière, et gardez bien que le prisonnier n'échappe pas;" so saying, monsieur le capitaine led the way to a large white house and buildings, about two hundred yards from the river's banks. On their arrival, Newton was surrounded by twenty or thirty slaves of both sexes, who chattered and jabbered a thousand questions concerning him to the negro captain and Gustave Adolphe, neither of whom condescended to reply.

"Monsieur de Fontanges, où est-il?" inquired the old negro.

"Monsieur dort," replied a little female voice.

The captain was taken aback at this unfortunate circumstance, for no one dared to wake their master.

"Et madame?" inquired he.

"Madame est dans sa chambre."

There again he was floored—he could not venture there; so he conducted Newton, who was not very sorry to escape from the burning rays of the sun, to his own habitation, where an old negress, his wife, soon obtained from the negro that information relative to the capture of Newton which the bevy of slaves in the yard had attempted in vain; but wives have winning ways with them!

CHAPTER XX

" What elegance and grandeur wide expand,
The pride of Turkey and of Persia land!
Soft quilts on quilts, on carpets carpets spread,
And couches stretched around in seemly band,
And endless pillows rise to prop the head.

    .   .   .   .

Here languid Beauty kept her pale-faced court."
—THOMSON.

THE female slaves who could not obtain the history of Newton immediately repaired to the chamber of their mistress, knowing that if they could succeed in raising her curiosity,

128

they would at the same time gratify their own. Madame de Fontanges was, as they asserted, in her chamber, or what may now be more correctly styled her boudoir. It was a room about fourteen feet square, the sides of which were covered with a beautiful paper, representing portions of the history of Paul and Virginia ; the floor was covered with fine matting, with here and there a small Persian carpet above it. Small marble tables were decorated with a variety of ornaments and French perfumes, or vases filled with the splendid flowers of a tropical clime. There was a large window at each end of the room, cut down to the ground in the French fashion, and outside of both was a little balcony—the trellis-work covered with passion-flower and clematis. The doors and other compartments of the room were not papered, but had French mirrors let into the panelling. On a low ottoman of elegant workmanship, covered with a damask French silk, reposed Madame de Fontanges, attended by three or four young female slaves, of different complexions, but none of pure African blood. Others were seated upon the different Persian carpets about the room in listless idleness, or strewing the petals of the orange-flower to perfume the apartment with its odour. The only negro was a little boy, about six years of age, dressed in a fantastic costume, who sat in a corner, apparently in a very sulky humour.

Madame de Fontanges was a creole—that is, born in the West Indies, of French parents. She had been sent home to France for her education, and had returned at the age of fourteen to Guadaloupe, where she soon after married Monsieur de Fontanges, an officer of rank and brother to the governor of the island. Her form was diminutive, but most perfect ; her hand and arm models for the statuary ; while her feet were so small as almost to excite risibility when you observed them. Her features were regular, and, when raised from their usual listlessness, full of expression. Large hazel eyes, beautifully pencilled eyebrows, with long fringed eyelashes, dark and luxuriant hair, Grecian nose, small mouth, with thin coral lips, were set off by a complexion which even the climate could not destroy, although it softened it into extreme delicacy.

Such was the person of Madame de Fontanges, now about

eighteen years old, and one of the most beautiful specimens of the French creole which could be imagined. Her perfect little figure needed no support; she was simply attired in a muslin *robe de chambre*, as she reposed upon the ottoman, waiting with all the impatience of her caste for the setting in of the sea-breeze, which would give some relief from the oppressive heat of the climate.

"Eventez, Nina! éventez!" cried she to one of her attendants, who was standing at the head of the sofa with a large feather fan.

"Oui, madame," replied the girl, stirring up the dormant atmosphere.

"Eventez, Caroline! éventez mes mains, vite."

"Oui, madame," replied the second, working away with another fan.

"Eventez! éventez mes pieds, Mimi."

"Oui, madame," replied the third, fanning in the direction pointed out.

"Louise," said Madame de Fontanges languidly, after a short pause, "apportez-moi de l'eau sucrée."

"Oui, madame," replied another, rising in obedience to the order.

"Non, non! Je n'en veux pas—mais j'ai soif horrible. Manchette, va chercher de l'eau cérise."

"Oui, madame," replied Manchette, rising from her seat. But she had not quitted the room before Madame de Fontanges had changed her mind.

"Attendez, Manchette. Ce n'est pas ça. Je voudrais de limonade. Charlotte, va l'en chercher."

"Oui, madame," said Charlotte, leaving the room to execute the order.

"Ah! mon Dieu! qu'il fait une chaleur épouvantable. Mimi, que tu es paresseuse? Eventez! vite, vite. Où est Monsieur?"

"Monsieur dort."

"Ah! qu'il est heureux. Et Cupidon—où est-il?"

"Il est ici, au coin, madame. Il boude."

"Qu'est-ce qu'il a fait donc?"

"Ah! madame, il a volé le dindon rôti, et l'a tout mangé."

"Ah! le petit polisson! Venez ici, Cupidon."

Cupidon, the little negro boy we have before mentioned as sitting in the corner of the room, walked up with a very deliberate pace to the side of the ottoman, his two thick lips sticking out about six inches in advance of the remainder of his person.

"Cupidon," said the lady, turning a little on one side to him, "tu as mangé le dindon entier. Tu as mal fait, mon ami. Tu seras malade. Comprends-tu, Cupidon, c'est une sottise que tu as fait?"

Cupidon made no reply; his head was hung down a little lower, and his lips extended a little farther out.

"Sache que tu es un petit voleur!" continued his mistress.

Cupidon did not condescend to answer.

"Allez, monsieur; ne m'approchez pas."

Cupidon turned short round without reply, and walked back to his corner with the same deliberate pace as before, when he came out of it.

Charlotte now returned with the lemonade for which she had been despatched, and informed her mistress as she presented it that Nicholas, who had charge of the schooner, had returned with an European prisoner; but that neither he nor Gustave would give her any further information, although she had requested it in the name of her mistress. This was quite an event, and gave a fillip to the inertness of Madame de Fontanges, whose curiosity was excited.

"A-t-il bonne mine, Charlotte?"

"Oui, madame, c'est un bel homme."

'Et où est-il?"

"Avec Nicholas."

'Et Monsieur?"

'Monsieur dort."

"Il faut l'éveiller. Faites bien mes compliments à Monsieur de Fontanges, et dites-lui que je me trouve fort malade, et que je voudrais lui parler. Entends-tu, Céleste; je parle à toi."

"Oui, madame," replied the girl, throwing some orange flowers off her lap and rising to deliver her message.

M. de Fontanges, who, like most of the Europeans, slept through the hottest portion of the day, rose in compliance with his wife's message, and made his appearance in the boudoir, dressed in a white cotton jacket and trousers. A few polite inquiries after the health of Madame de Fontanges, which, as he had conjectured from similar previous occurrences, was not worse than usual, were followed by his receiving from her the information of Newton's arrival, coupled with an observation that it would amuse her if the prisoner were interrogated in her presence.

Newton was summoned to the boudoir, where M. de Fontanges, who spoke very good English, received from him the history of his disasters, and translated them into French to gratify the curiosity of his wife.

"C'est un beau garçon," observed M. de Fontanges. "Mais quoi faire? Il est prisonnier. Il faut l'envoyer à mon frère, le gouverneur."

"Il est joli garçon," replied Madame de Fontanges. "Donnez-lui des habits, Fontanges, et ne l'envoyez pas encore."

"Et pourquoi, mon amie?"

"Je voudrais lui apprendre le Français."

"Cela ne se peut pas, ma chère; il est prisonnier."

"Cela se peut, Monsieur de Fontanges," replied the lady.

"Je n'ose pas," continued the husband.

"Moi j'ose," replied the lady decidedly.

"Je ne voudrais pas," said the gentleman.

"Moi, je veux," interrupted the lady.

"Mais il faut être raisonnable, madame."

"Il faut m'obéir, monsieur."

"Mais——"

"Pschut!" replied the lady; "c'est une affaire décidée. Monsieur le gouverneur ne parle pas l'Anglais. C'est *absolument nécessaire* que le jeune homme apprenne notre langue; et c'est mon plaisir de l'enseigner. Au revoir, Monsieur de Fontanges. Charlotte, va chercher des habits."

CHAPTER XXI

" 'Tis pleasing to be schooled in a strange tongue
By female lips and eyes ; that is, I mean,
When both the teacher and the taught are young,
As was the case, at least, where I had been.
They smile so when one's right, and when one's wrong
They smile still more."

—BYRON.

M. DE FONTANGES, aware of the impetuosity and caprice of his wife (at the same time that he acknowledged her many redeeming good qualities), did not further attempt to thwart her inclinations. His great objection to her plan was the impropriety of retaining a prisoner whom he was bound to give up to the proper authorities. He made a virtue of necessity, and having acquainted Newton with the wish of Madame de Fontanges, requested his parole of honour that he would not attempt to escape if he was not delivered up to the authorities, and remain some time at Lieu Désiré. Newton, who had no wish to be acquainted with a French *cachot* sooner than it was absolutely necessary, gave the promise required by M. de Fontanges, assuring him that ingratitude was not a part of his character. M. de Fontanges then requested that Newton would accept of a portion of his wardrobe, which he would direct to be sent to the room that would be prepared for him. This affair being arranged, Newton made his bow to the lady, and in company with M. de Fontanges retired from the boudoir.

It may be suspected by the reader that Madame de Fontanges was one of those ladies who cared a great deal about having her own way, and very little for her husband. As to the first part of the accusation, I can only observe that I never yet had the fortune to fall in with any lady who did not try all she could to have her own way, nor do I conceive it to be a crime. As to the second, if the reader has formed that supposition, he is much mistaken. Madame de Fontanges was very much attached to her husband, and the attachment as well as the confidence was reciprocal.

It was not, therefore, from any feeling of jealousy that M. de Fontanges had combated her resolution; but, as we have before observed, from a conviction that he was wanting in his duty when he did not report the arrival of Newton at the plantation. The wish of Madame de Fontanges to detain Newton was, as she declared, a caprice on her part, which had entered her head, to amuse herself by teaching him French. It is true that had not Newton been remarkably prepossessing in his appearance, the idea would in all probability have never been conceived; but, observing that he was much above the common class, and wishing to relieve the monotony of her life by anything which would create amusement, she had formed the idea, which, when combated by her husband, was immediately strengthened to a resolution.

Of this Newton received the benefit. An excellent dinner, or rather supper, with M. de Fontanges, a comfortable bed in a room supplied with all that convenience or luxury could demand, enabled him to pass a very different night from those which we have lately described.

About twelve o'clock the ensuing day, Newton was summoned by one of the slave girls to the boudoir of Madame de Fontanges. He found her on the ottoman as before. Newton, who had been operated upon by a black barber, and was dressed in the habiliments of M. de Fontanges, made a much more respectable appearance than upon his former introduction.

" Bon jour, monsieur," said the lady.

Newton bowed respectfully.

" Comment vous appelez-vous ? "

Newton, not understanding, answered with another bow.

" Le jeune homme n'entends pas, madame," observed Mimi.

" Que c'est ennuyant. Monsieur," said Madame de Fontanges, pointing to herself, " moi—Madame de Fontanges : vous ? " pointing to him.

" Newton Forster."

" Nu-tong Fasta—ah, c'est bon ; cela commence," said the lady. " Allons, mes enfans, répétez-lui tous vos noms."

" Moi—Mimi," said the girl bearing that name, going up to Newton and pointing to herself.

"Mimi," repeated Newton, with a smile and nod of his head.

"Moi—Charlotte."

"Moi—Louise."

"Moi—Céleste."

"Moi—Nina."

"Moi—Caroline."

"Moi—Manchette."

"Et moi—Cupidon," finished the little black boy, running up, and then retreating as fast back into his corner.

Newton repeated all the names, as the individuals respectively introduced themselves to him. Then there was a pause, during which, at the desire of Madame de Fontanges, Newton was offered a chair, and sat down.

"Allons, dites-lui les noms de toute la garniture," said Madame de Fontanges to her attendants.

"Oui, madame," said Mimi, going up to Newton, and, pointing to the fan in her hand—"éventail."

"Eventail," repeated Newton, who began to be amused, and who now repeated every French word after them.

"Flacon," said Charlotte, showing him the eau-de-Cologne bottle.

"Chaise,"cried Louise, holding up a chair.

"Livre," said Nina, pointing to a book.

"Mouchoir," said Caroline, holding up an embroidered handkerchief.

"Montre," followed up Manchette, pointing to her mis-tress's watch.

"Canapé," cried Céleste, pointing to the ottoman.

"Joli garçon," bawled out Cupidon, coming up to Newton, and pointing to himself.

This created a laugh, and then the lesson was continued. Every article in the room was successively pointed out to Newton, and he was obliged to repeat the name; and afterwards the articles of their dress were resorted to, much to his amusement. Then there was a dead stand: the fact is, that there is no talking with noun substantives only.

"Ah! mon Dieu! il faut envoyer pour Monsieur de Fontanges," cried the lady; "va le chercher, Louise."

M. de Fontanges soon made his appearance, when the lady explained to him their dilemma, and requested his assistance. M. de Fontanges laughed, and explained to Newton, and then, by means of his interpretation, connected sentences were made, according to the fancy of the lady, some of which were the cause of great merriment. After an hour, the gentlemen made their bows.

"I think," observed M. de Fontanges, as they walked away, "that if you really are as anxious to learn our language as madame is to teach you, you had better come to me every morning for an hour. I shall have great pleasure in giving you any assistance in my power, and I trust that in a very short time, with a little study of the grammar and dictionary, you will be able to hold a conversation with Madame de Fontanges, or even with her dark-complexioned page."

Newton expressed his acknowledgments, and the next day he received his first lesson; after which he was summoned to support the theory by practice in the boudoir of Madame de Fontanges. It is hardly necessary to observe that each day increased the facility of communication.

For three months Newton was domiciled with Monsieur and Madame de Fontanges, both of whom had gradually formed such an attachment to him, that the idea of parting never entered their head. He was now a very tolerable French scholar, and his narratives and adventures were to his benefactors a source of amusement, which amply repaid them for the trouble and kindness which they had shown to him. Newton was, in fact, a general favourite with every one on the plantation, from the highest to the lowest; and his presence received the same smile of welcome at the cottage of the slave as at the boudoir of Madame de Fontanges.

Whatever may have been the result of Newton's observations relative to slavery in the English colonies, his feelings of dislike insensibly wore away during his residence at Lieu Désiré: there he was at least convinced that a slave might be perfectly happy. It must be acknowledged that the French have invariably proved the kindest and most considerate of masters, and the state of bondage is much mitigated in the islands which appertain to that nation. The reason is obvious: in France there is a *bonhomie*, a degree of equality, established between the different grades of

136

society by universal politeness. A French servant is familiar with his master at the same time that he is respectful; and the master, in return, condescends to his inferior without forgetting their relative positions. This runs through society in general; and as no one can well be polite without some good-nature (for politeness, frivolous as it may appear, is a strong check upon those feelings of selfishness, too apt to be indulged in), it leads to a general feeling of good-will towards others. This has naturally been practised by Frenchmen wherever they may be; and the consequence is, that the slaves are treated with more consideration, and in return have warmer feelings of attachment towards their owners, than are to be found in colonies belonging to other nations. Newton perceived and acknowledged this, and comparing the condition of the people at Lieu Désiré with that of most of the peasantry of Europe, was unwillingly obliged to confess that the former were in every respect the more fortunate and the more happy of the two.

One morning, soon after Newton had breakfasted with M. de Fontanges, and had been summoned to the boudoir, a letter was brought in. It was from the governor to M. de Fontanges, stating that he had heard with great surprise that M. de Fontanges concealed an English prisoner in his house, and desiring that he might be immediately sent up to headquarters. That there might be no delay or refusal, a corporal, accompanied by two file of men, brought down the intimation to the plantation.

Newton was in the very middle of a long story, Madame de Fontanges on the ottoman, and her attendants collected round her, seated on the floor—even Cupidon had advanced from his corner to within half distance, his mouth and eyes wide open, when M. de Fontanges entered the boudoir with anxiety and chagrin expressed in his countenance.

"Qu'est-ce qu'il y a, mon ami?" said Madame de Fontanges, rising hastily and running up to her husband.

M. de Fontanges answered by putting the governor's letter into his wife's hands.

"Ah! les barbares!" cried Madame de Fontanges; "est-il possible? Pauvre Monsieur Nutong! On l'amène au cachot."

"Au cachot!" cried all the coloured girls in a breath, and bursting into tears—"O ciel!"

M. de Fontanges then explained to Newton the order which he had received. Newton replied that he had had no right to expect otherwise on his first landing on the island; that he had incurred a heavy debt of gratitude to them for having preserved him so long from a prison; and that the remembrance of their kindness would tend to beguile the tedious hours of captivity (from which it may appear that Newton, in point of expressing himself, was half a Frenchman already). He then kissed the hand of Madame de Fontanges, tried to console the little slave girls, who were all *au désespoir*, patted Cupidon on the head by way of farewell, and quitted the boudoir in which he had passed so many happy hours. When he was outside he again expressed his obligations to M. de Fontanges, who then stated his determination to call upon his brother, the governor, and try to alleviate the hardships of his lot as much as was possible. In less than an hour, Newton, in company with his host, was on the road to Basse Terre, leaving the corporal and his two file of men to walk back as fast as they could, the corporal having sufficient *savoir vivre* not to refuse the pledge of the governor's brother for the safe delivery of the prisoner.

It was not until late in the evening that they arrived at Basse Terre, when they immediately proceeded to the house of the governor, and were admitted to his presence.

The governor, who had been much displeased at the circumstance of Newton having remained so long on the island, was more pacified when M. de Fontanges explained to him the way in which he had been made prisoner, and the hardships which he had previously endured. M. de Fontanges accounted for his long detention at Lieu Désiré by stating the real fact, viz., the pertinacity of Madame de Fontanges; which, although it might have been considered a very poor argument in England, had its due weight in a French colony.

The governor entered into conversation with Newton, who detailed to him the horrors of the shipwreck which he had undergone. The narrative appeared to affect him much. He told Newton that under such circumstances he could hardly consider him as a prisoner, and would take the first opportunity of releasing him, and would accept his parole for not quitting the island. Newton returned his thanks for so much courtesy, and withdrew in company with M. de Fontanges.

"Monsieur le Marquis has much sympathy for those who have been shipwrecked," observed Monsieur de Fontanges, after they had quitted the room. "Poor man! he lost his wife, a beautiful young woman, and his only child, a little girl, about seven years back, when they were proceeding home in a vessel bound to Havre. The vessel has never been heard of since, and he has never recovered the loss."

"In what year was it?" inquired Newton.

"In the autumn of the year ——",

"There were many vessels wrecked on our coast during that dreadful winter," replied Newton. "I myself, when in a coaster, picked up several articles belonging to a French vessel. I have them in my possession now; they are of some value."

"What did they consist of?" inquired Monsieur de Fontanges.

"A large trunk, containing the wearing apparel of a female and a child; there were also several orders of knighthood, and some jewels; but I hardly know what they were, as it is some time since I have looked at them."

"How strange that you could find no clue to discover the names of the parties!"

"There were French letters," replied Newton, "which I could not read; they were only signed by initials, which did not correspond with the marks on the linen belonging to the lady, although the surname might have been the same as that of the child."

"Do you recollect the initials?"

"Perfectly well: the marks on the lady's apparel were L. C., that on the linen of the infant J. F."

"Mon Dieu! mon Dieu!" cried Monsieur de Fontanges; "then it may indeed have been the apparel of the Marquise de Fontanges. The linen must have been some marked with her maiden name, which was Louise de Colmar. The child was christened Julie de Fontanges, after her grandmother. My poor brother had intended to take his passage home in the same vessel, his successor being hourly expected; but the frigate in which the new governor had embarked was taken by an English squadron, and my brother was forced to remain here."

" Then the property must undoubtedly belong to the Marquis," replied Newton. " I only wish I could have been able to assure him that his wife and child were equally safe ; but that I am afraid is impossible, as there can be no doubt but that they were all lost. Do you mean to communicate what I have told you to the Marquis ? "

" By no means ; it will only tear open a wound which has but partially healed. If you will send me all the particulars when you return I shall feel much obliged; not that the effects are of any consequence. The Marquise and her child are undoubtedly lost, and it could be no consolation to my brother to ascertain that a trunk of their effects had been saved."

Here the conversation dropped, and was never again renewed.

Newton was heartily welcomed again at Lieu Désiré, where he remained three weeks, when a note from the governor informed him that a cartel was about to sail.

It was with mutual pain that Newton and his kind friends took their farewell of each other. In this instance M. de Fontanges did not accompany him to Basse Terre, but bade him adieu at his own door. Newton, soon after he was on the road, perceived that M. de Fontanges had acted from a motive of delicacy, that he might not receive the thanks of Newton for two valises, well furnished, which overtook Newton about a quarter of a mile from the plantation, slung on each side of a horse, under the guidance of a little negro perched on the middle. Newton made his acknowledgments to the governor for his kind consideration, then embarked on board of the *Marie Thérèse* schooner, and in three days he once more found himself on shore in an English colony; with which piece of information I conclude this chapter.

CHAPTER XXII

" Mercy on us ! a bairn, a very pretty bairn,
A boy, a child."
—SHAKSPEARE.

WHEN Newton was landed from the cartel at Jamaica, he found the advantage of not being clad in the garb of a sailor, as all those who were in such costume were immediately handed over to the admiral of the station, to celebrate their restoration to liberty on board of a man-of-war; but the clothes supplied to him by the generosity of M. de Fontanges had anything but a maritime appearance, and Newton was landed with his portmanteaus by one of the man-of-war's boats, whose crew had little idea of his being a person so peculiarly suited to their views, possessing as he did the necessary qualifications of youth, activity, and a thorough knowledge of his profession. Newton was so anxious to return home, that after a few days' expensive sojourn at an hotel, frequented chiefly by the officers of the man-of-war in port, he resolved to apply to the captain of a frigate ordered home with despatches to permit him to take a passage. He had formed a slight intimacy with some of the officers, who assured him that he would experience no difficulty in obtaining his request. His application was made in person ; and after his statement that he had been released in the last cartel which had come from Guadaloupe, his request was immediately granted without any further questions being put relative to his profession or the manner in which he had been captured. The captain very civilly gave him to understand that he might mess with the gunroom officers if he could arrange with them, and that he expected to sail on the evening of the ensuing day. Newton immediately repaired on board of the frigate, to ascertain if the officers would receive him as a mess-mate ; and further, whether the amount of his mess-money would be more than he could in prudence afford. At the bottom of one of the portmanteaus he had found a bag of two, hundred dollars, supplied by his generous host, and in the same bag there was also deposited a small note from Madame de Fontanges, wishing him success, and enclosing (as a souvenir) a ring, which he had often perceived on her finger; but adequate as was this supply to his own wants, Newton did not forget that his father was, in all probability, in great distress, and would require his assistance on his return. He was, therefore, naturally anxious not to expend more than was absolutely necessary in defraying his passage. The old first lieutenant, to whom, upon his arrival on board, he was introduced as commanding officer, received him with much urbanity, and when Newton stated that he had obtained the captain's permission to make the application, immediately acceded to his wishes on the part of his messmates as well as of himself, when Newton followed up his application by requesting to know the expense which he would incur, as in case of its being greater than his finances could meet, he would request permission to choose a less expensive mess.

"I am aware," replied the veteran, "that those who have been shipwrecked and in a French prison are not likely to be very flush of cash. It is, however, a point on which I must consult my messmates. Excuse me one moment, and I will bring you an answer. I have no doubt but that it will be satisfactorily arranged; but there is nothing like settling these points at once. Mr. Webster, see that the lighter shoves off the moment that she is clear," continued the first lieutenant to one of the midshipmen as he descended the quarter-deck ladder, leaving Newton to walk the quarter-deck.

In a few minutes the first lieutenant reappeared, with one or two officers of the gunroom mess, who greeted him most cordially.

"I have seen all that are requisite," said he to Newton. "Two I have not spoken to, the master and the purser; they are both poor men, with families. If, therefore, you will not be too proud to accept it, I am requested to offer you a free passage from the other officers of the mess, as we feel convinced that your company will more than repay us. The proportion of the expense of your passage to the other two will be but one or two pounds; a trifle, indeed, but still of consequence to them, and that is the only expense which you will incur. If you can afford to pay that any time after your arrival in England, we shall be most happy to receive

142

`you, and make the passage as comfortable and pleasant as circumstances will permit."

To this most liberal proposition Newton most gladly acceded. The officers who had come on deck with the first lieutenant invited Newton below, where he was introduced to the remainder of the mess, who were most of them fine young men, as happy and careless as if youth was to last for ever. Having pledged each other in a glass of grog, Newton returned on shore. The next morning he made his arrangements, paid his bill at the hotel, and before twelve o'clock was again on board of the frigate, which lay with the Blue Peter hoisted, and her fore-topsail loose, waiting for her captain, who was still detained on shore while the admiral and governor made up their despatches.

When Newton had applied to the captain of the frigate for a passage home, he could hardly believe it possible that the person to whom he was introduced could be entrusted with the command of so fine a vessel. He was a slight-made, fair-complexioned lad, of nineteen or twenty years at the most, without an incipient mark of manhood on his chin. He appeared lively, active, and good-natured; but what were the other qualifications he possessed to deserve such a mark of confidence were to Newton an enigma requiring solution.

It was, however, to be explained in very few words. He was the son of the admiral of the station, and (as at that period there was no regulation with respect to age to check the most rapid promotion), after he had served his time as midshipman, in less than two months he had been raised through the different ranks of lieutenant, commander, and post-captain. On receiving the latter step, he was at the same time appointed to the frigate in question, one of the finest which belonged to his Majesty's service. In order, however, that he should to a certain degree be in leading-strings, a very old and efficient officer had been selected by the admiral as his first lieutenant. Whether, in common justice, the captain and his subordinate ought not to have changed places, I leave the reader to guess; and it was the more unfair towards the worthy old first lieutenant, as, if the admiral had not entertained such a high opinion of his abilities and judgment as to confide to him the charge of his son, he would long before have been promoted himself to one of the many vacancies which so repeatedly occurred.

Captain Carrington had all the faults which, if not inherent, will naturally be acquired by those who are too early entrusted with power. He was self-sufficient, arbitrary, and passionate. His good qualities consisted in a generous disposition, a kindness of heart when not irritated, a manly courage, and a frank acknowledgment of his errors. Had he been allowed to serve a proper time in the various grades of his profession—had he been taught to obey before he had been permitted to command—he had within him all the materials for a good officer: as it was, he was neither officer, sailor, nor anything else, except a spoiled boy. He would often attempt to carry on the duty as captain, and as often failed from want of knowledge He would commence manœuvring the ship, but find himself unable to proceed. At these unfortunate break-downs he would be obliged to resign the speaking-trumpet to the first lieutenant; and if, as sometimes happened, the latter (either from accident, or perhaps from a pardonable pique at having the duty taken out of his hands) was not at his elbow to prompt him when at fault, at these times the cant phrase of the officers, taken from some farce, used to be, " York, you're wanted."

About an hour before sunset the juvenile captain made his appearance on board, rather *fresh* from taking leave of his companions and acquaintances on shore. The frigate was got under weigh by the first lieutenant, and before the sun had disappeared was bounding over the foaming seas in the direction of the country which had nurtured to maturity the gnarled oak selected for her beautiful frame. Newton joined his new messmates in drinking a prosperous passage to old England, and, with a heart grateful for his improved prospects, retired to the hammock which had been prepared for him.

When Newton rose in the morning, he found that the wind had shifted contrary during the night, and that the frigate was close-hauled, darting through the smooth water with her royals set. At ten o'clock the master proposed tacking the ship, and the first lieutenant went down to report his wish to the captain.

"Very well, Mr. Nourse," replied the captain; "turn the hands up."

"Ay, ay, sir," replied the first lieutenant, leaving the cabin.

"Call the boatswain, quartermaster—all hands 'bout ship."

"All hands 'bout ship," was now bellowed out by the boatswain, and re-echoed by his mates at the several hatchways, with a due proportion of whistling from their pipes.

"Tumble up, there—tumble up smartly, my lads."

In a minute every man was on deck and at his station; many of them, however, tumbling down in their laudable hurry to tumble up.

"Silence there, fore and aft—every man to his station," cried the first lieutenant through his speaking-trumpet. "All ready, sir," reported the first lieutenant to the captain, who had followed him on deck. "Shall we put the helm down?"

"If you please, Mr. Nourse."

"Down with the helm."

When the master reported it down, "The helm's a-lee," roared the first lieutenant.

But Captain Carrington, who thought light winds and smooth water a good opportunity for practice, interrupted him as he was walking towards the weather-gangway. "Mr. Nourse, Mr. Nourse, if you please, I'll work the ship."

"Very good, sir," replied the first lieutenant, handing him the speaking-trumpet. "Rise tacks and sheets, if you please, sir," continued the first lieutenant (*sotto voce*); "the sails are lifting."

"Tacks and sheets!" cried the captain.

"Gather in on the lee main-tack, my lads," said the first lieutenant, going to the lee gangway to see the duty performed.

Now, Captain Carrington did know that "mainsail haul" was the next word of command; but as this order requires a degree of precision as to the exact time at which it is given, he looked over his shoulder for the first lieutenant, who usually prompted him in this exigence. Not seeing him there, he became disconcerted; and during the few seconds that he cast his anxious eyes about the deck to discover where the first lieutenant was, the ship had passed head to wind.

"Mainsail haul!" at last cried the captain; but it was too late; the yards would not swing round; everything went wrong, and the ship was *in irons*.

145   K

"You hauled a little too late, sir," observed the first lieutenant, who had joined him. "You must box her off, sir, if
you please."

But Captain Carrington, although he could put the ship in
irons, did not know how to take her out.

"The ship is certainly most cursedly out of trim," observed
he ; "she'll neither wear nor stay. Try her yourself, Mr.
Nourse," continued the captain, "I'm sick of her ! "—and
with a heightened colour he handed the speaking-trumpet
over to the first lieutenant.

"York, you're wanted," observed the lieutenant abaft to
the marine officer, dropping down the corners of his mouth.

"York, you're wanted," tittered the midshipmen in whispers, as they passed each other.

"Well, I've won your grog, Jim," cried one of the marines
who was standing at the forebrace ; "I knew he'd never
do it."

"He's like me," observed another, in a low tone ; "he left
school too 'arly, and lost his edication."

Such were the results of injudicious patronage. A fine
ship entrusted to a boy ignorant of his duty ; laughed at,
not only by the officers, but even by the men ; and the
honour of the country at stake, and running no small risk
of being tarnished if the frigate met with a vigorous
opponent.[1] Thank God, this is now over ! Judicious
regulations have put a stop to such selfish and short-sighted
patronage. Selfish, because those who were guilty of it
risked the honour of the nation to advance the interests
of their protégés ; short-sighted, because it is of little use
making a young man a captain if you cannot make him an
officer. I might here enter into a discussion which might be
of some use, but it would be out of place in a work intended
more for amusement than for instruction ; nor would it in
all probability be read. I always make it a rule myself to
skip over all those parts introduced in a light work which

[1] It is true that an officer must now serve a certain time in the various
grades before promotion, which time is supposed to be sufficient for
him to acquire a knowledge of his profession ; but whether that
knowledge is obtained depends, as before, upon the young officer's
prospects in life. If from family interest he is sure of promotion, he
is not quite so sure of being a seaman.

146

are of denser materials than the rest, and I cannot expect but that others will do the same. There is a time and place for all things ; and, like the Master of Ravenswood, "I bide my time."

The frigate dashed gallantly through the water, at one time careening to an adverse wind, at another rolling before a favouring gale ; and to judge from her rapid motion, she was not in such very bad trim as Captain Carrington had found out. Each day rapidly brought her nearer to their cherished home, as "she walked the waters like a thing of life." I can conceive no prouder situation in this world than being captain of a fine frigate with a well-disciplined crew; but d—n your eight-and-twenties !

"We had better take in the royals, if you please, sir," said the first lieutenant, as he came, with his hat in his hand, into the cabin, where the captain was at dinner with several of the officers, the table crowded with a variety of decanters and French green bottles.

"Pho! nonsense! Mr. Nourse ; we'll carry them a little longer," replied the captain, who had been carrying too much sail another way. "Sit down and take a glass of wine with us. You always cry out before you're hurt, Nourse."

"I thank you, sir," replied the first lieutenant seriously ; "you will excuse me ; it is time to beat to quarters."

"Well then, do so ; I had no idea it was so late. Mr. Forster, you don't pass the bottle."

"I have taken enough, I thank you, sir."

The officers present also made the same statement.

"Well then, if you won't, gentlemen—steward, let's have some coffee."

The coffee appeared and disappeared, and the officers made their bows and quitted the cabin as the first lieutenant entered it to report the muster at quarters.

"All present and sober, sir. I am afraid, sir," continued he, "the masts will be over the side if we do not clew up the royals."

"Stop a moment, if you please, Mr. Nourse, until I go up and judge for myself," replied the captain, who was inclined to be pertinacious.

Captain Carrington went on deck. The men were still

ranged round the decks at their quarters; more than one
pair of eyes were raised aloft to watch the masts, which were
bending like coach-whips, and complaining bitterly.

"Shall we beat a retreat, and pipe hands to shorten sail,
sir ? We had better take in the third reefs, sir; it looks
very squally to-night," observed the first lieutenant.

"Really, Mr. Nourse, I don't exactly perceive the necessity——"

But at that moment the fore- and main-topgallant-masts
went over the side ; and the look-out man at the fore-top-
gallant-masthead, who had been called down by the first
lieutenant, but did not hear the injunction, was hurled into
the sea to leeward.

"Helm down !" cried the master.

"Man overboard !—man overboard !" echoed round the
decks; while some of the officers and men jumped into the
quarter-boats, and cast off the gripes and lashings.

Captain Carrington, who was immediately sobered by the
catastrophe, which he felt had been occasioned by his own
wilfulness, ran aft to the taffrail, and when he saw the poor
sailor struggling in the waves, impelled by his really fine
nature, he darted overboard to save him ; but he was not by
any means a powerful swimmer, and encumbered with his
apparel, it was soon evident that he could do no more than
keep himself afloat.

Newton, who perceived how matters stood, with great
presence of mind caught up two of the oars from the boat
hanging astern, and darted over to the assistance of both.
One oar he first carried to the seaman, who was exhausted
and sinking. Placing it under his arms, he then swam with
the other to Captain Carrington, who could not have remained above water but a few seconds more without the
timely relief. He then quietly swam by the side of Captain
Carrington, without any attempt at extra exertion.

The boat was soon lowered down, and in a few minutes
they were all three again on board and in safety. Captain
Carrington thanked Newton for his assistance, and acknowledged his error to the first lieutenant. The officers and
men looked upon Newton with respect and increased good-
will, and the sailors declared that the captain was a prime
little fellow, although he hadn't had an "edication."

Nothing worthy of remark occurred during the remainder of the passage. The ship arrived at Plymouth, and Newton took leave of his shipmates; Captain Carrington requesting that Newton would command any interest that he had if ever it should be required. It was with a throbbing heart that Newton descended from the outside of the coach which conveyed him to Liverpool, and hastened towards the obscure street in which he left his father residing. It was about four o'clock in the afternoon when Newton arrived at his father's door. To his delight he perceived through the shop-window that his father was sitting at his bench, but his joy was checked when he perceived his haggard countenance. The old man appeared to be absorbed in deep thought, his cheek resting upon his hand, and his eyes cast down upon the little bench, to which the vice used to be fixed, but from which it was now removed.

The door was ajar, and Newton entered with his portmanteau in his hand; but whatever noise he might have made was not sufficient to rouse Nicholas, who continued in the same position.

With one glance round the shop, Newton perceived that it was bare of everything; even the glazed cases on the counter, which contained the spectacles, &c., had disappeared. All bespoke the same tale, as did the appearance of his father—misery and starvation.

"My dearest father!" cried Newton, unable to contain himself any longer.

"How!—what?" cried Nicholas, starting at the voice, but not looking round. "Pho! nonsense!—he's dead," continued the old man, communing with himself, as he again settled into his former position. .

"My dearest father, I'm not dead!—look round—'tis Newton! alive and well."

"Newton!" replied the old man, rising from his stool and tottering to the counter, which was between them, on which he laid both his hands to support himself as he looked into his son's face. "'Tis Newton, sure enough! My dear, dear boy!—then you an't dead?"

"No, indeed, father; I am alive and well, thank God!"

"Thank God, too!" said Nicholas, dropping his face on the counter and bursting into tears.

149

Newton sprang over to the side where his father was and embraced him. For some time they were locked in each other's arms; when Nicholas, who had recovered his composure, looked at Newton, and said, "Are you hungry, my dear boy?"

"Yes, indeed I am," replied Newton, smiling, as the tears coursed down his cheeks, "for I have had nothing since breakfast."

"And I have had nothing for these two days," replied Nicholas, leaning back on the wall in evident exhaustion.

"Good God! you don't say so?" cried Newton; "where can I buy something ready cooked?"

"At the shop round the corner: there's a nice piece of boiled beef there; I saw it yesterday. I offered my improvement upon the duplex for a slice, but he would not trust me, even for that."

Newton ran out, and in a few minutes reappeared with the beef in question, some bread, and a pot of porter, with two plates and knives and forks, which the people had lent him upon his putting down a deposit. He laid them on the counter before his father, who, without saying a word, commenced his repast: the beef disappeared—the bread vanished—the porter-pot was raised to his mouth, and in a moment it was dry!

"Never made a better dinner, Newton," observed Nicholas; "but I wish there had been a little more of it."

Newton, who had only been a spectator, immediately went out for another supply, and on his return assisted his father in its demolition.

"Newton," said Nicholas, who for a few minutes had relinquished his task, "I've been thinking—that—I should like another slice of that beef; and Newton, as I said before—I'll trouble you for the porter."

CHAPTER XXIII

" *Orlando.* Then forbear your food a little while,
While, like a doe, I go to find my fawn
And give it food. There is a poor old man
Oppressed with two weak evils, age and hunger."
—SHAKSPEARE.

READER, were you ever really hungry? I do not mean
the common hunger arising from health and exercise, and
which you have the means of appeasing at the moment, when
it may be considered a source of pleasure rather than of pain
—I refer to the gnawing of starvation; because, if you have
not been, you can form no conception of the agony of the
suffering. Fortunately, but very few of my readers can have
any knowledge of it; the general sympathy which it creates
is from an ideal, not a practical knowledge. It has been my
lot during the vicissitudes of a maritime life to have suffered
hunger to extremity; and although impossible to express the
corporeal agony, yet some notion of it may be conceived from
the effect it had upon my mind. I felt that I hated the
whole world, kin or no kin; that theft was a virtue, murder
excusable, and cannibalism anything but disgusting; from
which the inference may be safely drawn, viz., that I was
devilish hungry.

I mention this, because Nicholas Forster, although he had
been two days without food, and had disposed of every article
which was saleable, was endued with so much strength of
principle as not to have thought (or if he had thought of it,
immediately to have dismissed the thought) of vending the
property found in the trunk by his son, and which had
remained so long in their possession. That few would have
been so scrupulous, I will acknowledge; whether Nicholas
was over-scrupulous, is a question I leave to be debated by
those who are fond of argument. I only state the fact.

Until the arrival of the ship brought home by Mr. Berecroft, the allotment of Newton's wages had been regularly
paid to his father; but when the owner discovered that the
brig had parted company with the convoy, and had not since

been heard of, the chance of capture was considered so great that the owner refused to advance any more on Newton's account. Nicholas was thus thrown upon his own resources, which were as small as they could be. The crew of the brig, who quitted her in the boat, were picked up by a homeward-bound vessel, and brought what was considered the certain intelligence of Jackson and Newton having perished on the wreck. Nicholas, who had frequently called at the owner's since his allowance had been stopped to obtain tidings of his son, was overwhelmed with the intelligence of his death. He returned to his own house, and never called there again. Mr. Berecroft, who wished to find him out and relieve him, could not ascertain in what quarter of the town he resided, and shortly after was obliged to proceed upon another voyage. Thus was the poor optician left to his fate; and it is probable that, but for the fortunate return of Newton, it would soon have been miserably decided.

Newton was much pleased when he learnt from his father that he had not disposed of the property which he had picked up at sea, for he now felt assured that he had discovered the owner at Guadaloupe, and intended to transmit it to M. de Fontanges as soon as he could find a safe conveyance; but this at present was not practicable. As soon as his father had been re-established in his several necessities and comforts, Newton, aware that his purse would not last for ever, applied to the owner of the brig for employment; but he was decidedly refused. The loss of the vessel had soured his temper against any one who had belonged to her. He replied that he considered Newton to be an unlucky person, and must decline his sailing in any of his vessels, even if a vacancy should occur.

To every other application made elsewhere, Newton met with the same ill-fortune. Mr. Berecroft was not there to recommend or to assist him, and months passed away in anxious expectation of his patron's return, when the intelligence was brought home that he had been carried off by yellow fever, which that year had been particularly malignant and fatal. The loss of his only protector was a heavy blow to poor Newton; but he bore up against his fortune and redoubled his exertions. As before, he could always obtain employment before the mast; but this he refused, knowing that if again impressed, however well he might be off himself, and however fortunate in prize-money, his father would be left destitute, and in all probability be starved before he could return. The recollection of the situation in which he had found him on his return from the West Indies made Newton resolve not to leave his father without some surety of his being provided with the means of subsistence. He was not without some employment, and earned sufficient for their mutual maintenance by working as a rigger on board of the ships fitting for sea; and he adhered to this means of a livelihood until something better should present itself. Had Newton been alone in the world, or his father able to support himself, he would have immediately applied to Captain Carrington to receive him in some capacity on board of his frigate, or have entered on board some other man-of-war. Newton's heart was too generous, and his mind too truly English, not to bound when he read or heard of the gallant encounters between the vessels of the rival nations, and he longed to be one of the many thousands so diligently employed in twining the wreath of laurel round their country's brow.

Nearly one year of constant fatigue, constant expectation, and constant disappointment was thus passed away; affairs grew daily worse, employment scarce, money scarcer. Newton, who had been put off from receiving his wages until the ensuing day, which, as they had no credit, was in fact putting off their dinner also to the morrow, went home, and dropped on a chair in a despondent mood at the table where Nicholas was already seated.

" Well, Newton, what's for dinner?" said Nicholas, drawing his chair close to the table in preparation.

" I have not been paid the money due to me," replied Newton; "and, father, I'm afraid there's nothing."

Nicholas backed his chair from the table again with an air of resignation as Newton continued—

" Indeed, father, I think we must try our fortune elsewhere. What's the use of staying where we cannot get employment? Everything is now gone except our wearing apparel. We might raise some money upon mine, it is true; but had we not better, before we spend it, try if fortune will be more favourable to us in some other place?"

"Why, yes, Newton, I've been thinking that if we were to go to London, my improvement on the duplex——"

"Is that our only chance there, sir?" replied Newton, half smiling.

"Why, no; now I think of it, I've a brother there, John Forster, or Jack, as we used to call him. It's near thirty years since I heard of him; but somebody told me, when you were in the West Indies, that he had become a great lawyer, and was making a large fortune. I quite forgot the circumstance till just now."

Newton had before heard his father mention that he had two brothers, but whether dead or alive he could not tell. The present intelligence appeared to hold out some prospect of relief, for Newton could not for a moment doubt that if his uncle was in such flourishing circumstances, he would not refuse assistance to his brother. He therefore resolved not to wait until their means were totally exhausted. The next day he disposed of all his clothes except one suit, and found himself richer than he had imagined. Having paid his landlord the trifle due of rent, without any other incumbrance than the packet of articles picked up in the trunk at sea, three pounds sterling in his pocket, and the ring of Madame de Fontanges on his little finger, Newton, with his father, set off on foot for the metropolis.

CHAPTER XXIV

> "I labour to diffuse the important good
> Till this great truth by all be understood,
> That all the pious duty which we owe
> Our parents, friends, our country, and our God,
> The seed of every virtue here below,
> From discipline and early culture grow."
>
> —WEST.

THE different chapters of a novel remind me of a convoy of vessels. The incidents and *dramatis personæ* are so many respective freights, all under the charge of the inventor, who, like a man-of-war, must see them all safely and together into port. And as the commanding officer when towing one

154

vessel which has lagged behind up to the rest, finds that in
the meantime another has dropped nearly out of sight, and
is obliged to cast off the one in tow to perform the same
necessary duty towards the sternmost, so am I necessitated
for the present to quit Nicholas and Newton while I run
down to Edward Forster and his protégée.

It must be recollected that during our narrative "Time has
rolled his ceaseless course," and season has succeeded season,
until the infant, in its utter helplessness to lift its little
hands for succour, has sprung up into a fair, blue-eyed little
maiden of nearly eight years old, light as a fairy in her proportions, bounding as a fawn in her gait ; her eyes beaming with
joy, and her cheeks suffused with the blush of health, when
tripping over the sea-girt hills ; meek and attentive when
listening to the precepts of her fond and adopted parent.

"Faithful," the Newfoundland dog, is no more, but his
portrait hangs over the mantelpiece in the little parlour.
Mrs. Beazely, the housekeeper, has become inert and querulous from rheumatism and the burden of added years. A
little girl, daughter of Robinson the fisherman, has been
called in to perform her duties, while she basks in the
summer's sun or hangs over the winter's fire. Edward
Forster's whole employment and whole delight has long
been centred in his darling child, whose beauty of person,
quickness of intellect, generous disposition, and affectionate
heart, amply repay him for his kind protection.

Of all chapters which can be ventured upon, one upon
education is perhaps the most tiresome. Most willingly
would I pass it over, not only for the reader's sake, but for
mine own : for his, because it cannot well be otherwise than
dry and uninteresting ; for mine, because I do not exactly
know how to write it.

But this cannot be. Amber was not brought up according
to the prescribed maxims of Mesdames Appleton and Hamil-
ton ; and as effects cannot be satisfactorily comprehended
without the causes are made known, so it becomes necessary,
not only that the chapter should be written, but, what is still
more vexatious, absolutely necessary that it should be read.

Before I enter upon this most unpleasant theme—unpleasant to all parties, for no one likes to teach, and no one
likes to learn—I cannot help remarking how excessively *au*

fail we find most elderly maiden ladies upon every point connected with our unprofitable species. They are erudite upon every point *ab ovo*, and it would appear that their peculiar knowledge of the theory can but arise from their attentions having never been diverted by the practice.

Let it be the teeming mother or the new-born babe—the teething infant or the fractious child—the dirty, pin-before urchin or sampler-spoiling girl—schoolboy lout or sapling Miss —voice-broken, self-admiring hobbledehoy, or expanding conscious and blushing maiden, the whole arcana of Nature and of Art has been revealed to them alone.

Let it be the scarlet-fever or a fit of passion, the measles or a shocking fib—whooping-cough or apple-stealing—learning too slow or eating too fast—slapping a sister or clawing a brother —let the disease be bodily or mental, they alone possess the panacea; and blooming matrons, spreading out in their pride, like the anxious chuckling hen over their numerous encircling offspring, who have borne them with a mother's throes, watched over them with a mother's anxious mind, and reared them with a mother's ardent love, are considered to be wholly incompetent, in the opinion of these dessicated and barren branches of Nature's stupendous ever-bearing tree.

Mrs. Beazely, who had lost her husband soon after marriage, was not fond of children, as they interfered with her habits of extreme neatness. As far as Amber's education was concerned, all we can say is, that if the old housekeeper did her no good, she certainly did her no harm. As Amber increased in years and intelligence, so did her thirst for knowledge on topics upon which Mrs. Beazely was unable to give her any correct information. Under these circumstances, when applied to, Mrs. Beazely, who was too conscientious to mislead the child, was accustomed to place her hand upon her back, and complain of the rheumatiz—"Such a stitch, my dear love; can't talk now—ask your pa when he comes home."

Edward Forster had maturely weighed the difficulties of the charge imposed upon him, that of educating a female. The peculiarity of her situation, without a friend in the wide world except himself; and his days, in all probability, numbered to that period at which she would most require an adviser—that period when the heart rebels against the head and too often overthrows the legitimate dynasty of reason-

156

determined him to give a masculine character to her education, as most likely to prove the surest safeguard through a deceitful world.

Aware that more knowledge is to be imparted to a child by conversation than by any other means (for by this system education is divested of its drudgery), during the first six years of her life Amber knew little more than the letters of the alphabet. It was not until her desire of information was excited to such a degree as to render her anxious to obtain her own means of acquiring it that Amber was taught to read, and then it was at her own request. Edward Forster was aware that a child six years old, willing to learn, would soon pass by another who had been drilled to it at an earlier age and against its will, and whose mind had been checked in its expansive powers by the weight which constantly oppressed its infant memory. Until the above age, the mind of Amber had been permitted to run as unconfined through its own little regions of fancy as her active body had been allowed to spring up the adjacent hills—and both were equally beautified and strengthened by the healthy exercise.

Religion was deeply impressed upon her grateful heart ; but it was simplified almost to unity, that it might be clearly understood. It was conveyed to her through the glorious channel of Nature, and God was loved and feared from the contemplation and admiration of His works.

Did Amber fix her eyes upon the distant ocean, or watch the rolling of the surf; did they wander over the verdant hills, or settle on the beetling cliff; did she raise her cherub-face to the heavens, and wonder at the studded firmament of stars, or the moon sailing in her cold beauty, or the sun blinding her in his warmth and splendour—she knew that it was God who made them all. Did she ponder over the variety of the leaf ; did she admire the painting of the flower, or watch the motions of the minute insect, which, but for her casual observation, might have lived and died unseen—she felt, she knew that all was made for man's advantage or enjoyment, and that God was great and good. Her orisons were short, but they were sincere ; unlike the child who, night and morning, stammers through a " Belief" which it cannot comprehend, and whose ideas of religion are, from injudicious treatment, too soon con‑ nected with feelings of impatience and disgust.

Curiosity has been much abused. From a habit we have contracted in this world of not calling things by their right names, it has been decried as a vice, whereas it ought to have been classed as a virtue. Had Adam first discovered the forbidden fruit he would have tasted it, without, like Eve, requiring the suggestions of the devil to urge him on to disobedience. But if by curiosity was occasioned the fall of man, it is the same passion by which he is spurred to rise again, and reappear only inferior to the Deity. The curiosity of little minds may be impertinent, but the curiosity of great minds is the thirst for knowledge—the daring of our immortal powers—the enterprise of the soul to raise itself again to its original high estate. It was curiosity which stimulated the great Newton to search into the laws of heaven, and enabled his master-mind to translate the vast mysterious page of Nature, ever before our eyes since the creation of the world, but never, till he appeared, to be read by mortal man. It is this passion which must be nurtured in our childhood, for upon its healthy growth and vigour depends the future expansion of the mind.

How little money need be expended to teach a child, and yet what a quantity of books we have to pay for! Amber had hardly ever looked into a book, and yet she knew more, that is, had more general useful knowledge, than others who were twice her age. How small was Edward Forster's little parlour —how humble the furniture it contained !—a carpet, a table, a few chairs, a small china vase as an ornament on the mantelpiece. How few were the objects brought to Amber's view in their small secluded home ! The plates and knives for dinner, a silver spoon or two, and their articles of wearing apparel. Yet how endless, how inexhaustible were the amusement and instruction derived from these trifling sources !—for these were Forster's books.

The carpet—its hempen ground carried them to the north, from whence the material came, the inhabitants of the frozen world, their manners and their customs, the climate and their cities, their productions and their sources of wealth. Its woollen surface, with its various dyes—each dye containing an episode of an island or a state, a point of natural history, or of art and manufacture.

The mahogany table, like some magic vehicle, transported them in a second to the torrid zone, where the various tropical flowers and fruit, the towering cocoa-nut, the spread-ing palm, the broad-leaved banana, the fragrant pine—all that was indigenous to the country, all that was peculiar in the scenery and the clime, were pictured to the imagination of the delighted Amber.

The little vase upon the mantelpiece swelled into a splendid atlas of Eastern geography, an inexhaustible folio, describing Indian costumes, the Asiatic splendour of costume, the gorgeous thrones of the descendants of the Prophet, the history of the Prophet himself, the superior instinct and stupendous body of the elephant; all that Edward Forster had collected of Nature or of Art through these extensive regions were successively displayed, until they returned to China, from whence they had commenced their travels. Thus did the little vase, like the vessel taken up by the fisherman in the "Arabian Nights," contain a giant confined by the seal of Solomon—Knowledge.

The knife and spoon brought food unto the mind as well as to the body. The mines were entered, the countries pointed out in which they were to be found, the various metals, their value, and the uses to which they were applied. The dress again led them abroad; the cotton hung in pods upon the tree, the silkworm spun its yellow tomb, all the process of manufacture was explained. The loom again was worked by fancy, until the article in comment was again produced.

Thus was Amber instructed and amused; and thus, with Nature for his hornbook and Art for his primer, did the little parlour of Edward Forster expand into "the universe."

CHAPTER XXV

" They boast
Their noble birth : conduct us to the tombs
Of their forefathers, and from age to age
Ascending, trumpet to their illustrious race."

DEVOTED as he was to the instruction of his adopted child, Edward Forster was nevertheless aware that more was required in the education of a female than he was competent to fulfil. Many and melancholy were his reveries

159

on the forlorn prospects of the little girl (considering his own precarious life and the little chance that appeared of restoring her to her friends and relations). Still he resolved that all that could should be done; the issue he left to Providence. That she might not be cast wholly unknown upon the world in case of his death, he had often taken Amber to a neighbouring mansion, with the owner of which, Lord Aveleyn, he had long been on friendly terms, although, until latterly, he had declined mixing with the society which was there collected. Many years before, the possessor had entered the naval service, and had, during the few months that he had served in the capacity of midshipman, been entrusted to the charge of Edward Forster.

It is a curious fact, although little commented upon, how much society in general is affected by the entailment of property in aristocratical families upon the male heir; we may add, how much it is demoralised. The eldest son, accustomed from his earliest days to the flattery and adulation of dependents, is impressed with but one single idea, namely, that he is the fortunate person deputed by chance to spend so many thousands per annum, and that his brothers and sisters, with equal claims upon the parent, are to be almost dependent upon him for support. Of this the latter are but too soon made conscious, by the difference of treatment which they experience from those around them; and feelings of envy and ill-will towards their eldest brother are but too often the result of such inequality. Thus, one of the greatest charms of life, unity between brethren, is destroyed.

The possessor of the title and the estates is at last borne to his long home, there to lie until summoned before that Presence where he, and those who were kings, and those who were clowns, will stand trembling as erring men, awaiting the fiat of eternal justice. In his turn, the young lord revels in his youth.

Then how much more trying is the situation of the younger brothers. During their father's lifetime they had a home, and were brought up in scenes and with ideas commensurate with the fortune which had been entailed. Now, they find themselves thrown upon the world, without the means of support even adequate to their wants. Like the steward in the parable, " They cannot dig, to beg they are ashamed;"

and, like him, they too often resort to unworthy means to supply their exigencies.

Should the young heir prove sickly, what speculations on his demise ! The worldly stake is so enormous that the ties of nature are dissolved, and a brother rejoices at a brother's death ! One generation is not sufficient to remove these feelings ; the barrenness of his marriage-bed, or the weakly state of his children, are successively speculated upon by the presumptive heir. Let it not be supposed that I would infer this always to be the fact. I have put the extreme case, to point out what must ensue according to the feelings of our nature, if care is not taken to prevent its occurrence. There is a cruelty, a more than cruelty, in parents bringing up their children with ideas which seldom can be realised, and rendering their future lives a pilgrimage of misery and discontent, if not of depravity.

But the major part of our aristocracy are neither deficient in talent nor in worth. They set a bright example to the nobles of other countries, and very frequently even to the less demoralised society of our own. Trammelled by the deeds of their forefathers, they employ every means in their power to remedy the evil ; and a large proportion of their younger branches find useful and honourable employment in the army, the navy, or the Church. But their numbers cannot all be provided for by these channels ; and it is the country at large which is taxed to supply the means of sustenance to the younger scions of nobility—taxed directly in the shape of place and sinecure, indirectly in various ways ; but in no way so heavily as by the monopoly of the East India Company, which has so long been permitted to oppress the nation, that these *detrimentals* (as they have named themselves) may be provided for. It is a well-known fact that there is hardly a peer in the Upper House, or many representatives of the people in the Lower, who are not, or who anticipate to be, under some obligation to this Company by their relations or connections being provided for in those distant climes ; and it is this bribery (for bribery it is, in whatever guise it may appear) that upholds one of the most glaring, the most oppressive of all monopolies, in the face of common sense, common justice, and common decency. Other taxes are principally felt by the higher and middling classes ; but this most odious, this most galling tax is felt even in the cot-

L

tage of the labourer, who cannot return to refresh himself after his day of toil with his favourite beverage, without paying twice its value out of his hard-earned pittance, to swell the dividend of the Company, and support these *pruriencies* of noble blood.

And yet, deprecating the evils arising from the system of entail, I must acknowledge that there are no other means by which (in a monarchical government) the desirable end of upholding rank is to be obtained. I remember once, when conversing with an American, I inquired after one or two of his countrymen who but a few years before were of great wealth and influence. To one of my remarks he answered, " In our country all the wealth and power at the time attached to it does not prevent a name from sinking into insignificance, or from being forgotten soon after its possessor is dead, for we do not entail property. The distribution scatters the amassed heap, by which the world around him has been attracted ; and although the distribution tends to the general fertilisation of the country, yet with the disappearance, the influence of the possessor, and even his name, are soon forgotten."

These remarks, as will appear in the sequel, are apposite to the parties whom I am about to introduce to the reader. As, however, they are people of some consequence, it may appear to be a want of due respect on my part if I were to introduce them at the fag-end of a chapter.

CHAPTER XXVI

" 'Twas his the vast and trackless deep to rove :
Alternate change of climates has he known,
And felt the fierce extremes of either zone,
Where polar skies congeal th' eternal snow,
Or equinoctial suns for ever glow ;
Smote by the freezing or the scorching blast,
A ship-boy on the high and giddy mast."

—FALCONER.

THE father of the present Lord Aveleyn had three sons, and, in conformity with the usages commented upon in the preceding chapter, the two youngest were condemned to the army and navy; the second, who had priority of choice, being dismissed to gather laurels in a red coat, while the third was recommended to do the same, if he could, in a suit of blue. Fairly embarked in their several professions, a sum of fifty pounds per annum was placed in the hands of their respective agents, and no more was thought about a pair of "detrimentals."

Lord Aveleyn's father, who had married late in life, was summoned away when the eldest brother of the present Lord Aveleyn, the heir, was yet a minor, about two years after he had embarked in the ship to which Edward Forster belonged. Now it was the will of Providence that, about six months after the old nobleman's decease, the young lord and his second brother, who had obtained a short furlough, should most unadvisedly embark in a small sailing boat on the lake close to the mansion, and that, owing to some mismanagement of the sail, the boat upset, and they were both drowned.

· As soon as the melancholy intelligence was made known to the trustees, a letter was despatched to Captain L——, who commanded the ship in which young Aveleyn was serving his time, acquainting him with the catastrophe, and requesting the immediate discharge of the young midshipman. The captain repaired on board; when he arrived on the quarter-deck, he desired the first lieutenant to send down for young Aveleyn.

"He is at the mast-head, sir," replied the first lieutenant, "for neglect of duty."

"Really, Mr. W——," replied the captain, who had witnessed the boy's ascent at least a hundred times before with perfect indifference, and had often sent him up himself, "you appear to be very sharp upon that poor lad; you make no allowance for youth—boys will be boys."

· "He's the most troublesome young monkey in the ship, sir," replied the first lieutenant, surprised at this unusual interference.

"He has always appeared to me to be a well-disposed, intelligent lad, Mr. W——; and I wish you to understand that I do not approve of this system of eternal mast-heading. However, he will not trouble you any more, as his discharge is to be immediately made out. He is now," continued the

163

captain, pausing to give more effect to his communication, "Lord Aveleyn."

"Whew! now the murder's out," mentally exclaimed the first lieutenant.

"Call him down immediately, Mr. W——, if you please, and recollect that I disapprove of the system."

"Certainly, sir; but really, Captain L——, I don't know what I shall do if you restrict my power of punishing the young gentlemen; they are so extremely unruly. There's Mr. Malcolm," continued the first lieutenant, pointing to a youngster who was walking on the other side of the deck with his hands in his pockets, "it was but yesterday that he chopped off at least four inches from the tail of your dog Ponto at the beef-block, and pretends it was an accident."

"What! my setter's tail?"

"Yes, sir, he did, I can assure you."

"Mr. Malcolm," cried the captain, in great wrath, "how came you to cut off my dog's tail?"

Before I went to sea I had always considered a London cock-sparrow to be the truest emblem of consummate impudence, but I have since discovered that he is quite modest compared to a midshipman.

"Me, sir?" replied the youngster demurely. "I didn't cut off his tail, sir; he *cut it off himself!*"

"What, sir!" roared the captain.

"If you please, sir, I was chopping a piece of beef, and the dog, who was standing by, turned short round, and put his tail under the chopper."

"Put his tail under the chopper, you little scamp!" replied Captain L——, in a fury. "Now just put your head above the maintop-gallant cross-trees, and stay there until you are called down. Mr. W——, you'll keep him up till sunset."

"Ay, ay, sir," replied the first lieutenant, with a satisfactory smile at the description of punishment inflicted.

When I was a midshipman, it was extremely difficult to avoid the mast-head. Out of six years served in that capacity, I once made a calculation that two of them were passed away perched upon the cross-trees, looking down, with calm philosophy, upon the microcosm below. Yet, although I never deserved it, I derived much future advantage from my

164

repeated punishments. The mast-head, for want of something worse to do, became my study; and during the time spent there, I in a manner finished my education. Volumes after volumes were perused to while away the tedious hours; and I conscientiously believe it is to this mode of punishment adopted by my rigid superiors that the world is indebted for all the pretty books which I am writing.

I was generally exalted either for thinking or not thinking; and as I am not aware of any medium between the active and passive state of our minds (except dreaming, which is still more unpardonable), the reader may suppose that there is no exaggeration in my previous calculation of one-third of my midshipman existence having been passed away upon "the high and giddy mast."

"Mr. M——," would the first lieutenant cry out, "why did you stay so long on shore with the jolly-boat?"

"I went to the post-office for the officers' letters, sir."

"And pray, sir, who ordered you?"

"No one, sir; but I thought——"

"You thought, sir! How dare you think?—go up to the mast-head, sir."

So much for thinking.

"Mr. M——," would he say at another time, when I came on board, "did you call at the admiral's office?"

"No, sir; I had no orders. I didn't think——"

"Then why didn't you think, sir? Up to the mast-head, and stay there till I call you down."

So much for not thinking. Like the fable of the wolf and the lamb, it was all the same; bleat as I pleased, my defence was useless, and I could not avert my barbarous doom.

To proceed: Captain L—— went over the side; the last pipe had been given, and the boatswain had returned his call into his jacket-pocket and walked forward, when the first lieutenant, in pursuance of his orders, looked up aloft, intending to have hailed the new lord, and have requested the pleasure of his company on deck; but the youngster, feeling a slight degree of appetite, after enjoying the fresh air for seven hours without any breakfast, had just ventured down the top-mast rigging, that he might obtain possession of a bottle of tea and some biscuit, which one of his messmates had carried up for him, and stowed away in the bunt of the maintopsail. Young Aveleyn, who thought that the departure of the captain would occupy the attention of the first lieutenant, had just descended to, and was placing his foot on, the topsail yard, when Mr. W—— looked up, and witnessed this act of disobedience. As this was a fresh offence committed, he thought himself warranted in not complying with the captain's mandate, and the boy was ordered up again, to remain till sunset. " I would have called him down," muttered Mr. W——, whose temper had been soured from long disappointment, " but since he's a lord, he shall have a good spell of it before he quits the service ; and then we shall not have his recommendation to others in his own rank to come into it, and interfere with our promotion."

Now it happened that Mr. W——, who had an eye like a hawk, when he cast his eyes aloft, observed that the bunt of the maintopsail was not exactly so well stowed as it ought to be on board of a man-of-war ; which is not to be wondered at, when it is recollected that the midshipmen had been very busy enlarging it to make a pantry. He therefore turned the hands up, "mend sails," and took his station amidship on the booms, to see that this, the most delinquent sail, was properly furled.—"Trice up—lay out.—All ready forward ? " —" All ready, sir."—" All ready abaft ? "—" All ready, sir." —" Let fall."—Down came the sails from the yards, and down also came the bottle of tea and biscuit upon the face of the first lieutenant, who was looking up ; the former knocking out three of his front teeth, besides splitting open both his lips and chin.

Young Aveleyn, who witnessed the catastrophe, was delighted ; the other midshipmen on deck crowded round their superior to offer their condolements, winking and making faces at each other in by-play, until the first lieutenant descended to his cabin, when they no longer restrained their mirth.

About an hour afterwards, Mr. W—— reappeared with his face bound up, and summoned all the young gentlemen on deck, insisting upon being informed who it was who had stowed away the bottle in the bunt of the sail ; but midshipmen have most treacherous memories, and not one of them knew anything about it. As a last resource young Aveleyn was called down from the mast-head,

166

"Now, sir," said Mr. W——, "either inform me directly who it was who stowed away the bottle aloft, or I pledge you my word you shall be discharged from his Majesty's service to-morrow morning. Don't pretend to say that you don't know, for you must."

"I do know," replied the youngster boldly, "but I never will tell."

"Then either you or I shall leave the service. Man the first cutter;" and when the boat was manned, the first lieutenant sent some papers on shore, which he had been desired to do by the captain.

When the boat returned, the clerk was sent for, and desired by Mr. W—— to make out Mr. Aveleyn's discharge, as the officers and midshipmen thought (for Mr. W—— had kept his secret) for his disobedient conduct. The poor boy, who thought all his prospects blighted, was sent on shore, the tears running down his cheeks, as much from the applause and kind farewells of his shipmates, as from the idea of the degradation which he underwent. Now the real culprit was young Malcolm, who, to oblige the captain, had taken his station at the fore-top-gallant mast-head because the dog Ponto thought proper to cut off his own tail. The first lieutenant, in his own woe, forgot that of others; and it was not until nine o'clock at night, that Malcolm, who thought that he had stayed up quite long enough, ventured below, when he was informed of what had taken place.

The youngster immediately penned a letter to the captain, acknowledging that he was the offender, and requesting that Mr. Aveleyn might not be discharged from the service; he also ventured to add a postscript, begging that the same lenity might be extended towards himself; which letter was sent on shore by the captain's gig when it left the ship the next morning, and was received by Captain L—— at the very same time that young Aveleyn, who had not been sent on shore till late in the evening, called upon the captain to request a reprieve from his hard sentence.

The boy sent up his name and was immediately admitted.

"I presume you know why you are discharged from the service?" said Captain L——, smiling benignantly.

"Yes, sir," replied the boy, holding his head down submissively, "because of that accident—I'm very sorry, sir."

167

"Of course you must, and ought to be. Such heavy blows are not common, and hard to bear. I presume you go immediately to Buckhurst?"

"I suppose I must, sir; but I hope, Captain L——, th t you'll look over it."

"I shall have very great pleasure in so doing," replied Captain L——; "I hear that it is——"

"Thanky, sir, thanky," replied the youngster, interrupting the captain. "Then I may go on board again and tell the first lieutenant?"

"Tell the first lieutenant what?" cried Captain L——, perceiving some mistake. "Why, has not Mr. W—— told you?"

"Yes, sir, he told me it was your orders that I should be dismissed his Majesty's service."

"Discharged—not dismissed. And I presume he told you why: because your two elder brothers are dead, and you are now Lord Aveleyn."

"No, sir!" cried the youngster with astonishment; "because his three front teeth are knocked out with a bottle of *scaldchops*, and I would not peach who stowed it away in the bunt of the sail."

"This is excessively strange!" replied Captain L——. "Do me the favour to sit down, my lord; the letters from the ship will probably explain the affair."

There was, however, no explanation, except from young Malcolm. The captain read his letter, and put it into the hands of Lord Aveleyn, who entered into a detail of the whole.

Captain L—— produced the letter from the trustees, and, desiring his lordship to command him as to any funds he might require, requested the pleasure of his company to dinner. The boy, whose head wheeled with the sudden change in his prospects, was glad to retire, having first obtained permission to return on board with young Malcolm's pardon, which had been most graciously acceded to. To the astonishment of everybody on board, young Aveleyn came alongside in the captain's own gig, when the scene in the midshipmen's berth and the discomfiture of the first lieutenant may be imagined.

"You don't belong to the service, Frank," said the old

master's mate; "and, as peer of the realm, coming on board to visit the ship, you are entitled to a salute. Send up and say you expect one, and then W—— must have the guard up, and pay you proper respect. I'll be hanged if I don't take the message, if you consent to it."

But Lord Aveleyn had come on board to pay a debt of gratitude, not to inflict mortification. He soon quitted the ship, promising never to forget Malcolm; and, unlike the promises of most great men, it was fulfilled, and Malcolm rose to be a captain from his own merit, backed by the exertions of his youthful patron.

For the next week the three mast-heads were so loaded with midshipmen, that the boatswain proposed a preventer backstay, that the top-masts might not go over the side; but shortly after, Captain L——, who was not pleased at the falsehood which Mr. W—— had circulated, and who had many other reasons for parting with him, succeeded in having him appointed to another ship; after which the midshipmen walked up and down the quarter-deck with their hands in their pockets, as before.

CHAPTER XXVII

" But Adeline determined Juan's wedding
    In her own mind, and that's enough for woman ;
    But then with whom ? There was the sage Miss Redding,
    Miss Raw, Miss Flaw, Miss Showman and Miss Knowman,
    And the two fair co-heiresses Giltbedding.
    She deemed his merits something more than common.
    All these were unobjectionable matches,
    And might go on, if well wound up, like watches."
                                                —BYRON.

THE young Lord Aveleyn returned to the hall of his ancestors, exchanging the gloomy cockpit for the gay saloon, the ship's allowance for sumptuous fare, the tyranny of his messmates and the harshness of his superiors for adulation and respect. Was he happier? No. In this world, whether in boyhood or riper years, the happiest state of existence is when under control. Although contrary to received opinion, this is a fact ; but I cannot now stop to demonstrate the truth of the assertion.

Life may be compared to a gamut of music: there are seven notes from our birth to our marriage ; and thus may we run up the first octave—milk, sugar-plums, apples, cricket, cravat, gun, horse ; then comes the wife, a *da capo* to a new existence, which is to continue until the whole diapason is gone through. Lord Aveleyn ran up his scale like others before him.

" Why do you not marry, my dear Frank ? " said the Dowager Lady Aveleyn one day, when a thick fog debarred her son of his usual pastime.

" Why, mother, I have no objection to marry ; and I suppose I must one of these days, as a matter of duty . but I really am very difficult to please ; and if I were to make a bad choice, you know a wife is not like this gun, which will *go off* when I please."

" But still, my dear Frank, there are many very eligible matches to be made just now."

" I do not doubt it, madame ; but pray who are they ? "

" Why, Miss Riddlesworth——"

" A very pretty girl, and I am told a large fortune. But let me hear the others first."

" Clara Beauchamp, well connected, and a very sweet girl."

" Granted also, for anything I know to the contrary. Have you more on your list ? "

" Certainly. Emily Riddlesdale ; not much fortune, but very highly connected indeed. Her brother, Lord Riddlesdale, is a man of great influence."

" Her want of money is no object, my dear mother, and the influence of her brother no inducement ; I covet neither. I grant you that she is a very nice girl. Proceed."

" Why, Frank, one would think that you were a sultan with his handkerchief. There is Lady Selina Armstrong."

" Well, she is a very fine girl, and talks well."

" There is Harriet Butler, who has just come out."

" I saw her at the last ball we were at—a very pretty creature."

" Lady Jemima Calthorpe." .

" Not very good-looking, but clever and agreeable."

"There is Louisa Manners, who is very much admired."

"I admire her very much myself"

"Well, Frank, you have exhausted my catalogue. There is not one I have mentioned who is not unexceptionable, and whom I would gladly embrace as a daughter-in-law. You are now turned of forty, my dear son, and must make up your mind to have heirs to the title and estates. I am, however, afraid that your admiration is so general that you will be puzzled in your choice.'

"I will confess to you, my dearest mother, that I have many years thought of the necessity of taking to myself a wife, but have never yet had courage to decide. I admit that if all the young women you have mentioned were what they appear to be, a man need not long hesitate in his choice; but the great difficulty is that their real tempers and dispositions are not to be ascertained till it is too late. Allow that I should attempt to discover the peculiar disposition of every one of them, what would be the consequence? —that my attentions would be perceived. I do not exactly mean to accuse them of deceit; but a woman is naturally flattered by perceiving herself an object of attraction, and when flattered, is pleased. It is not likely, therefore, that the infirmities of her temper (if she have any) should be discovered by a man whose presence is a source of gratification. If artful, she will conceal her faults; if not so, there will be no occasion to bring them to light. And even if, after a long courtship, something wrong should be discovered, either you have proceeded too far in honour to retract, or are so blinded by your own feelings as to extenuate it. Now, it is only the parents and near relations of a young woman who can be witnesses to her real character, unless it be, indeed, her own maid, whom one could not condescend to interrogate."

"That is all very true, Frank; but recollect the same observations apply to your sex as well as ours. Lovers and husbands are very different beings. It is quite a lottery on both sides."

"I agree with you, my dear mother; and, as marry I must, so shall it be a lottery with me—I will leave it to chance, and not to myself. then if I am unfortunate, I will blame my stars, and not have to accuse myself of a want of proper discrimination." Lord Aveleyn took up a sheet of paper, and

171

dividing it into small slips, wrote upon them the names of the different young ladies proposed by his mother. Folding them up, he threw them on the table before her, and requested that she would select any one of the papers.

The dowager took up one.

"I thank you, madam," said Lord Aveleyn, taking the paper from her hand, and opening it—"'Louisa Manners.' Well, then, Louisa Manners it shall be ; always provided that she does not refuse me. I will make my first advances this very afternoon—that is, if it does not clear up, and I can take out the pointers."

"You surely are joking, Frank ? "

"Never was more serious. I have my mother's recommendation, backed by fate. Marry I must, but choose I will not. I feel myself desperately in love with the fair Louisa already. I will report my progress to you, my dear madam, in less than a fortnight."

Lord Aveleyn adhered to his singular resolution, courted, and was accepted. He never had reason to repent his choice ; who proved to be as amiable as her countenance would have indicated. The fruits of his marriage was one son, who was watched over with mingled pride and anxiety, and who had now arrived at the age of fifteen years.

Such was the history of Lord Aveleyn, who continued to extend his friendship to Edward Forster, and, if he had required it, would gladly have proffered his assistance, in return for the kindness which Forster had shown towards him when he was a midshipman. The circumstances connected with the history of the little Amber were known to Lord Aveleyn and his lady ; and the wish of Forster, that his little charge should derive the advantage of mixing in good female society, was gladly acceded to, both on his account and on her own. Amber would often remain for days at the mansion, and was a general favourite, as well as an object of sympathy.

But the growth of their son, too rapid for his years, and which brought with it symptoms of pulmonary disease, alarmed Lord and Lady Aveleyn ; and, by the advice of the physicians, they broke up their establishment, and hastened with him to Madeira, to re-establish his health. Their departure was deeply felt both by Forster and his charge ; and before they could recover from the loss, another severe trial awaited them in the death of Mrs. Beazely, who, full of years and rheumatism, was gathered to her fathers. Forster, habituated as he was to the old lady, felt her loss severely : he was now with Amber quite alone ; and it so happened that in the following winter his wound broke out, and confined him to his bed until the spring.

As he lay in a precarious state, the thought naturally occurred to him, " What will become of this poor child if I am called away ? There is not the slightest provision for her : she has no friends, and I have not even made it known to any of my own that there is such a person in existence." Edward Forster thought of his brother, the lawyer, whom he knew still to be flourishing, although he had never corresponded with him ; and resolved that, as soon as he was able to undertake the journey, he would go to town, and secure his interest for the little Amber, in case of any accident happening to himself.

The spring and summer passed away before he found himself strong enough to undertake the journey. It was late in the autumn that Edward Forster and Amber took their places in a heavy coach for the metropolis, and arrived without accident on the day or two subsequent to that on which Nicholas and Newton had entered it on foot.

CHAPTER XXVIII

" Through coaches, drays, choked turnpikes, and a whirl
    Of wheels, and roar of voices, and confusion,
Here taverns wooing to a pint of ' purl,'
    There mails fast flying off like a delusion.

Through this, and much and more, is the approach
    Of travellers to mighty Babylon ;
Whether they come by horse, or chair, or coach,
    With slight exceptions, all the ways seem one."
                          —BYRON.

WHEN Newton Forster and his father arrived at London, they put up at an obscure inn in the Borough. The next day Newton set off to discover the residence of his uncle. The people of the inn had recommended him to apply to some stationer or bookseller, who would allow him to look over a red-book; and, in compliance with these instructions, Newton stopped at a shop in Fleet Street, on the doors of which was written in large gilt letters—"Law Bookseller." The young men in the shop were very civil and obliging, and, without referring to the "Guide," immediately told him the residence of a man so well known as his uncle, and Newton hastened in the direction pointed out.

It was one of those melancholy days in which London wears the appearance of a huge scavenger's cart. A lurid fog and mizzling rain, which had been incessant for the previous twenty-four hours; sloppy pavements, and kennels down which the muddy torrents hastened to precipitate themselves into the sewers below; armies of umbrellas, as far as the eye could reach, now rising, now lowering, to avoid collision; hackney-coaches in active sloth, their miserable cattle plodding along with their backs arched and heads and tails drooping like barn-door fowls crouching under the cataract of a gutter; clacking of pattens and pestering of sweepers; not a smile upon the countenance of one individual of the multitude which passed him;—all appeared anxiety, bustle, and selfishness. Newton was not sorry when he turned down the narrow court which had been indicated to him, and, disengaged from the throng of men, commenced a more rapid course. In two minutes he was at the door of his uncle's chambers; which, notwithstanding the inclemency of the weather, stood wide open, as if there should be no obstacle in a man's way, or a single moment for reflection allowed him, if he wished to entangle himself in the expenses and difficulties of the law. Newton furled his weeping umbrella; and first looking with astonishment at the mud which had accumulated above the calves of his legs, raised his eyes to the jambs on each side, where in large letters he read at the head of a long list of occupants, "Mr. Forster, Ground Floor." A door with Mr. Forster's name on it, within a few feet of him, next caught his eye. He knocked, and was admitted by the clerk, who stated that his master was at a consultation, but was expected back in half-an-hour, if he could wait so long. Newton assented, and was ushered into the parlour, where the clerk presented the newspaper of the day to amuse him until the arrival of his uncle.

174

THE MERCHANT SERVICE

As soon as the door was closed, Newton's curiosity as to the character of his uncle induced him to scrutinise the apartment and its contents. In the centre of the room, which might have been about fourteen feet square, stood a table, with a shadow lamp placed before the only part of it which was left vacant for the use of the pen. The remainder of the space was loaded with parchment upon parchment, deed upon deed, paper upon paper. Some, especially those underneath, had become dark and discoloured by time; the ink had changed to a dull red, and the imprint of many a thumb inferred how many years they had been in existence, and how long they had lain as sad mementoes of the law's delay. Others were fresh and clean, the japanned ink in strong contrast with the glossy parchment—new cases of litigation, fresh as the hopes of those who had been persuaded by flattering assurances to enter into a labyrinth of vexation, from which, perhaps, not to be extricated until these documents should assume the hue of the others, which silently indicated the blighted hopes of protracted litigation. Two massive iron chests occupied the walls on each side of the fireplace, and round the whole area of the room were piled 'one upon another large tin boxes, on which, in legible Roman characters, were written the names of the parties whose property was thus immured. There they stood like so many sepulchres of happiness, mausoleums raised over departed competence; while the names of the parties inscribed appeared as so many registers of the folly and contention of man.

But from all this Newton could draw no other conclusion than that his uncle had plenty of business. The fire in the grate was on so small a scale, that, although he shivered with wet and cold, Newton was afraid to stir it lest it should go out altogether. From this circumstance he drew a hasty and unsatisfactory conclusion that his uncle was not very partial to spending his money.

But he hardly had time to draw these inferences, and then take up the newspaper, when the door opened, and another party was ushered into the room by the clerk, who informed him, as he handed a chair, that Mr. Forster would return in a few minutes.

The personage thus introduced was a short young man,

with a round face, bushy eyebrows, and dogged countenance, implying wilfulness without ill-nature. As soon as he entered, he proceeded to divest his throat of a large shawl, which he hung over the back of a chair; then doffing his great-coat, which was placed in a similar position, he rubbed his hands, and walked up to the fire, into which he insinuated the poker, and immediately destroyed the small symptoms of combustion which remained, reducing the whole to one chaos of smoke.

" Better have left it alone, I believe," observed he, re-inserting the poker, and again stirring up the black mass, for the fire was now virtually defunct.

" You're not cold, I hope, sir?" said the party, turning to Newton.

" No, sir, not very," replied Newton good-humouredly.

" I thought so; clients never are; nothing like law for keeping you warm, sir. Always bring on your cause in the winter months. I do, if I can; for it's positive suffocation in the dog-days!"

" I really never was at law," replied Newton, laughing; "but if ever I have the misfortune, I shall recollect your advice."

" Never was at law! I was going to say, what the devil brings you here? but that would have been an impertinent question. Well, sir, do you know, there was a time at which I never knew what law was," continued the young man, seating himself in a chair opposite to Newton. " It was many years ago, when I was a younger brother, and had no pro-perty: no one took the trouble to go to law with me; for if they gained their cause, there were no effects. Within the last six years I have inherited considerable property, and am always in hot water. I heard that the lawyers say, ' causes produce effects.' I am sure I can say that ' effects have pro-duced causes!' "

" I am sorry that your good fortune should be coupled with such a drawback."

" Oh, it's nothing! It's just to a man what a clog is to a horse in a field—you know pretty well where to find him. I'm so used to it—indeed so much so, that I should feel rather uncomfortable if I had nothing on my hands: just keeps me from being idle. I've been into every court in the metropolis, and have no fault to find with one of them except the Court of R——ts."

" And pray, sir, what is that court, and the objection you have to it ? "

" Why, as to the court, it's the most confounded ras—— ; but I must be careful how I speak before strangers : you'll excuse me, sir; not that I suspect you, but I know what may be considered as a libel. I shall, therefore, just state that it is a court at which no gentleman can appear; and if he does, it's of no use, for he'll never get a verdict in his favour."

" What ! then it is not a court of justice ? "

" Court of justice ! no, it's a court for the recovery of small debts ; but I'll just tell you, sir, exactly what took place with me in that court, and then you will be able to judge for yourself. I had a dog, sir; it was just after I came into my property; his name was Cæsar, and a very good dog he was. Well, sir, riding out one day about four miles from town, a rabbit put his nose out of a cellar where they retailed potatoes. Cæsar pounced upon him, and the rabbit was dead in a moment. The man who owned the rabbit and the potatoes came up to me and asked my name, which I told him ; at the same time I expressed my sorrow at the accident, and advised him in future to keep his rabbits in hutches. He said he would, and demanded three shillings and sixpence for the one which the dog had killed. Now, although he was welcome to advice, money was quite another thing ; so he went one way muttering something about law, and I another, with Cæsar at my heels, taking no notice of his threat. Well, sir, in a few days my servant came up to say that somebody wished to see me upon particular business, and I ordered him to be shown up. It was a blackguard-looking fellow, who put a piece of dirty paper in my hand ; summoned me to appear at some dog-hole or another, I forget where. Not understanding the business, I enclosed it to a legal friend, who returned an answer that it was a summons to the Court of R——ts, that no gentleman could go there, and that I had better let the thing take its course. I had forgotten all about it, when, in a few days, a piece of paper was brought to me, by which I found that the court adjudged me to pay £1, 2s. 6d. for damages and costs. I asked who brought it, and was told it was the son of the potato-merchant, accompanied by a tipstaff. I requested the pleasure of their company, and asked the legal gentleman what it was for.

" ' Eighteen shillings for ten rabbits destroyed by your dog, and 4s. 6d. for costs of court.'

" ' Ten rabbits ! ' exclaimed I ; ' why, he only killed one.'

" ' Yes, sir,' squeaked out the young potato-merchant; ' but it was a doe rabbit in the family way ; we counted nine young ones, all killed too ! '

" ' Shameful ! ' replied I. ' Pray, sir, did your father tell the court that the rabbits were not born ? '

" ' No, sir; father only said there was one doe rabbit and nine little ones killed. He asked 4s. 6d. for the old one, but only 1s. 6d. apiece for the young ones.'

" ' You should have been there yourself, sir,' observed the tipstaff.

" ' I wish Cæsar had left the rabbit alone. So it appears,' replied I, ' he only asked 3s. 6d. at first ; but by this Cæsarean operation I am nineteen shillings out of pocket.'—Now, sir, what do you think of that ? "

" I think that you should exclaim against the dishonesty of the potato-merchant, rather than the judgment of the court. Had you defended your own cause, you might have had justice."

" I don't know that. A man makes a claim against another, and takes his oath to it ; you must then either disprove it or pay the sum ; your own oath is of no avail against his. I called upon my legal friend, and told him how I had been treated, and he then narrated the following circumstance, which will explain what I mean :—

" He told me that he never knew of but one instance in which a respectable person had gained his cause, and in which, he was ashamed to say, that he was a party implicated. The means resorted to were as follows :—A Jew upholsterer sent in a bill to a relation of his for a chest of drawers, which had never been purchased or received. Refusing to pay, he was summoned to the Court of R——ts. Not knowing how to act, he applied to my informant, who, being under some obligations to his relative, did not like to refuse.

178

" ' I am afraid that you will have to pay,' said the attorney to his relation, when he heard the story.

" ' But I never had them, I can swear to it.'

" ' That's of no consequence; he will bring men to swear to the delivery. There are hundreds who are about the court who are ready to take any oath, at half-a-crown a head; and that will be sufficient. But, to oblige you, I will see what I can do.'

" They parted, and in a day or two my legal acquaintance called upon his relation, and told him that he had gained his cause. 'Rather at the expense of my conscience, I must acknowledge,' continued he; 'but one must fight these scoundrels with their own weapons '

" ' Well, and how was it?' inquired the other.

" ' Why, as I prophesied, he brought three men forward, who swore to the delivery of the goods. Aware that this would be the case, I had provided three others, who swore to their having been witness to the payment of the bill! This he was not prepared for, and the verdict was given in your favour.' "

"Is it possible," exclaimed Newton, "that such a court of Belial can exist in England?"

"Even so; and as there is no appeal, pray keep out of it. For my——"

But here the conversation was interrupted by the entrance of Mr. John Forster, who had returned from his consultation.

We have already described Mr. John Forster's character; we have now only to introduce his person. Mr. John Forster was about the middle height, rather inclined to corpulency, but with great show of muscular strength. His black nether garments and silk stockings fitted a leg which might have been envied by a porter, and his breadth of shoulder was extreme. He had a slouch, probably contracted by long poring over the desk; and his address was as abrupt as his appearance was unpolished. His forehead was large and bald, eye small and brilliant, and his cheeks had dropped down so as to increase the width of his lower jaw. Deep, yet not harsh lines were imprinted on the whole of his countenance, which indicated inflexibility and self-possession.

179

"Good morning, gentlemen," said he, as he entered the room; "I hope you have not been waiting long. May I request the pleasure of knowing who came first? 'First come, first served,' is an old motto."

"I believe this gentleman came first," replied the young man.

"Don't you *know*, sir? Is it only a *believe*?"

"I did arrive first, sir," said Newton; "but as I am not here upon legal business, I had rather wait until this gentleman has spoken to you."

"Not upon legal business—humph!" replied Mr. Forster, eyeing Newton. "Well, then, if that is the case, do me the favour to sit down in the office until I have communicated with this gentleman."

Newton, taking up his hat, walked out of the door, which was opened by Mr. Forster, and sat down in the next room until he should be summoned. Although the door between them was closed, it was easy to hear the sound of the voices within. For some minutes they fell upon Newton's ears; that of the young man like the loud yelping of a cur, that of his uncle like the surly growl of some ferocious beast. At last the door opened:

"But, sir," cried the young man in alto.

"Pay, sir, pay! I tell you, pay!" answered the lawyer, in a stentorian voice.

"But he has cheated me, sir!"

"Never mind—pay!"

"Charged twice their value, sir!"

"I tell you, pay!"

"But, sir, such imposition!"

"I have told you twenty times, sir, and now tell you again —and for the last time—pay!"

"Won't you take up my cause, sir, then?"

"No, sir! I have given you advice, and I will not pick your pocket! Good morning, sir;" and Mr. Forster, who had backed his client out of the room, shut the door in his face to prevent further discussion.

The young man looked a moment at the door after it was closed, and then turned round to Newton.

"If yours is really law business, take my advice, don't stay to see him; I'll take you to a man who *is* a lawyer. Here you'll get no law at all."

180

"Thank ye," replied Newton, laughing; "but mine is really not law business."

The noise of the handle of the door indicated that Mr. Forster was about to reopen it to summon Newton, and the young man, with a hasty good morning, brushed by Newton and hastened into the street.

CHAPTER XXIX

"*Hamlet.* Is not parchment made of sheepskin?
Horatio. Ay, my lord, and of calves' skins too.
Hamlet. They are sheep and calves which
   Seek out their assurance in that."
   —SHAKSPEARE.

THE door opened as intimated at the end of our last chapter, and Newton obeyed the injunction from the lawyer's eye to follow him into the room.

"Now, sir, your pleasure?" said Mr. Forster.

"I must introduce myself," replied Newton; "I am your nephew, Newton Forster."

"Humph! where's your documents in proof of your assertion?"

"I did not consider that anything further than my word was necessary. I am the son of your brother, Nicholas Forster, who resided many years at Overton."

"I never heard of Overton; Nicholas I recollect to have been the name of my third brother; but it is upwards of thirty years since I have seen or heard of him. I did not know whether he was alive or dead. Well, for the sake of argument, we'll allow that you are my nephew, what then?"

Newton coloured up at this peculiar reception. "What then, uncle? why, I did hope that you would have been glad to have seen me; but as you appear to be otherwise, I will wish you good morning;" and Newton moved towards the door.

"Stop, young man; I presume that you did not come for nothing! Before you go, tell me what you came for."

181

"To tell you the truth," replied Newton with emotion, "it was to ask your assistance and your advice; but——"

"But jumping up in a huff is not the way to obtain either. Sit down on that chair, and tell me what you came for."

"To request you would interest yourself in behalf of my father and myself; we are both out of employ, and require your assistance."

"Or probably I never should have seen you!"

"Most probably; we knew that you were in good circumstances and thriving in the world; and as long as we could support ourselves honestly, should not have thrust ourselves upon you. All we wish now is that you will, by your interest and recommendation, put us in the way of being again independent by our own exertions; which we did not consider too much to ask from a brother and an uncle."

"Humph! so first you keep aloof from me because you knew that I was able to assist you, and now you come to me for the same reason!"

"Had we received the least intimation from you that our presence would have been welcome, you would have seen us before."

"Perhaps so; but I did not know whether I had any relations alive."

"Had I been in your circumstances, uncle, I should have inquired."

"Humph! Well, young man, as I find that I have relations, I should like to hear a little about them; so now tell me all about your father and yourself."

Newton entered into a detail of the circumstances, with which the reader is already acquainted. When he had finished, his uncle, who had listened with profound attention, his eye fixed upon that of Newton as if to read his inmost thoughts, said, "It appears, then, that your father wishes to prosecute his business as optician. I am afraid that I cannot help him. I wear spectacles certainly when I read; but this pair has lasted me eleven years, and probably will as many more. You wish me to procure you a situation in an East Indiaman as third or fourth mate. I know nothing about the sea; I never saw it in my life; nor am I aware that I have a sailor in my acquaintance."

"Then, uncle, I will take my leave."

182

THE MERCHANT SERVICE

"Not so fast, young man; you said that you wanted my assistance and my advice. My assistance I cannot promise you, for the reasons I have stated; but my advice is at your service. Is it a legal point?"

"Not exactly, sir," replied Newton, who was mortified almost to tears; "still I must acknowledge that I now more than ever wish that the articles were in safe keeping and out of my hands." Newton then entered into a detail of the trunk being picked up at sea, and stated his having brought with him the most valuable of the property, that it might be deposited in safe hands.

"Humph!" observed his uncle, when he had finished. "You say that the articles are of value."

"Those who are judges consider the diamonds and the other articles to be worth nearly one hundred pounds; I cannot pretend to say what their real value is."

"And you have had these things in your possession these seven years?"

"I have, sir."

"Did it never occur to you, since you have been in distress, that the sale of these articles would have assisted you?"

"It often has occurred to me when I have found that the little I could earn was not sufficient for my father's support; but we had already decided that the property was not legally mine, and I dismissed the idea as soon as I could from my thoughts. Since then I have ascertained to whom the property belongs, and of course it has become more sacred."

"You said a minute ago that you now more than ever wished the property in safe keeping. Why so?"

"Because, disappointed in the hopes I had entertained of receiving your assistance, I foresaw that we should have more difficulties than ever to struggle against, and wished not to be in the way of temptation."

"You were right. Well then, bring me those articles to-morrow by one o'clock precisely; I will take charge of them, and give you a receipt. Good morning, nephew; very happy to have had the pleasure of making your acquaintance. Remember me kindly to my brother, and tell him I shall be happy to see him at one, precisely."

"Good morning, sir," replied Newton, with a faltering voice, as he hurried away to conceal the disappointment and indignation which he felt at this cool reception and dismissal.

"Not legally mine—humph! I like that boy," muttered the old lawyer to himself when Newton had disappeared. "Scratton!"

"Yes, sir," replied the clerk, opening the door.

"Fill up a cheque for five hundred pounds, self or bearer, and bring it to me to sign."

"Yes, sir."

"Is it this evening or to-morrow that I attend the arbitration meeting?"

"This evening, seven o'clock."

"What is the name of the party by whom I am employed?"

"Bosanquet, sir."

"East India director, is he not?"

"Yes, sir."

"Humph! that will do."

The clerk brought in the draft, which was put into his pocket-book without being signed; his coat was then buttoned up, and Mr. John Forster repaired to the chop-house, at which for twenty-five years he had seldom failed to make his appearance at the hour of three or four at the latest.

It was with a heavy heart that Newton returned to the inn in the Borough at which he left his father, whom he found looking out of window, precisely in the same seat and position where he had left him.

"Well, Newton, my boy, did you see my brother?"

"Yes, sir; but I am sorry to say that I have little hope of his being of service to us."

Newton then entered into a narration of what had passed.

"Why, really, Newton," said his father, in his single-heartedness, "I do not see such cause of despair. If he did doubt your being his nephew, how could he tell that you were? and if he had no interest with naval people, why, it's not his fault. As for my expecting him to break his spectacles on purpose to buy new ones of me, that's too much, and it would be foolish on his part. He said that he was very happy to have made your acquaintance, and that he should be glad to see me. I really don't know what more you could expect. I will call upon him to-morrow, since he wishes it. At five o'clock precisely, don't you say?"

"No, sir, at one."

"Well, then, at one; those who have nothing to do must suit their hours to those who are full of business. Recollect now, two o'clock precisely."

"One o'clock, sir."

"Ay, very true, one o'clock I meant; now let's go to dinner."

Nicholas Forster appeared in excellent spirits, and Newton, who did not like to undeceive him, was glad to retire at an early hour that he might be left to his own reflections, and form some plan as to their proceedings in consequence of this unexpected disappointment.

CHAPTER XXX

> " Now, by two-headed Janus,
> Nature hath framed strange fellows in her time ;
> Some that will ever more peep through their eyes,
> And laugh like parrots at a bagpiper ;
> And others of such vinegar aspect,
> That they'll not show their teeth in way of smile,
> Though Nestor swear the jest be laughable."
> —SHAKSPEARE.

THE next forenoon Nicholas and his son left the inn in good time to keep their appointment. The weather had changed, and the streets through which they passed were crowded with people who had taken advantage of the fine weather to prosecute business which had admitted of being postponed. Nicholas, who stared every way except the right, received many shoves and pushes, at which he expostulated, without the parties taking even the trouble to look behind them as they continued their course. This conduct produced a fit of reverie, out of which he was soon roused by another blow on the shoulder, which would twist him half round ; and thus he continued in an alternate state of reverie and excitement, until he was dragged by Newton to his brother's chambers. The clerk, who had been ordered to admit them, opened the parlour door, where they found Mr. John Forster sitting at his table, with his spectacles on, running through a brief.

185

"Your servant, young man. Nicholas Forster, I presume," said he, taking his eyes off the brief, and looking
at Forster without rising from his chair. "How do you do,
brother?"

"Are you my brother John?" interrogated Nicholas.

"I am John Forster," replied the lawyer.

"Well, then, I am really very glad to see you, brother,"
said Nicholas, extending his hand, which was taken with a
"Humph!"—(A minute's pause.)

"Young man, you're ten minutes past your time," said
John, turning to Newton. "I told you one o'clock precisely."

"I am afraid so," replied Newton; "but the streets were
crowded, and my father stopped several times."

"Why did he stop?"

"To expostulate with those who elbowed him; he is not
used to it."

"He soon will be if he stays here long. Brother Nicholas,"
said Forster, turning round; but perceiving that Nicholas had
taken up his watch, and was examining the interior, his intended remark was changed. "Brother Nicholas, what are
you doing with my watch?"

"It's very dirty," replied Nicholas, continuing his examination; "it must be taken to pieces."

"Indeed it shall not," replied John.

"Don't be alarmed, I'll do it myself, and charge you
nothing."

"Indeed you will not do it yourself, brother. My watch
goes very well when it's left alone. Do me the favour to
hand it to me."

Nicholas shut up the watch, and handed it to his brother
over the table. "It ought not to go well in that state,
brother."

"But I tell you that it does, brother," replied John, putting
the watch into his fob.

"I have brought the things that I mentioned, sir," said
Newton, taking them out of his handkerchief.

"Very well; have you the inventory?"

"Yes, sir, here it is."

"No. 1, a diamond ring.

"No. 2——"

"I should rather think that they were No. 3," observed

186

Nicholas, who had taken up his brother's spectacles. "You're not very short-sighted, brother."

"I am not, brother Nicholas; will you oblige me by giving me my spectacles?"

"Yes, I'll wipe them for you first," said Nicholas, commencing his polish with an old cotton handkerchief.

"Thanky, thanky, brother, that will do," replied John, holding out his hand for the spectacles, which he immediately put in the case and conveyed into his pocket. The lawyer then continued the inventory.

"It is all right, young man, and I will sign a receipt."

The receipt was signed, and the articles deposited in the iron chest.

"Now, brother Nicholas, I have no time to spare; have you anything to say to me?"

"No," replied Nicholas, starting up.

"Well, then, I have something to say to you. In the first place, I cannot help you in your profession (as I told my nephew yesterday), neither can I afford you any time, which is precious; so good-bye, brother. Here is something for you to read when you go home." John Forster took out his pocket-book, and gave him a sealed letter.

"Nephew, although I never saw the sea or knew a sailor in my life, yet the law pervades everywhere. An East India director, who is under obligations to me, has promised a situation for you as third mate on board of the *Bombay Castle*. Here is his address; call upon him, and all will be arranged. You may come here again before you sail; and I expect you will make proper arrangements for your father, who, if I can judge from what I have already seen, will lose that paper I have given him, which contains what is not to be picked up every day." Nicholas was in a deep reverie; the letter had dropped from his hand, and had fallen, unnoticed by him, on the carpet. Newton picked it up, and without Nicholas observing him, put it into his own pocket. "Now, good-bye, nephew take away my brother, pray. It's a good thing, I can tell you, sometimes to find out an uncle."

"I trust my conduct will prove me deserving of your kindness,' replied Newton, who was overjoyed at the unexpected issue of the meeting.

"I hope it will, young man. Good morning. Now, take

187

away your father; I'm busy;" and old Forster pulled out his spectacles and recommenced his brief.

Newton went up to his father, touched him on the shoulder, and said in a low tone, and nodding his head towards the door, "Come, father."

Nicholas got upon his legs, retreated a few steps, then turned round—"Brother, didn't you say something about a letter I was to put in the post?"

"No, I didn't," replied John shortly, not raising his eyes from the brief.

"Well, I really thought I heard something——"

"Come, father, my uncle's busy"

"Well, then, good-bye, brother."

"Good-bye," replied John, without looking up; and Newton with his father quitted the room.

No conversation passed during the walk to the inn, except an incidental remark of Nicholas, that it appeared to him that his brother was very busy.

When they arrived, Newton hastened to open the inclosure, and found it to be a draft for £500, which his uncle had ordered to be filled up the day before. Nicholas was lost in astonishment; and Newton, although he had already gained some insight into his uncle's character, was not a little surprised at his extreme liberality

"Now," cried Nicholas, rubbing his hands, "my improvement upon the duplex;" and the subject, brought up by himself, again led him away, and he was in deep thought.

There was a little piece of advice upon the envelope —"When you cash the draft, take the number of your notes." This was all; and it was carefully attended to by Newton, who took but £20, and left the remainder in the hands of the banker. The next day Newton called on the East India director, who gave him a letter to the captain of the ship, lying at Gravesend, and expecting to sail in a few days. To Gravesend he immediately repaired, and presenting his credentials, was favourably received, with an intimation that his company was required as soon as convenient.

Newton had now no other object to occupy him than to secure an asylum for his father, and this he was fortunate enough to meet with when he little expected. He

188

had disembarked at Greenwich, intending to return to London by the coach, when, having an hour to spare, he sauntered into the Hospital, to view a building which had so much of interest to a sailor. After a few minutes' survey he sat down on a bench occupied by several pensioners outside of the gate, wishing to enter into conversation with them relative to their condition, when one addressed the other—"Why, Stephen, since the old man's dead, there's no one that'll suit us; and I expects that we must contrive to do without blinkers at all. Jim Nelson told me the other day that the fellow in town as has his shop full of polished brass, all the world like the quarter-deck of the *Le Amphitrite,* when that sucking Honourable (what was his name?) commanded her —Jim said to me as how he charged him one-and-sixpence for a new piece of flint for his starboard eye. Now you know that old Wilkins never axed no more than three-pence. Now, how we're to pay at that rate comes to more than my knowledge. Jim hadn't the dirt, although he had brought his threepence; so his blinkers are left there in limbo."

"We must find out another man; the shop's to let, and all handy. Suppose we speak to the governor?"

"No use to speak to the governor; he don't use blinkers, and so won't have no fellow-feeling."

Newton entered into conversation, and found that an old man who gained his livelihood in a small shop close to the gate by repairing the spectacles of the pensioners had lately died, and that his loss was severely felt by them, as the opticians in town did not work at so reasonable a rate. Newton looked at the shop, which was small and comfortable, commanding a pleasant view of the river, and he was immediately convinced that it would suit his father. On his return he proposed it to Nicholas, who was delighted at the idea, and the next day they viewed the premises together, and took a short lease. In a few days Nicholas was settled in his new habitation, and busily employed in enabling the old pensioners to read the newspapers and count their points at cribbage. He liked his customers, and they liked him. His gains were equal to his wants; and, unless on particular occasions—such as a new coat, which, like his birthday, occurred but once a year—he never applied to the banker's for

189

assistance. Newton, as soon as his father was settled, and his own affairs arranged, called upon his uncle previous to his embarkation. Old Forster gave a satisfactory "Humph!" to his communication; and Newton, who had tact enough to make his visit short, received a cordial shake of the hand when he quitted the room.

CHAPTER XXXI

" Poor, short-lived things ! what plans we lay !
   Ah ! why forsake our native home,
   To distant climates speed away ?
   For self sticks close, where'er we roam.

Care follows hard, and soon o'ertakes
   The well-rigged ship ; the warlike steed
   Her destined quarry neeer forsakes ;
   Nor the wind flees with half the speed."

—COWPER.

NEWTON, who had made every preparation, as soon as he had taken leave of his uncle hastened to join his ship, which still remained at Gravesend waiting for the despatches to be closed by the twenty-four leaden heads presiding at Leadenhall Street. The passengers, with the exception of two, a Scotch Presbyterian divine and his wife, were still on shore, divided amongst the inns of the town, unwilling until the last moment to quit *terra firma* for so many months of sky and water, daily receiving a visit from the captain of the ship, who paid his respects to them all round, imparting any little intelligence he might have received as to the probable time of his departure.

When Newton arrived on board, he was received by the first mate, a rough, good-humoured, and intelligent man, about forty years of age, to whom he had already been introduced by the captain on his previous appearance with the letter from the director.

" Well, Mr. Forster, you're in very good time. As in all probability we shall be shipmates for a voyage or two, I trust that we shall be good friends. Now for your traps;" then

190

turning round, he addressed, in the Hindostanee language, two or three Lascars (fine, olive-coloured men, with black, curling, bushy hair), who immediately proceeded to hoist in the luggage.

The first mate, with an "Excuse me a moment," went forward to give some directions to the English seamen, leaving Forster to look about him. What he observed, we shall describe for the benefit of our readers.

The Indiaman was a twelve-hundred-ton ship, as large as one of the small class seventy-fours in the king's service, strongly built, with lofty bulwarks, and pierced on the upper deck for eighteen guns, which were mounted on the quarter-deck and forecastle. Abaft, a poop, higher than the bulwarks, extended forward between thirty and forty feet, under which was the cuddy or dining-room and state cabins appropriated to passengers. The poop, upon which you ascended by ladders on each side, was crowded with long ranges of coops, tenanted by every variety of domestic fowl, awaiting, in happy unconsciousness, the day when they should be required to supply the luxurious table provided by the captain. In some, turkeys stretched forth their long necks, and tapped the decks as they picked up some ant who crossed it in his industry. In others, the crowing of cocks and calling of the hens were incessant; or the geese, ranged up rank and file, waited but the signal from one of the party to raise up a simultaneous clamour, which as suddenly was remitted. Coop answered coop in variety of discord while the poulterer walked round and round to supply the wants of so many hundreds committed to his charge.

The booms before the mainmast were occupied by the large boats, which had been hoisted in preparatory to the voyage. They also composed a portion of the farmyard. The launch contained about fifty sheep, wedged together so close that it was with difficulty they could find room to twist their jaws round as they chewed the cud. The stern-sheets of the barge and yawl were filled with goats and two calves, who were the first destined victims to the butcher's knife; while the remainder of their space was occupied by hay and other provender, pressed down by powerful machinery into the smallest compass. The occasional baa-ing and bleating on the booms were answered by the lowing of the three milch-

191

cows between the hatchways of the deck below; where also were to be descried a few more coops, containing fowls and rabbits. The manger, forward, had been dedicated to the pigs; but as the cables were not yet unbent or bucklers shipped, they at present were confined by gratings between the main-deck guns, where they grunted at each passer-by, as if to ask for food.

The boats, hoisted up on the quarters, and the guys of the davits, to which they were suspended, formed the kitchen-gardens from which the passengers were to be supplied, and were loaded with bags containing onions, potatoes, turnips, carrots, beets, and cabbages, the latter in their full, round proportions hanging in a row upon the guys, like strings of heads which had been demanded in the wrath or the caprice of some despot of Mahomet's creed.

Forster descended the ladder to the main-deck, which he found equally encumbered with cabins for the passengers, trunks and bedding belonging to them, and many other articles which had not yet found their way into the hold, the hatches of which were open, and in which lanterns in every direction partially dispelled the gloom, and offered to his view a confused outline of bales and packages. Carpenters sawing deals, sailmakers roping the foot of an old mainsail, servants passing to and fro with dishes, Lascars jabbering in their own language, British seamen d—g their eyes, as usual, in plain English, gave an idea of confusion and want of method to Newton Forster, which, in a short time, he acknow-ledged himself to have been premature in having conceived. Where you have to provide for such a number, to separate the luggage of so many parties, from the heavy chest to the fragile bandbox, to take in cargo, and prepare for sea, all at the same time, there must be apparently confusion. In a few days everything finds its place; and what is of more consequence, is itself to be found as soon as it may be re-quired.

According to the regulations on board of East India ships, Forster messed below with the junior mates, midshipmen, surgeon's assistant, &c.; the first and second mates only having the privilege of constantly appearing at the captain's table, while the others receive but an occasional invitation. Forster soon became on intimate terms with his shipmates.

As they will, however, appear upon the stage when required to perform their parts, we shall at present confine ourselves to a description of the captain and the passengers.

Captain Drawlock was a man of about fifty years of age. Report said that in his youth he had been wild; and some of his contemporary commanders in the service were. wont to plague him by narrating divers freaks of former days, the recollection of which would create anything but a smile upon his face. Whether report and the other captains were correct or not in their assertions, Captain Drawlock was in appearance quite a different character at the time we introduce him. He was of sedate aspect, seldom smiled, and appeared to be wrapt up in the importance of the trust confided to him, particularly with respect to the young women who were sent out under his protection. He talked much of his responsibility, and divided the whole of his time between his chronometers and his young ladies, in both of which a trifling error was a source of irritation. Upon any deviation on the part of either, the first were rated carefully, the latter were rated soundly; considering the safety of the ship to be endangered on the one hand, and the character of his ship to be equally at stake on the other. It was maliciously observed that the latter were by far the more erratic of the two; and still more maliciously, that the austere behaviour on the part of Captain Drawlock was all pretence; that he was as susceptible as the youngest officer in the ship, and that the women found it out long before the voyage was completed.

It has been previously mentioned that all the passengers were on shore except two, a Presbyterian divine and his wife, the expenses attending whose passage out were provided for by a subscription which had been put on foot by some of the serious people of Glasgow, who prayed fervently, and enlivened their devotions with most excellent punch. The worthy clergyman (for worthy he was) thought of little else but his calling, and was a sincere, enthusiastic man, who was not to be checked by any consideration in what he considered to be his duty; but although he rebuked, he rebuked mildly, and never lost his temper. Stern in his creed, which allowed no loophole by which the offender might escape, still there was a kindness, and even a humility in his expostulation, which caused his zeal never to offend, and often to create serious reflection. His wife was a tall, handsome woman, who evidently had usurped an ascendency over her husband in all points unconnected with his calling. She, too, was devout; but hers was not the true religion, for it had not charity for its basis. She was clever and severe; spoke seldom, but the few words which escaped from her lips were sarcastic in their tendency.

The passengers who still remained on shore were numerous. There was an old colonel, returning from a three years' furlough, the major part of which had been spent at Cheltenham. He was an Adonis of sixty, with yellow cheeks and white teeth; a man who had passed through life doing nothing; had risen in his profession without having seen service, except on one occasion, and of that circumstance he made the most. With a good constitution and happy temperament, constantly in society, and constantly in requisition, he had grown old without being aware of it, and considered himself as much an object of interest with the other sex as he was formerly when a gay captain of five-and-twenty with good prospects. Amusing and easily amused, he had turned over the pages of the novel of life so uninterruptedly, that he had nearly arrived at the last page without being conscious that the finis was at hand.

Then there were two cadets from the college, full of themselves and their own consequence, fitted out with plenty of money and plenty of advice, both of which were destined to be thrown away. There was also a young writer, who talked of his mother, Lady Elizabeth, and other high relations, who had despatched him to India that he might be provided for by a cholera morbus or a lucrative post, a matter of perfect indifference to those who had sent him from England. Then, let me see—oh! there were two officers of a regiment at St. Helena, with tongues much longer than their purses, who in the fore part of the day condescended to talk nonsense to the fairer of the other sex, and in the evening to win a few pounds from the weaker of their own.

But all these were nobodies in the eyes of Captain Drawlock; they were a part of his cargo for which he was not responsible. The important part of his consignment were

THE MERCHANT SERVICE

four unmarried women; three of them were young, good-looking, and poor; the other ill-favoured, old, but rich. We must give precedence to wealth and age. The lady last mentioned was a Miss Tavistock, born and educated in the City, where her father had long been at the head of the well-established firm of Tavistock, Bottlecock & Co., dyers, calenderers, and scourers. As we before observed, she was the fortunate sole heiress to her father's accumulation, which might amount to nearly thirty thousand pounds, but had been little gifted by Nature. In fact, she was what you may style most preposterously ugly; her figure was large and masculine, her hair red, and her face very deeply indented with the smallpox. As a man, she would have been considered the essence of vulgarity; as a woman, she was the quintessence—so much so, that she had arrived at the age of thirty-six without having, notwithstanding her property, received any attentions which could be construed into an offer. As we always seek most eagerly that which we find most difficult to obtain, she was possessed with *une fureur de se marier*, and as a last resource had resolved to go out to India, where she had been informed that "anything white" was acceptable. This passion for matrimony (for with her it had so become, if not a disease) occupied her whole thoughts; but she attempted to veil them by always pretending to be extremely sensitive and refined; to be shocked at anything which had the slightest allusion to the "increase and multiply," and constantly lamented the extreme fragility of her constitution, to which her athletic bony frame gave so determined a lie, that her hearers were struck dumb with the barefaced assertion. Miss Tavistock had kept up a correspondence with an old schoolmate, who had been taken away early to join her friends in India, and had there married. As her hopes of matrimony dwindled away, so did her affection for her old friend appear, by her letters, to increase. At last, in answer to a letter, in which she declared that she would like to come out and (as she had long made a resolution to continue single) adopt one of her friend's children, and pass her days with them, she received an answer, stating how happy they would be to receive her, and personally renew the old friendship, if indeed she could be persuaded to venture upon so long and venturous a passage. Whether this answer was sincere or not,

195

Miss Tavistock took advantage of the invitation, and writing to intimate her speedy arrival, took her passage in the *Bombay Castle.*

The other three spinsters were sisters—Charlotte, Laura, and Isabel Revel, daughters of the Honourable Mr. Revel, a roué of excellent family, who had married for money, and had dissipated all his wife's fortune except the marriage settlement of £600 per annum. Their mother was a selfish, short-sighted, manœuvring woman, whose great anxiety was to form establishments for her daughters, or, in other terms, remove the expense of their maintenance from her own to the shoulders of other people, very indifferent whether the change might contribute to their happiness or not. Mr. Revel may be said to have long deserted his family; he lived nobody knew where, and seldom called, unless it was to "raise the wind" upon his wife, who by entreaties and threats was necessitated to purchase his absence by a sacrifice of more than half her income. Of his daughters he took little notice when he did make his appearance; and if so, it was generally in terms more calculated to raise the blush of indignant modesty than to stimulate the natural feelings of affection of a daughter towards a parent. Their mother, whose income was not sufficient to meet the demands of a worthless husband in addition to the necessary expenses attendant on three grown-up women, was unceasing in her attempts to get them off her hands; but we will introduce a conversation which took place between her and a sedate-looking, powdered old gentleman, who had long been considered as a "friend of the family," as thereby more light will perhaps be thrown upon her character.

"The fact is, my dear Mr. Heaviside, that I hardly know what to do. Mr. Revel, who is very intimate with theatre people, proposed that they should try their fortune on the stage. He says (and indeed there is some truth in it) that nowadays the best plan for a man to make himself popular is to be sent to Newgate, and the best chance that a girl has of a coronet is to become an actress. Well, I did not much like the idea, but at last I consented. Isabel, my youngest, is, you know, very handsome in her person, and sings remarkably well, and we arranged that she should go on first, and if she succeeded, that her sister Charlotte should follow her; but Isabel is of a very obstinate disposition, and when we

196

proposed it to her she peremptorily refused, and declared that she would go out as governess, or anything, rather than consent. I tried what coaxing would do, and her father tried threatening; but all in vain. This was about a year ago, and she is now only seventeen; but she ever was a most decided, a most obstinate character."

"Very undutiful, indeed, ma'am; she might have been a duchess before this—a very foolish girl, indeed, ma'am," observed the gentleman.

"Well, Mr. Heaviside, we then thought that Charlotte, our eldest, had the next best chance of success. Although not by any means so good-looking as her sister—indeed, to tell you the truth, Mr. Heaviside, which I would not do to everybody, but I know that you can keep a secret—Charlotte is now nearly thirty years old, and her sister, Laura, only one year younger."

"Is it possible, madam?" replied Mr. Heaviside, looking at the lady with well-feigned astonishment.

"Yes, indeed," replied the lady, who had forgotten that in telling her daughters' secrets she had let out her own; "but I was married so young, so very young, that I am almost ashamed to think of it. Well, Mr. Heaviside, as I was saying, although not so good-looking as her sister, Mr. Revel, who is a good judge in these matters, declared that by the theatre lights Charlotte would be reckoned a very fine woman. We proposed it to her, and after a little pouting she consented; the only difficulty was, whether she should attempt tragedy or comedy. Her features were considered rather too sharp for comedy, and her figure not quite tall enough for tragedy. She herself preferred tragedy, which decided the point; and Mr. Revel, who knows all the actors, persuaded Mr. Y—— (you know who I mean, the great tragic actor) to come here and give his opinion of her recitation. Mr. Y—— was excessively polite; declared that she was a young lady of great talent, but that a slight lisp, which she has, unfitted her most decidedly for tragedy. Of course it was abandoned for comedy, which she studied some time; and when we considered her competent, Mr. Revel had interest enough to induce the great Mr. M—— to come and give his opinion. Charlotte performed her part, as I thought, remarkably well, and when she had finished she left the room that Mr. M——

197

might not be checked by her presence from giving me his unbiassed opinion."

"Which was favourable, ma'am, I presume; for if not fitted for the one, she naturally must have been fit for the other."

"So I thought," replied the lady to this polite *non sequitur* of the gentleman. "But Mr. M—— is a very odd man, and, if I must say it, not very polite. What do you think, Mr. Heaviside? As soon as she left the room he rose from his chair, and, twisting up the corner of his mouth as he looked me in the face, he said, 'Madam, it is my opinion that your daughter's comedy, whenever she makes her appearance on the boards, will, to use a Yankee expression, be most particularly damned! I wish you a very good morning.'"

"Very rude indeed, madam; most excessively unpolite of Mr. M——. I should not have thought it possible."

"Well, Mr. Heaviside, as for Laura, poor thing! you are aware that she is not quite so clever as she might be; she never had any memory when a child—she never could recollect the evening hymn if she missed it two nights running, so that acting was out of the question with her. So that all my hopes of their forming a splendid establishment by that channel have vanished. Now, my dear Mr. Heaviside, what would you propose?"

"Why, really, ma'am, it is so difficult to advise in these times; but if anxious to dispose of your daughters, why not send them out to India?"

"We have thought of it several times; for Mr. Revel has an uncle there unmarried, and they say very rich. He is a colonel in the Bombay marine, I believe."

"More probably in the Bengal army, ma'am."

"Well, I believe you are right; but I know it is in the Company's service. But the old gentleman hates my husband, and will not have anything to say to him. I did write a very civil letter to him, in which I just hinted how glad one or two of my daughters would be to take care of his house, but he never condescended to give me an answer. I am told that he is a very unpleasant man."

"A difficult thing to advise, ma'am, very difficult indeed; but I can tell you a circumstance which occurred about five years ago, when a similar application to a relative in India was made by a friend of mine. It was no more attended to than yours has been. Nevertheless, as it was supposed the answer had miscarried, the young lady was sent out to her relative with a decent equipment and a letter of introduction. Her relation was very much surprised; but what could he do? he could not permit the young lady to remain without a roof over her head, so he received her; and as he did not like to say how he had been treated, he held his tongue. The young lady in the course of three months made a very good match, and is, to my knowledge, constantly sending home India shawls and other handsome presents to her mother.

"Indeed, Mr. Heaviside, then do you advise——"

"It is difficult, extremely difficult, to advise upon so nice a point. I only state the fact, my dear madam; I should think the colonel must feel the want of female society; but, God bless me! it's nearly two o'clock. Good morning, my dear Mrs. Revel—good morning."

"Good morning, my dear Mr. Heaviside; 'tis very kind of you to call in this sociable way and chat an hour or two. Good morning."

The result of the above conversation was a consultation between Mr. Revel and his wife upon their first meeting. Mr. Revel was delighted with the plan, not so much caring at the disposal of his daughters as he was pleased with the idea of annoying his uncle, from whom he at one time had great expectations; but as it was necessary to be circumspect, especially with Isabel, Mr. Revel took the opportunity of a subsequent visit to state that he had received a letter from his uncle in India wishing one of his daughters to go out and live with him. In a few months he read another letter (composed by himself, and copied in another hand), earnestly desiring that they might all come out to him, as it would be much to their advantage. The reluctance of the two eldest was removed by pointing out the magnificent establishments they might secure; the consent of Isabel by a statement of difficulty and debt on the part of her parents, which would end in beggary if not relieved from the burden of their support.

By insuring her life, a sum of money sufficient for their outfit and passage was raised on Mrs. Revel's marriage settlement; and the three Miss Revels were thus shipped off by their affectionate parents as a "venture" in the *Bombay Castle*.

CHAPTER XXXII

" Thus the rich vessel moves in trim array,
Like some fair virgin on her bridal day :
Thus like a swan she cleaves the watery plain,
The pride and wonder of the Ægean main.

The natives, while the ship departs the land,
Ashore, with admiration gazing stand ;
Majestically slow before the breeze,
In silent pomp she marches on the seas."

—FALCONER.

MUCH to the satisfaction of Captain Drawlock, the chrono-meters and the ladies were safe on board, and the *Bombay Castle* proceeded to the Downs, where she was joined by the purser, charged with the despatches of the august directors. Once upon a time a director was a very great man, and the India Board a very great Board. There must have been a very great many plums in the pudding, for in this world people do not take trouble for nothing ; and until later years, how eagerly, how perseveringly was this situation applied for— what supplicating advertisements—what fawning and wheed-ling promises of attention to the interests of the proprietors— "your voices, good people !" But now nobody is so particu-larly anxious to be a director, because another Board "bigger than he" has played the kittiwake, and forced it to disgorge for the consumption of its superior—I mean the Board of Control; the reader has probably heard of it; the Board which, not content with the European residents in India being deprived of their proudest birthright, "the liberty of the press," would even prevent them from having justice awarded to them, by directing two tame elephants (thereby implying two —— ——) to be placed on each side of a wild one (thereby implying an honest and conscientious man). Notwithstanding all which, for the present, the tongue, the ears, and the eyes are permitted to be made discreet use of, although I believe that the new charter is to have a clause introduced to the contrary.

The prevalent disease of the time we live in is ophthalmia

THE MERCHANT SERVICE

of intellect, affecting the higher classes. Monarchs, stone-blind, have tumbled headlong from their thrones, and princes have been conducted by their subjects out of their principali-ties. The aristocracy are purblind, and cannot distinctly decipher the "signs of the times." The hierarchy cannot discover why people would have religion at a reduced price; in fact, they are all blind, and will not perceive that an enormous mass, in the shape of public opinion, hangs over their heads and threatens to annihilate them. Forgetting that kings, and princes, and lords, spiritual or temporal, have all been raised to their various degrees of exaltation by public opinion alone, they talk of legitimacy, of vested rights, and Deuteronomy. Well, if there is to be a general tumble, thank God, I can't fall far!

We left the *Bombay Castle* in the Downs, where she re-mained until joined by several other India vessels. On the arrival of a large frigate, who had orders to escort them as far as the island of St. Helena, they all weighed, and bore down the Channel before a strong S.E. gale. The first ten days of a voyage there is seldom much communication between those belonging to the ship and the passengers; the former are too much occupied in making things ship-shape, and the latter with the miseries of sea-sickness. An adverse gale in the Bay of Biscay, with which they had to contend, did not at all contribute to the recovery of the digestive powers of the latter; and it was not until a day or two before the arrival of the convoy at Madeira that the ribbon of a bonnet was to be seen fluttering in the breeze which swept the decks of the *Bombay Castle*.

The first which rose up from the quarter-deck hatchway was one that encircled the head of Mrs. Ferguson, the wife of the Presbyterian divine, who crawled up the ladder, sup-ported on one side by her husband, and on the other by the assiduous Captain Drawlock.

"Very well done, ma'am, indeed!" said the captain, with an encouraging smile, as the lady seized hold of the copper stanchions which surrounded the skylights to support herself when she had gained the deck. "You're a capital sailor, and have by your conduct set an example to other ladies, as I have no doubt your husband does to the gentlemen. Now allow me to offer you my arm."

201

"Will you take mine also, my dear," said Mr. Ferguson.

"No, Mr. Ferguson," replied the lady tartly; "I think it is enough for you to take care of yourself. Recollect your Scripture proverb of 'the blind leading the blind.' I have no inclination to tumble into one of those pits," added she, pointing to the hatchway.

Captain Drawlock very civilly dragged the lady to the weather-side of the quarter-deck, where, after in vain attempting to walk, she sat down on one of the carronade slides.

"The fresh air will soon revive you, ma'am; you'll be much better directly," observed the attentive captain. "I beg your pardon one moment, but there is another lady coming out of the cuddy."

The cabins abaft the cuddy, or dining-room, were generally occupied by the more distinguished and wealthy passengers (a proportionate sum being charged extra for them). The good people of Glasgow, with a due regard to economy, had not run themselves into such unnecessary expenses for the passage of Mr. and Mrs. Ferguson. Mr. Revel, aware of the effect produced by an appearance of wealth, had taken one of them for his daughters. The other had been secured by Miss Tavistock, much to the gratification of the captain, who thus had his unmarried ladies and his chronometers both immediately under his own eye.

The personage who had thus called the attention of the captain was Isabel Revel, whom, although she has already been mentioned, it will be necessary to describe more particularly to the reader.

Isabel Revel was now eighteen years old, endowed with a mind so superior, that had not her talents been checked by a natural reserve, she might have stepped from the crowd and have been hailed as a genius. She had been brought up by a foolish mother, and had in her earlier years been checked by her two insipid sisters, who assumed over her an authority which their age alone could warrant. Seldom, if ever, permitted to appear when there was company, that she might not "spoil the market" of the eldest, she had in her solitude applied much to reading, and thus had her mind been highly cultivated.

The conduct of her father entitled him to no respect, the

heartlessness of her mother to no esteem, the tyranny of her sisters to no affection, yet did she strive to render all. Until the age of sixteen she had been the Cinderella of the family, during which period of seclusion she had learned to think and to act for herself.

. Her figure was a little above the middle size, light and elegant; her features beautiful, with an expression of seriousness, arising probably from speaking little and reflecting much. Yet she possessed a mind ardent and enthusiastic, which often bore her away in animated discourse, until the eye of admiration fixed upon her would suddenly close her lips, for her modesty and her genius were at perpetual variance.

It is well known to most of my readers that woman is a problem; but it may not be as well known that nowadays she is a mathematical problem. Yet so it is. As in the latter you have certain known quantities given by which you are to find a quantity unknown, so in a lady you have the hand, the foot, the mouth, &c., apparent; and 'tis only by calculation, now that modern dresses are made so full, that you can arrive at a just estimate of her approach to total perfection. All good arithmeticians, as they scrutinised the outward and the visible of Isabel Revel, were perfectly assured as to her quotient. But if I talked for hours, I could say no more than that she was one of those ideal images created in the dream of youth and poetry, fairly embodied in flesh and blood. As her father had justly surmised, could she have been persuaded to have tried her fortune on the stage, she had personal attractions, depth of feeling, and vivacity of mind to have rendered her one of the very first of the profession, to excel in which, perhaps, there is more correct judgment and versatility of talent required than any other, and would have had a fair prospect of obtaining that coronet which has occasionally been the reward of those fair dames who "stoop to conquer."

Mr. Revel, who had been made acquainted with the customs on board of East India ships, had been introduced to Mrs. Ferguson, and had requested her to take upon herself the office of chaperon to his daughters during the passage—a nominal charge indeed, yet considered to be etiquette. Mrs. Ferguson, pleased with the gentlemanlike demeanour and personal appearance of Mr Revel, and perhaps at the same time not sorry to have an authority to find fault, had most graciously acquiesced; and the three Miss Revels were considered to be under her protection.

As I said before, Miss Isabel Revel made her appearance not unattended, for she was escorted by Doctor Plausible, the surgeon of the ship. And now I must again digress while I introduce that gentleman. I never shall get that poor girl from the cuddy-door.

Doctor Plausible had been summoned to prescribe for Miss Laura Revel, who suffered extremely from the motion of the vessel and the remedies which she had applied to relieve her uneasiness. Miss Laura Revel had been told by somebody previous to her embarkation that the most effectual remedy for sea-sickness was gingerbread. In pursuance of the advice received, she had provided herself with ten or twelve squares of this commodity, about one foot by eighteen inches, which squares she had commenced upon as soon as she came on board, and had never ceased to swallow, notwithstanding various interruptions. The more did her stomach reject it the more did she force it down, until, what with deglutition *et vice versâ*, she had been reduced to a state of extreme weakness, attended with fever.

How many panaceas have been offered without success for two evils—sea-sickness and hydrophobia! and between these two there appears to be a link, for sea-sickness as surely ends in hydrophobia, as hydrophobia does in death. The sovereign remedy prescribed when I first went to sea was a piece of fat pork tied to a string, to be swallowed, and then pulled up again; the dose to be repeated until effective. I should not have mentioned this well known remedy, as it has long been superseded by other nostrums, were it not that this maritime prescription has been the origin of two modern improvements in the medical catalogue—one is the stomach-pump, evidently borrowed from this simple engine; the other is the very successful prescription now in vogue, to those who are weak in the digestive organs, to eat fat bacon for breakfast, which I have no doubt was suggested to Dr. Vance from what he had been eye-witness to on board of a man-of-war.

But here I am digressing again from Doctor Plausible to Dr. Vance. Reader, I never lose the opportunity of drawing a moral; and what an important one is here! Observe how difficult it is to regain the right path when once you have

204

quitted it. Let my error be a warning to you in your journey
through life, and my digressions preserve you from diverging
from the beaten track, which, as the Americans would say,
leads clean slick on to happiness and peace.

Doctor Plausible was a personable man, apparently about
five-and-thirty years old; he wore a little powder in his hair,
black silk stockings, and knee-breeches. In this I consider
Doctor Plausible was right; the above look much more scientific than Wellington trousers; and much depends upon the
exterior. He was quite a ladies' man; talked to them about
their extreme sensibility, their peculiar fineness of organic
structure, their delicacy of nerves, and soothed his patients
more by flattery than by physic. Having discovered that
Miss Laura was not inclined to give up her gingerbread, he
immediately acknowledged its virtues, but recommended that
it should be cut into extremely small dice, and allowed, as it
were, to melt away upon the tongue; stating that her digestive organs were so refined and delicate, that they would not
permit themselves to be loaded with any large particles, even
of farinaceous compound. Isabel Revel, who had been informed that Mrs. Ferguson was on deck, expressed a wish to
escape from the confined atmosphere of the cabin; and Doctor
Plausible, as soon as he had prescribed for Miss Laura, offered
Miss Isabel his services, which, for want of a better perhaps,
were accepted.

The ship at this time had a great deal of motion. The gale
was spent; but the sea created by the violence of the wind
had not yet subsided, and the waves continued still to rise
and fall again, like the panting breasts of men who have just
desisted from fierce contention. Captain Drawlock hastened
over to receive his charge from the hands of the medical
attendant; and paying Isabel some compliments on her appearance, was handing her over to the weather-side, where
Mrs. Ferguson was seated, when a sea of larger dimensions
than usual careened the ship to what the sailors term a "heavy
lurch." The decks were wet and slippery. Captain Drawlock
lost his footing, and was thrown to leeward. Isabel would
most certainly have kept him company, and indeed was
already under weigh for the lee-scuppers, had not it been
that Newton Forster, who stood near, caught her round the
waist, and prevented her from falling.

It certainly was a great presumption to take a young lady round the waist previous to any introduction; but at sea we are not very particular; and if we do perceive that a lady is in danger of a severe fall, we do not stand upon etiquette. What is more remarkable, we generally find that the ladies excuse our unpolished manners, either upon the score of our good intentions, or because there is nothing so very impertinent in them after all. Certain it is that Isabel, as soon as she had recovered from her alarm, thanked Newton Forster, with a sweet smile, for his timely aid, as she again took the arm of Captain Drawlock, who escorted her to the weather side of the quarter-deck.

"I have brought you one of your protégées, Mrs. Ferguson," said Captain Drawlock. "How do you feel, Miss Revel?"

"Like most young ladies, sir, a little giddy," replied Isabel. "I hope you were not hurt, Captain Drawlock; I'm afraid that you fell by paying more attention to me than to yourself."

"My duty, Miss Revel. Allow me to add, my pleasure," replied the captain, bowing.

"That's very politely said, Captain Drawlock," replied Isabel.

"Almost too polite, I think," observed Mrs. Ferguson (who was out of humour at not being the first object of attention), "considering that Captain Drawlock is a married man with seven children." The captain looked glum, and Miss Revel observing it, turned the conversation by inquiring, "Who was that gentleman who saved me from falling?"

"Mr. Newton Forster, one of the mates of the vessel. Would you like to walk, Miss Revel, or remain where you are?"

"Thank you, I will stay with Mrs. Ferguson."

The gentlemen passengers had as yet but occasionally appeared on deck. Men generally suffer more from the distressing sickness than women. As soon, however, as the news had been communicated below that the ladies were on deck, some of the gentlemen immediately repaired to their trunks to make themselves presentable, and then hastened on deck. The first on deck was the old colonel, who tottered up the hatchway, and by dint of seizing rope after rope, at last succeeded in advancing his lines to within hearing range of Mrs. Ferguson, to whom he had been formally introduced.

THE MERCHANT SERVICE

He commenced by lamenting his unfortunate sufferings, which had prevented him from paying those attentions, ever to him a source of enjoyment and gratification; but he was a martyr —quite a martyr; never felt any sensation which could be compared to it, except when he was struck in the breast with a spent ball in the battle of ——; that their appearance had made him feel revived already; that as the world would be a dark prison without the sun, so would a ship be without the society of ladies; commenced a description of Calcutta, and then—made a hasty retreat to the lee-gangway.

The young writer next made his appearance, followed by two boys, who were going out as cadets; the first, with a new pair of grey kid gloves, the others in their uniforms. The writer descanted long upon his own miseries, without any inquiry or condolement for the sufferings of the ladies. The cadets said nothing, but stared so much at Isabel Revel that she dropped her veil.

The ladies had been about a quarter of an hour on deck when the sun, which had not shown itself for two days, gleamed through the clouds. Newton, who was officer of the watch, and had been accustomed, when with Mr. Berecroft, to work a chronometer, interrupted the captain, who was leaning on the carronade talking to Mrs. Ferguson.

"The sun is out, and the horizon pretty clear, sir; you may have sights for the chronometers."

"Yes, indeed," said the captain, looking up; "be quick, and fetch my sextant. You'll excuse me, ladies, but the chronometers must be attended to."

"In preference to us, Captain Drawlock? Fie, for shame!" replied Mrs. Ferguson.

"Why, not exactly," replied the captain, "not exactly; but the fact is, that the sun may go in again."

"And we can stay out, I presume?" replied Isabel, laughing. "I think, Mrs. Ferguson, we ought to go in too."

"But, my dear young lady, if the sun goes in, I shall not get a sight!"

"And if we go in, you will not get a sight either," replied Mrs. Ferguson.

"Between the two, sir," observed Newton, handing Captain Drawlock his sextant, "you stand a chance of losing both. There's no time to spare; I'm all ready."

Captain Drawlock walked to the break of the gangway, so far concealed from the ladies that they c uld not perceive that he was looking through his sextant, the use of which they did not comprehend, having never seen one before. Newton stood at the capstern, with his eyes fixed on the watch.

"Captain Drawlock," said Mrs. Ferguson, calling to him, "allow me to observe——"

"Stop," cried Captain Drawlock, in a loud voice. Newton, to whom this was addressed, noted the time.

"Good heavens! what can be the matter?" said Mrs. Ferguson, with astonishment, to those near her; "how excessively rude of Captain Drawlock; what can it be?" continued she, addressing the colonel, who had rejoined them.

"Really, madam, I cannot tell; but it is my duty to inquire," replied the colonel, who, going up to Captain Drawlock, said, "Have the ladies already so fallen in your estimation——."

"Forty degrees!" cried Captain Drawlock, who was intent upon his sextant. "Excuse me, sir, just now."

"When will you be at leisure, sir?" resumed the colonel haughtily.

"Twenty-six minutes," continued the captain, reading off his sextant.

"A little sooner, I should hope, sir," retorted the colonel.

"Forty-five seconds."

"This is really quite insufferable! Miss Revel, we had better go in."

"Stop!" again cried Captain Drawlock, in a loud voice.

"Stop!" repeated Mrs. Ferguson angrily; "surely we are not slaves."

Newton, who heard what was passing, could not repress his laughter.

"Indeed, I am sure there must be some mistake, Mrs. Ferguson," observed Isabel. "Wait a little."

"Forty-six minutes, thirty seconds," again read off the captain. "Capital sights both! but the sun is behind that dark cloud, and we shall have no more of his presence."

"Nor of ours, I assure you, sir," said Mrs. Ferguson, rising as Captain Drawlock walked from the gangway to the capstern.

"Why, my dear madam, what is the matter?"

"We have not been accustomed to such peremptory language, sir. It may be the custom on board ship to holla 'stop' to ladies when they address you, or express a wish to leave the deck."

"My dearest madam, I do assure you, upon my honour, that you are under a mistake. I ordered Mr. Forster to stop, not you."

"Mr. Forster!" replied the lady; "why, he was standing still the whole time!"

It was not until the whole system of taking sights for chronometers had been satisfactorily explained that the lady recovered her good-humour. While the captain was thus employed with Mrs. Ferguson, Newton, although it was not necessary, explained the mystery to Miss Revel, who, with Mrs. Ferguson, soon after quitted the deck.

The sights taken proved the ship to be to the eastward of her reckoning. The other ships in company had made the same discovery, and the course was altered one quarter of a point. In two days they dropped their anchor in Funchal Roads.

But I must for a little while recross the Bay of Biscay, and, with my reader, look into the chambers of Mr. John Forster.

CHAPTER XXXIII

" Look
Upon this child—I saved her, must not leave
Her life to chance ; but point me out some nook
Of safety, where she less may shrink and grieve.

.   .   .   .   .   .

This child, who, parentless, is therefore mine."

—BYRON.

A FEW minutes after Newton had quitted the chambers of his uncle the clerk made his appearance, announcing to Mr. John Forster that a gentleman requested to speak to him.

"I asked the gentleman's name, sir," observed the clerk, shutting-to the door, "but he did not choose to give it. He has a little girl with him."

"Very well, Scratton; the little girl cannot concern me," replied the old lawyer; "ask him to walk in;" and he again conned over the brief, not choosing to lose the minute which might elapse before he was again to be interrupted. The door was reopened, and Edward Forster, with Amber holding him by the hand, entered the room.

"Your servant, sir. Scratton, a chair—two chairs, Scratton. I beg your pardon, young lady."

When the clerk had retired, Mr. John Forster commenced as usual. "Now, sir, may I request the favour of asking your business with me?"

"You do not recollect me; nor am I surprised at it, as it is fifteen years since we last met. Time and suffering, which have worn me to a skeleton, have also worn out the remembrance of a brother. I am Edward Forster."

"Edward Forster! humph! Well, I did not recollect you; but I'm very glad to see you, brother. Very strange— never have heard of one of my family for years, and now they all turn up at once! No sooner get rid of one, than up starts another. Nicholas came from the Lord knows where the other day."

Edward Forster, who was better acquainted with his brother's character than Newton, took no notice of the abruptness of his remarks, but replied—

"Nicholas! Is he, then, alive? I shall be delighted to see him."

"Humph!" replied John, "I was delighted to get rid of him. Take care of your watch or spectacles when you meet him."

"Indeed, brother! I trust he is not such a character."

"But he is a character, I can tell you; not what you suppose—he's honest enough. Let me see—if my memory serves me, brother Edward, we last met when you were passing through London on your way to ——, having been invalided, and having obtained a pension of forty pounds per annum for a severe wound received in action. And pray, brother, where have you been ever since?"

"At the same spot, from which I probably never should have been induced to remove, had it not been for the sake of this little girl who is now with me."

"And pray who may be that little girl? Is she your daughter?"

"Only by adoption."

"Humph, brother! for a half-pay lieutenant, that appears rather an expensive whim!—bad enough to maintain children of our own begetting."

"You say true," replied Edward; "but if in this instance I have incurred an expense and responsibility, it must be considered to be more my misfortune than my fault." Edward Forster then entered into the particulars connected with Amber's rescue. "You must acknowledge, brother John," observed Edward, as he closed his narrative, "that I could not well have acted otherwise; you would not yourself."

"Humph! I don't know that; but this I do know, that you had better have stayed at home!"

"Perhaps so, considering the forlorn prospects of the child; but we must not judge. The same Providence which willed that she should be so miraculously saved, also willed that I should be her protector;—why otherwise did the dog lay her at my feet?"

"Because it had been taught to 'fetch and carry,' I suppose; but however, brother Edward, I have no right to question your conduct. If the girl is as good as she is pretty, why all the better for her; but as I am rather busy, let me ask if you have any more to say to me?"

"I have, John; and the discourse we have had is preliminary. I am here with a child, forced upon me, I may say, but still as dear to me as if she were mine own. You must be aware that I have nothing but my pension and half-pay to subsist upon. I can save nothing. My health is undermined and my life precarious. Last winter I never expected to quit my bed again; and as I lay in it, the thought naturally occurred of the forlorn and helpless state in which this poor little girl would be in case of my decease. In a lonely cottage, without money, without family or friends to apply to, without any one near her being made acquainted with her unfortunate history, what would have become of her? It was this reflection which determined me, if my life was spared, as soon as my health would permit, to come to you, the only relative I was certain of still having in the world, that I might acquaint you with her existence, and, with her history, confide to you the few articles of dress which she wore when rescued, and which may eventually lead

211

to her recognition—a case of extreme doubt and difficulty,
I grant; but the ways of Providence are mysterious, and her
return to the arms of her friends will not be more wonderful
than her preservation on that dreadful night.   Brother! I
never have applied to you in my own behalf, although conscious how ample are your means—and I never will; but I
do now plead in favour of this dear child.   Worn out as I am,
my pilgrimage on earth can be but short; and if you would
smooth the pillow of a dying brother, promise him now that
you will extend your bounty to this poor orphan when I'm
no more ! ''

Edward Forster's voice was tremulous at the close of his
appeal, and his brother appeared to be affected.   There was
a silence of a minute, when the customary "humph !" was
ejaculated, and John Forster then continued : " A very foolish
business, brother—very foolish, indeed.   When Nicholas and
his son came here the other day and applied to me, why it
was all very well—there was relationship ; but really, to put
another man's child upon me ! ''

" Not while it pleases Heaven to spare my life, brother.''

" ' May you live a thousand years ! ' then, as the Spanish
say ; but however, brother Edward, as you say, the poor
thing must not starve ; so if I am to take care of a child of
another man's begetting as soon as you are dead, I can only
say it will very much increase my sorrow at your loss.   Come
here, little one.   What's your name ? ''

" Amber.''

" Amber ! who the devil gave you that fool's name ? ''

" I did, brother,'' replied Edward ; " I thought it appropriate.''

" Humph ! really can't see why.   Why did you not call her
Sukey, or some name fit for a Christian ?   Amber !   Amber's
a gum, is it not ?   Stop, let's see what Johnson says.''

The lawyer went to a case of books which were in the next
room, and returned with a quarto.

" Now,'' said he, seating himself; " AG—AL—AM—Am-
bassador—Ambassadress—Amber !—humph ! here it is : ' A
yellow, transparent substance of a gummous or bituminous
consistence, but of a resinous taste, and a smell like oil of
turpentine ; chiefly found in the Baltic Sea or the coast of
Prussia.'   Humph !   ' Some have imagined it to consist of the

212

tears of birds ; others the '—humph !—' of a beast ; others the scum of the Lake Cephesis, near the Atlantic ; others a congelation in some fountains, where it is found swimming like pitch.' Really, brother," continued the lawyer, fixing his eyes on the little girl and shutting the book, "I can't see the analogy."

"Be her godfather, my dear brother, and call her any name you please."

"Humph !"

"Pray, papa," said Amber, turning to Edward Forster, "what's the meaning of 'humph'?"

"Humph !" repeated the lawyer, looking hard at Amber.

"It implies yes or no, as it may be," replied Edward Forster, smiling.

"I never heard any one say it before, papa. You're not angry with me, sir?" continued Amber, turning round to John Forster.

"No, not angry, little girl ; but I'm too busy to talk to you, or indeed with you, brother Edward. Have you anything more to say ?"

"Nothing, my dear brother, if I have your promise."

"Well, you have it ; but what I am to do with her, God only knows ! I wish you had kept better hours. You mentioned some clothes which might identify her to her relations ; pray let me have them, for I shall have the greatest pleasure in restoring her to them as soon as possible after she is once in my hands."

"Here they are, brother," replied Edward, taking a small packet from his coat-pocket ; "you had better take charge of them now ; and may God bless you for having relieved my mind from so heavy a load !"

"Humph ! by taking it on my own shoulders," muttered John, as he walked to the iron safe to deposit the packet of linen ; then returning to the table, "Have you anything more to say, brother ?"

"Only to ask you where I may find my brother Nicholas ?"

"That I can't tell ; my nephew told me somewhere down the river ; but it's a long way from here to the Nore. Nephew's a fine lad ; I sent him off to the East Indies."

"I am sorry, then, that I have no chance of seeing him : but you are busy, brother ?"

213

"I have told you so three times, as plain as I could speak."

"I will no longer trespass on your time. We return home to-morrow morning; and as I cannot expect ever to see you again, God bless you, my dear John, and farewell; I am afraid I may say, in this world at least, farewell for ever!"

Edward held out his hand to his brother. It was taken with considerable emotion. "Farewell, brother, farewell!— I'll not forget."

"Good-bye, sir," said Amber, going close up to John Forster.

"Good-bye, my little girl," replied he, looking earnestly in her face; and then, as if thawing towards her, as he scanned her beautiful and expressive features, removing his spectacles and kissing her, "Good-bye."

"O papa," cried Amber, as she went out of the room, "he kissed me!"

"Humph!" said John Forster, as the door closed upon them.

The spectacles were put on, and the reading of the brief immediately continued.

CHAPTER XXXIV

" *Strickland.* These doings in my house distract me.
I met a fine gentleman ; when I inquired who
He was—why, he came to Clarinda. I met
A footman too, and he came to Clarinda.
My wife had the character of a virtuous
Woman————."
—*Suspicious Husband.*

" Let us no more contend
Each other, blamed enough elsewhere, but strive
In offices of love, how we may lighten
Each other's burden in our share of woe."
—MILTON.

I DO not know a spot on the globe which astonishes and delights, upon your first landing, as the island of Madeira. The voyager embarks, and is in all probability confined to his cabin, suffering under the dreadful protraction of sea-sickness. Perhaps he has left England in the gloomy close of autumn, or the frigid concentration of an English winter. In a week, or even in a shorter period, he again views that *terra firma* which he had quitted with regret, and which in his sufferings he would have given half that he possessed to regain.

When he lands upon the island, what a change! Winter has become summer; the naked trees which he left are exchanged for the most luxuriant and varied foliage, snow and frost for warmth and splendour; the scenery of the temperate zone for the profusion and magnificence of the tropics; fruit which he had never before seen; supplies for the table unknown to him; a bright sky, a glowing sun, hills covered with vines, a deep blue sea, a picturesque and novel costume— all meet and delight the eye, just at the precise moment when to have been landed, even upon a barren island, would have been considered as a luxury. Add to all this the unbounded hospitality of the English residents, a sojourn too short to permit satiety, and then is it to be wondered that the island of Madeira is a "green spot" in the memory of all those who land there, or that they quit it with regret?

The *Bombay Castle* had not been two hours at anchor before the passengers had availed themselves of an invitation from one of the English residents, and were quartered in a splendid house, which looked upon a square and one of the principal churches in the city of Funchal. While the gentlemen amused themselves at the extensive range of windows with the novelty of the scene, and the ladies retired to their apartments to complete the hasty toilet of their disembarkation, Captain Drawlock was very busy in the counting-house below with the master of the house. There were so many pipes of Madeira for the Honourable Company, so many for the directors' private cellars, besides many other commissions for friends, which Captain Drawlock had undertaken to execute; for at that period Madeira wine had not been so calumniated as it latterly has been.

A word upon this subject. I am a mortal enemy to every description of humbug; and I believe there is as much in the medical world as in any other. Madeira wine had for a century been in high and deserved reputation, when on a sudden some fashionable physician discovers that it contained more acid than sherry. Whether he was a sleeping partner in some Spanish house, or whether he had received a present of a few pipes of sherry that he might turn the scale of public favour towards that wine, I know not ; but certain it is that it became fashionable with all medical gentlemen to prescribe sherry ; and when once anything becomes fashionable, *c'est une affaire decidée.*

I do not pretend to be much of a pathologist ; but on reading Mr. F——'s analysis on the component parts of wine, I observed that in one hundred parts there are perhaps twenty-two parts of acid in Madeira and nineteen in sherry ; so that, in fact, if you reduce your glass of Madeira wine just one sip in quantity, you will imbibe no more acid than in a full glass of sherry ; and when we consider the variety of acids in sugar and other compounds which abound in culinary preparations, the fractional quantity upon which has been grounded the abuse of Madeira wine appears to be most ridiculous.

But if not a pathologist, I have a most decided knowledge of what is good wine ; and if the gout should some day honour me with a visit, I shall at least have the consolation to know that I have by potation most honestly earned it.

But allowing that the medical gentlemen are correct, still their good intentions are frustrated by the knavery of the world ; and the result of their prescriptions is that people drink much more acid than they did before. I do every justice to good old sherry when it does make its appearance at table ; it is a noble wine when aged and unsophisticated from its youth ; but for once that you meet with it genuine, you are twenty times disappointed. When Madeira wine was in vogue, the island could not produce the quantity required for consumption, and the vintage from the north side of the island, or of Teneriffe, was substituted. This adulteration no doubt was one of the causes of its losing its well-established reputation. But Madeira wine has a quality which in itself proves its superiority over all other wines, namely, that although no other wine can be passed off as Madeira, yet with Madeira the wine-merchants may imitate any other wine that is in demand. What is the consequence ? that Madeira, not being any longer in request as Madeira, now that sherry is the " correct thing," and there not being sufficient of the latter to meet the increased demand, most of the wine vended as sherry is made from the inferior Madeira wines. Reader, if you have ever been in Spain, you may have seen the Xerez or sherry wine brought from the mountains to be put into the cask. A raw goat-skin, with the neck-part and the four legs sewed up, forms a leathern bag, containing perhaps from fifteen to twenty gallons. This is the load of one man, who brings it down on his shoulder exposed to the burning rays of the sun. When it arrives, it is thrown down on the sand, to swelter in the heat with the rest, and remains there probably for days before it is transferred into the cask. It is this proceeding which gives to sherry that peculiar leather twang which distinguishes it from other wines—a twang easy to imitate by throwing into a cask of Cape wine a pair of old boots and allowing them to remain a proper time. Although the public refuse to drink Madeira as Madeira, they are in fact drinking it in every way disguised—as port, as sherry, &c.; and it is a well-known fact that the poorer wines from the north side of the island are landed in the London docks and shipped off to the Continent, from whence they reappear in bottles as " peculiarly fine-flavoured hock ! "

Now, as it is only the indifferent wines which are thus turned into sherry—and the more inferior the wine, the more acid it contains—I think I have made out a clear case that people are drinking more acid than they did before this wonderful discovery of the medical gentlemen, who have for some years led the public by the nose.

There are, however, some elderly persons of my acquaintance who are not to be dissuaded from drinking Madeira, but who continue to destroy themselves by the use of this acid, which perfumes the room when the cork is extracted. I did represent to one of them that it was a species of suicide after what the doctors had discovered; but he replied in a very gruff tone of voice, " Maybe, sir ; but you can't teach an old dog new tricks ! "

I consider that the public ought to feel very much indebted to me for this *exposé*. Madeira wine is very low, while sherry is high in price. They have only to purchase a cask of Madeira and flavour it with Wellington boots or ladies' slippers, as it may suit their palates. The former will produce the high-coloured, the latter the pale sherry. Further, I

consider that the merchants of Madeira are bound to send
me a letter of thanks, with a pipe of Bual to prove its
sincerity. Now I recollect Stoddart did promise me some
wine when he was last in England; but I suppose he has
forgotten it.

But from the produce I must return to the island and
my passengers. The first day of their arrival they ate their
dinner, took their coffee, and returned to bed early to enjoy a
comfortable night after so many of constant pitching and
tossing. The next morning the ladies were much better,
and received the visits of all the captains of the India ships,
and also of the captain of the frigate who escorted them.

The officers of the *Bombay Castle* had been invited to
dinner; and the first mate not being inclined to leave the
ship, Newton had for one accepted the invitation. On his
arrival he discovered, in the captain of the frigate, his
former acquaintance, Captain Carrington, in whose ship he
had obtained a passage from the West Indies, and who,
on the former being paid off, had been appointed to the
command of the *Boadicea*. Captain Carrington was delighted
to meet Newton; and the attention which he paid to him,
added to the encomiums bestowed when Newton was out of
hearing, raised him very high in the opinion, not only of
Captain Drawlock, but also in the estimation of the ladies.
At the request of Captain Carrington, Newton was allowed
to remain on shore till the departure from the island; and
from this circumstance he became more intimate with the
ladies than he would in all probability have otherwise been
in the whole course of the voyage. We must pass over the
gallop up to Nostra Senhora da Monte—an expedition opposed
by Captain Drawlock on the score of his responsibility; but he
was overruled by Captain Carrington, who declared that Newton
and he were quite sufficient convoy. We must pass over the
many compliments paid to Isabel Revel by Captain Carrington,
who appeared desperately in love after an acquaintance of
four-and-twenty hours, and who discovered a defect in the
Boadicea which would occupy two or three days to make
good, that he might be longer in her company; but we will
not pass over one circumstance which occurred during their
week's sojourn at this delightful island.

A certain Portuguese lady, of noble birth, had been left

a widow, with two daughters and a fine estate to share between them. The daughters were handsome, but the estate
was so much handsomer, that it set all the mandolins of the
Portuguese inamoratos strumming under the windows of the
lady's abode from sunset to the dawn of day.

Now, it did so occur that a young English clerk in a
mercantile house, who had a fresh complexion and a clean
shirt to boast of (qualifications unknown to the Portuguese),
won the heart of the eldest daughter; and the old lady, who
was not a very strict Catholic, gave her consent to this
heretical union. The Catholic priests, who had long been
trying to persuade the old lady to shut up her daughters in
a convent and endow the Church with her property, expressed
a holy indignation at the intended marriage. The Portuguese
gentlemen, who could not brook the idea of so many fair hills
of vines going away to a stranger, were equally indignant; in
short, the whole Portuguese population of the island were in
arms; but the old lady, who had always contrived to have
her way before her husband's death, was not inclined to be
thwarted now that she was her own mistress; and notwithstanding threats and expostulations from all quarters, she
awaited but the arrival of an English man-of-war that the
ceremony might be performed, there being at that time
no Protestant clergyman on the island; for the reader must
know that a marriage on board of a king's ship, by the captain, duly entered in the log-book, is considered as valid as
if the ceremony were performed by the Archbishop of Can-
terbury.

I once married a couple on board of a little ten-gun brig,
of which I condescended to take the command to oblige the
First Lord of the Admiralty; offered, I believe, to "provide" for
me, and rid the Board of all future solicitations for employment
or promotion.

It was one of my sailors, who had come to a determination
to make an honest woman of Poll and an ass of himself at one
and the same time. The ceremony took place on the quarter-
deck. "Who gives this woman away?" said I, with due
emphasis, according to the ritual. "I do," cried the boatswain in a gruff voice, taking the said lady by the arm and
shoving her towards me, as if he thought her not worth
keeping. Everything went on seriously, nevertheless. The

219

happy pair were kneeling down on the Union Jack, which had been folded on the deck in consideration of the lady's knees, and I was in the middle of the blessing, when two pigs, which we had procured at St. Jago's, being then off that island (creatures more like English pigs on stilts than anything else, unless you could imagine a cross between a pig and a greyhound), in the lightness of their hearts and happy ignorance of their doom took a frisk, as you often see pigs do on shore, commenced a run from forward right aft, and galloping to the spot where we all were collected, rushed against the two just made one, destroying their centre of gravity and upsetting them; and, indeed, destroying the gravity and upsetting the seriousness of myself and the whole of the ship's company. The lady recovered her legs, d——d the pigs, and taking her husband's arm, hastened down the hatchway; so that I lost the kiss to which I was entitled for my services. I consoled myself by the reflection that, "please the pigs," I might be more fortunate the next time that I officiated in my clerical capacity. This is a digression, I grant, but I cannot help it; it is the nature of man to digress. Who can say that he has through life kept in the straight path? This is a world of digression; and I beg that critics will take no notice of mine, as I have an idea that my digressions in this work are as agreeable to my readers as my digressions in life have been agreeable to myself.

When Captain Carrington anchored with his convoy in Funchal Roads, immediate application was made by the parties for the ceremony to be performed on board of his ship. It is true that, as Mr. Ferguson had arrived, it might have taken place on shore; but it was considered advisable, to avoid interruption and insult, that the parties should be under the sanctuary of a British man-of-war. On the fourth day after the *Boadicea's* arrival the ceremony was performed on board of her by Mr. Ferguson; and the passengers of the *Bombay*, residing at the house of Mr. ——, who was an intimate friend of the bridegroom, received and accepted the invitation to the marriage-dinner. The feast was splendid, and after the Portuguese custom. The first course was boiled. It consisted of boiled beef, boiled mutton, boiled hams, boiled tongues, boiled bacon, boiled fowls, boiled turkeys, boiled sausages, boiled cabbages, boiled potatoes, and boiled carrots. Duplicates of each were ranged in opposition, until the table groaned with its superincumbent weight. All were cut up, placed in one dish, and handed round to the guests. When they drank wine, every glass was filled, and everybody who filled his glass was expected to drink the health of every guest separately and by name before he emptied it. The first course was removed, and the second made its appearance, all roasted. Roast beef, roast veal, roast mutton, roast lamb, roast joints of pork, roasted turkeys, roasted fowls, roasted sausages, roasted everything; the centre dish being a side of a large hog, rolled up like an enormous fillet of veal. This, too, was done ample justice to, by the Portuguese part of the company at least; and all was cleared away for the dessert, consisting of oranges, melons, pine-apples, guavas, citrons, bananas, peaches, strawberries, apples, pears, and, indeed, of almost every fruit which can be found in the whole world; all of which appear to naturalise themselves at Madeira. It was now supposed by the uninitiated that the dinner was over; but not so: the dessert was cleared away, and on came a *husteron proteron* medley of pies and puddings, in all their varieties, smoking hot, boiled and baked; custards and sweet-meats, cheese and olives, fruits of all kinds preserved, and a hundred other things, from which the gods preserve us! At last the feast was really over—the Portuguese picked their teeth with their forks, and the wine was circulated briskly. On such an occasion as the marriage of her daughter, the old lady had resolved to tap a pipe of Madeira which was at the very least fifty years old, very fine in flavour, but from having been so long in the wood, little inferior in strength to genuine Cognac. The consequence was that many of the gentlemen became noisy before the dinner was over; and their mirth was increased to positive uproar upon a message being sent by the bishop, ordering, upon pain of excommunication, that the ceremony should proceed no further. The ladies retired to the withdrawing-room; the gentlemen soon followed; but the effects of the wine were so apparent upon most of them, that Captain Drawlock summoned Newton to his assistance, and was in a state of extreme anxiety until his " responsibilities " were safe at home. Shortly afterwards, Captain Carrington, and those who were the least affected, by persuasion or force, removed the others from the house; and the bridal party were left to themselves, to deliberate whether they should or should not obey the preposterous demands of the reverend bishop.

Captain Carrington was excessively fond of a joke, and never lost the opportunity when it occurred. Now it happened that in the party invited there was a merchant of the name of Sullivan, who upon his last visit to England had returned with a very pretty, and at the same time a very coquettish, young lady as his wife. It happened, in the casualties of a large dinner-party, that the old colonel (Ellice was his name, if I have not mentioned it before) was seated next to her, and, as usual, was remarkably attentive. Mr. Sullivan, like many other gentlemen, was very inattentive to his wife, and, unlike most Irishmen, was very jealous of her. The very marked attention of the colonel had not escaped his notice; neither did his fidgeting upon this occasion escape the notice of those about him, who were aware of his disposition. The poor colonel was one of those upon whose brain the wine had taken the most effect; and it was not until after sundry falls, and being again placed upon his legs, that he had been conveyed home between Captain Carrington and Mr. ——, the merchant at whose house the party from the *Bombay Castle* were residing. The ensuing morning he did not make his appearance at breakfast; and the gentlemen residing on the island, commenting upon the events of the evening before, declared in a joking way that they should not be surprised at Mr. Sullivan sending him a challenge in the course of the morning; that was, if he was up so soon, as he had quitted the house in a greater state of inebriety than even the colonel. It was upon this hint that Captain Carrington proposed to have some amusement; and having arranged with one of the junior partners of the house, he went into the room of the colonel, whom he found still in bed.

"Well, colonel, how do you find yourself?" said Captain Carrington, when he had roused him.

"Oh! very bad, indeed; my head is ready to split; never felt such a sensation in my head before, except when I was struck with a spent ball at the battle of ——"

"I am very sorry for your headache, colonel; but more

sorry that the wine should have played you such a trick last night."

"Trick, indeed!" replied the colonel; "I was completely overcome; I do not recollect a word that passed after I had quitted the dinner-table."

"Are you serious? Do you not recollect the scene with Mrs. Sullivan?"

"Mrs. Sullivan! My dear sir, what scene? I certainly paid every attention due to a very pretty woman; but I recollect no further."

"Not the scene in the drawing-room?"

"God bless me!—No—I do not even recollect ever going into the drawing-room! Pray tell me what I said or did; I hope nothing improper."

"Why, that depends very much whether a lady likes it or not; but in the presence of so many people——"

"Merciful powers! Captain Carrington, pray let me know at once what folly it was that I committed."

"Why, really, I am almost ashamed to enter into particulars; suffice to say, that you used most unwarrantable freedom towards her."

"Is it possible?" cried the colonel. "Now, Captain Carrington, are you not joking?"

"Ask this gentleman; he was present."

The assertion of the captain was immediately corroborated, and the colonel was quite aghast.

"Excuse me, gentlemen; I will run immediately—that abominable wine. I must go and make a most ample apology. I am bound to do it, as a gentleman, as an officer, and as a man of honour."

Captain Carrington and his confederate quitted the room, satisfied with the success of their plot. The colonel rose, and soon afterwards made his appearance. He swallowed a cup of coffee, and then proceeded on his visit to make the *amende honorable*.

When Mr. Sullivan awoke from the lethargy produced from the stupefying effects of the wine, he tried to recollect the circumstances of the preceding evening; but he could trace no further than to the end of the dinner, after which his senses had been overpowered. All that he could call to memory was, that somebody had paid great attention to his wife, and that what had passed afterwards was unknown. This occasioned him to rise in a very jealous humour; and he had not been up more than an hour when the colonel sent up his card, requesting, as a particular favour, that the lady would admit him.

The card and messenger were taken by the servant to Mr. Sullivan, whose jealousy was again roused by the circumstance; and wishing to know if the person who had now called was the same who had been so attentive to his wife on the preceding evening, and the motives of the call, he requested that the colonel might be shown in, without acquainting his wife, whom he had not yet seen, with his arrival. The colonel, who intended to have made an apology to the lady without the presence of a third person, least of all of her husband, ascended the stairs, adjusting his hair and cravat, and prepared with all the penitent assurance and complimentary excuses of a too ardent lover. The fact was, that although the colonel had expressed to Captain Carrington his regret and distress at the circumstance, yet, as an old Adonis, he was rather proud of this instance of juvenile indiscretion. When, therefore, he entered the room, and perceived, instead of the lady, Mr. Sullivan raised up to his utmost height, and looking anything but good-humoured, he naturally started back, and stammered out something which was unintelligible. His behaviour did not allay the suspicions of Mr. Sullivan, who requested in a haughty tone to be informed of the reason why he had been honoured with a visit. The colonel became more confused, and totally losing his presence of mind, replied—

"I called, sir—on Mrs. Sullivan—to offer an apology for my conduct last night; but as I perceive that she is not visible, I will take a more favourable opportunity."

"Any apology you may have to offer to my wife, sir," replied Mr. Sullivan, "may be confided to me. May I inquire the circumstances which have occurred to render an apology necessary?" and Mr. Sullivan walked to the door and closed it.

"Why, really, Mr. Sullivan, you must be aware that circumstances may occur," replied the colonel, more confused; "the fact is, that I consider it my duty, as a gentleman and a man of honour, to express my regrets to your fair lady."

"My fair lady! for what, sir, may I ask?"

"Why, sir," stammered the colonel, "to state the truth, for, as a gentleman and a man of honour, I ought not to be ashamed to acknowledge my error—for the very improper behaviour which I was guilty of last night."

"Improper behaviour, sir!—d—nation! with my wife?" roared Mr. Sullivan in his rage. "What behaviour, sir? and when, sir?"

"Really, sir, I was too much affected with the wine to know anything which passed. I did hope to have addressed the lady in person on the subject, and I came here with that intention."

"I daresay you did, sir."

"But," continued the colonel, "as it appears I am not to have that honour, I consider that I have done my duty in requesting that you will convey my sentiments of regret for what has passed;—and now, sir, I wish you a good morning."

"Good morning," retorted the husband, with a sneer, "and observe, sir, I will not trouble you to call again. William, show this gentleman outside the door."

The colonel, who was descending the stairs, turned round to Mr. Sullivan at the latter part of his speech, and then, as if thinking better of it, he resumed his descent, and the door was immediately closed upon him.

Mr. Sullivan, as soon as he was satisfied that the colonel was shut out, immediately repaired to his wife's dressing-room, where he found her reading.

"Madam," said he, fixing his eyes sternly on her, "I have been informed of what took place last night."

"I'm sure I do not know what that was," replied the lady, coolly, "except that you were very tipsy."

"Granted, madam; you took advantage of it; and your conduct——"

"My conduct, Mr. Sullivan!" replied his wife, kindling with anger.

"Yes, Mrs. Sullivan, your conduct. A married woman, madam, who allows gentlemen——"

"Gentlemen, Mr. Sullivan! I allow no gentleman but yourself. Are you sure that you are quite sober?"

"Yes, madam, I am; but this affected coolness will not

avail you : deny, if you can, that Colonel Ellice did not last night——"

"Well, then, I do deny it. Neither Colonel Ellice nor any other man ever did——"

"Did what, madam?" interrupted the husband in a rage.

"I was going to observe, if you had not interrupted me, that no one was wanting in proper respect towards me," replied the lady, who grew more cool as her husband increased in choler. "Pray, Mr. Sullivan, may I inquire who is the author of this slander?"

"The author, madam! look at me—to your confusion look at me!"

"Well, I'm looking."

"'Twas, madam—the colonel himself."

"The colonel himself!"

"Yes, madam, the colonel himself, who called this morning to see you and renew the intimacy, I presume; but by mistake was shown up to me, and then made an apology for his conduct."

"It's excessively strange : first the colonel is rude without my knowledge, and then apologises to you! Mr. Sullivan, I'm afraid that your head is not right this morning."

"Indeed, madam, I only wish that your heart was as sound," replied the husband with a sneer; "but, madam, I am not quite blind. An honest woman—a virtuous woman, Mrs. Sullivan, would have immediately acquainted her husband with what had passed—not have concealed it; still less have had the effrontery to deny it, when acknowledged by her *paramour.*"

"*Paramour!*" cried the lady, with an hysterical laugh; "Mr. Sullivan, when I select a paramour, it shall be a handsome young man—not an old, yellow-faced——"

"Pshaw, madam! there's no accounting for taste; when a woman deviates from the right path——"

"Right path! if ever I deviated from the right path, as you call it, it was when I married such a wretch as you! Yes, sir," continued the lady, bursting into tears, "I tell you now —my life has been a torment to me ever since I married (sobbing)—always suspected for nothing (sob, sob)—jealous, detestable temper (sob)—go to my friends (sob)—hereafter may repent (sob)—then know what you've lost" (sob, sob, sob).

226

"And, madam," replied Mr. Sullivan, "so may you also know what you have lost before a few hours have passed away; then, madam, the time may come when the veil of folly may be rent from your eyes, and your conduct appear in all its deformity. Farewell, madam—perhaps for ever!"

The lady made no reply; Mr. Sullivan quitted the room, and, repairing to his counting-house, wrote a challenge to the colonel and confided the delivery of it to one of his friends, who unwillingly accepted the office of second.

CHAPTER XXXV.

" He's truly valiant that can wisely suffer
The worst that man can breathe, and make his wrongs
His outsides; to wear them, like his raiment, carelessly,
And ne'er prefer his injuries to his heart,
To bring it into danger."

—SHAKSPEARE.

THE colonel in the meantime had returned to the house where he was residing, when he was immediately accosted by Captain Carrington and the other gentlemen who had been let into the secret of the plot. During his walk home the colonel had been ruminating on his dismissal, and had not quite made up his mind whether he ought or ought not to resent the conduct of Mr. Sullivan. Naturally more inclined for peace than war, by the time that he had arrived home he had resolved to pocket the affront, when Captain Carrington called him on one side, and obtained from him a recapitulation of what had passed; which probably never would have been given if the colonel had not considered the communication as confidential. This, however, did not suit the intentions of Captain Carrington, who felt inclined for more mischief; and, when the colonel had concluded his narrative, he replied, "Upon my word, colonel, as you observe, this conduct on the part of Mr. Sullivan is not exactly what can be permitted by us military men. I hardly know how to advise; indeed, I would not take the responsibility; however, I will consult with Mr. S—— and Mr. G——, and if you will leave your honour in our hands, depend upon it we will do you strict justice;" and Captain Carrington quitted the colonel, who would have expostulated, and, walking up to the other gentlemen, entered into a recapitulation of the circumstances. A wink of his eye, as his back was turned to the colonel, fully expressed to the others the tenor of the advice which they were to offer.

" Well, gentlemen, what is your opinion ? " said the captain, as he concluded his narrative.

" I think," replied Mr. S——, with a serious face, " there can be but one—our gallant friend has been most grossly insulted. I think," continued he, addressing the colonel, who had quitted the sofa, in his anxiety to know the issue of their debate, " that I should most decidedly ask him what he meant."

" Or rather demand an apology," observed Mr. G——.

" Which Mr. Sullivan, as a man of honour, is bound to offer, and the colonel, as a gentleman and an officer, has a right to insist upon. Do you not think so, Captain Carrington ? " said Mr. S——.

" Why, I have always been more inclined to be a peacemaker than otherwise, if I can," replied Captain Carrington. " If our gallant friend the colonel is not sure that Mr. Sullivan did use the words, ' I won't trouble you to call again,'—are you positive as to the exact words, colonel ? "

" Why, to the best of my recollection," replied the colonel, " I rather think those were the words. I may be mistaken: it was certainly—most certainly, something to that effect."

" Were they ' requesting you to call again ' ? " said Captain Carrington.

" No, no, that they were certainly not."

" Well, they could be but one or the other. Then, gentlemen, the case is clear—the words were uttered," said Mr. S——. " Now, Captain Carrington, what would you advise ? "

" I really am vexed to say that I do not see how our friend, Colonel Ellice, can do otherwise than demand an apology or a meeting."

" Could not I treat him with contempt, Captain Carrington ? " demanded the colonel.

" Why, not exactly," replied Mr. S——. " Sullivan is of

good family — the Sullivans of Bally-cum-Poop. He was some time in the 48th Regiment, and was obliged to retire from it for challenging his colonel."

" Well, gentlemen," replied the colonel, " I suppose I must leave my honour in your hands, although it does appear to me that 'our time is very short for such arrangements. We sail early to-morrow morning, Captain Carrington—at daylight, I think you said, and it will be too late to-night."

" My dear colonel, I will risk a rebuke from the Admiralty," replied the captain, " rather than not allow you to heal your wounded honour. I will stay till the day after to-morrow, should it be requisite for the arrangement of this business."

" Thank you, many thanks," replied the colonel, with an expression of disappointment. " Then I had better prepare the letter ? "

" Carta por senhor commandate," interrupted a Portuguese, presenting a letter to the colonel ; " O senhor embaixo ; queir risposta."

The colonel opened the letter, which contained Mr. Sullivan's challenge,—pistols—to-morrow morning, at daylight— one mile on the road to Machico.

The colonel's countenance changed two or three shades less yellow as he read the contents : recovering himself with a giggle, he handed the letter to Captain Carrington. " You see, captain, the gentleman has saved me the trouble—he, he, he ! these little affairs are common to gentlemen of our profession—he, he ! and, since the gentleman wishes it, why, I presume—he, he ! that we must not disappoint him."

" Since you are both of one mind, I think there will be some business done," observed Mr. S——. " I perceive that he is in earnest by the place named for the meeting We generally settle our affairs of honour in the Loo-fields ; but I suppose he is afraid of interruption. They want an answer, colonel."

" Oh ! he shall have one," replied the colonel, tittering with excitement ; " he shall have one. What hour does he say ? "

" Oh, we will arrange all that. Come, colonel," said Captain Carrington, taking him familiarly by the arm, and leading him away.

The answer was despatched, and they sat down to dinner. Many were the friendly and encouraging glasses of wine drank with the colonel, who recovered his confidence, and was then most assiduous in his attentions to the ladies, to prove his perfect indifference. He retired at an early hour, nevertheless.

In the meantime Mr. Sullivan had received the answer, and had retired to his counting-house to arrange his affairs in case of accident. He had not seen his wife since the *fracas*. And now we will leave them for a while, and make a few remarks upon duelling.

Most people lament, many abuse, the custom as barbarous; but barbarous it is not, or it would not be necessary in a state of high civilisation. It is true that by the practice we offend laws human and divine; but, at the same time, it must be acknowledged that neither law nor religion can keep society in such good order, or so restrain crime. The man who would defy the penalty of the law and the commandments of his God against seduction will, however, pause in his career when he finds that there are brothers to avenge an injured sister. And why so?—because in this world we live, as it were, in a tavern, careless of what the bill is we run up, but dreading the day of reckoning, which the pistol of our adversary may bring at once. Thus, duelling may be considered as a necessary evil, arising out of our wickedness; a crime in itself rare in occurrence, but which prevents others of equal magnitude from occurring every day; and, until the world is reformed, nothing can prevent it. Men will ever be governed by the estimation of the world; and until the whole world decide against duelling—until it has become the usage to offer the other cheek upon the first having been smitten—then, and not till then, will the practice be discontinued. When a man refuses to fight a duel, he is stigmatised as a coward, his company is shunned; and, unless he is a wretch without feeling, his life becomes a burden. Men have refused from purely conscientious motives, and have subsequently found themselves so miserable, from the neglect and contumely of the world, that they have *backslided*, and have fought to recover their place in society. There have been some few—very few—who, having refused from conscientious motives, have adhered to these resolutions, because they feared

God and not man. There was more courage in their refusal than if they had run the gauntlet of a hundred duels; a moral courage which is most rare,—preferring the contempt of man to the wrath of God. It is, however, the most trying situation on this side of the grave. To refuse to fight a duel is, in fact, to obey the stern injunction, " Leave all and follow Me."

For my part, I never have and never will fight a duel, if I can help it. I have a double motive for my refusal: in the first place, I am afraid to offend the Deity; and in the next, I am afraid of being shot. I have, therefore, made up my mind never to meet a man except upon what I consider fair terms; for when a man stakes his life, the gambling becomes rather serious, and an equal value should be laid down by each party. If, then, a man is not so big—not of equal consequence in the consideration of his fellow-mites —not married, with five small children, as I am—not having so much to lose,—why, it is clear that I risk more than he does; the stake is not equal, and I, therefore, shall not meet him. If, on the contrary, he presents a broader target—if he is my superior in rank, more patriarchal at home, or has so many hundreds per annum more—why, then the disadvantages will be on his side; and I trust I am too much of a gentleman, even if he offers to waive all these considerations, to permit him to fight. It would be swindling the man out of his life.

The best advice I can offer to my friends under these unpleasant circumstances is, first to try if they cannot persuade their adversaries to make an apology; and if they will not, why, then, let them make one themselves; for although the making an apology creates a very uneasy sensation, and goes very much *against* the stomach, yet, depend upon it, a well-directed bullet creates a much more uneasy feeling, and, what is worse, goes *directly into it.*

We left Mrs. Sullivan sobbing in her anger, when her husband bounded out of the room in his heroics. At the time that he made the threat she was in no humour to regard it; but as her anger gradually subsided, so did her alarm increase. Notwithstanding that she was a coquette, she was as warmly attached to her husband as he was to her; if she trifled, it was only for her amusement, and to attract that meed of admiration to which she had been accustomed previous to her marriage, and which no woman can renounce on her first entry into that state. Men cannot easily pardon jealousy in their wives, but women are more lenient towards their husbands. Love, hand-in-hand with confidence, is the more endearing; yet, when confidence happens to be out of the way, Love will sometimes associate with Jealousy; still, as this disagreeable companion proves that Love is present, and as his presence is what a woman, and all a woman asks, she suffers Jealousy, nay, sometimes even becomes partial to him, for the sake of Love.

Now that Mrs. Sullivan had been most unjustly accused, the reader must know, and, moreover, that she had great reason to feel irritated. When her tears had subsided, for some time she continued in her chair, awaiting with predetermined dignity the appearance and apology of Mr. Sullivan. After some time had elapsed she wondered why he did not come. Dinner was announced, and she certainly expected to meet him then, and she waited for some minutes to see if he would not take this opportunity of coming up to her;—but no. She then presumed that he was still in the sulks, and had sat down to table without her, and therefore, as he would not come—why, she went; but he was not at the table. Every minute she expected him. Had he been told? Where was he? He was in the counting-house, was the reply. Mrs. Sullivan swallowed a few mouthfuls and then returned upstairs. Tea was made—announced to Mr. Sullivan, yet he came not. It remained on the table; the cup poured out for him was cold. The urn had been sent down, with strict injunctions to keep the water boiling, and all was cleared away. Mrs. Sullivan fidgeted and ruminated, and became uneasy. He never had been at variance for many hours since their marriage, and all for nothing! At last the clock struck ten, and she rang the bell. "Where is Mr. Sullivan?"—"In the counting-house."—"Tell him that I wish to speak with him." Mr. Sullivan had not answered him, and the door was locked inside. This intelligence created a little irritation and checked the tide of affection. "Before all the servants—so inconsiderate—it was quite insulting!" With a heavy heart Mrs. Sullivan lighted the chamber candle and went upstairs to bed. Once she turned down the stairs two or three steps, intending to go to the counting-house door; but her pride restrained her, and she reascended. In an hour Mrs. Sullivan was in bed, expecting her husband every minute, listening at the slightest sound for his footstep; but two o'clock came and he was still away. She could bear up against her suspense and agitation no longer; she rose, threw on her *robe de nuit*, and descended the stairs. All the family had long retired, and everything was still; her light foot made no noise as she tripped along. As she neared the door she perceived the light gleaming through the keyhole. Whether to peep or to speak first—he might be fast asleep. Curiosity prevailed—she looked through the keyhole, and perceived her husband very busy writing. After he had finished his letter he threw down his pen, pressed his forehead with both hands, and groaned deeply. Mrs. Sullivan could refrain no longer. "William! William!" cried she, in a soft, imploring voice; but she was not answered. Again and again did she repeat his name, until an answer, evidently wrung from him by impatience, was returned—"It is too late now."

"Too late, dear William! Yes, it is very late—it's almost three o'clock. Let me in, William—pray do!"

"Leave me alone. it's the last favour I shall probably ever request of you."

"The last favour! O William! you frighten me so. Dear William—do—do let me in. I'm so cold—I shall die. Only for one moment, and I'll bless you. Pray do, William!"

It was not until after repeated and repeated entreaties of this kind that Mr. Sullivan, worn-out by importunity, at last opened the door.

"Mary, I am very busy; I have opened the door to tell you so, and to request that you will not interrupt me. Now oblige me by going to bed."

But getting in was everything; and a young and pretty wife, in *déshabille* and in tears, imploring, entreating, conjuring, promising, coaxing, and fondling, is not quite so easy to be detached when once she has gained access. In less than half-an-hour Mr. Sullivan was obliged to confess that her conduct had been the occasion of a meeting being agreed upon for that morning, and that he was arranging his affairs in case of a melancholy termination.

"You now, Mary, must see the consequences of your conduct. By your imprudence your husband's life is risked, probably sacrificed ; but this is no time to be at variance. I forgive you, Mary—from my soul I do, as I hope for pardon myself."

Mrs. Sullivan burst into a paroxysm of tears, and it was some time before she could answer. "William," cried she energetically, "as you well say, this is no time to be at variance, neither is it a time for falsehood. What I stated to you this morning was true ;—if not, may I never hope for pardon, and may heaven never be opened to me ! You have been deceived—grossly deceived ; for what purpose I know not: but so it is. Do not, therefore, be rash. Send for all who were present, and examine them ; and if I have told you a falsehood, put me away from you, to the shame and seclusion I shall so well deserve."

"It is too late, Mary ; I have challenged him, and he has accepted it. I fain would believe you, but he told me so himself."

"Then he told a lie ! a base, cowardly lie ! which sinks him beneath the notice of a gentleman. Let me go with you and confront him. Only let him dare to say it to my face ; 'tis all I ask, William, that I may clear my fame with you. Come to my bed—nay, nay, don't refuse me ; " and poor Mrs. Sullivan again burst into tears.

We must leave the couple to pass the remaining hours in misery, which, however, reclaimed them both from faults. Mrs. Sullivan never coquetted more, and her husband was, after this, never jealous but on trifles.

The colonel was just as busy on his side in preparing for the chances of the morrow . these chances, however, were never tried ; for Captain Carrington and his confederates had made their arrangements. Mr. Sullivan was already dressed, his wife clinging to him in frantic despair, when a letter was left at his door, the purport of which was that Colonel Ellice had discovered that his companions had been joking with him when they had asserted that during his state of inebriety he had offered any rudeness to Mrs. Sullivan. As, therefore, no offence had been committed, Colonel Ellice took it for granted that Mr. Sullivan would be satisfied with the explanation.

THE MERCHANT SERVICE

Mrs. Sullivan, who devoured the writing over her husband's shoulder, sank down on her knees in gratitude, and was raised to her husband's arms, who, as he embraced her, acknowledged his injustice.

The same party who wrote this epistle also framed another in imitation of Mr. Sullivan's handwriting, in which Mr. Sullivan acquainted the colonel, that having been informed by a mutual friend that he had been in error relative to Colonel Ellice's behaviour of the night before, he begged to withdraw the challenge, and apologise for having suspected the colonel of incivility, &c. ; that having been informed that Colonel Ellice embarked at an early hour, he regretted that he would not be able to pay his respects to him, and assure him, &c.

The receipt of this letter, just as the colonel had finished a cup of coffee preparatory to starting, made him, as a single man, quite as happy as the married couple ; he hastened to put the letter into the hands of Captain Carrington, little thinking that he was handing it over to the writer.

"You observe, Captain Carrington, he won't come to the scratch. Perhaps as well for him that he does not," said the colonel, chuckling in his glee.

The breakfast was early ; the colonel talked big, and explained the whole affair to the ladies, quite unconscious that every one in the company knew that the hoax had been played upon him. Before noon every one had embarked on board of their respective ships, and their lofty sails were expanded to a light and favouring breeze.

CHAPTER XXXVI

"Isabel. Anywhere to avoid matrimony: the thought of a husband is terrible to me.

Inis. But if you might choose for yourself, I fancy matrimony would be no such frightful thing to you."—*The Wonder.*

THE *Boadicea,* with the Indiamen, proceeded on to their destination, Captain Carrington taking every opportunity which light winds and smooth water afforded him of paying

235

his respects to the ladies on board of the *Bombay Castle,* or of inviting them on board of the frigate. The fact was that he had fallen most desperately in love with Isabel Revel, and paid her the most marked attention; but, although a pleasant, light-hearted companion, and a young man of good family and prospects, Isabel Revel had not fallen in love with him; she liked his company, but nothing more.

In a month the squadron had arrived at the island of St. Helena, to which Captain Carrington had been ordered to convoy them: his directions were then to cruise in a certain latitude, and ultimately to proceed on to the East Indies, if he did not fall in with the vessels he expected. It was, therefore, but parting to meet again; but during the short time that they refitted and completed their water at St. Helena, Captain Carrington proposed, and was politely refused by Isabel Revel. Impatient as a boy who has been denied his plaything, he ordered his stores immediately on board, and the next day quitted the island. It may appear strange that a young lady obviously sent out on speculation, should have refused so advantageous an offer; for the speculation commences with the voyage. Some ladies are selected at Madeira. Since the Cape has been in our possession, several have been induced to stay in that colony; and very often ships arrive with only the refuse of their cargo for the intended market in the East. But Isabel Revel had consented to embark on the score of filial duty, not to obtain a husband, unless she liked the gentleman who proposed; and Captain Carrington did not happen to come up to her fanciful ideas of the person to be chosen for life. Captain Carrington did not impart the intelligence of his ill-success to any one but Newton, who was employed to carry his farewell message. His secret was faithfully kept by both. Isabel Revel was not one of those young ladies who would make use of such an unworthy advantage to heighten her consequence in the eyes of others. But there was another reason, not exactly known to Isabel herself at the time, which prevented her from listening to the proposals of Captain Carrington. Had she questioned her own heart, she would have discovered that she was prepossessed in favour of one who as unconsciously had become attached to her. He knew his own feelings, but had checked them in the bud, aware that he had nothing to offer but himself.. This person was Newton Forster. His intimacy with Captain Carrington, the attention shown him by Captain Drawlock. (who entrusted him to work the chronometers!), his own excellent character and handsome person, had raised him to more importance than his situation as a junior officer would have warranted ; and his behaviour was such as to have secured him the good-will of every one on board of the ship. Newton's unassuming, frank manner, added to a large stock of general information, occasioned his society to be courted, even by those who would otherwise have been inclined to keep at a distance one in his subordinate rank.

When they arrived at St. Helena, the first mate, for a wonder, no longer made any difficulty of going on shore for an hour or two, if he knew that Newton would be the commanding officer during his absence; nay, so high did he stand in the opinion of his captain, that not only was he permitted to take charge of the chronometers, but if called away for a time below, Captain Drawlock would hand over to Newton's charge any one of the unmarried *responsibilities* who might happen to be leaning on his arm.

The Indiamen being now left to protect themselves, the senior officer, Commodore Bottlecock, issued most elaborate memoranda as to the order of sailing, exercise of the men at the great guns and small arms, and every other point which could tend to their security by due preparation. Nevertheless the ladies continued to appear on deck. Mrs. Ferguson sat in her majesty ; the young ladies tittered, and were reprimanded ; the young gentlemen were facetious and were rebuked ; the old colonel talked of his adventure at Madeira, and compared everything to the spent ball at the battle of ——. Dr. Plausible had become a most assiduous attendant upon Miss Tavistock ever since he had satisfactorily ascertained that she had property of her own ; everybody had become intimate ; every one was becoming tired, when the bearings and distance at noon placed them about two hundred miles from Point de Galle, the southernmost extremity of Ceylon. The wind was fresh and fair, and they congratulated each other upon a speedy termination to their tedious voyage.

Dinner was announced by the old tune of "Oh! the roast beef of Old England;" and during a long voyage

237

the announcement of dinner is a very great relief every way. As had been the invariable rule throughout the whole of the voyage, Miss Charlotte and Miss Laura Revel were placed on the one side of Captain Drawlock, Miss Tavistock and Isabel Revel on the other. They were flanked on the other side by Mrs. and Mr. Ferguson, who thus separated them from any undue collision with the gentlemen passengers or officers of the ship. The colonel was placed next to Mrs. Ferguson, the young writer next to her husband : then the two cadets, supported by the doctor and purser, the remainder of the table being filled up with the officers of the ship, with the first mate at the foot. Such was the order of Captain Drawlock's dinner-sailing; as strictly adhered to as the memoranda of Commodore Bottlecock: the only communication permitted with the young ladies under his charge (unless married men) being to "request the honour of drinking a glass of wine with them."

All this may appear very absurd, but a little reflection will convince the reader to the contrary. There is a serious responsibility on a captain of an Indiaman who takes charge of perhaps a dozen young women, who are to be cooped up for months in the same ship with as many young men. Love, powerful everywhere, has on the waters even more potent sway, hereditary, I presume, from his mother's nativity. Idleness is the friend of love; and passengers have little or nothing to do to while away the tedium of a voyage. In another point, he has great advantage from the limited number of the fair sex. In a ball or in general society, a man may see hundreds of women, admire many, yet fall in love with none. Numbers increase the difficulty of choice, and he remains delighted, but not enslaved. But on board of a ship, the continued presence of one whom he admires by comparison out of the few—one who, perhaps, if on shore, would in a short time be eclipsed by another, but who here shines without competition — gives her an advantage which, assisted by idleness and opportunity, magnifies her attractions, and sharpens the arrow of all-conquering Love. Captain Drawlock perhaps knew this from experience; he knew also that the friends of one party, if not of both, might be displeased by any contract formed when under his surveillance, and that his character and the character of his ship (for ships nowadays have characters, and very much depend upon them for their well-doing) might suffer in consequence. Strict as he might therefore appear, he was only doing his duty.

Grace being requested from Mr. Ferguson, he indulged the company with one quite as long as usual; rather too long, considering that the ship was very unsteady, and the ladies had to cling to the table for support. But Mr. Ferguson was not a sailor, or he would have known that it is the custom to reduce the grace in proportion with the canvas. When the royals are set, we submit to a homily; under double-reefed topsails, a blessing; but under storm stay-sails, an ejaculation is considered as orthodox.

"Mrs. Ferguson, will you permit me to send you a little mulligatawney?" said Captain Drawlock · "if you prefer it, there is sheep's-head broth at the other end of the table."

"Then I will take a little of the broth, if you please, Captain Drawlock."

"Mr. Mathews, Mrs. Ferguson will take some broth. I am sorry, Mrs. Ferguson, that our table is so ill-supplied; but a long voyage and bad weather has been very fatal to our hencoops."

"Indeed, Captain Drawlock, you need not apologise." Nor was there any occasion, for the table was loaded.

"Perhaps Miss Laura Revel will permit me to send her a slice of this mutton?" said the obsequious colonel.

"No, I thank you; I have eaten nothing but mutton lately. I think I shall be a sheep myself soon," added the young lady, tittering.

"That would be very much against your inclination, I should think, Miss Laura," observed Mrs. Ferguson tartly.

"La! why so? how do you know, Mrs. Ferguson?"

"Because a sheep never changes its name until after it is dead. I shrewdly suspect you would like to change yours before."—(This was a hard hit.)

"As you have yours, Mrs. Ferguson," quietly answered Isabel, in support of her sister.

"Very fair on both sides," said the colonel, bowing to the ladies, who sat together. "Pray, Miss Laura, don't talk of being a sheep; we are all ready to devour you as it is."

"La! you don't say so?" replied the young lady, much pleased.

"Colonel Ellice," interrupted Captain Drawlock, with a serious air, "several of the company will thank you to carve that joint, when you have finished paying your compliments. Miss Tavistock, the honour of a glass of wine. We have not had the pleasure of your company on deck to-day."

"No, Captain Drawlock. I did intend to come, but my health is in such a delicate state, that by the advice of Dr. Plausible I remained below."

"Miss Tavistock, will you allow me to send you some mutton?"

"If you please, colonel; a very small slice."

"Mr. Forster, what have you in that dish before you?"

"A chicken, Captain Drawlock."

"Miss Isabel Revel, will you take some chicken?"

"No, I thank you, Captain Drawlock," replied Isabel.

"Did you say yes or no?" inquired Newton, who had caught her eye.

"I'll change my mind," said Isabel, smiling.

Now, I know it for a fact, although I shall not give up my authority, that Isabel Revel never wanted any chicken until she perceived that Newton was to help her. So, if Love occasionally takes away the appetite, let us do him justice—he sometimes creates one.

"Miss Tavistock, allow me to send you a little of this turkey," said Dr. Plausible; "it is easy of digestion."

"If you please, doctor," replied Miss Tavistock, cramming the last mouthful of mutton into her mouth, and sending away her plate to be changed.

"Will you not take a little ham with it, Miss Tavistock?" said Captain Drawlock.

"If you please, sir."

"The honour of a glass of wine, Miss Tavistock," said the colonel.

"With pleasure, sir."

"Miss Charlotte Revel, you have really eaten nothing," said Captain Drawlock.

"That proves you have not paid me the least attention," replied the young lady. "Had you honoured me with a single glance during dinner, you could not but have observed that I have been dining very heartily."

"I really am quite shocked, Miss Charlotte, and bow to your reproof. Will you take a glass of wine with me, in reconciliation ? "

"I consider a glass of Madeira a very poor bribe, sir."

"Well then, Miss Charlotte, it shall be champagne," replied Captain Drawlock in his gallantry. "Steward, champagne." A fortunate hit for the company; as champagne was in general only produced upon what sailors call "clean shirt days," viz., Sundays and Thursdays.

"We are highly indebted to Miss Revel," observed the colonel, bowing to her, "and I think we ought to drink her health in a bumper."

Agreed to *nem. con.*

Champagne, thou darling of my heart ! To stupefy oneself with other wines is brutal; but to raise oneself to the seventh heaven with thee is quite ethereal. The soul appears to spurn the body, and take a transient flight without its dull associate—the—the—broke down, by Jupiter ! All I meant to say was that champagne is very pretty tipple ; and so thought the dinner-party, who were proportionally enlivened.

"Is this orthodox, Mr. Ferguson," inquired the colonel, holding up his glass.

"So far orthodox that it is very good ; and what is orthodox is good," replied the divine, with good-humour.

"The *Asia* has made the signal for 'a strange sail—suspicious,' " said the second mate to Captain Drawlock, putting his head into the cabin.

"Very well, Mr. Jones, keep a glass upon the commodore."

"Mrs. Ferguson, will you take some of this tart ?—Damascene, I believe," said the first mate.

"If you please, Mr. Mathews, did not Mr. Jones say 'suspicious' ? What does that imply ? "

"Imply, madam ! why, that he don't like the cut of her jib ! "

"And pray, what does that mean ? "

"Mean, madam ! why, that for all he knows to the contrary, she may be a French frigate."

"A French frigate ! a French frigate ! O dear ! O dear !" cried two or three ladies at a breath.

"Mr. Mathews," said Captain Drawlock, "I am really surprised at your indiscretion. You have alarmed the ladies. A suspicious sail, Mrs. Ferguson, merely implies—in fact, that they do not know what she is."

"Is that *all* it means?" replied Mrs. Ferguson, with an incredulous look.

"Nothing more, madam; nothing more, I assure you."

"Commodore has made a signal that the strange vessel is a man-of-war bearing down," said the second mate, again entering the cabin.

"Very well, Mr. Jones," said Captain Drawlock, with assumed indifference, but at the same time fidgeting on his chair.

The first mate and Newton immediately quitted the cabin.

"Miss Tavistock, will you take a little of this pudding?"

"If you please, sir, a very little"

"A man-of-war! I'll go and have a look at her," said the colonel, who rose up, bowed to the ladies, and left the cuddy.

"Most probably one of our cruisers," observed Captain Drawlock.

"The commodore has made the signal to prepare for action, sir," said the second mate.

"Very well, Mr. Jones," said Captain Drawlock, who could now restrain himself no longer. "You must excuse me, ladies, for a moment or two; but our commodore is so very prudent a man, and I am under his orders. In a short time I hope to return to the pleasure of your society."

Captain Drawlock's departure was followed by that of all the male party, with the exception of Dr. Plausible and Mr. Ferguson, both of whom, however, were anxious to go upon deck and ascertain how matters stood.

"Mr. Ferguson, where are you going?" said his wife sharply. "Pray, sir, do us the favour to remain. Your profession, if I mistake not, is one of peace."

"Oh! Doctor Plausible, I feel very unwell," cried Miss Tavistock.

"I will stay with you, my dear madam," replied the doctor.

A gun from the commodore's ship, which was close to

windward of them, burst upon their ears, rattling the cabin windows, and making every wine-glass on the table to dance with the concussion.

"Oh! oh! oh!" screamed Miss Tavistock, throwing herself back in her chair and expanding her arms and fingers.

Doctor Plausible flew to the lady's assistance.

"The extreme fineness of her organic structure,—a little water, if you please, Miss Charlotte Revel."

A tumbler of water was poured out, and Doctor Plausible, dipping the tip of his forefinger into it, passed it lightly over the lady's brow. "She will be better directly."

But the lady did not think proper to come-to as soon as the doctor prophesied, and Mrs. Ferguson, snatching up the tumbler, dashed the contents with violence in Miss Tavistock's face; at which Miss Tavistock not only revived, but jumped up from her chair, blowing and spluttering.

"Are you better now, Miss Tavistock?" said Mrs. Ferguson soothingly, at the same time glancing her eyes at the other ladies, who could not restrain their mirth.

"Oh! Doctor Plausible, that shock has so affected my nerves, I feel that I shall faint again, I do indeed—I'm going——"

"Lean upon me, Miss Tavistock, and permit me to conduct you to your cabin," replied the doctor; "the extreme delicacy of your constitution," continued he, whispering, as they left the cuddy, "is not equal to the boisterous remedies of Mrs. Ferguson."

As they went out, Newton Forster came in.

"You must not be alarmed, ladies, when I state that I am commissioned by Captain Drawlock to inform you that the stranger's manœuvres are so doubtful, that we think she is an enemy. He has desired me to request you will accept my convoy to the lower deck, where you will be safe from accident, in the event of our coming to an engagement. Mr. Ferguson, the captain entrusts the ladies to your charge, and requests that you will not leave them upon any consideration. Now, Mrs. Ferguson, will you permit me to escort you to a place of security?"

At this intelligence Laura Revel stared, Charlotte burst into tears, and Isabel turned pale. Mrs. Ferguson took the arm of Newton without saying a word, when the other was offered and accepted by Isabel. Mr. Ferguson, with the two other sisters, brought up the rear. The ladies had to pass the quarter-deck, and when they saw the preparations—the guns cast loose, the shot lying on the deck, and all the various apparatus for destruction—their fears increased. When they had been conducted to their place of safety, Newton was about to return on deck, when he was seized by Miss Charlotte and Laura Revel, who entreated him not to leave them.

" Do stay with us, Mr. Forster; pray, don't go," cried they both.

" I must indeed, ladies ; you are perfectly safe here."

" For God's sake, don't you go away, Mr. Forster!" cried Laura, falling on her knees. " I shall die of fright. You shan't go !" screamed Laura, as the two sisters clung on to the skirts of his jacket, and effectually prevented his escape, unless, like the patriarch, he had left his garment behind.

Newton cast an appealing glance at Isabel, who immediately interfered—" Charlotte, for shame ! you are preventing Mr. Forster from going to his duty. My dear Laura, do not be so foolish ; Mr. Forster can be of no service to us, but he will be on deck. Let go, Laura."

Newton was released. " I am much obliged to you, Miss Isabel," said Newton, with his foot on the ladder; " but I have no time now to express my thanks. Not to be on deck——"

" I know it, Mr. Forster: go up, I beseech you ; do not wait a moment;" and Newton sprang up the ladder, but not before he had exchanged with Isabel a glance which, had he been deficient in courage, would have nerved him for the approaching combat. We must leave the ladies with Mr. Ferguson (who had no pleasant office), while we follow Newton on deck. The stranger had borne down with studding sails, until within three miles of the Indiamen, when she rounded to. She then kept away a little, to close nearer, evidently examining the force opposed to her. The Indiamen had formed line of battle in close order, the private signal between English men-of-war and East India ships flying at their mast-heads.

" Extremely strange that she does not answer the private signal," said the colonel to the second mate.

244

" Not at all, if she don't know how."

" You are convinced, then, that she is a French frigate ? "

" No, not positive ; but I'll bet you ten to one she is :—bet off if either of us are killed, of course ! "

" Thanky ; I never bet," answered the colonel, turning away.

" What do you think of her, Mr. Mathews ? " said Captain Drawlock to the first mate, who had his eyes on the ship.

" She is English built and English rigged, sir, that I'll swear ; look at her lower yard-arms, the squaring of her top-sails. She may be French now, but the oak in her timbers grew in Old England."

" I agree with you," said Newton. " Look at the rake of her stern ; she is English all over."

" Then why don't she answer the private signal ? " said Captain Drawlock.

" She's right in the wind's eye of us, sir, and our flags are blowing end on from her."

" There goes up her bunting, sir," cried the first mate.

" English, as I said. The commodore is answering, sir. Up with the ensign there abaft. All's right, tell the ladies."

" I will ; I'll go and inform them," said the colonel, who immediately descended to impart the joyful intelligence.

The frigate bore down and hove to. The commodore of the India squadron went on board, when he found that she was cruising for some large Dutch store-ships and vessels armed *en flute,* which were supposed to have sailed from Java. In a quarter of an hour she again made sail, and parted company, leaving the Indiamen to secure their guns and pursue their course.

There are two parties whose proceedings we had overlooked ; we refer to Miss Tavistock and Dr. Plausible. The latter handed the lady to her cabin, assisted her to lie down upon her couch, and taking her hand gently, retained it in his own, while with his other he continued to watch her pulse.

" Do not alarm yourself, my dear Miss Tavistock ; your sensibility is immense. I will not leave you. I cannot think what could have induced you to trust yourself on such a voyage of danger and excitement."

" Oh ! Dr. Plausible, where my affections are centred

there is nothing, weak creature that I am, but my soul would carry me through: indeed I am all soul. I have a dear friend in India."

" He is most happy," observed the doctor, with a sigh.

" He, Dr. Plausible! you quite shock me! Do you imagine for a moment that I would go out to follow any gentleman? No, indeed, I am not going out on speculation, as some young ladies. I have enough of my own, thank God! I keep my carriage and corresponding establishment, I assure you."—(The very thing that Dr. Plausible required.)

"Indeed! my dear Miss Tavistock, is it then really a female friend?"

"Yes! the friend of my childhood. I have ventured this tedious, dangerous voyage, once more to fold her in my arms."

" Disinterested affection! a heart like yours, miss, were indeed a treasure to be won. What a happy man would your husband be!"

" Husband! Oh, Dr. Plausible, don't mention it: I feel convinced,—positively convinced, that my constitution is not strong enough to bear matrimony."

The doctor's answer was too prolix for insertion; it was a curious compound dissertation upon love and physic united. There was devoted attention, extreme gentle treatment, study of pathology, advantage of medical attendance always at hand, careful nursing, extreme solicitude, fragility of constitution restored, propriety of enlarging the circle of her innocent affections, ending at last in devoted love, and a proposal—to share her carriage and establishment.

Miss Tavistock assumed another faint — the shock was so great; but the doctor knelt by her and kissed her hand with well-affected rapture. At last, she murmured out a low assent, and fell back, as if exhausted with the effort. The doctor removed his lips from her hand to her mouth, to seal the contract; and, as she yielded to his wishes, almost regretted that he had not adhered to his previous less assuming gallantry.

CHAPTER XXXVII

" 'Tis sweet to hear the watch-dog's honest bark
Bay deep-mouthed welcome as we draw near home ;
'Tis sweet to know there is an eye will mark
Our coming—and look brighter when we come."

—BYRON.

EDWARD FORSTER returned home with his little *protégée*, his mind relieved from the weight which had oppressed it : he knew that the word of his brother was his bond, and that under a rough exterior he concealed a generous and sympathising heart. It was in the early part of the autumn that he again took possession of the cottage ; and as he once more seated himself in his old arm-chair, he mentally exclaimed, " Here then am I again at anchor for a short time until summoned to another world." His prophecy was correct ; during the severe winter that followed, his wound opened again, and his constitution, worn out, gave way to repeated suffering. He had not been confined to his bed more than a fortnight when he felt that his end was approaching. He had long been prepared : nothing remained to be done but to write a letter to his brother, which he confided to Robinson, the fisherman, with directions that it should be put in the post-office immediately after his death, and a strict charge to watch over the little girl until she should be sent for by his brother.

This last necessary act had been completed when Robinson, who was standing by the side of the bed with the letter in his hand, informed him that the family at the Hall had returned from the Continent on the evening before, with their only son, who was now restored to health. This intelligence induced Forster to alter his plans ; and trusting to the former friendship of Lord Aveleyn, he despatched Robinson to the Hall, stating his own condition, and requesting that his lordship would come to the cottage. Lord Aveleyn immediately obeyed the summons ; and perceiving at the first glance that Forster's situation debarred all chance of recovery, took upon himself with willingness the charge of

247

the letter, and promised to receive Amber into his house until it was convenient that she should be removed. It was dark when Lord Aveleyn, with melancholy foreboding, took his last farewell; for, ere the sun had risen again, the spirit of Edward Forster had regained its liberty, and soared to the empyrean, while the deserted Amber wept and prayed.

Edward Forster had not concealed from her the precarious tenure of his existence, and since their return from London had made her fully acquainted with all the particulars connected with her own history. The last few weeks, every interval of suffering had been devoted by him to enforce those principles which he ever had inculcated, and to prepare for the event which had now taken place.

Amber was kneeling by the side of the bed; she had been there so long that she was not aware that it was broad day. Her face, laid upon her hands, was completely hidden by her luxuriant hair, which had escaped from the confinement of the comb, when the door of the chamber of death was softly opened. Amber, who either did not hear the noise or thought it was the daughter of Robinson, who lived as servant in the cottage, raised not her head. The steps continued to approach, then the sound ceased, and Amber felt the arms of some one encircling her waist to raise her from her kneeling posture. She lifted up her head, and dividing the hair from her forehead that she might see who it was, perceived that it was young Aveleyn who was hanging over her.

"My poor little girl!" said he in a tone of commiseration.

"Oh! William Aveleyn," cried Amber, bursting into a paroxysm of tears, as she was folded in his arms.

The sorrow of youth is sympathetic, and William Aveleyn, although seventeen years old, and fast advancing to manhood, did not disdain to mingle his tears with those of his former playmate. It was some time before he could persuade Amber, who clung to him in her grief, to any degree of serenity.

"Amber dear, you must come to us at the Hall; this is no place for you now."

"And why not, William? Why should I leave so soon? I'm not afraid of being here, or lying by his side alone:

I've seen other people die. I saw Mrs. Beazely die—I saw poor 'Faithful' die; and now, they all are dead," said Amber, bursting into tears, and burying her face in William Aveleyn's bosom. "I knew that he was to die," said she, raising her head, after a time—"he told me so; but to think that I shall never hear him speak again—that very soon I shall never see him more—I must cry, William."

"But your father is happy, Amber."

"He is happy, I know; but he was not my father, William. I have no father—no friend on earth I know of. He told me all before he died; 'Faithful' brought me from the sea."

This intelligence roused the curiosity of William Aveleyn, who interrogated Amber, and obtained from her the whole of the particulars communicated by Edward Forster; and as she answered to his many questions, she grew more composed.

The narrative had scarcely been finished, when Lord Aveleyn, who had been summoned by Robinson, drove to the door accompanied by Lady Aveleyn, who thought that her presence and persuasion would more readily induce Amber to leave the cottage. Convinced by her of the propriety of the proposal, Amber was put into the carriage without resistance, and conveyed to the Hall, where everything that kindness and sympathy could suggest was resorted to, to assuage her grief. There we must leave her, and repair to the metropolis.

"Scratton," said Mr. John Forster to his clerk, who had answered the bell, "recollect I cannot see any one to-day."

"You have several appointments, sir," replied the clerk.

"Then send and put them all off."

"Yes, sir; and if any one calls, I am to say that you are not at home?"

"No, I am at home; why tell a lie? but I cannot see anybody."

The clerk shut the door; John Forster put on his spectacles to reperuse the letter which lay before him. It was the one from Edward, enclosed in a frank by Lord Aveleyn, with a few lines announcing his brother's death, and stating that Amber was at the Hall, where they should be glad that she should remain until it was convenient to send for her. Edward's letter repeated his thanks to his brother for his kind promise, and took a last and affectionate farewell. John Forster struggled for a time with his feelings, but the more he attempted to repress them the more violent they became. He was alone, and he gave them vent. The legal documents before him, arising from the bitterness of strife, were thus unusually moistened with a tribute to a brother's memory. But in a few moments the old lawyer was himself again; all traces of emotion had disappeared, and no one who had seen him then would ever have imagined that John Forster could have been thus moved. The next day he was not as usual to be found at his chambers: the fact was that he had set off immediately after breakfast upon what is generally termed "house-hunting." The apartments which he occupied in his chambers were not sufficient for the intended increase of his establishment; and when he had given his promise to Edward, he was fully aware of the expense which would be entailed by receiving Amber, and had made up his mind to incur it. He therefore fixed upon a convenient house in Lincoln's Inn Fields, which would not detach him far from his chambers. Having arranged for a lease of twelve years, John Forster returned to his chambers

"Scratton," said he, "look out for a man-servant, a cook, housemaid, and a steady woman as housekeeper—good characters and undeniable reference. The housekeeper must be a somewhat superior person, as she will have to take charge of a young miss, and I do not want her spoiled by keeping company with the general description of servants. Do you understand?"

Scratton did; and in less than a month, as everything is to be obtained for money in the city of London, the house was furnished by a city upholsterer in a plain way, and all the servants installed in their respective situations.

Mr. John Forster took possession of his new house, and tried for a week if all worked well. Ascertaining that the furniture was complete, the under-servants well-behaved, and the housekeeper a mild and very intelligent personage, fit to be entrusted with the charge of a little girl, he then wrote to Lord Aveleyn, reiterating the thanks conveyed in his former letter, and requesting that Amber might be delivered into the charge of the bearer. With this letter Mr. Scratton was despatched, and, in due time, arrived at the Hall. Amber wept bitterly at the idea of parting with those who had been so kind to her, and passing into the hands of one who was a stranger. Having exacted a promise from William Aveleyn that he would call as he passed through on his way to Cambridge, she bade her kind friends farewell, entered the chaise in company with Mr. Scratton, and was hurried off to London.

Mr. Scratton was one of those personages who never spoke except on business, and having no business to transact with a girl of twelve years old, he never spoke at all, except when necessity rendered it imperative. Amber was, therefore, left to her own reflections. What they all were, I cannot tell, but one certainly was that travelling in a chaise for two days with Mr. Scratton was not very agreeable. Most happy was she when they drove up to the door of Mr. John Forster's new habitation. The old gentleman, who had calculated the hour of her arrival after the receipt of a letter from her companion, was there to receive her. Amber, who had been prepossessed in his favour by Edward Forster, who had told her that in his brother she would find a protector and indulgent parent, ran up to him when she entered the room, and burst into tears as the injunctions of Edward Forster returned to her memory. John Forster took her in his arms and kissed her. "My little girl," said he, "what my brother was, such will I be to you. Consider me as your father; for his memory, and I hope soon for your own sake, I shall rejoice to be so."

After an hour, by which time Amber had recovered her serenity and become almost cheerful, she was consigned to the charge of Mrs. Smith, the housekeeper, and John Forster hastened back to his chambers and his clients, to make up for so much lost time.

It was not long before the old gentleman discovered that the trouble and expense that he had incurred to please his brother was the occasion of pleasure and gratification. He no longer felt isolated in the world: in short, he had a home, where a beaming eye met his return, and an affectionate heart ministered to his wishes; where his well-known rap at the door was a source of delight, and his departure one of regret.

In a few months Amber had entwined herself round the old man's heart: the best masters were procured for her, and all the affection of a doting parent upon an only child was bestowed by him who, when the proposition was made, had declared that it was bad enough to maintain children of one's own begetting.

Bless my soul! how poor authors are obliged to gallop about. Now I must be off again to India, and get on board of the *Bombay Castle*.

CHAPTER XXXVIII

" A green and gilded snake had wreathed itself,
Who, with her head, nimble in threats, approached
The opening of his mouth."

—SHAKSPEARE.

THE *Bombay Castle* arrived at Madras without further adventure. A few hours after she had anchored, all the passengers, receiving kind messages from, or escorted on shore by their relatives or consignees, had landed—all, with the exception of the three Miss Revels, whose anxiety to land was increased by the departure of the others, and the unpleasant situation in which they were placed by remaining a clog upon Captain Drawlock, who would not quit his ship until he had surrendered up his charge. By inquiry of the dubashes, Captain Drawlock found out that an old Colonel Revel was residing at his bungalow, about two miles distant from the fort; and supposing him not to be aware of the arrival of his grand-nieces, he despatched Newton Forster to acquaint him with the circumstance. It was late in the afternoon when Newton arrived at the residence of the colonel, when he perceived immediately that everything was on the establishment of an old Indian nabob. A double set of palanquin-bearers were stretched under the verandahs, syces were fanning the horses with their chowries, tailors and various craftsmen were at work in the shade, while a herd of consumers, butlers, and other Indian domestics, were loitering about, or very busy doing nothing.

It will be necessary before Newton is introduced to the colonel that the colonel should be introduced to the reader. He was a man of nearly sixty years of age, forty-five of which, with the exception of occasional furlough, had been passed in the country.   Having held several lucrative situations for many years, and, although not parsimonious, being very prudent in money concerns, he had amassed a very large fortune.   More than once he had returned to England on leave, and with the full intention of remaining there, if he could be comfortable ; but a few months in his native country only made him more anxious to return to India.   His habits, his tastes, were all Eastern; the close hospitality, the cold winter of England, the loss of consequence, naturally resulting when a man mixes in the crowd of London, all disgusted him, and he invariably returned to India long before his furlough had expired.   He was a bachelor from choice. When young he had been very cruelly treated by the object of his admiration, who deserted him for a few lacs of rupees, which offered themselves with an old man as their appendage.   This had raised his bile against the sex in general, whom he considered as mercenary and treacherous.   His parties were numerous and expensive, but women were never to be seen in his house; and his confirmed dislike to them was the occasion of his seldom visiting, except to those who were, like himself, in a state of happy singleness.   In other points he was a liberal, worthy man, and a perfect gentleman, but extremely choleric in his disposition.

Newton addressed himself to one of the butlers, requesting to be announced.   The man led the way to a spacious hall, coated and floored with chunam, when Newton perceived the colonel, who presented rather a curious spectacle.   " Burra Saib ; Saib," said the Indian, and immediately retired.

The colonel was a tall, gaunt man, with high cheek-bones, bushy eyebrows, and white hair.   He was seated on a solitary chair in the centre of the hall; his dress consisting of a pair of white nankeen trousers and a white shirt, the sleeves of the latter tucked up to his shoulders, and exposing sinewy arms covered with hair.   By his side lay a basket of mangoes, and before his chair a large tub of water.   As Newton entered, he had an opportunity of witnessing the most approved method of eating this exquisite fruit.   The colonel had then one as large as a cassowary's egg held in both hands, and applied to his mouth, while he held his head over the tub of water, to catch the superabundant juice which flowed over his face, hands, and arms, and covered them with a yellow stain.   The contents of the mango were soon exhausted; the stone and pulp were dropped into the tub of water, and the colonel's hand was extended to the basket for a repetition of his luxurious feast, when Newton was announced. Newton was sorry to interrupt him, and would have made an apology, had he not observed that the colonel, whose back was towards him, continued his pleasing avocation : the fact was that the colonel was so intent upon his occupation that he had neither heard the announcement nor could he perceive Newton, who thus had an opportunity of witnessing the demolition of at least two dozen more mangoes without the colonel having turned his eyes in that direction, or being aware that he was not alone. But something at length attracted the attention of Newton, and induced him to come forward and put an end to the colonel's repast. The colonel had just taken another mango out of the basket, when Newton perceived a small snake wind itself over the rim, and curl up one of the feet of the colonel's chair, in such a position that the very next time that the colonel reached out his hand he must have come in contact with the reptile. Newton hardly knew how to act; the slightest movement of the old gentleman might be fatal to him; he therefore walked up softly and was about to strike the reptile on the head with his stick, when the colonel, as he leant over the tub, half rose from the chair. In an instant, Newton snatched it from under him, and jerked it, with the snake, to the corner of the hall. The colonel, whose centre of gravity had not been sufficiently forward to enable him to keep his feet, fell backward, when Newton and he both rolled on the floor together, and also both recovered their legs at the same time.

" You'll excuse me, sir," said Newton.

" I'll be d—d if I do, sir !" interrupted the colonel, in a rage. " Who the devil are you ? and how dare you presume to play off such impertinent jokes upon a stranger ? Where did you come from ? How did you get in, sir ? "

" Is that a joke, sir ? " replied Newton, calmly pointing to the snake, which was still hissing in its wrath at the corner of the room where the chair lay. Newton then briefly explained the circumstances.

" Sir, I beg your pardon a thousand times, and am very much your debtor. It is the most venomous snake that we have in the country. I trust you will accept my apology for a moment's irritation, and at the same time my sincere thanks." The colonel then summoned the servants, who provided them. selves with bamboos, and soon despatched the ol ject which had occasioned the misunderstanding. The colonel then apologised to Newton, while he repaired to the bath, and in a few minutes returned, having undergone the necessary ablution after a mango feast. His dress was changed, and he offered the appearance of an upright, gentleman-like, hard-featured man, who had apparently gone through a great deal of service without his stamina having been much impaired.

" I beg your pardon, my dear sir, for detaining you. May I request the pleasure of your name and the occasion of your providential visit ? "

" I have a letter for you, sir," replied Newton, who had been entrusted with the one which Mr. Revel had given to his daughters on their embarkation.

" Oh ! a letter of introduction. It is now quite superfluous, you have already introduced yourself."

" No, sir, it is not a letter of recommendation in my behalf, but to announce the arrival of your three grand-nieces—daughters of the Honourable Mr. Revel—in the *Bombay Castle*, the ship to which I belong."

" What ? " roared the colonel, " my three grand-nieces ! daughters of Mr. Revel ! "

" So I have understood from them, sir."

The colonel tore open the letter, in which Mr. Revel very coolly informed him that, not having received any answers to his former epistles on the subject, he presumed that they had miscarried, and had therefore been induced, in consequence of the difficulties which he laboured under, to send his daughters out to his kind protection. The colonel, as soon as he had finished the perusal of the letter, tore it into pieces again and again, every renewed action showing an increase of excitement. He then threw the fragments on the floor, stamping upon them in an ecstasy of rage.

" The d—d scoundrel !—the villain !—the rascal ! Do you know, sir, that when I was last in England this fellow swindled me out of a thousand pounds ? Yes, sir, a thousand pounds, by G—d ! promised to pay me in three weeks ; and when I was coming back, and asked for my money, he laughed at me, and ordered his servant not to let me in. And now he has sent out his three daughters to me—pawned them off upon me, laughing, I suppose, in his sleeve, as he did when he cheated me before. I'll not receive them, by G—d! they may find their way back again how they can;" and the colonel paced the room up and down, throwing his arms about in his fury.

Newton waited some time before he ventured to make any observation; indeed, he was so astonished at such an unheard-of proceeding, and so shocked at the unfortunate situation of Isabel, that he hardly knew what to say.

"Am I to inform the young ladies that you will not receive them?"

"You don't know me, sir. When did I ever receive a woman into my house? They are all alike, sir. Plotted with their father, I'll answer for, with the hopes of getting husbands. Tell them, sir, that I'll see them d—d first! Swindling scoundrel!—first cheats me out of a thousand pounds, and then tries to cheat me into providing for his family!"

Newton paused a little, to allow the colonel's wrath to subside, and then observed—"I never was so much distressed as to be the bearer of your message. The young ladies are certainly no parties to their father's dishonesty, and are in a situation much to be pitied. In a foreign country, thousands of miles from their friends, without means of subsistence, or of paying their passage home. What is to become of them?"

"I don't care."

"That your indignation is just, Colonel Revel, I admit; but allowing that you will not receive them, how are they to return home? Captain Drawlock, I am sure, would give them a passage; but we proceed to China. Poor girls!" continued Newton, with a sigh. "I should like to make a remark, Colonel Revel, if it were not considered too great a liberty in a stranger."

"You have already taken a liberty which in all probability has saved my life I shall be happy to listen to any remark that you may wish to offer."

"It was, sir, that, reprehensible as their father's conduct may be, common humanity, and a regard for your own character, will hardly warrant their being left thus destitute. They, at least, are your relations, and have neither offended nor deceived you; on the contrary, are with you joint victims of their father's deception."

"You appear to take a great interest in these young ladies," observed the colonel sharply.

"If I had never seen them, sir, their present unfortunate dilemma would be sufficient. Knowing them intimately as I do, I must say that this intelligence will be to one, at least, a death-blow. I would to God that I were able to assist and protect her!"

"Very handsome, then, I presume?" replied the colonel, with a sneer.

"She certainly is, sir; but it was not admiration of her beauty which occasioned the remark. If you knew her, sir, you would be as sorry to part with her as you now appear to be to receive her."

The colonel continued to pace the room, but with less violence than before. Newton observed this, and therefore was silent, hoping that reflection would induce him to alter his resolution. In a few minutes, apparently forgetting the presence of Newton, the colonel commenced talking to himself aloud, muttering out a few detached phrases: "Must take them in, by G—d! Couldn't show my face—nowhere —d—d scoundrel! Keep them here till next ship—till they are as yellow as gamboge, then send them home—revenge in that."

Thus did the old gentleman mutter loud enough for Newton to hear. A few minutes more were spent in perambulation, when he threw himself into the chair.

"I think, my young acquaintance, you appear to be interested for these relations of mine, or at least for one of them."

"I certainly am, sir; and so is every one who is acquainted with her."

"Well, I am glad to hear that there is one good out of the three. I have been put in a passion—no wonder; and I have said more than should be repeated. Were it known that these girls had been sent out to me in this way, the laugh would be raised against me, as it is known that I am not very partial to women; and it would also be of serious injury to them and their prospects. I have determined upon receiving them for the best of all possible reasons—I can't help

257   R

myself. You will, therefore, add to the obligations of this day by saying nothing about what has been made known to you "

" Most certainly, sir ; I will pledge you my honour, if it is requested."

" When I say not mention it, I mean to other parties ; but to the girls I must request you to state the facts. I will not have them come here, pawing and fondling and wheedling me as an old bachelor with a few lacs of rupees to be coaxed out of. It would make me sick ; I detest women and their ways. Now, if they are informed of the real state of the case, that they are here only on sufferance, that I neither wished nor want them, and that I have been imposed upon by their scoundrel of a father, I may keep them at the other end of the bungalow, and not be annoyed with their company ; until upon plea of bad health, or some other excuse, I can pay their passage back again."

" Could you not state these facts yourself, sir ? "

" No, I never meddle with women ; besides, it is better that they should know it before they come here. If you will promise me what I now request, why, I will consent to give them house-room ; if not, they may stay where they are. It will be but a few days' laugh at me, or abuse of me, I care little which "

" Well, sir, unpleasant as this intelligence must be, their present suspense is still more so. You will allow me to disclose it in as delicate a manner as possible."

" You may be as refined as you please, provided that you tell the exact truth, which I am convinced that you will by your countenance " .

" Then I will take my leave, sir," replied Newton.

" Fare you well, my dear sir ; recollect that my house is your home ; and although not fond of the society of women, I shall be delighted with yours. The young ladies may be brought on shore to the hotel, and I will send a carriage for them   Good-bye. What is your name ? "

" Forster, sir."

" Good-bye then, Mr. Forster, for the present ; " and the colonel quitted the room.

CHAPTER XXXIX

" Then there were sighs, the deeper for suppression,
    And stolen glances, sweeter for the theft,
And burning blushes, though for no transgression,
    Tremblings when met, and restlessness when left.
All these are little preludes to possession,
    Of which young passion cannot be bereft,
And merely tend to show how greatly love is
    Embarrassed, at first starting, with a novice."

                                        —BYRON.

IT was in no very happy frame of mind that Newton quitted
the colonel's house to execute his mission to the Miss Revels.
That the two eldest, provided they were admitted, would not
much take to heart either the conduct of their father or the
coolness of their relation, he was pretty well assured; but he
was too well acquainted with Isabel's character not to know
that she would deeply feel the humiliating situation in which
she was placed, and that it would prey upon her generous
and sensitive mind. As, however, there was no remedy, he
almost congratulated himself that as the colonel's message
was to be delivered, the commission had been placed in
his trust.

Captain Drawlock, tired of waiting, had escorted the young
ladies on shore to the hotel, anxiously expecting the arrival
of Newton, who was conducted there by a messenger despatched to intercept him.

" Well, Mr. Forster, is it all right?" said Captain Drawlock,
on his appearance.

" The colonel's carriage will be here for the ladies in less
than half-an-hour," replied Newton evasively.

" Then, Miss Revels, as I am extremely busy, I shall wish
you good morning, and will have the pleasure of paying my
respects before I sail. Allow me to offer you my best thanks
for your company during our voyage, and to assure you how
much your presence has contributed to enliven it. Forster,
you will, of course, remain with the Miss Revels, and see
them safe in the carriage;" and Captain Drawlock, who

259

appeared to consider his responsibility over with the voyage, shook hands with them, and quitted the hotel.

"Mr. Forster," said Isabel, as soon as Captain Drawlock was out of hearing, "I am sure, by your countenance, that there has been something unpleasant. Is it not so?"

"I am sorry to answer in the affirmative, and more sorry to be forced to impart the cause." Newton then entered into a detail of what had passed at the colonel's house. Isabel listened to it with attention, her sisters with impatience. Miss Charlotte, with an air of consternation, inquired whether the colonel had refused to receive them. On being informed to the contrary, she appeared to be satisfied. Laura simpered, and observed, "How very odd of papa!" and then seemed to think no more about it. Isabel made no observation; she remained on her chair, apparently in deep and painful thought.

A few minutes after the communication the colonel's carriage made its appearance, and Newton proposed that they should quit the hotel. Charlotte and Laura were all ready and impatient, but Isabel remained seated by the table.

"Come, Isabel," cried Charlotte.

"I cannot go, my dear Charlotte," replied Isabel; "but do not let me prevent you or Laura from deciding for yourselves."

"Not go!" cried the two sisters at once. Isabel was firm; and Newton, who did not think himself authorised to interfere, was a silent witness to the continued persuasions and expostulations of the two elder, and the refusal of the younger sister. Nearly half-an-hour thus passed away, when Charlotte and Laura decided that they would go, and send back the carriage for Isabel, who by that time would have come to her senses. The heartless, unthinking girls tripped gaily down to the carriage, and drove off. Newton, who had escorted them, retraced his steps, with a beating heart, to the room where he had left Isabel.

She was in tears.

"Do I intrude, Miss Revel?" said Newton, who could not repress his emotion at the sight.

"Oh no! I expected and wished that you would return, Mr. Forster. Do you think that you could find Captain Drawlock? I should feel much obliged if you would take that trouble for me."

THE MERCHANT SERVICE

"I will immediately go in search of him, if you wish it. Believe me, Miss Revel, I feel most sincerely for your situation; and if it were not considered an impertinent question, I should ask you what may be your present intentions?"

"Acquainted as you are with all the circumstances, Mr. Forster, the question is not impertinent, but kind. God knows that I require an adviser. I would, if possible, conceal the facts from Captain Drawlock. It is not for a daughter to publish a father's errors; but you know all, and I can therefore have no scruple in consulting with you: I do not see why I should. My resolution is at best a hasty one; but it is, never to enter the house of my relation under such humiliating circumstances — that is decided; but how to act, or what to do, is where I require advice. I am in a cruel situation. What a helpless creature is a woman! Were I a man, I could have worked my passage home, or have honestly obtained my bread in this place; but a woman—a young and unprotected woman—in a distant clime, and without a friend——"

"Do not say that you are without a friend; one who has at least the will, if not the power to serve you," replied Newton.

"No—not without a friend; but what avails a friend whose assistance I could not accept? It is to Captain Drawlock, therefore, that I must apply, and, painful as it may be, throw myself upon his generosity; for that reason I wish to see him. He may advise some means by which I may obtain a passage home. I will return in any capacity—as a nurse to children, as an attendant—anything that is creditable. I would watch over the couch of fever, pestilence, and plague, for months, rather than appear to be a party to my father's duplicity. O Mr. Forster! what must you think of the daughters after what you have heard of the parent's conduct?" and Isabel burst into tears.

Newton could contain himself no longer. "My dear Miss Revel, let me persuade you to compose yourself," said he, taking her hand, which was not withdrawn. "If you feel on this occasion, so do I most deeply—most deeply, because I can only lament, and dare not offer to assist you. The means of returning to your own country I can easily procure from Captain Drawlock; but would you accept

it from me ? I know—I cannot expect that you would;
and that, under such circumstances, it would be insulting
in me to offer it. Think, then, what pain I must feel to
witness your distress, and yet dare not offer to assist one
for whom—O my God——" ended Newton, checking his
feelings.

"I feel the kindness and the delicacy of your conduct,
Mr. Forster; and I will candidly acknowledge that, could
I accept it, there is no one to whom I would more cheerfully
be under an obligation; but the world will not permit it."

"What shall I do, Miss Revel?—shall I go for Captain
Drawlock?"

"Stay a little while; I wish to reflect. What would you
advise?—as a friend, tell me candidly, Mr. Forster."

"I am indeed proud that you allow me that title. It is
all that I ever dare hope for; but Isabel (I beg your pardon,
Miss Revel, I should have said)——"

"Nay, nay, I am not displeased. Why not Isabel? We
have known one another long enough; and deserted as I
feel, a kind word now——" Isabel covered her face with
her hand. Newton, who was standing by her, was overcome
by the intensity of his feelings; gradually they approached
nearer, until by, I suppose, the same principle which holds
the universe together—the attraction of cohesion—Newton's
arm encircled the waist of Isabel, and she sobbed upon his
shoulder. It was with difficulty that Newton refrained from
pouring out his soul, and expressing the ardent love which
he had so long felt for her; but it was taking advantage of
her situation. He had nothing to offer but himself and
beggary. He did refrain. The words were not spoken;
yet Isabel divined his thoughts, appreciated his forbearance,
and loved him more for his resolution.

"Isabel," said Newton at length, with a sigh, "I never
valued or wished for wealth till now. Till this hour I never
felt the misery of being poor."

"I believe you, Mr. Forster; and I am grateful, as I know
that it is for my sake that you feel it; but," continued she,
recovering herself, "crying will do no good. I asked you
for your advice, and you have only given me your arm."

"I am afraid it is all I shall ever have to offer," replied Newton. "But, Isabel, allow me to ask you one

question: Are you resolved never to enter your relation's house?"

"Not on the humiliating terms which he has proposed. Let the colonel come here for me and take me home with him, and then I will remain there until I can return to England; if not, I will submit to any privation, to any honest humiliation, rather than enter under his roof. But indeed, Mr. Forster, it is necessary that Captain Drawlock should be summoned. We are here alone; it is not correct; you must feel that it is not."

"I do feel that it is not; but, Isabel, I was this morning of some trifling service to the colonel, and may have some little weight with him. Will you allow me to return to him, and try what I can do? It will not be dark for these two hours, and I will soon be back."

Isabel assented. Newton hastened to the colonel, who had already been much surprised when he had been informed by his domestics (for he had not seen them) that only two ladies had arrived. The old gentleman was now cool. The explanation and strong persuasions of Newton, coupled with the spirited behaviour of Isabel, whose determination was made known to him, and which was so different from the general estimate he had formed of the sex, at last prevailed. The colonel ordered his carriage, and in company with Newton drove to the hotel, made a sort of apology—a wonderful effort on his part, and requested his grand-niece to accept of his hospitality. In a few minutes Isabel and the colonel were out of sight, and Newton was left to his own reflections.

A few days afterwards Newton accepted the colonel's invitation to dine, when he found that affairs were going on better than he expected. The old gentleman had been severely quizzed by those who were intimate with him, at the addition to his establishment, and had winced not a little under the lash; but on the whole, he appeared more reconciled than could have been expected. Newton, however, observed that, when speaking of the three sisters, he invariably designated them as "my grand-niece and the two other young women."

CHAPTER XL

" Rich in the gems of India's gaudy zone,
    And plunder piled from kingdoms not their own,
    Degenerate trade ; thy minions could despise
    Thy heart-born anguish of a thousand cries :
    Could lock, with impious hands, their teeming store,
    While famished nations died along the shore ;
    Could mock the groans of fellow-men, and bear
    The curse of kingdoms, peopled with despair ;
    Could stamp disgrace on man's polluted name,
    And barter with their gold eternal shame."
                                        —CAMPBELL.

GOLD!—gold ! for thee, what will man not attempt ?—for thee, to what degradation will he not submit ?—for thee, what will he not risk in this world, or prospectively in the next ?   Industry is rewarded by thee ; enterprise is supported by thee ; crime is cherished, and heaven itself is bartered for thee, thou powerful auxiliary of the devil !   One tempter was sufficient for the fall of man ; but thou wert added, that he ne'er might rise again.

Survey the empire of India ; calculate the millions of acres, the billions with which it is peopled, and then pause while you ask yourself the question—How is it that a company of merchants claim it as their own ? By what means did it come into their possession ?

Honestly, they will reply. Honestly ! you went there as suppliants ; you were received with kindness and hospitality, and your request was granted, by which you obtained a footing on the soil. . Now you are lords of countless acres, masters of millions, who live or perish as you will ; receivers of enormous tribute. Why, how is this ?

Honestly, again you say ; by treaty, by surrender, by taking from those who would have destroyed us the means of doing injury. Honestly ! say it again, that heaven may register, and hell may chuckle at your barefaced, impudent assertion.

No ! by every breach of faith which could disgrace an

infidel; by every act of cruelty which could disgrace our nature; by extortion, by rapine, by injustice, by mockery of all laws human or divine. The thirst for gold, and a golden country, led you on; and in these scorching regions you have raised the devil on his throne, and worshipped him in his proud pre-eminence as Mammon.

Let us think. Is not the thirst for gold a temptation to which our natures are doomed to be subjected—part of the ordeal which we have to pass? or why is it that there never is sufficient?

It appears to be ordained by Providence that this metal, obtained from the earth to feed the avarice of man, should again return to it. If all the precious ore which for a series of ages has been raised from the dark mine were now in tangible existence, how trifling would be its value! how inadequate as a medium of exchange for the other productions of Nature or of Art! If all the diamonds and other precious stones which have been collected from the decomposed rocks (for hard as they once were, like all sublunary matter, they too yield to time), why, if all were remaining on the earth, the frolic gambols of the May-day sweep would shake about those gems, which now are to be found in profusion only where rank and beauty pay homage to the thrones of kings. Arts and manufactures consume a large proportion of the treasures of the mine, and as the objects fall into decay, so does the metal return to the earth again. But it is in Eastern climes, where it is collected, that it soonest disappears. Where the despot reigns, and the knowledge of an individual's wealth is sufficient warranty to seal his doom, it is to the care of the silent earth alone that the possessor will commit his treasures; he trusts not to relation or to friend, for gold is too powerful for human ties. It is but on his deathbed that he imparts the secret of his deposit to those he leaves behind him. Often called away before he has time to make it known, reserving the fond secret till too late, still clinging to life and all that makes life dear to him; often does the communication, made from the couch of death, in half-articulated words, prove so imperfect, that the knowledge of its existence is of no avail unto his intended heirs; and thus it is that millions return again to the earth from which they have been gathered with such toil. What

avarice has dug up avarice buries again ; perhaps in future
ages to be regained by labour, when, from the chemical
powers of eternal and mysterious Nature, they have again
been filtered through the indurated earth, and reassumed
the form and the appearance of the metal which has .lain
in darkness since the creation of the world.

Is not this part of the grand principle of the universe?
—the eternal cycle of reproduction and decay, pervading
all and everything—blindly contributed to by the folly
and wickedness of man! "So far shalt thou go, but no
further," was the fiat ; and arrived at the prescribed limit,
we must commence again. At this moment intellect has
seized upon the seven-league boots of the fable, which
fitted everybody who drew them on, and strides over the
universe. How soon, as on the decay of the Roman Empire,
may all the piles of learning which human endeavours would
rear as a tower of Babel to scale the heavens disappear,
leaving but fragments to future generations as proofs of pre-
existent knowledge ! Whether we refer to nature or to art,
to knowledge or to power, to accumulation or destruction,
bounds have been prescribed which man can never pass,
guarded as they are by the same unerring and unseen Power
which threw the planets from His hand to roll into their
appointed orbits. All appears confused below, but all is
clear in heaven.

I have somewhere heard it said, that wherever heaven may
be, those who reach it will behold the mechanism of the universe in its perfection. The stars now studding the firmament
in such apparent confusion, will there appear in all their
regularity, as worlds revolving in their several orbits round
suns which gladden them with light and heat, all in harmony,
all in beauty, rejoicing as they roll their destined course in
obedience to the Almighty fiat ; one vast, stupendous, and,
to the limits of our present senses, incomprehensible mechanism, perfect in all its parts, most wonderful in the whole.
Nor do I doubt it : it is but reasonable to suppose it. He
that hath made this world and all upon it, can have no limits
to His power.

I wonder whether I shall ever see it.

I said just now, let us think. I had better have said, let us
not think ; for thought is painful, even dangerous, when carried

to excess. Happy is he who thinks but little, whose ideas are so confined as not to cause the intellectual fever, wearing out the mind and body, and often threatening both with dissolution. There is a happy medium of intellect, sufficient to convince us that all is good—sufficient to enable us to comprehend that which is revealed, without a vain endeavour to pry into the hidden; to understand the one, and lend our faith unto the other; but when the mind would soar unto the heaven not opened to it, or dive into sealed and dark futurity, how does it return from its several expeditions? Confused, alarmed, unhappy; willing to rest, yet restless; willing to believe, yet doubting; willing to end its futile travels, yet setting forth anew. Yet, how is a superior understanding envied! how coveted by all!—a gift which always leads to danger, and often to perdition.

Thank Heaven! I have not been entrusted with one of those thoroughbred, snorting, champing, foaming sort of intellects, which run away with Common Sense, who is jerked from his saddle at the beginning of its wild career. Mine is a good, steady, useful hack, who trots along the highroad of life, keeping on his own side, and only stumbling a little now and then, when I happen to be careless—ambitious only to arrive safely at the end of his journey, not to pass by others.

Why am I no longer ambitious? Once I was, but 'twas when I was young and foolish. Then methought " It were an easy leap to pluck bright honour from the pale-faced moon;" but now I am old and fat, and there is something in fat which chokes or destroys ambition. It would appear that it is requisite for the body to be active and springing as the mind; and if it is not, it weighs the latter down to its own gravity. Who ever heard of a fat man being ambitious? Cæsar was a spare man; Buonaparte was thin as long as he climbed the ladder; Nelson was a shadow. The Duke of Wellington had not sufficient fat in his composition to grease his own Wellington boots. In short, I think my hypothesis to be fairly borne out, that fat and ambition are incompatible.

It is very melancholy to be forced to acknowledge this, for I am convinced that it may be of serious injury to my works. An author with a genteel figure will always be more read

than one who is corpulent. All his etherealness departs.
Some young ladies may have fancied me an elegant young
man, like Lytton Bulwer, full of fun and humour, concealing
all my profound knowledge under the mask of levity, and
have therefore read my books with as much delight as has
been afforded by " Pelham." But the truth must be told.
I am a grave, heavy man, with my finger continually laid
along my temple, seldom speaking unless spoken to—and
when ladies talk, I never open my mouth; the consequence
is, that sometimes, when there is a succession of company, I
do not speak for a week. Moreover, I am married, with five
small children; and now all I look forward to, and all I
covet, is to live in peace, and die in my bed.

I wonder why I did not commence authorship before!
How true it is that a man never knows what he can do until
he tries! The fact is, I never thought that I could make a
novel; and I was thirty years old before I stumbled on the
fact. What a pity!

Writing a book reminds me very much of making a passage
across the Atlantic. At one moment, when the ideas flow,
you have the wind aft, and away you scud, with a flowing
sheet, and a rapidity which delights you; at other times,
when your spirit flags, and you gnaw your pen (I have lately
used iron pens, for I'm a devil of a crib-biter), it is like unto
a foul wind, tack and tack, requiring a long time to get a
short distance. But still you do go, although but slowly;
and in both cases we must take the foul wind with the fair.
If a ship were to furl her sails until the wind was again
favourable, her voyage would be protracted to an indefinite
time; and if an author were to wait until he again felt in a
humour, it would take a life to write a novel.

Whenever the wind is foul, which it now most certainly is,
for I am writing anything but " Newton Forster," and which
will account for this rambling, ·stupid chapter, made up of
odds and ends, strung together like what we call "skewer
pieces" on board of a man-of-war; when the wind is foul,
as I said before, I have, however, a way of going ahead by
getting up the steam, which I am now about to resort to—
and the fuel is brandy. All on this side of the world are
asleep, except gamblers, housebreakers, the new police, and
authors. My wife is in the arms of Morpheus—an allegorical

crim. con., which we husbands are obliged to wink at ; and I am making love to ₁ the brandy-bottle, that I may stimulate my ideas, as unwilling to be roused from their dark cells of the brain as the spirit summoned by Lochiel, who implored at each response, " Leave me, oh ! leave me to repose."

Now I'll invoke them, conjure them up, like little imps, **to** do my bidding :

> By this glass which now I drain,
> By this spirit, which shall cheer you,
> As its fumes mount to my brain,
> From thy torpid slumbers rear you.

> By this head, so tired with thinking,
> By this hand, no longer trembling,
> By these lips, so fond of drinking,
> Let me feel that you're assembling.

> By the bottle placed before me
> (Food for you, ere morrow's sun),
> By this second glass I pour me,
> Come, you *little beggars*, come.

CHAPTER XLI

> " British sailors have a knack,
> Haul away, yo ho, boys,
> Of hauling down a Frenchman's jack
> 'Gainst any odds, you know, boys."
> —*Old Song.*

THERE was, I flatter myself, some little skill in the introduction of the foregoing chapter, which has played the part of chorus during the time that the *Bombay Castle* has proceeded on to Canton, has taken in her cargo, and is on her passage home, in company with fifteen other East Indiamen and several country ships, all laden with the riches of the East, and hastening to pour their treasures into the lap of their country. Millions were floating on the waters, entrusted to the skill of merchant seamen to convey them home in safety, and to their courage to defend them from the enemy, which had long been lying in wait to intercept them. By a .very unusual chance or oversight there had been no men-of-war despatched to protect property of such enormous value.

The Indian fleet had just entered the Straits of Malacca, and were sailing in open order, with a fresh breeze and smooth water. The hammocks had been stowed, the decks washed, and the awnings spread. Shoals of albicore were darting across the bows of the different ships; and the seamen, perched upon the catheads and spritsail-yard, had succeeded in piercing with their harpoons many, which were immediately cut up, and in the frying-pans for break-fast. But very soon they had "other fish to fry;" for one of the Indiamen, the *Royal George*, made the signal that there were four strange sail in the S.W.

"A gun from the commodore, sir," reported Newton, who was officer of the watch. "The flags are up—they are not our pennants."

It was an order to four ships of the fleet to run down and examine the strange vessels.

Half-an-hour elapsed, during which time the glasses were at every masthead. Captain Drawlock himself, although not much given to climbing, having probably had enough of it during his long career in the service, was to be seen in the maintop. Doubts, suspicions, declarations, surmises, and positive assertions were bandied about, until they were all dispelled by the reconnoitring ships telegraphing, "A French squadron, consisting of one line-of-battle ship, three frigates, and a brig." It was, in fact, the well-known squadron of Admiral Linois, who had scoured the Indian Seas, ranging it up and down with the velocity as well as the appetite of a shark. His force consisted of the *Marengo*, of eighty guns; the famed *Belle Poule*, a forty-gun frigate, which outstripped the wind; the *Sémillante*, of thirty-six guns; the *Berceau*, ship corvette, of twenty-two, and a brig of sixteen. They had sailed from Batavia on purpose to intercept the China fleet, having received intelligence that it was unprotected, and anticipating an easy conquest, if not an immediate sur-render, to their overpowering force.

"The recall is up on board of the commodore," said Mathews, the first mate, to Captain Drawlock.

270

THE MERCHANT SERVICE

"Very well, keep a good look-out; he intends to fight, I'll answer for it. We must not surrender up millions to these French scoundrels without a tussle."

"I should hope not," replied Mathews; "but that big fellow will make a general average among our tea canisters, I expect, when we do come to the scratch. There go the flags, sir," continued Mathews, repeating the number to Captain Drawlock, who had the signal-book in his hand.

"Form line of battle in close order, and prepare for action," read Captain Drawlock from the signal-book.

A cheer resounded through the fleet when the signal was made known. The ships were already near enough to each other to hear the shouting, and the confidence of others added to their own.

"If we only had *all* English seamen on board, instead of these Lascars and Chinamen, who look so blank," observed Newton to Mathews, "I think we should show them some play."

"Yes," growled Mathews; "John Company will some day find out the truth of the old proverb, ' Penny wise and pound foolish ! ' "

The French squadron, which had continued on the wind to leeward until they could fetch the India fleet, now tacked, and laid up directly for them. In the meantime, the English vessels were preparing for action ; the clearing of their lumbered decks was the occasion of many a coop of fowls, or pig of the true China breed, exchanging their destiny for a watery grave. Fortunately, there were no passengers. Homeward-bound China ships are not encumbered in that way, unless to astonish the metropolis with such monstrosities as the mermaid, or as the Siamese twins, coupled by Nature like two hounds (separated lately indeed by Lytton Bulwer, who has satisfactorily proved that "unity between brethren," so generally esteemed a blessing, on the contrary is a bore). In a short time all was ready, and the India fleet continued their course under easy sail, neither courting nor avoiding the conflict.

At nightfall the French squadron hauled to the wind; the conduct of the China fleet rendered them cautious, and the French admiral considered it advisable to ascertain, by broad daylight, whether a portion of the English ships were not men-of-war; their cool and determined behaviour certainly warranted the suspicion. It was now to be decided whether the Indiamen should take advantage of the darkness of the night to escape, or wait the result of the ensuing day. The force opposed to them was formidable and concentrated; their own, on the contrary, was weak from division, each ship not having more than sixty English seamen on board, the country ships none at all, the few belonging to them having volunteered on board the Indiamen. In this decision, Commodore Dance proved his judgment as well as his courage. In an attempt to escape the fleet would separate; and from the well-known superior sailing of the French squadron, most of them would be overtaken, and being attacked single-handed, fall an easy prey to the enemy.

In this opinion the captains of the Indiamen, who had communicated during the night, were unanimous, and equally so in the resolution founded upon it, "to keep together and fight to the last." The India fleet lay-to for the night, keeping their lights up and the men at their quarters, most of the English seamen sound asleep, the Lascars and Chinese sitting up in groups, expressing, in their own tongues, their fear of the approaching combat, in which, whether risked for national honour or individual property, they could have no interest.

The morning broke, and discovered the French squadron about three miles to windward. Admiral Linois had calculated that if the fleet consisted only of merchant vessels they would have profited by the darkness to have attempted to escape, and he had worked to windward during the night, that he might be all ready to pounce down upon his quarry. But when he perceived that the English ships did not attempt to increase their distance, he was sadly puzzled.

The French tricolour hardly had time to blow clear from their taffrails, when the English unions waved aloft in defiance; and that Admiral Linois might be more perplexed by the arrangements of the night, three of the most warlike Indiamen displayed the red ensign, while the remainder of the ships hoisted up the blue. This ruse led the French admiral to suppose that these three vessels were men-of-war, composing the escort of the fleet.

"The *Royal George* leading into action, followed by the other ships in close order."

At nine o'clock the commodore made the signal to fill; and the French squadron not bearing down, the India fleet continued its course under easy sail. The French admiral then edged away with his squadron, with the intention of cutting off the country ships, which had been stationed to leeward, but which, since the British fleet had hauled their wind, had been left in the rear. It was now requisite for the British commander to act decidedly and firmly. Captain Timmins, an officer for courage and conduct not surpassed by any in our naval service, who commanded the *Royal George*, edged to within hail of the commodore, and recommended that the order should be given to tack in succession, bear down in a line ahead, and engage the enemy. This spirited advice was acted upon; the *Royal George* leading into action, followed by the other ships in such close order that their flying jib-booms were often pointed over the taffrails of their predecessors.

In a quarter of an hour was to be witnessed the unusual spectacle of a fleet of merchant ships exchanging broadsides with the best equipped and highest disciplined squadron that ever sailed from France. In less than an hour was presented the more unusual sight of this squadron flying from the merchant ships, and the signal for a general chase answered with enthusiastic cheers.

That Admiral Linois might have supposed, previous to the engagement, that some of the British ships were men-of-war is probable; but that he knew otherwise after they had commenced action must also have been the case. The fact was, he was frightened at their determined courage and their decided conduct; and he fled, not from the guns, but from the *men*.

I do not know on record any greater instance of heroism on the part of British seamen; and I am delighted that Newton Forster was in the conflict, or of course I could not have introduced it in this work.

And now, those who read for amusement may, if they please, skip over the rest of the chapter. There are points connected with the India service which I intend to comment upon; and as all the wisdom of the age is confined to novels, and nobody reads pamphlets, I introduce them here.

When one man is empowered to hold in check, and to

s

insist upon the obedience of, a large proportion of his fellows, it can only be by "opinion" that his authority can be supported.

By "opinion" I mean the knowledge that he is so empowered by the laws of the country to which they all belong, and by which laws they will be punished if they act in opposition to his authority. The fiat of the individual commanding is in this case the fiat of the nation at large; to contend with this fiat is not contending with the individual, but with the nation, to whose laws they must submit, or return to their country no more. A commander of a vessel, therefore, armed with martial law, is, in fact, representing and executing not his own will, but that of the nation who have made the law; for he is amenable, as well as his inferiors, if he acts contrary to or misuses it.

In the merchant service martial law is not permitted; the bye-laws relative to shipping, and the common law of the country, are supposed to be sufficient; and certainly the present system is more advisable than to vest such excessive power in the hands of men who, generally speaking, neither require nor are fit to be entrusted with it. Where, as in the greater number of merchant vessels, the master and his subordinate officers compose one-third, if not one-half, of the complement on board, nothing but the most flagrant conduct is likely to produce insubordination.

But in the East India service the case is different. The vessels themselves are of dimensions equal, if not superior, to our largest class of frigates, and they carry from thirty to forty guns; the property embarked in them is also of such an extent, that the loss almost becomes national; their commanders are men of superior attainments, as gentlemen and as officers; finally, the complement of seamen under their command is larger than on board of many of the king's ships.

The above considerations will at once establish that those bye-laws which afford protection to the well-governing of the merchant service in general are not sufficient to maintain the necessary discipline on board of the East India ships. The greater the disproportion between the unit who commands and the numbers who obey, the greater the chance of mutiny. Sedition is the progeny of assembly. Even where grievances may be real, if there is no contact and no discussion, there will be no insubordination; but imaginary grievances, canvassed and discussed in assembly, swell into disaffection and mutiny. When, therefore, numbers are collected together, as in the vessels of the East India service, martial law becomes indispensable; and the proof of it is, that the commanders of these vessels have been forced to exercise it upon their own responsibility. A letter of marque should be granted to all vessels carrying a certain number of men, empowering the commanders, under certain sureties and penalties, to exercise this power. It would be a boon to the East India ships, and ultimately a benefit to the navy.

To proceed. The merchant ships of the Company are men-of-war; the men-of-war of the Company are—what shall I call them? By their right names—they are all *Bombay Marine;* but let me at once assert, in applying their own name to them as a reproach, that the officers commanding them are not included in the stigma. I have served with them, and have pleasure in stating that, taking the average, the vessels are as well officered as those in our own service; but let us describe the vessels and their crews. Most of the vessels are smaller in scantling than the run down (and constantly *going down*) ten-gun brigs in our own service, built for a light draught of water (as they were originally intended to act against the pirates which occasionally infest the Indian Seas), and unfit to contend with anything like a heavy sea. Many of them are pierced for, and actually carry, fourteen or sixteen guns, but as effective fighting vessels, ought not to have been pierced for more than eight. I have no hesitation in asserting that an English cutter is a match for any of them, and a French privateer has before now proved that she was superior. The crews are composed of a small proportion of English seamen, a small proportion of Portuguese sea-cunnies, a proportion of Lascars, and a proportion of Hindoo Bombay marines. It requires two or three languages to carry on the duty; customs, religions, provisions, all different, and all living and messing separate. How is it possible that any officer can discipline a ship's company of this incongruous description so as to make them "pull together"? In short, the vessels and the crews are equally contemptible, and the officers, in cases of difficulty, must be sacrificed to the pride and meanness of the Company. My reason for taking notice

of the "Bombay Marine" arises from an order lately pro-
mulgated, in which the officers of this service were to take
rank and precedence with those of the navy. Now, as far as
the officers themselves are concerned, so far from having any
objection to it, I wish, for their own merits and the good-
will that I bear them, that they were incorporated into our
navy-list; but as long as they command vessels of the above
description, in the event of a war, I will put a case to prove
the absurdity and danger which may result. There is not
one vessel at this present time in their service which would
not be sunk by one well-directed broadside from a large
frigate; yet as many of their officers are of long standing, it
is very probable that a squadron of English frigates may fall
in with one of these vessels, the captain of which would
be authorised by his seniority to take the command of the
whole of them. We will suppose that this squadron falls in
with the enemy, of equal or superior force; can the officer
in command lead on the attack? If so, he will be sent
down by the first broadside. If he does not, from whom are
the orders to proceed during the action? The consequences
would be as injurious as the arrangement is ridiculous.

The charter of the East India Company will soon expire;
and if it is to be renewed, the country ought to have some
indemnification for the three millions which this colony or
conquest (which you please) annually draws from it. Now
there is one point which deserves consideration: the con-
stitutional protection of all property is by the nation, and as
a naval force is required in India, that force should be
supplied by the armaments of the nation, at the expense of
the Company. I have already proved that the "Bombay
Marine" is a useless and incompetent service: let it be
abolished altogether, and men-of-war be sent out to supply
their place. It is most important that our navy should be
employed in time of peace, and our officers gain that practical
knowledge without which the theoretical is useless. Was
this insisted upon, a considerable force would be actively
employed, at no expense to the country, and many officers
become valuable who now are remaining inactive and forgetting what previous knowledge they may have acquired of
their nautical duties.

At the same time, every East India ship should be compelled to take on board her whole complement of English seamen, and not be half manned by Lascars and Chinamen.

But I presume I must be careful how I attempt to legislate for that country, or I shall have two tame elephants sent after me by the man *what* puts his hair in papers!

CHAPTER XLII

" What singular emotions fill
Their bosoms, who have been induced to roam,
With fluttering doubts, if all be well or ill,
With love for many, and with fears for some !"
—BYRON.

THE China fleet arrived without encountering any further danger ; the commodore and commanders of the several ships composing the fleet received that praise from their country-men to which their conduct had so fully entitled them. As soon as the *Bombay Castle* had entered the basin of the East India docks, Newton requested, and easily obtained, per-mission to leave the ship. He immediately directed his steps to Greenwich, that he might ascertain if his father was in existence ; for he had received no letters since his departure, although he had taken several opportunities to write. It is true that he had not expected any ; he knew that his father was too absent ever to think about writing to him, and his uncle much too busy to throw away any portion of his time in unnecessary correspondence.

When we approach the dwelling containing, or supposed to contain, an object of solicitude, of whose existence we are uncertain, what a thrill of anxiety pervades the frame ! How quickened is the throbbing of the heart ! how checked the respiration ! Thus it was with Newton Forster as he raised his hand to the latch of the door. He opened it, and the first object which delighted his eyes was his father seated upon a high stool smoking his pipe in the company of two veterans of the Hospital, who had brought their old bones to an anchor upon a large trunk. They were in earnest con-versation, and did not perceive the company of Newton, who waited a little while, holding the door ajar, as he contemplated the group.

One of the pensioners was speaking, and continued : " May be, or may not be, Mr. Forster, that's *dubersome ;* but if so be as how he is alive, why, you'll see him soon, that's sartin —take my word for it. A good son, as you say he was, as soon as he can get over the side of the ship always bears up for his parent's house. With the help of your barnacles, I worked my way clean through the whole yarn, and I seed the report of killed and wounded ; and I'll take my affidavy that there warn't an officer in the fleet as lost the number of his mess in that action, and a most clipping affair it was. Only think of mounseer turning tail to marchant vessels ! Damn my old buttons ! what will our jolly fellows do next ? "

" Next, Bill ! why, there be nothing to do, 'less they shave off the beard of the Grand Turk to make a swab for the cabin of the king's yacht, and sarve out his seven hundred wives amongst the fleet. I say, I wonder how he keeps so many of them craft in good order ? "

" I knows," replied the other, " for I axed the very question when I was up the Dardanelles. There be a big black fellow, a *unique* they calls him, with a large sword and a bag of sawdust, as always stands sentry at the door, and if so be a wom'un kicks up a bobbery, why, plump her head goes into the bag."

" Well, that's one way to make a good woman on her ; but as I was saying, Mr. Forster, you mustn't be down in the mouth ; a seaman as knows his duty never cares for leave till all the work be done. I'd bet a yard of pigtail that Mr. Newton——"

" Is here, my good fellow !" interrupted Newton. " My dear father !"

Nicholas sprang off his seat and embraced his son.

" My dear, dear boy ! why did you not come to me before ? I was afraid that you had been killed. Well, I'm glad to see you, Newton. How did you like the West Indies ? "

" The East Hinges, you mean, Mr. Forster. Newton," continued the old pensioner, wiping both sides of his hand upon his blue breeches, and then extending it, " tip us your daddle, my lad ; I like to touch the flipper of one who has helped to shame the enemy, and it will be no disgrace for you to grapple with an old seaman, who did his duty as long as he had a pin to stand upon."

"With pleasure, my friend," replied Newton, taking the old man's hand, while the other veteran seized the one unoccupied, and surveying Newton from top to toe, observed, "If your ship be manned with all such lads as you—why, she be damned well manned, that's all."

Newton laughed and turned to his father.

"Well, father, how are you? have you been quite well? And how do you like your berth here?"

"Why, Newton, I get on much better than I did at Bristol."

"It be Liverpool he mean, Mr. Newton; but your good father be a little damaged in his upper works; his memory-box is like a sieve. Come, Bill, we be two too many. When father and son meet after a India voyage, there be much to say as wants no listeners. Good-bye, Mr. Forster; may you never want a son, and may he never want a ship!"

Newton smiled his thanks to the considerate old pensioners, as they stumped out of the door and left him alone with his father. The communications of Nicholas were as concise as usual. He liked his situation, liked his company, had as much work as he wished for, and had enjoyed good health. When Newton entered upon pecuniary matters, which he was the sooner induced to do by observing that his father's coat and smallclothes were in a most ruinous condition, he discovered, that though the old gentleman had provided himself with money from the bankers during the first year to purchase a new suit of clothes, latterly he not only had quite forgotten that there were funds at his disposal, but even that he had procured the clothes, which had remained in the chest from the day they had been sent home without having been tried on.

"Dear me! now I recollect, so I did; and I put them upstairs somewhere. I was busy at the time with my improvement on the duplex."

"Have you seen much of my uncle, sir?" inquired Newton.

"Your uncle!—dear me, no! I don't know where he lives; so I waited until you came back. We'll go to-morrow, Newton, or he may think me unkind. I'll see if his watch goes well; I recollect he said it did. But, Newton, tell me all about your voyage, and the action with the French ships."

Newton entered into a detail, during which he perceived by his father's questions that his memory had become more impaired, and that he was more absent than ever. He arranged to call upon his uncle the ensuing day; and then it was his intention, without communicating it to his father, to make every inquiry and advertise to ascertain the fate of his mother. This was a duty which he had long wished to repeat; but his necessities and want of time had hitherto prevented the renewal of the task.

Early the next morning Newton and his father went up to London by the Greenwich coach; and a walk of a few minutes after they were put down brought them to the chambers of Mr. John Forster.

"How do you do, Mr. Scratton? Is my uncle at home?" inquired Newton.

Mr. Scratton immediately recognised him, and very graciously replied that his uncle was at home, and would be very glad to see him, having talked very often of him lately.

Newton and his father were ushered into the parlour, where he found his uncle precisely in the same position as when he last saw him; it would almost have appeared that he had not quitted his seat during Newton's tedious voyage.

"Nephew," said Mr. John Forster, without rising from his chair, "I am very glad to see you. Brother Nicholas, I am very glad to see you too. Chairs, Scratton," continued the old lawyer, taking his watch off the table and placing it in his fob. "Well, nephew, I am very glad to hear such good accounts of you. I saw Mr. Bosanquet yesterday, and he told me that you had for your good conduct been promoted to the rank of second mate."

"It is more than I am aware of," replied Newton, much pleased with the information. "I am much obliged to you for the intelligence, as I am for your many other acts of kindness."

"Well, so you ought to be; it's no bad thing, as I told you before, to find out an uncle. By-the-bye, there has been some alteration in my establishment since we parted, nephew. I have a house in Lincoln's Inn Fields, and a spare bed, if you will accept of it. We dine at six; brother Nicholas, I shall be very happy to see you, if you can stay.

It will be too late to go home after dinner, but you can share my nephew's bed."

"I shall be most happy to accept your kind offer for a few days, sir, if it does not incommode you," replied Newton.

"No; you will not incommode me there, but you do very much here, where I am always busy. So good-bye, my boy; I shall be at home at six. Brother Nicholas, you did not vouchsafe me an answer."

"About what, brother John?" replied Nicholas, who had been in the clouds.

"Oh, I'll tell you all about it, father," said Newton, laughing. "Come away now—my uncle is busy." And Nicholas rose up, with the observation—

"Brother John, you appear to me to read a great deal."

"Yes, I do, brother."

"How much do you read a day?"

"I really cannot say; much depends upon whether I am interrupted or not."

"It must be very bad for your eyes, brother John."

"It certainly does not improve them," replied the lawyer impatiently.

"Come, father, my uncle is very busy," said Newton, touching Nicholas on the arm.

"Well, good-bye, brother John. I had something to say —oh! I hope you are not displeased at my not coming to see you before?"

"Humph! not in the least, I can assure you, brother Nicholas; so good-bye. Newton, you'll bring him with you at six," said Mr. John Forster; and he resumed his brief before they had quitted the room.

Newton was much surprised to hear that his uncle had taken a house, and he surmised whether he had not also been induced to take a wife. He felt an inclination to put the question to Mr. Scratton as he passed through the office, but checked the wish, lest it should appear like prying into his uncle's affairs. Being the month of February, it was dark long before six o'clock, and Newton was puzzled what to do with his father until that time. He returned to the Salopian Coffee-house, opposite to which they had been put down by the Greenwich coach; and

281

taking possession of a box, called for some biscuits and a pint of sherry; and requesting his father to stay there until his return, went out to purchase a sextant and some other nautical luxuries, which his pay enabled him to procure without trespassing upon the funds supplied by the generosity of his uncle. He then returned to his father, who had finished the wine and biscuits, and had his eyes fixed upon the ceiling of the room; and calling a hackney coach, drove to the direction which his uncle had pointed out as his residence.

Mr. John Forster had already come home, and they found him in the dining-room decanting the wine for dinner, with Amber by his side. Newton was surprised at the appearance of a little girl; and as he took her proffered hand, inquired her name.

"Amber. Papa says it's a very foolish name; don't you, papa?"

"Yes, my dear, I do; but now we are going to dinner, and you must go to Mrs. Smith; so good-night."

Amber kissed the old lawyer as he stooped to her; and wishing the company good-night, she left the room.

"Brother John," said Nicholas, "I really had no idea that you were a married man."

"Humph! I am not a married man, brother."

"Then pray, brother, how is it possible for that little girl to be your daughter?"

"I did not say she was my daughter; but now we will go upstairs into the drawing-room, while they put the dinner on the table."

The dinner was soon announced; the cookery was plain, but good, the wine excellent. When the dessert was placed on the table, Mr. John Forster rose, and taking two bottles of port wine from the sideboard, placed them on the table, and addressed Newton.

"Nephew, I have no time to *sip* wine, although it is necessary that I drink it. Now, we must drink fast, as I have only ten minutes to spare; not that I wish you to drink more than you like, but I must push the bottle round, whether you fill or no, as I have an appointment, what we call a consultation, at my chambers. Pass the bottle, brother," continued the lawyer, helping himself, and shoving the decanter to Nicholas.

THE MERCHANT SERVICE

Nicholas, who had been little accustomed to wine, obeyed mechanically, swallowing down each glass *à gorge déployée,* as he was awoke from his meditations by the return of the bottle, and then filling up his glass again. Newton, who could take his allowance as well as most people, could not, however, venture to drink glass for glass with his uncle, and the bottle was passed several times without his filling. When the ten minutes had elapsed, Mr. John Forster took his watch from the table, replaced it in his fob, and rose from his chair. Locking up the remainder of the wine, he quitted the house without apology, leaving his guests to entertain themselves, and order tea when they felt inclined.

" My brother seems to be very busy, Newton," observed Nicholas. " What wine was that we have been drinking ? It was very strong ; I declare my head turns round ; " and in a few moments more Nicholas dropped his head upon the table and was fast asleep.

Newton, who perceived that his father was affected by the wine which he had been drinking, which was, in the sum total, a pint of sherry at the coffee-house before dinner, and at least a bottle during and after his meal, thought it better that he should be allowed to take his nap. He therefore put out the candles, and went up into the drawing-room, where he amused himself with a book until the clock struck twelve. According to the regulations of the house, the servants had retired to bed, leaving a light in the passage for their master on his return, which sometimes was at a very late hour, or rather, it should be said, at a very early one. Newton lighted a chamber-candlestick and went down into the parlour to rouse his father ; but all his attempts were in vain. The wine had taken such an effect upon him, that he was in a state of lethargy. Newton observed that the servant had cleared the table, and that the fire was out ; and as there was no help for it, he removed the chairs to the end of the room, that his father might not tumble over them if he awoke in the dark, and then retired to his own bed.

CHAPTER XLIII

" Angels and ministers of grace defend us !

. . . . . .

Be thy intents wicked or charitable,
Thou com'st in such a questionable shape
That I will speak to thee."

—SHAKSPEARE.

IT was past two o'clock when Mr. John Forster returned from his chambers and let himself in with a pass-key. Having secured the street door, the old gentleman lighted his candle from the lamp, which he blew out, and had his foot upon the first step of the stairs, when he was startled by a loud snore from Nicholas in the dining-room. He immediately proceeded there, and found his brother, with his head still lying on the table.

"Humph!" ejaculated the lawyer. "Why, brother Nicholas — brother Nicholas ! "

Nicholas, who had nearly slept off the effects of the wine, answered with an unintelligible sort of growling.

" Brother Nicholas, I say—brother Nicholas—will you get up, or lie here all night ? "

" They shall be cleaned and ready by to-morrow morning," replied Nicholas, dreaming.

" Humph ! that's more than you will be, apparently. I say, brother Nicholas."

" Yes, brother," replied Nicholas, raising his head and staring at the candle. " Why, what's the matter ? "

" The matter is, that I wish to go to bed, and wish to see you in bed before I go myself."

" Yes, brother John, if you please, certainly. Where's my bed ? I do believe I have been asleep."

" Humph ! I have no doubt upon the subject," replied John Forster, lighting another candle. " Come this way, brother Nicholas," and they both ascended the stairs.

When Mr. John Forster arrived at the door of his own room, on the first storey, he stopped. " Now, brother Nicholas, are you quite awake ? Do you think that I may trust you with a candle ? "

"I should hope so," replied Nicholas; "I see that it is silver, but I hope I'm honest, brother John."

"Humph! I mean, can I trust you to put it out?"

"Yes, I think that you may. Pray, which is my room?"

"The first door on the left, when you are at the top of the stairs."

"The first door."

"Yes, the first on the left; do you understand?"

"Yes, brother, I do; the first door on the left."

"Very well; then I wish you a good-night."

"Good-night, brother," replied Nicholas, ascending the stairs as John Forster entered his room.

Nicholas arrived at the head of the stairs; but his brain was not very clear. He muttered to himself, "I think I'm right—yes, I'm right—the first door—to the right—yes—that's it;" and instead of the room to the left, where Newton was, he walked into the one to the right, which appertained to the housekeeper, Mrs. Smith.

The old lady was fast asleep. Nicholas threw off his clothes, put out his candle, and stepped into bed without waking the old lady, whom he supposed to be his son, and in a few minutes they snored in concert.

The morning dawned. The watchmen (London nightingales) ceased their notes and retired to their beds. The chimney-sweeps (larks of the metropolis) raised their shrill cry as they paced along with chattering teeth. Housemaids and kitchenmaids presented their back views to the early passengers as they washed off the accumulation of the previous day from the steps of the front door. "Milk below" (certainly much below "proof") was answered by the ascent of the busy cooks, when a knock at the door of Mrs. Smith's room from the red knuckles of the housemaid awoke her to a sense of her equivocal situation.

At her first discovery that a man was in her bed she uttered a scream of horror, throwing herself upon her knees, and extending her hands before her in her amazement. The scream awoke Nicholas, who, astonished at the sight, and his modesty equally outraged, also threw himself in the same posture, facing her, and recoiling. Each looked aghast at each; each considered the other as the lawless invader; but before a word of explanation could pass between them, their countenances changed from horror to surprise, from surprise to anxiety and doubt.

" Why," screamed the housekeeper, losing her breath with astonishment.

" It is ! " cried Nicholas, retreating further.

" Yes—yes—it is—my *dear* Nicholas ! "

" No—it can't be," replied Nicholas, hearing the fond appellation.

" It is—oh ! yes—it is your poor unhappy wife, who begs your pardon, Nicholas," cried the housekeeper, bursting into tears, and falling into his arms.

" My dear—dear wife ! " exclaimed Nicholas, as he threw his arms around her, and each sobbed upon the other's shoulder.

In this position they remained a minute, when Mr. John Forster, who heard the scream and subsequent exclamations, and had taken it for granted that his brother had been guilty of some *contretemps,* first wiped the remaining lather from his half-shaved chin, and then ascended to the housekeeper's room, from whence the noise had proceeded. When he opened the door, he found them in the position we have described, both kneeling in the centre of the bed embracing and sobbing. They were so wrapt in each other, that they did not perceive his entrance. Mr. John Forster stared with amazement for a few seconds, and thus growled out—

" Why, what are you two old fools about ? "

" It's my husband, sir,"—" It's my wife, brother John," cried they, both at once, as the tears coursed down their cheeks

" Humph ! " ejaculated the lawyer, and he quitted the room.

We must let the reader imagine the various explanations which took place between Nicholas and his truly reformed wife, Newton and his uncle, Amber, and everybody in the household, while we narrate the events which had brought about this singular *dénouement.*

The reader may recollect that we left Mrs. Forster in the lunatic asylum, slowly recovering from an attack of brain fever, which had been attended with a relapse. For many weeks she continued in a state of great feebleness, and during that time, when in the garden in company with other denizens of this melancholy abode (wishing to be usefully employed), she greatly assisted the keepers in restraining them, and in a short time established that superiority over them which is invariably the result of a sane intellect. This was soon perceived by Doctor Beddington, who (aware of her destitute condition) offered her a situation as nurse in the establishment until the inspecting magistrates should make their appearance, with the promise that she might continue in it afterwards if she thought proper. This proposal was accepted by Mrs. Forster until she might resolve what course to take, and she soon became a most invaluable person in the establishment, effecting more by lenient and kind treatment than the keepers were able to do by their violence. So completely changed was Mrs. Forster in disposition, that so far from feeling any resentment against those who had been the means of her confinement, she acknowledged to herself that her own conduct had been the occasion of her misfortune, and that those who had contributed to open her eyes to her former insanity were her best friends. She was humbled, and unhappy; but she kissed the rod. All that she now wished was to find out her husband, and by her future conduct to make reparation for the past. One of the gaolers, at her request, made every inquiry as to the part of England to which Nicholas had removed; but it was without success. All trace was lost; and Mrs. Forster accepted the situation of nurse until she might be enabled to prosecute her search, or obtain the intelligence which she desired.

For nine months Mrs. Forster remained in the establishment, during which time she had saved a sum of money sufficient for her support and travelling expenses. She then resolved to search after her husband, whose pardon for her previous conduct seemed to be the *sine quâ non* for which she continued to exist. She took leave of the doctor; and, strange to say, it was with feelings of regret that she quitted an abode, once a source of horror and disgust; but time reconciles us to everything, and she made a half promise to Dr. Beddington, that if she could not hear any tidings of her husband, or should discover that he was no more, she would return to the situation.

Mrs. Forster directed her course to London, why or wherefore she hardly knew; but she had imbibed the idea that the metropolis was the most likely place to meet with him. Her first inquiries were about any families of the name of Forster; but the Directory gave such an enormous list of Forsters, of all trades and callings, and in every situation in life, that she closed it with despair. She had a faint recollection that her husband (who was not very communicative, and least of all to her) had stated that he had a brother alive somewhere; but this was all that she knew. Nevertheless, she set about her task in good earnest, and called upon every one of the name in the middling classes of life, to ascertain if they were relations of her husband. There were many in high life whose names and addresses she had obtained from the Red-book, but to them she dared not apply. All she could do was to question the servants, but every answer was unsatisfactory; and Mis. Forster, whose money was nearly expended, had serious thoughts of returning to the lunatic establishment, when the advertisement in the newspapers, of Mr. Scratton, for a housekeeper, which Mr. John Forster had desired him to procure, met her eye. Unwilling to leave London, she applied for and obtained the situation, having received an excellent character from Doctor Beddington, to whom she had written and explained her views.

Her heart leapt when she discovered that her master's name was Forster; and when she first saw him she could not but persuade herself that there was a family likeness. The germs of hope were, however, soon withered when Amber, in answer to her inquiries, stated that Mr. Forster had a brother lately dead, who had never been married, and that she never heard of his having another. Her fellow-servants were all as strange as herself, and Mrs. Forster (who had assumed the name of Smith) was obliged to have recourse to the patience and resignation which had been so severely inculcated. The charge of Amber soon proved a source of delight; the control which she had over the household a source of gratification (not, as before, for the pleasure of domineering, but for the sake of exercising kindness and forbearance); and Mrs. Forster was happy and resigned.

It may be surmised as strange that during the period which she remained in this capacity she had never heard mention of her husband or her son; but it must be remembered that Nicholas had never called upon his brother, and that Newton was in the East Indies; and, moreover, that Mr. John Forster was just as little inclined to be communicative as her husband. Indeed, he never came in contact with his house-keeper, except to pay the bills, which was regularly once a month, when he called her down after dinner; and after the accounts were settled, offered her a glass of wine, as a proof of his being satisfied with her conduct. When Newton and his father arrived at the chambers on the day before the dis-covery, and were invited to dinner, his note of communication was as laconic as usual.

"MRS. SMITH,—I have invited two gentlemen to dine with me to-day, six precisely.   JOHN FORSTER.

"P.S.—Let the spare bed be ready."

Mrs. Forster prepared everything as directed; and having done her duties below, retired to her room, where she usually sat with Amber. She did not therefore see the parties when they entered; and Amber, who had run down to meet her protector, heard nothing during her short stay in the room to suppose that they were relatives of Mr. John Forster. All that she had to communicate was, that the parties were an elderly gentleman and a very handsome young man.

Yet even this simple communication caused the pulse of Mrs. Forster to accelerate. They might be her husband and her son. It was the first time the spare bed had been ordered. Reflection, however, convinced her that her hopes were strung upon too slight a thread; and musing on the improbability of not having ascertained during a year the fact of her master having so near a relative—moreover, her son was not in existence—she sighed, and dismissed the idea as ridiculous. Before the gentlemen had finished their wine, Amber was in bed, and Mrs. Forster invariably sat at the side of it until her own hour of repose had arrived. A certain in-definable curiosity still remained lurking; yet as she could not gratify it without intrusion (if the strangers were still up), she retired to bed, with the reflection that all her doubts would be relieved in the morning; and after lying awake for some hours in a state of suspense, she at last fell into that sound sleep which is usually produced by previous excitement. How she was awakened from it, the reader has been already informed.

"It's rather awkward, Newton," said Mr. John Forster, about ten days afterwards. "I cannot do without your mother, that's certain; but what am I to do with your father? Humph! Well, she must take charge of him as well as Amber. She must teach him——"

"Teach him what, sir?" replied Newton, laughing.

"Teach him what? Why, to leave my watch and spectacles alone. I dare not lay them down for a moment."

"I think we may teach him that, sir, if it is all you require."

"I ask no more; then he may go about the house like a tame rabbit. When will your ship be ready, boy?"

"In about a fortnight, sir. I called upon Captain Oughton the day before yesterday, but he was not at home. His steward gave me the information."

"What is the name of the ship?"

"The *Windsor Castle,* sir."

"Why, all the India ships appear to be called Castles. Your last ship was called the *Bombay Castle,* I think?"

"Yes, sir; there are a great many of them so named—they really are floating castles."

"And full of ladies. You 'castle your queens, as they do at chess.' Humph!"

A pun from Mr. John Forster was a rarity; he never had been known to make one before; and Newton asserts that he never heard him guilty of it afterwards. It deserves, therefore, bad as it was, to be recorded.

CHAPTER XLIV

" But to stick to my route
'Twill be hard, if some novelty can't be struck out.
Is there no Algerine, no Kamschatkan arrived ?
No plenipo-pacha, three-tailed and three-wived ?
No Russian, whose dissonant, consonant name
Almost rattles to fragments the trumpet of fame ?

POSTSCRIPT

By-the-bye, have you found any friend who can construe
That Latin account, t'other day, of a monster ?
If we can't get a Russian—and that story in Latin
Be not *too* improper, I think I'll bring that in."

—MOORE.

A FEW mornings after this colloquy with his uncle, Newton
was very busy perambulating the streets of London in search
of various requisites for his trip to India, when his hand was
seized before he had time to call to mind the features of the
party who shook it with such apparent warmth.

"My dear Mr. Forster, I am so delighted to see you,
so happy to hear of your gallant adventure with the French
squadron. Mrs. Plausible will be quite pleased at meeting her
old shipmate; she often talks about you. I must make sure of
you," continued the doctor, drawing from his pocket a large
packet of cards, and inserting, at the top of one of them,
Newton Forster's name with his pencil. "This is an invitation
to our conversazione of to-morrow night, which you must do
us the honour to accept. We shall have all the scientific men
of the day, and a very pretty sprinkling of nobility, if not something more. However, you will see. Shall I tell Mrs. Plausible that you will come, or will you disappoint her ?"

"Why," replied Newton, "if I possibly can, I will. I presume the hour is not very precise ?"

"Oh no, from nine until two or three ; but if you wish to
see great people, about eleven is the exact time."

"Well then," replied Newton, "the time which suits great
people also suits me. I hope Mrs. Plausible is quite well."

"Quite well, I thank you. Good-bye ;" and Dr. Plausible

291

hurried off so quickly, that Newton was induced to look after him to ascertain what could induce such precipitation. He perceived Dr. Plausible shaking hands warmly with another gentleman, and after a few seconds the packet of cards was again pulled out of his pocket, and the pencil in requisition. It will be necessary to go back a little to acquaint the reader with what had occurred since the acceptation of Dr. Plausible by Miss Tavistock, when they were on board of the *Bombay Castle.* On their arrival at Madras, Miss Tavistock's early and dearest friend, who resided in the up-country, had commissioned an acquaintance to receive Miss Tavistock until they could make arrangements for her journey to the interior. By this female acquaintance Miss Tavistock was kindly welcomed, and received into her house; but Miss Tavistock's prospects having altered, so had all her devoted attachment to the friend of her early years. She wrote, announcing her intended change of condition, and regretting that Dr. Plausible's affairs requiring his immediate presence in England, would prevent her having the delight of embracing one who was so entwined round her heart. The letter was nevertheless very cold, and Miss Tavistock was very much abused by her dearest friend, who, disappointed in her expectations, did not condescend an answer. In a week Miss Tavistock was united to Dr. Plausible; and in less than a fortnight afterwards they were on their passage home. Dr. Plausible found that his wife's report of her circumstances was correct, and that now he had the means of keeping his carriage and of seeing company in moderation. Shortly after their return, Dr. Plausible took the lease of a house in a betwixt and between fashionable street, and not wishing to remain idle, attempted to get into practice as an accoucheur; for although the fortune brought by his wife was considerable, still, to keep his carriage in London, he was obliged "to sail nearer to the wind" in other points than he found agreeable; moreover, he was ambitious. A night-bell, with "night-bell" in capital letters over it, that people might be aware in the broad day that it was a night-bell, which of course they could not read in the dark, was attached to one side of the street door. It was as loud as an alarm-bell, and when rung, was to be heard from No. 12 to 44 in the street where Dr. Plausible resided.

THE MERCHANT SERVICE

· There are little secrets in all trades; and one is, how to obtain practice as a medical man, which whole mystery consists in making people believe that you have a great deal. When this is credited, practice immediately follows; and Dr. Plausible was aware of the fact. At first setting off, the carriage drew up to the door occasionally, and stood there for some time, when the doctor made his appearance, and stepped in. He then took a round of about three hours through every fashionable part of the town, sitting well forward, that everybody might see him, apparently examining his visiting-book. At times he would pull up at some distinguished person's door, where were two or three carriages before him, and getting out, would go in to the porter to ask some frivolous question. Another ruse was to hammer at some titled mansion and inquire for another titled person, by mistake. This occupied the morning, after which Dr. Plausible returned home. During the first month the night-bell was rung two or three times a week by the watchman, who was fee'd for his trouble; but after that period it increased its duties, until it was in motion once, if not twice, every night, and his disturbed neighbours wished Dr. Plausible and his extensive practice at the devil. The carriage also was now rattled to the door in a hurry, and Dr. Plausible was seen to enter with his case of instruments and drive off with rapidity, sometimes twice a day. In the meantime, Mrs. Plausible did her part, as she extended her acquaintance with her neighbours. She constantly railed against a medical husband; declared that Dr. Plausible was never at home, and it was impossible to say at what hour they might dine. The tables also were strewed with the cards of great and fashionable people, obtained by Dr. Plausible from a celebrated engraver's shop by a douceur to the shopman, when the master was absent. At last Dr. Plausible's instruments were used in good earnest; and although not known or even heard of in the fashionable world, he was sent for by the would-be fashionables, because they imagined that he was employed by their betters. Now it so happened that in the same street there lived another medical man, almost a prototype of Dr. Plausible, only not quite so well off in the world. His name was Dr. Feasible. His practice was not extensive, and he was encumbered with a wife and large family. He also very naturally wished to extend his practice and his reputation; and after many fruitless attempts, he at last hit upon a scheme which he thought promised to be successful.

" My dear," said he one morning to his wife, " I am thinking of getting up a conversazione."

" A conversazione, my love; why, is not that a very expensive affair ? "

" Why, not very. But if it brings me practice, it will be money well laid out."

" Yes, my love, if it does, and if we have the money to lay out."

" Something must be done. I have hardly a patient left. I have an idea that it will succeed. Go, my dear, and make up this prescription, and let the boy take it to Mrs. Bluestone's. I wish I had a couple of dozen patients like her. I write her prescriptions, take my fee, and then, that I may be sure that it is properly made up, I volunteer to take it to the chemist's myself."

" Pray, what is the complaint of Mrs. Bluestone, my love ? "

" Nothing; she over-eats herself—that's all. Abernethy would cure her in twenty-four hours."

" Well, but, my love, about this conversazione ? "

" Go and make up the prescription, my dear, and we'll talk the matter over afterwards."

They did so. A list of the people they were acquainted with was drawn out, the expense calculated, and the affair settled.

The first point to be considered was the size of the cards.

" These, my love," said Mrs. Feasible, who came in from a long walk with her bonnet still on, " these are three shillings and sixpence a hundred; and these, which are a size larger, are four-and-sixpence. Which do you think we ought to have ? "

" Why, really, my dear, when one sends out so many, I do not see why we should incur unnecessary expense. The three-and-sixpenny ones are quite large enough."

" And the engraving will be fourteen shillings."

" Well, that will only be a first expense. Conversazione, in old English, of course."

" And here, my love, are the ribbons for the maids' caps

and sashes; I bought them at Waterloo House, very cheap, and a very pretty candlelight colour."

" Did you speak to them about their gowns ? "

" Yes, my love ; Sally and Peggy have each a white gown, Betty I can lend one of my own."

The difference between a conversazione and a rout is simply this : In the former you are expected to talk or listen, but to be too ethereal to eat. In the latter, to be squeezed in a crowd, and eat ices, &c., to cool yourself. A conversazione has, therefore, a great advantage over the latter, as far as the pocket is concerned, it being much cheaper to procure food for the mind than food for the body. It would appear that tea has been as completely established as the beverage of modern scientific men, as nectar was formerly that of the gods. The Athenæum gives tea ; and I observed in a late newspaper, that Lord G—— has promised tea to the Geographical Society. Had his lordship been aware that there was a beverage invented on board a ship much more appropriate to the science over which he presides than tea, I feel convinced he would have substituted it immediately ; and I therefore take this opportunity of informing him that sailors have long made use of a compound which actually goes by the name of *geograffy*, which is only a trifling corruption of the name of the science, arising from their laying the accent on the penultimate. I will now give his lordship the receipt, which is most simple.

Take a tin-pot, go to the scuttle-butt (having obtained permission from the quarter-deck), and draw off about half a pint of very offensive-smelling water. To this add a gill of vinegar and a ship's biscuit broken up into small pieces. Stir it well up with the forefinger ; and then, with the forefinger and thumb, you may pull out the pieces of biscuit, and eat them as fast as you please, drinking the liquor to wash all down.

Now this would be the very composition to hand round to the Geographical Society. It is not christened geography without a reason; the vinegar and water representing the green sea, and the pieces of biscuit floating in it the continents and islands which are washed by it.

Now, my lord, do not you thank me for my communication ?

But we must return to the conversazione of Doctor and Mrs. Feasible.

295

The company arrived. There was rap after rap. The whole street was astonished with the noise of the wheels and the rattling of the iron steps of the hackney-coaches. Doctor Feasible had procured some portfolios of prints; some Indian idols from a shop in Wardour Street, duly labelled and christened, and several other odds and ends to create matter of conversation. The company consisted of several medical gentlemen and their wives, the great Mr. B—— and the facetious Mr. C——. There were ten or twelve authors, or gentlemen suspected of authorship, fourteen or fifteen chemists, all scientific of course, one colonel, half-a-dozen captains, and, to crown all, a city knight and his lady, besides their general acquaintance, unscientific and unprofessional. For a beginning this was very well; and the company departed very hungry, but highly delighted with their evening's entertainment.

"What can all that noise be about?" said Mrs. Plausible to her husband, who was sitting with her in the drawing-room reading the *Lancet*, while she knotted, or *did not*.

"I am sure I cannot tell, Mrs. Plausible."

"There, again! I'm sure if I have heard one, I have heard thirty raps at a door within this quarter of an hour. I'm determined I will know what it is," continued Mrs. Plausible, getting up and ringing the bell.

"Thomas, do you know what all that noise is about?" said Mrs. Plausible, when the servant answered the bell.

"No, ma'am, I doesn't."

"Well, then, go and see."

"Yes, ma'am."

The impatience of Mrs. Plausible during the absence of Thomas increased with the repetition of the knocks.

"Well, Thomas?" said she, as the footman entered.

"If you please, ma'am, Mr. Feasible has got a conwersation—that's all."

"Got a what?"

"A conversazione he means, my dear. It's very strange that Mr. Feasible should pretend to give such a thing!"

"I think so too," replied the lady. "He keeps no carriage. What can be his inducement?"

"I perceive," replied Dr. Plausible, "he wants to get practice. Depend upon it, that's his plan. A sprat to catch a mackerel!"

Husband and wife were again silent, and resumed their occupations; but the *Lancet* was not read, and the knotting was all in knots, for they were both in a brown study. At last Mrs. Plausible commenced—

" I really do not see, my dear, why we should not give a conversazione as well as Dr. Feasible."

"I was just thinking that we could give them much better ; our acquaintance now is very numerous."

" And very respectable," replied the lady ; " it will make us more known in the world."

" And add to my practice. I'll soon beat Dr. Feasible out of the field ! "

The result of this conversation was a conversazione, which certainly was on a much better scale, and better attended, than the one collected by Dr. Feasible. Dr. Plausible had pumped a mutual acquaintance as to the merits of his rival, and had set to work with great diligence.

He ordered his carriage, and for two or three days previous to the one fixed went round to all his friends who had curiosities, foreign, indigenous, or continental, admired them, talked learnedly, expressed a wish to exhibit them to several gentlemen of talent at his next conversazione, pulled out a card for the party, and succeeded in returning home with his carriage stuffed with curiosities and monstrosities.

Negus and cherry-water were added to tea in the refreshment-room ; and the conversazione of Dr. Plausible was pronounced by those who had been invited to both, infinitely superior to that of Dr. Feasible. A good-natured friend called upon Dr. and Mrs. Feasible with the news. They pretended indifference, as they bit their lips to conceal their vexation. As soon as he took his leave—

" Well, my dear," said Mrs. Feasible, " what do you think of this ? Very unhandsome on the part of Dr. Plausible ! I was told this morning that several of our acquaintances have expressed a wish to be introduced to him."

"We must not give up the point, my love. Dr. Plausible may make a splash once ; but I suspect that his horses eat him out of house and home, and interfere very much with the butcher's bills. If so, we who keep no carriage can afford it better. But it's very annoying, as there will be an increase of expense."

" Very annoying, indeed ! " replied the lady. " Look at his

card, my dear, it is nearly twice as large as ours. I begged it of Mr. Tomkins, on purpose to compare it."

"Well then, my dear, we must order others, and mind that they measure an inch more than his. It shall cost him something before we have done, I'm determined."

"You heard what Mr. Smithson said? They gave negus and cherry-water."

"We must do the same. I've a great mind to give ices."

"Oh! my love, remember the expense."

"Very true; but we can ice our negus and cherry-water. Rough ice is only twopence a pound, I believe."

"Well, that will be an improvement."

"And there shall be more, or I'll be in the Bench," replied the doctor, in his wrath.

The next conversazione for which cards were issued by Dr. Feasible was on a superior scale. There was a considerable increase of company. He had persuaded a country baronet, secured the patronage of two ladies of rank (with a slight blot on their escutcheons), and collected, amongst others, a French count (or adventurer), a baron with mustachios, two German students in their costumes and long hair, and an actress of some reputation. He had also procured the head of a New Zealand chief; some red snow, or rather, red water (for it was melted), brought home by Captain Ross; a piece of granite from the Croker mountains; a kitten in spirits, with two heads and twelve legs; and half-a-dozen abortions of the feathered or creeping tribes. Everything went off well. The two last fees he had received were sacrificed to have the party announced in the *Morning Post*, and Dr. Feasible's triumph was complete.

But it was not to last long. In ten days Dr. Plausible's cards were again issued, larger than Dr. Feasible's, and with a handsome embossed border of lilies and roses. Male attendants, tea and coffee, ices and liqueurs were prepared; and Dr. Feasible's heart failed him when he witnessed the ingress and egress of the pastrycooks, with their boxes on their heads. Among his company he had already mustered up five celebrated blues; four ladies of quality, of better reputation than Dr. Feasible's; seven or eight baronets and knights; a bishop of Fernando Po; three or four general officers; and a dozen French and German visitors to the country, who had not only titles, but wore orders at their button-holes. Thus far had he advanced when he met Newton Forster and added him to the list of the invited. In about two hours afterwards Dr. Plausible returned home to his wife, radiant with smiles.

"My dear, who do you think has promised to come to-morrow night?"

"Who, my love?"

"Prince Fizzybelli!"

"You don't say so?" screamed the lady with delight.

"Yes, most faithfully promised."

"What will the Feasibles say?" cried the lady; "but—is he a real prince?"

"A real prince! Oh yes, indeed he is! well known in Tartary."

"Well, Dr. Plausible, I have good news for you. Here is a note from Mr. H——, in answer to yours, in which he promises you the loan of the wax figure from Germany, of a female in the first stage of par—partu—I can't make out the word."

"Excellent! most excellent!" cried the doctor, rubbing his hands; "now we shall do."

Newton, who had some curiosity to see a conversazione, which to him was a *terra incognita*, did not fail to go at the appointed hour. He was ushered upstairs into the drawing-room, at the door of which he was received by Mrs. Plausible in blue and silver. The rooms not being very large were extremely crowded, and Newton at one moment found himself jammed against some curiosity, and at another treading on the toes or heels of people, who accepted his apologies, looking daggers, and with a snarling "don't mention it."

But a thundering knock at the door was followed by the announcement of his Highness Prince Fizzybelli—Prince Fizzybelli at the door—Prince Fizzybelli coming up—Prince Fizzybelli (enters).

Had it been permitted, Dr. Plausible would have received his guest with a flourish of trumpets, as great men are upon the stage, without which it is impossible nowadays to know a great man from a little one. However, the hired servants did their duty, and the name of Fizzybelli was fizzed about the room in every direction. Dr. Plausible trod on the corns of old Lady G——, upset Miss Periwinkle, and nearly knocked down a French savant in his struggle to obtain the door to receive his honoured guest, who made a bow, looked at the crowd—looked at the chandelier—looked at his watch, and looked very tired in the course of five minutes, when Prince Fizzybelli ordered his carriage and was off.

Newton, who had examined several very strange things which occupied the tables about the room, at last made his way to the anteroom, where the crowd was much more dense than elsewhere. Taking it for granted that there was something interesting to be seen, he persevered until he had forced his way to the centre, when what was his astonishment when he beheld under a long glass case a figure of a woman modelled in wax, of exact and certainly of beautiful proportion! It was as large as life, and in a state of perfect nudity. The face lifted up, and discovered the muscles beneath; in fact, every part of the image could be removed, and presented to the curious every part of the human frame, modelled exact, and coloured. Newton was indeed astonished: he had witnessed several articles in the other room, which he had considered more fitted for the museum of an institution than a drawing-room; but this was indeed a novelty; and when, to crown all, he witnessed certain little *demireps* of science, who fancied that not to be ashamed was now as much a proof of knowledge as in our first parents it was of innocence, and who eyed the figure without turning away from it or blushing, he quitted the room with disgust, and returned home quite satisfied with one conversazione.

I am not partial to blues: generally speaking, ladies do not take up science until they find that the men will not take up them; and a remarkably clever woman by reputation is too often a remarkably unpleasant or a remarkably ugly one. But there are exceptions; exceptions that a nation may be proud of—women who can fulfil their duties to their husbands and their children, to their God, and to their neigh bour, although endowed with minds more powerful than is allotted to one man in tens of thousands. These are heavenly blues; and, among the few, no one shines more pre-eminent than my dear Mrs. S——e.

However, whether Newton was satisfied or not, this conversazione was a finisher to Dr. Feasible, who resigned the contest. Dr. Plausible not only carried away the palm—but, what was still worse, he carried off the "practice!"

CHAPTER XLV

" Their only labour is to kill the time ;
    And labour dire it is, and weary woe ;
 They sit—they lounge—turn o'er some idle rhyme :
    Then rising sudden—to the glass they go,
    Or saunter forth with loitering step and slow."
                                                  —*Castle of Indolence.*

CAPTAIN OUGHTON, who commanded the *Windsor Castle,*
was an original. His figure was short and thick-set, his face
broad, and deeply pitted with the smallpox ; his nose, an
apology for a nose, being a small tubercle arising midway
between his eyes and mouth, the former of which were small,
the latter wide, and displaying a magnificent row of white
teeth. On the whole, it was impossible to look in his face
without being immediately struck with his likeness to a bull-
dog. His temperament and his pursuits were also analogous ;
he was a great pugilist, knew the merits of every man in the
ring, and the precise date and circumstances attending every
battle which had been fought for the previous thirty years.
His conversation was at all times interlarded with the slang
terms appropriated to the science to which he was so devoted.
In other points he was a brave and trustworthy officer, although
he valued the practical above the theoretical branches of his
profession, and was better pleased when superintending the
mousing of a stay or the strapping of a block than when
"flooring" the sun, as he termed it, to ascertain the latitude,
or "breaking his noddle against the old woman's" in taking
a lunar observation. Newton had been strongly recommended
to him, and Captain Oughton extended his hand as to an old
acquaintance, when they met on the quarter-deck. Before
they had taken a dozen turns up and down, Captain Oughton
inquired if Newton could handle the mauleys ; and on being
assured in the negative, volunteered his instruction during
their passage out.

"You heard the end of it, I suppose?" said Captain
Oughton, in continuance.

"The end of what, sir?"

"What!—why, the fight. Spring beat. I've cleared three hundred by him."

"Then, sir, I am very glad that Spring beat," replied Newton.

"I'll back him against a stone heavier any day in the week. I've got the newspaper in the cabin with the fight—forty-seven rounds; but we can't read it now—we must see after these soldiers and their traps. Look at them," continued Captain Oughton, turning to a party of the troops ordered for the passage, who were standing in the gangway and booms; "every man Jack with his tin pot in his hand and his greatcoat on. Twig the drum-boy; he has turned his coat—do you see?—with the lining outwards to keep it clean. By Jove, that's a wrinkle!"

"How many officers do you expect, Captain Oughton?"

"I hardly know—they make such alterations in their arrangements; five or six, I believe. The boat went on shore for them at nine o'clock. They have sent her back, with their compliments, seven times already, full of luggage. There's one lieutenant—I forget his name—whose chests alone would fill up the main-deck. There's six under the half-deck," said Captain Oughton, pointing to them.

"Lieutenant Winterbottom," said Newton, reading the name.

"I wish to Heaven that he had remained the winter, or that his chests were all to the bottom! I don't know where the devil we are to stow them. Oh, here they come! Boatswain's mate, tend the side there."

In a minute or thereabouts the military gentlemen made their appearance, one by one, on the quarter-deck, scrutinising their gloves as they bade adieu to the side-ropes, to ascertain if they had in any degree been defiled by the adhesive properties of the pitch and tar.

Captain Oughton advanced to receive them. "Welcome, gentlemen," said he—"welcome on board. We trip our anchor in half-an-hour. I am afraid that I have not the pleasure of knowing your names, and must request the honour of being introduced."

"Major Clavering, sir," said the major, a tall, handsome man, gracefully taking off his hat; "the officers who accompany me are (waving his hand towards them in succession), Lieutenant Winterbottom——"

Lieutenant Winterbottom bowed.

"I've had the pleasure of reading Lieutenant Winter-bottom's name several times this forenoon," observed Captain Oughton, as he returned the salute.

"You refer to my luggage, I'm afraid, Captain Oughton."

"Why, if I must say it, I certainly think you have enough for a general."

"I can only reply that I wish my rank were equal to my luggage; but it is a *general* complaint every time I have the misfortune to embark. I trust, Captain Oughton, it will be the only one you will have to make of me during the passage."

Major Clavering, who had waited during this dialogue, continued—"Captain Majoribanks, whom I ought to apologise to for not having introduced first——"

"Not at all, major; you just heard the brevet rank which Winterbottom's baggage has procured him."

"Not the first time a man has obtained rank through his 'baggage,'" observed one of the officers, *sotto voce.*

"Mr. Ansell, Mr. Petres, Mr. Irving."

The necessary bows were exchanged, and Mr. Williams, the first mate, desired to show the officers to their respective accommodations, when he would be able to ascertain what part of their luggage was required, and be enabled to strike the remainder down into the after-hold.

As the officers followed the first mate down the companion-ladder, Captain Oughton looked at Mr. Ansell, and observed to Newton, "That fellow would *peel* well."

The *Windsor Castle* sailed, and in a few days was clear of the channel. Newton, whose thoughts were of Isabel Revel, felt not that regret at quitting the country usually attached to those who leave all dear to them behind. He knew that it was by following up his profession alone that he ever could have a chance of obtaining her; and this recollection, with the hopes of again beholding the object of his affections, lightened his heart to joy as the ship scudded across the Bay of Biscay before a N.E. gale. That he had little chance at present of possessing her, he knew; but hope leads us on, and no one more than the youth who is in love.

The table of Captain Oughton was liberally supplied, and the officers embarked proved (as they almost invariably do) to be pleasant, gentleman-like companions. The boxing-gloves were soon produced by Captain Oughton, who soon ascertained that in the officer who "would *peel* so well" he had found his match. The mornings were passed away in sparring, fencing, reading, walking the deck, or lolling on the hen-coops upon the poop. The announcement of the dinner-hour was a signal for rejoicing, and they remained late at the table, doing ample justice to the captain's excellent claret. The evening was finished with cards, cigars, and brandy pawnee. Thus passed the time away for the first three weeks of the passage, during which period all parties had become upon intimate terms.

But the voyage is, in itself, most tedious; and more tedious to those who not only have no duty to perform, but have few resources. As soon as the younger officers thought they might take a liberty, they examined the hen-coops, and selecting the most promising-looking cocks, trimmed them for fighting; chose between themselves, as their own property, those which they most approved of, and for some days fed and sparred them, to get them into wind, and ascertain the proper way in which they should be spurred. In the meantime two pairs of spurs were by their directions clandestinely made by the armourer of the ship, and when ready, they took advantage of the time when Captain Oughton was every day employed with the ship's reckoning, and the poulterer was at his dinner (viz., from twelve to one), to fight a main. The cocks which were killed in these combats were returned to the hen-coops, and supposed by the poulterer, who very often had a glass of grog, to have quarrelled within the bars.

"Steward," said Captain Oughton, "why the devil do you give us so many fowls for dinner? the stock will never last out the voyage: two roast fowls, two boiled fowls, curried fowl, and chicken pie! What can you be thinking of?"

"I spoke to the poulterer on the subject, sir; he constantly brings me down fowls, and he tells me that they kill each other fighting"

"Fighting! never heard of fowls fighting in a coop before. They must be all game fowls."

"That they are, most of them," said Mr. Petres; "I have often seen them fighting when I have been on the poop."

"So have I," continued Ansell; "I have seen worse cocks in the pit."

"Well, it's very odd; I never lost a cock in this way in all my voyages. Send the poulterer here; I must inquire about it."

"Yes, sir," replied the steward; and he quitted the cabin.

With the exception of the major, who knew nothing of the circumstances, the officers thought it advisable to decamp, that they might not be present when the *dénouement* took place. The poulterer made his appearance, was interrogated, and obliged in his own defence to criminate the parties, corroborating his assertions by producing a pair of spurs found upon a cock which had been killed, and thrown behind the coop in a hurry at the appearance of Captain Oughton on deck.

"I am sorry that my officers should have taken such a liberty," observed the major gravely.

"Oh, never mind, major, only allow me to be even with them; I shouldn't have minded if I had seen the fighting. I think you said that you would like to exercise your men a little this afternoon?"

"I did; that is, if not inconvenient."

"Not in the least, major; the quarter-deck is at your service. I presume you do not superintend yourself."

"Yes, I generally do."

"Well, don't this time; but let all the officers; and then I shall be able to play them a little trick that will make us all square."

Major Clavering consented. The officers were ordered up to drill their men. Captain Majoribanks and Mr. Irving had one party at the platoon exercise.

"Third man, your hand a little higher on the barrel of your musket. As you were; support—the word support is only a caution—arms—too—too."

"Two and two make four," observed one of the seamen.

Lieutenant Winterbottom had another party on the lee-side of the quarter-deck. "Ram down—cartridge. No. 12, slope your musket a little more—too—too—only two taps at the bottom of the barrel. Return—ramrods. No. 4, why don't you draw up the heel of your right leg level with the other? Recollect now, when you shoulder arms, to throw your musket up smartly.—Shoulder—as you were—the word shoulder is only a caution; shoulder—arms. Dress up a little, No. 8, and don't stick your stomach out in that way."

Mr. Ansell and Mr. Petres had two fatigue parties on the poop, without muskets. "To the right—face—to the right face. To the right—face—to the right—face."

"It's a dead calm with them soldiers—head round the compass," said one of the seamen to another.

"To the left—face—quick march, to the left—turn—to the right—turn—close files—mark time—right—left—right—left—forward."

"Them 'ere chaps' legs all going together put one in mind of a centipee—don't they, Tom?"

"Yes, but they don't get on quite so fast. Hollo, what pipe's that?—'All hands, air bedding.'"

The ship was hauled close to the wind, which was light. At the pipe, the sailors below ran up the hatchway, and those on deck threw down their work. In a minute every hammock was out of the netting, and every seaman busy at unlashing.

"Now, major, we had better go into the cabin," said Captain Oughton, laughing. "I shall, I can assure you."

Beds and blankets which are not shook more than once a month are apt to be very full of what is termed *fluff* and blanket *hairs*, and they have a close smell, by no means agreeable. The sailors, who had an idea that the order had been given inconsiderately, were quite delighted, and commenced shaking their blankets on the forecastle and weather gangway, raising a cloud, which the wind carried aft upon the parties exercising upon the quarter-deck.

"What the devil is all this?" cried Captain Majoribanks, looking forward with dismay. "Order—arms."

Lieutenant Winterbottom and half of his party were now seized with a fit of coughing. "Confound it!—shut—pans—handle—upon my soul I'm choked."

"This is most excessively disagreeable," observed Mr. Petres; "I made up my mind to be *tarred* when I came on board, but I had no idea that we should be *feathered*."

"Support—d——n it, there's no supporting this!" cried Captain Majoribanks. "Where's Major Clavering? I'll ask to dismiss the men."

"They are dismissing a great many little men forward, I suspect," said the first mate, laughing. "I cannot imagine what induced Captain Oughton to give the order; we never shake bedding except when the ship's before the wind."

This last very consoling remark made it worse than all; the officers were in an agony. There was not one of them who would not have stood the chance of a volley from a French regiment rather than what they considered that they were exposed to. But without Major Clavering's permission they could not dismiss their men. Captain Majoribanks hastened to the cabin to explain their very unpleasant situation, and received the major's permission to defer the exercise.

"Well, gentlemen," said Captain Oughton, "what is the matter?"

"The matter!" replied Ansell. "Why, my flesh creeps all over me. Of all the thoughtless acts, Captain Oughton, it really beats——"

"Cock-fighting," interrupted the captain, with a loud laugh. "Now we are quits."

The officers hastened below to wash and change their dress after this very annoying retaliation on the part of Captain Oughton. When they felt themselves again clean and comfortable, their good-humour returned, although they voted their captain not to be very refined in his ideas, and agreed with him that his practical joke beat "cock-fighting."

I believe there are no classes of people who embark with more regret, or quit a ship with more pleasure, than military men. Nor is it to be wondered at, if we consider the antithesis which is presented to their usual mode of life. Few military men are studious, or inclined to reading, which is almost the only resource which is to be found against the tedium of long confinement and daily monotony. I do not say this reproachfully, as I consider it arises from the peculiarity of their profession, and must be considered to be more their misfortune than their fault. They enter upon a military life just after they have left school—the very period at which, from previous and forced application, they have been surfeited with books *usque ad nauseam*. The parade, dress, the attention paid to them, which demands civilities in return; society, and the preference shown by the fair sex; their happy and well-conducted mess; the collecting together of so many young men, with all their varied plans of amusement, into which the others are easily persuaded to enter, with just sufficient duty on guard, or otherwise, not to make the duty irksome—all delights too much at first, and eventually, from habit, too much occupy their minds, to afford time for study.

In making this observation I must be considered to speak generally. There are many studious, many well-stored minds, many men of brilliant talents, who have improved the gift of nature by constant study and reflection, and whose conduct must be considered as the more meritorious from having resisted or overcome the strong temptation to do otherwise, which is offered by their profession.

" I wish," said Irving, who was stretched out his full length on one of the coops abaft, with the front of his cap drawn over his eyes—" I wish this cursed voyage was at an end. Every day the same thing; no variety—no amusement;—curry for breakfast—brandy pawnee as a finish. I really begin to detest the sight of a cigar or a pack of cards."

" Very true," replied Ansell, who was stretched upon an adjacent coop in all the listlessness of idleness personified—" very true, Irving. I begin to think it worse than being quartered in a country town inhabited by nobodies, where one has nothing to do but to loll and spit over the bridge all day till the bugle sounds for dinner."

" Oh! that was infinitely better; at least, you could walk away when you were tired, or exchange a word or two with a girl as she passed over it on her way to market."

" Why don't you take a book, Irving?" observed the major, laying down the one with which he had been occupied to join the conversation.

" A book, major? Oh, I've read until I am tired."

" What have you read since you embarked?" inquired his senior.

" Let me see—Ansell, what have I read?"

" Read!—nothing at all—you know that."

" Well, perhaps so; we have no mess newspapers here: the fact is, major, I am not very partial to reading—I am not in the habit of it. When on shore I have too much to do; but I mean to read by-and-by."

"And pray, when may that by-and-by be supposed to arrive?"

"Oh! some day when I am wounded or taken prisoner, and cannot do anything else; then I shall read a good deal. Here's Captain Oughton—Captain Oughton, do you read much?"

"Yes, Mr. Irving, I read a great deal."

"Pray, may I take the liberty to ask you what you read?"

"What I read! Why, I read Horsburgh's Directory—and I read—I read all the fights."

"I think," observed Ansell, "that if a man gets through the newspaper and the novels of the day, he does a great deal."

"He reads a great deal, I grant you," replied the major; "but of what value is that description of reading?"

"There, major," replied Ansell, "we are at issue. I consider a knowledge of the passing events of the day, and a recollection of the facts which have occurred during the last twenty years, to be more valuable than all the ancient records in existence. Who talks of Cæsar or Xenophon nowadays, except some Cambridge or Oxford prig? and of what value is that knowledge in society? The escape of a modern pickpocket will afford more matter of conversation than the famous retreat of the ten thousand."

"To be sure," replied Captain Oughton; "and a fair stand-up fight between Humphreys and Mendoza create more interest than the famous battles of ——, I'm sure I forget."

"Of Marathon and Thermopylæ; they will do," added Ansell.

"I grant," replied the major, "that it is not only unnecessary, but conceited in those who would show their reading; but this does not disprove the advantages which are obtained. The mind, well fed, becomes enlarged: and if I may use a simile, in the same way as your horse proves his good condition by his appearance, without ascertaining the precise quantity of oats which has been given him, so the mind shows, by its general vigour and power of demonstration, that it has been well supplied with 'hard food.'"

"Very hard food indeed," replied Captain Oughton; "nuts that I never could crack when I was at school, and don't mean to break my teeth with now. I agree with Mr. Ansell, 'that sufficient for the day is the knowledge thereof.'"

"Well, as the tree of knowledge was the tree of evil, perhaps that is the correct reading," replied Ansell, laughing. "Captain Oughton, you are a very sensible man; I hope we shall see you often at our mess when we're again on shore.

"You may say so now," replied Captain Oughton bluntly, "and so have many more said the same thing to me; but you soldiers have cursed short memories in that way after you have landed."

"I trust, Captain Oughton," replied Major Clavering, "that you will not have to make that accusation general."

"Oh! never mind, major; I never am affronted; the offer is made in kindness, and at the time sincere; but when people get on shore, and are so occupied with their own amusements, it is not to be wondered at if they are thoughtless and forget. At one time it did annoy me, I confess; for when I say I should be happy to see a man, I mean it; and if I did not mean it, I never would ask him. I thought that other people did the same; but I have lived long enough to discover that a 'general invitation' means 'don't come at all.'"

"Then I most certainly shall not say one word on the subject at present," replied the major. "How many bells was that?"

"Six; dinner will be on the table in a few minutes."

"Then, gentlemen, we had better go down and prepare. Why, Mr. Irving, you have not shaved this morning!"

"No, major, I mean to do it after dinner."

"I should rather think that you intended to say before," replied Major Clavering.

This gentleman-like hint was taken by the young ensign, who was aware that Major Clavering, although invariably polite, even in reproof, was not a commanding officer to be trifled with; and Mr. Irving made his appearance at the dinner-table with his "chin new reaped," and smooth, as if appertaining to one of the fairer sex.

CHAPTER XLVI

" Come o'er the sea,
Maiden, with me,
Mine through sunshine, storm, and snows ;
Seasons may roll,
But the true soul
Burns the same where'er it goes.
Let Fate frown on, so we love and part not,
'Tis life where thou art, 'tis death where thou'rt not."
—MOORE.

THE voyage was at last accomplished without adventure or interest, the *Windsor Castle* not having fallen in with more than two or three vessels during her passage. Happy were the military officers to hear the order given for the anchor to be let go upon their arrival in Madras Roads ; more happy were they to find themselves again on shore ; and most happy were Captain Oughton and his officers to witness the debarkation of the troops, who had so long crowded their decks and impeded their motions. Parting was indeed "sweet sorrow," as it always will be when there is short allowance of room, and still shorter allowance of water.

Newton Forster was in a state of anxiety during the quarter of an hour in which he was obliged to attend to his duty, furling the sails and squaring the yards ; and the time appeared most insupportably long until he could venture aft to make some inquiries from the dubashes, who were crowding alongside, as to the fate of Isabel Revel. Time and absence had but matured his passion, and it was seldom that Isabel was away from his thoughts. He had a faint idea formed by hope that she was partial to him ; but this was almost smothered by the fears which opposed it, when he reflected upon what might be produced by absence, importunity, and her independent spirit, which might, if not well treated by her relation, reconcile her to a marriage which, although not in every way eligible, secured her a prospect of contentment and of peace.

At last the yards were squared to the satisfaction of the

boatswain, the ropes were hauled taut, and coiled down, and the men sent below to their dinners. Newton walked aft, and the first person he met was the dubash who had attended the *Bombay Castle*. The cheeks of Newton flushed, and his heart throbbed quick, and his lips quivered, as he asked intelligence of the colonel and his family.

"Colonel Saib quite well, sir. Two ladies marry officer."

"Which two?" demanded Newton eagerly.

"Not know how call Bibi Saib's names. But one not marry—she very handsome—more handsome than all."

The heart of Newton bounded at this intelligence, as he knew that it must be Isabel who was still a spinster. This was shortly after corroborated by an English gentleman who came on board. Their stay at Madras was intended to be short, and Newton resolved to ask immediate leave on shore. Apologising to Captain Oughton for making such an unusual request, which he was induced to do from intelligence he had just received relative to his friends, he expressed his anxious wish. Captain Oughton, who had reason to be highly satisfied with Newton, gave his consent in the kindest manner; "and Forster, if you wish to remain, you have my permission. We will manage without you; only recollect, we sail on Thursday night." Newton was soon ready, and quitted the ship with Major Clavering; to whose credit it ought here to be observed, that a daily note was despatched to Captain Oughton, requesting the pleasure of his company at the mess, until he was satisfied that, in this instance, the general invitation was sincere.

As soon as he was clear of the surf and out of the masulah boat, Newton hired a conveyance, and drove out to the bungalow of the old colonel. He trembled as he announced his name to the butler, who ushered him half-way to the receiving-room; and, like most of the natives, finding some difficulty in pronouncing English, contented himself with calling out "Burrah Saib," and then walked off. Newton found himself in the presence of the old veteran and Isabel. The latter had been reading a new publication, which she laid down at the voice of the butler announcing a visitor. But "Burrah Saib" may be anybody; it implies a gentleman. What then was the surprise of Isabel, who had no intimation of his arrival, when Newton Forster made his appearance? Her

312 ·

exclamation of delight, as she ran to him and extended her hand, made Newton Forster but too happy ; and as for a few seconds he held the hand not withdrawn, and looked in her beaming eyes, he quite forgot the presence of the colonel. A glance from the eye of Isabel in the direction where the old gentleman was seated brought Newton to his recollection. He walked up to the colonel, who shook hands, and declared that he was most glad to see him.

"You take up your quarters here, of course, Mr. Forster ? "

" I shall have great pleasure in availing myself of your kind offer for a day or two," replied Newton. "I trust that you have been in good health since we parted."

" Not very ; that is, latterly. I am thinking of a change of climate. I intend to go home in October. I suppose you have been informed that the two young women have married ? "

" I was told so by some one who came on board."

" Yes. Isabel, my dear, order a chamber for Mr. Forster." Isabel left the room. "Yes, both married—thought of nothing else—regularly came out on spec. In less than a month they knew the exact rank of every gentleman in the Presidency ; ascertained their prospects, and the value of their appointments ; turned the rupees into pounds sterling ; broke off the conversation with an ensign at the sight of a lieutenant ; cut the lieutenant for a captain ; were all smiles for a major ; and actually made love themselves to anybody who was above that rank, and a bachelor. They made their decision at last ; indeed, pretty quick. They were only four months on my hands. Both up the country now."

" I trust they have married well, sir ? "

" That depends upon circumstances. They have married young men not used to the climate. May be widows in half a year. If their husbands weather it, of course, they will come in for their share of the good things ; but I'll warrant they will never be able to leave the country."

" Not leave the country, sir ! May I ask why ? "

" Because they have married foolish, extravagant wives, who will run them in debt ; and when once in debt, it is no easy matter in this country to get out of it. They must insure their lives for the money which they borrow ; and as the house of agency will be gainers by their demise, of course they will not be permitted to leave the country and their chance of the *cholera morbus*. Don't you think that my niece looks remarkably well?"

"I do; the climate does not appear to have affected her."

"Rather improved her," replied the colonel; "she is not so thin as when she came on shore. God bless her! I'm sure, Mr. Forster, I am under great obligations to you for having persuaded me to go for the dear girl when she arrived. She has been a treasure to me! If she has had one, she has had twenty offers since you left; many unexceptionable; but she has refused them all. In some instances I have persuaded her—I thought it was my duty. But no; she has but one answer, and that is a decided one. She will not leave me. She has watched and attended me in my sickness as my own daughter. I say again, God bless her!"

It was with delight that Newton heard these encomiums upon Isabel, and her resolution not to marry. Whether it was wholly on account of not wishing to leave the colonel or not, still every delay gave him more chance of ultimate success. Isabel, who had stayed away that the colonel might have time to make any communications to Newton, now returned, and the conversation became general. Newton entered into a narrative of what had occurred during his passage home, and amused them with his anecdotes and conversation.

In about an hour the colonel rose from his chair that he might prepare for dinner; and then it was that Newton perceived the great change which had taken place. He was no longer upright, but bowed down; his step was no longer firm, it was almost tottering; and as he left the room, Newton's eyes met those of Isabel.

"You think him ill?" said Isabel inquiringly.

"Yes, I do, Miss Revel. He is very much changed; his stamina appears to have been exhausted by the climate. I trust he will go home as he proposes."

"He has been ill—very ill indeed. He talks constantly of home; he has done so for months; but when the time comes he puts it off. I wish you would persuade him."

"I will do all I can; but if you cannot prevail, I'm afraid that my persuasion will be of little use."

" Indeed, I think otherwise ; you have power over him, Mr Forster. I have not forgotten how kindly you exercised it in my behalf. We—that is," continued Isabel, colouring up, "the colonel has often talked of you since you quitted us."

"I feel highly flattered by his remembrance," replied Newton; " but you are in mourning, Miss Revel. If not a liberty from one who feels an interest in all concerning you, may I inquire for whom?"

" It is for my father," replied Isabel, with emotion, sitting down, and passing her hand across her eyes.

" I never heard of his death, and must apologise for having been so indiscreet as to renew your sorrow. How long is it since? and what was his complaint?"

" He had no complaint—would to God that he had! He was shot in a duel," replied Isabel, as the tears coursed down her cheeks. "O Mr. Forster, I trust I am resigned to the dispensations of Providence, but—that he should be summoned away at the moment when he was seeking the life of his fellow-creature, with all the worst passions in excitement— unprepared—for he was killed on the spot. These reflections will make his death a source of bitter regret, which can terminate but with existence."

" Your mother is still alive?" inquired Newton, to change the painful subject.

" Yes, but very ill; the last accounts were very distressing; they say that her complaint is incurable."

Newton regretted having brought up so painful a subject. A few words of condolence and sympathy were offered, and they separated to prepare for dinner.

Newton remained four days under the roof of the colonel, during which time he was constantly in the society of Isabel ; and when the period of his departure arrived, he had just grounds to imagine that, were all obstacles in other points removed, Isabel Revel would not, on her part, have raised any against the accomplishment of his wishes ; but their mutual dependent situations chased away all ideas of the kind for the present, and although they parted with unconcealed emotion, not a word which could be construed into a declaration of attachment was permitted to escape his lips.

The *Windsor Castle* sailed for Calcutta, and in a few days anchored at Kedgeree to wait for a pilot to come down the river. During their short stay at this anchorage, Mr. Williams, the first mate, who was an old Indian voyager, went on shore every evening to follow up his darling amusement of shooting jackals, a description of game by no means scarce in that quarter of the world. Often remonstrated with for his imprudence in exposing himself to the heavy night-dew, he would listen to no advice. " It was very true," he acknowledged, " that his brother had died of a jungle fever in pursuing the same amusement, and what was more, the fowling-piece in his hand belonged to his brother, who had bequeathed it to him; but as he had never heard of two brothers dying from a jungle fever taken by shooting jackals, he considered that the odds were strongly in his favour." This argument, however specious, did not prove good. The third morning he returned on board, complaining of a headache and shivering. He was bled and put into his bed, which he never left again.

Before the *Windsor Castle* was ready to sail, the remains of Mr. Williams were consigned to the burying ground at Diamond Harbour, and Newton Forster was promoted to the rank of first mate of the *Windsor Castle*. This, as will hereafter be proved, was a most fortunate occurrence to Newton Forster. The *Windsor Castle* sailed with leave to call at Madras for letters or passengers, and in a few days was again at anchor in the roadstead. The first intelligence which they received upon their arrival was that the *cholera morbus* had been very fatal, and that among others the old colonel had fallen a victim to the disease. Newton again obtained permission to go on shore to Isabel. He found her in distress at the house of a Mrs. Enderby, a lady who had lost her husband by the same ravaging epidemic, and who had long been the intimate friend of the colonel and of Isabel. Mrs. Enderby was about to return to England by the first vessel, and had advised Isabel to take so favourable an opportunity of a chaperon. Isabel, who had many reasons for wishing to leave the country, particularly the declining state of her mother's health, had consented; and it was with great pleasure that she received from Newton the information of the best cabins of the *Windsor Castle* not having been hitherto engaged.

The colonel's will had been opened. He had bequeathed

his property, the whole of which, with the exception of his establishment in India, was invested in the English funds, to his grand-niece, Isabel Revel. It amounted to nearly seventy thousand pounds. It would be difficult to say whether Newton Forster felt glad or sorry at this intelligence. For Isabel's sake he undoubtedly was glad; but he could not but feel that it increased the distance between them, and on that account, and on that alone, his reflections were painful. " Had it," thought he, " been five thousand, or ten thousand pounds, it would have been different. In the course of a few years I might have been able to produce an equivalent to it, and—but this fortune has raised her above my hopes; even if she had a prepossession in my favour, it would be dishonest to take advantage of it."

Isabel Revel had very different feelings on the subject —she was her own mistress, and her manner to Newton was more cordial, more confidential than before. She had not forgotten that Newton had shown the same regard and partiality for her when she was going out to India; and afterwards, when in distress, he had been her friend and admirer when in adversity. She knew his feelings towards her, and she had appreciated his delicacy and forbearance. Lately she had seriously analysed her own, and her analysis was wound up by a mental acknowledgment that her wealth would be valueless if she could not share it with Newton Forster.

At the request of Mrs. Enderby, the poop cabins were engaged for Isabel and herself. Their time for preparation was short; but one day more having been obtained from Captain Oughton, through the influence of Newton, Mrs. Enderby and Isabel embarked, and the *Windsor Castle* spread her canvas, sailing away from pestilence and death.

CHAPTER XLVII

" Britannia needs no bulwark,
No towers along the steep,
Her march is o'er the mountain waves,
Her home is on the deep."
—CAMPBELL.

THE *Windsor Castle* ploughed through the vast ocean of waters before a propitious gale, laden with treasure, in the safe arrival of which so many were interested. But what were all the valuables stowed away in her frame, in the opinion of Newton Forster, in comparison with the lovely being who had entrusted them with her safe conduct to her native country! The extreme precautions adopted or suggested by Newton for security during the night—his nervous anxiety during the day—became a source of laughter and ridicule to Captain Oughton; who once observed to him, " Newton, my boy, I see how the land lies, but depend upon it, the old ship won't tumble overboard a bit sooner than before; so one reef in the topsails will be quite sufficient."

Indeed, although they " never mentioned it," it was impossible for either of them to disguise their feelings. Their very attempts at concealment only rendered them more palpable to every one on board. Captain Oughton, who was very partial to Newton, rejoiced in his good fortune. He had no objection to young people falling or being in love on board of his ship, although he would not have sanctioned or permitted a marriage to take place during the period that a young lady was under his protection. Once landed on Deal beach, as he observed, they might " buckle to " as soon as they pleased.

The *Windsor Castle* was within two hundred miles of the Mauritius, when a strange vessel was discovered on the weather beam, bearing down to them with all the canvas she could spread. Her appearance was warlike; but what her force might be it was impossible to ascertain at the distance she was off, and the position which she then offered, being then nearly " end on."

" Can you make out her hull, Mr. Forster ? " cried Captain

318

Oughton, hailing Newton, who was at the masthead with a glass.

"No, sir; her foreyard is but now clear of the water, but she rises very fast."

"What do you think of her spars, Forster?" said Captain Oughton to Newton, who had just descended to the last rattling of the main-rigging.

"She is very taut, sir, and her canvas appears to be foreign."

"I'll bet you what you please it's that d——d fellow Surcœuf. This is just his cruising-ground, if the report of that neutral vessel was correct."

"Another hour will decide the point, sir," replied Newton; "but I must say I think your surmise likely to prove correct. We may as well be ready for him; a cruiser she certainly is."

"The sooner the better, Mr. Forster. He's but a 'rum customer,' and 'a hard hitter' by all accounts. Clear up the decks, and beat to quarters."

The strange vessel came down with such rapidity, that by the time the captain's orders were obeyed she was not more than two miles distant.

"There's 'in studding-sails'—and in devilish good style too!" observed Captain Oughton. "Now we shall see what he's made of."

The vessel rounded to the wind as soon as she had reduced her sails, on the same tack as the *Windsor Castle,* displaying her broadside, as the French would say, *hérissée des canons.*

"A corvette, sir," said Newton, reconnoitring through his glass; "two-and-twenty guns, besides her bridle ports. She is French rigged;—the rake of her stern is French;—in fact, she is French all over."

"All Lombard Street to a China orange, 'tis Surcœuf," replied Captain Oughton, who with the rest of his officers had his glass upon the vessel. There goes the tricoloured flag to prove I've won my bet. Answer the challenge. Toss my hat up.—Pshaw! I mean hoist the colours there abaft. Mr. Thomas," continued Captain Oughton, addressing the boatswain, "send the ship's company aft. Forster, you had better see the ladies down below."

At the summons of the boatswain the men came aft, and

stood in a body on the lee-side of the quarter-deck, with their hats off, and impatience in their looks.

"Now, my lads," said Captain Oughton, "if I am not mistaken, that vessel is commanded by the very best seaman that ever left a French port, and to do him justice, he's a damnation fine fellow !—a severe punisher, and can take a mauling as well as give one."

"Yes, sir, so can we," replied several of the men together.

"I know you can, my lads; and give and take is fair play. All I say is, let it be a fair stand-up fight, and 'may the best man win.' So now, my lads, if you're ready to come to the scratch, why, the sooner we peel the better—that's all."

"Hurrah!" cried the seamen, as they separated to their quarters; and in compliance with the injunctions of the captain, threw off their jackets, and many of them their shirts, to prepare for the conflict.

The corvette, after she had rounded to and exchanged colours, reduced her sails to precisely the same canvas as that carried by the *Windsor Castle*. This was to try her rate of sailing. In a quarter of an hour her superiority was manifest. She then hauled up her courses, and dropped to her former position on the *Windsor Castle's* weather-beam.

"The fellow has the heels of us, at all events," observed Captain Oughton; "but, Forster, the ladies are not yet below. Mrs. Enderby, I am sorry to be obliged to put you in confinement for a short time. Miss Revel, you must do me the favour to accept of Mr. Forster's convoy below the water-line."

Newton offered his arm to Isabel, and followed Captain Oughton, who escorted Mrs. Enderby. His heart was swelling with such variety of feeling that he could not at first trust himself to speak. When they had descended the ladder, and were picking their way, stepping over the rammers, sponges, and tackles stretched across the main-deck, Newton observed, "This is not the first time I have been commissioned to place you in security. I trust I shall again have the pleasure of relieving you from your bondage."

Isabel's lips quivered as she replied, "I trust in God that you may, Mr. Forster !—but—I feel more anxious now than I did on the former occasion. I—— "

"I have a foreboding," interrupted Newton, "that this

day's work is to make or mar me! Why, I cannot tell, but
I feel more confident than the chances would warrant; but
farewell, Isabel—God bless you!" and Newton, pressing
her hand, sprang up the ladder to his station on the quarter-
deck.

I have before observed that a man's courage much depends
upon his worldly means or prospects. A man who has much
to lose, whatever the property may consist of, will be less
inclined to fight than another whose whole capital consists
of "a light heart and a thin pair of breeches." Upon the
same reasoning, a man in love will not be so inclined to fight
as another. Death then cuts off the sweetest prospects in
existence. Lord St. Vincent used to say that a married man
was d—d for the service. Now (bating the honeymoon) I
do not agree with his lordship. A man in love may be inclined to play the Mark Antony; but a married man, "come
what will, he has been blessed." Once fairly into action, it
then is of little consequence whether a man is a bachelor,
or married, or in love; the all-absorbing occupation of killing
your fellow-creatures makes you for the time forget whether
you are a beggar or a prince.

When Newton returned on deck, he found that the corvette had gradually edged down until nearly within point-
blank range.

"Shall we lay the main-topsail to the mast?" observed
Newton. "We shall see his manœuvres."

"Why, he hardly would be fool enough to bear down to
us," replied Captain Oughton; "he is a determined fellow,
I know, but I believe not a rash one. However, we can
but try. Square the main-yard."

As soon as the *Windsor Castle* was hove-to, the courses of
the enemy were seen to flutter a few moments in the breeze,
and then the canvas was expanded. When the vessel had
gathered sufficient way, she hove in stays, and crossed the
Windsor Castle on the opposite tack.

"I thought so," observed Captain Oughton. "The fellow
knows what he is about. He'll not 'put his head in chancery,'
that's clear. How cautious the rascal is! It's very like the
first round of a fight—much manœuvring and wary sparring
before they begin to make play."

The corvette stood on the opposite tack until well abaft

the beam. She then wore round, and ranged up on the weather quarter of the Indiaman. When within two cables' length of the *Windsor Castle,* who had a little before filled her main-topsail to be in command, the Frenchman hauled up his foresail, and discovered his lower rigging manned by the ship's company, who gave a loud but hasty cheer, and then disappeared.

One cock crowing is a challenge sure to be answered if the antagonist is game. The English seamen sprang up to return the compliment, when Captain Oughton roared out, "To your guns, you fools! Hard down with the helm—fly the jib-sheet—check headbraces—look out now, my lads."

The corvette had already put her helm up and paid off to pass under the stern of the *Windsor Castle,* with the intention of raking her. The promptitude of Captain Oughton foiled the manœuvre of the Frenchman, which would have been more fatal had the English seamen been in the rigging to have been swept off by his grapeshot. As the *Windsor Castle* was thrown upon the wind, an exchange of broadsides took place, which, according to the usual custom of all well-regulated broadsides in close conflict, cut away a certain proportion of the spars and rigging, and cut up a proportion of the ships' companies. The *Windsor Castle,* worked by Newton, bracing round on the other tack, and the corvette rounding to on the same, the two vessels separated for a few minutes.

"Devilish well stopped, Newton, wasn't it?" said Captain Oughton, showing his white teeth. "Look out again—here she comes."

The corvette again attempted to rake as she ranged up after tacking, by throwing herself up in the wind; but Captain Oughton, watching the slightest variation of his adversary's career, gradually edging away, and then putting his helm up, manœuvred that the broadsides should again be exchanged. This second exchange was more effectual than the first.

"A stomacher, and both down!" cried Captain Oughton, as he surveyed the deck. "Be quick, Newton, hand the men below. Don't bring her to the wind yet; he has lost his way by luffing up, and cannot make play again for a few minutes."

After the second broadside, the vessels were much further apart, from the *Windsor Castle* running off the wind, while the corvette was too much crippled to work with her usual rapidity. This was convenient to both parties, as the last broadside had been very mischievous. The Frenchman, low in the water, had suffered less in her hull and ship's company, but more in·her spars and rigging. The foremast was nearly cut in half by the carronade shot of her antagonist; her main-yard was badly wounded, and her wheel knocked to atoms, which obliged them to steer on the lower deck. The *Windsor Castle* had received five shots in her hull, three men killed, and six wounded; three of her main shrouds cut in two, and her mizzen-mast badly wounded.

It was a quarter of an hour before the Frenchman returned to the attack. Captain Oughton had again hauled his wind, as if not wishing to decline the combat; which, indeed, the superior sailing of his antagonist prevented. The corvette appeared to have given up manœuvring, whether from the crippled state of her spars and sails, or from perceiving that he had hitherto gained nothing by his attempts. He now ranged up to within two cables' lengths of the *Windsor Castle*, and recommenced the action, broadside to broadside.

The breeze was lulled by the concussion of the air; and both vessels continued in the same position and at the same distance for upwards of an hour, pouring in their broadsides, every shot of which was effectual.

" Now this is what I call a reg'lar set-to. Fire away, my lads," cried Captain Oughton, rubbing his hands. " A proper rally this. D—n it, but he's game ! "

The wounded mizzen-mast of the *Windsor Castle* received another shot in the heart of it, which threw it over the side. Every part of her hull proved the severe and well-directed fire of the enemy ; her sails were as ragged as Jeremy Diddler's pocket-handkerchief ; her remaining masts pitted with shot ; the bulwarks torn away in several places; the boats on the booms in shivers ; rigging cut away fore and aft, and the ends swinging to and fro with the motion of the vessel; her decks in confusion ; and some of her guns, from necessity, deserted. Captain Oughton, Newton, and the rest of the officers continued' to encourage the men, giving them assistance in working the guns; and the ship's company.

appeared to have fully imbibed the bull-dog spirit of their commander.

The fire of the *Windsor Castle* had been equally destructive. The vessels had gradually neared each other in the calm; and the height of the *Windsor Castle* out of the water, in comparison with the corvette, had given her the advantage in sweeping the decks of the enemy. The contending vessels were in this situation, when for a minute or two a cessation of firing took place in consequence of the accumulation of smoke, which had so completely enshrouded them both that they knew not where to direct their guns; and they waited until it should clear away, that the firing might recommence. A light air gradually swept the veil to leeward, and discovered both vessels to each other at the distance of half a cable's length. Captain Oughton was with Newton on the poop, and the commander of the French corvette was standing on the hammock nettings of his own vessel. The latter took off his hat and courteously saluted his adversary. Captain Oughton answered the salutation; and then waving his hat, pointed to the English colours, which had been hoisted at the main; as much as to say, "They never shall come down!" The Frenchman (it was Surcœuf) did the same to the tricolour, and the action recommenced.

"Well done, my lads!" cried Captain Oughton; "well done! that broadside was a staggerer—right into his ribs. Hurrah now, my hearts of oak! this fellow's worth fighting. Aim at his foremast—another broadside will floor it. It's on the reel. Newton, jump forward, and——"

But the order was stopped by a grape-shot, which struck Captain Oughton in the breast. He staggered and fell from the poop to the quarter-deck. Newton leapt down, and went to him. The torrents of blood from his breast at once told the tale; and Newton called to some of the men that his commander might be taken below.

"Wait a moment, my dear lad," said Captain Oughton faintly, and catching his breath at every word; "it's a finisher—can't come to time—I die game." His head fell on his breast, and the blood poured out of his mouth.

Newton directed the body to be taken into the cuddy, that the men might not be dispirited by the sight. He then hastened to the poop, that he might reconnoitre the enemy.

He perceived that the corvette had hauled on board his tattered courses, and was standing ahead of them.

"He's off, sir," cried one of the quartermasters.

"I suspect not," replied Newton, who had his glass to his eye, looking upon the decks of the French vessel. "They are preparing to board, and will be round again in five minutes. Cutlasses and pikes ready—forward, my lads, all of us! We must beat them off!"

"And will, too," cried the seamen, as in obedience to their orders they collected on the forecastle. But they mustered thin; nearly half of the ship's company were either lying dead or under the hands of the surgeon; and as Newton surveyed his little force, fatigued as they were with their exertions, black with powder, stained with blood, and reeking with perspiration, he could not but acknowledge how heavy were the odds against the attack of a vessel so well manned as the corvette appeared to be. Newton said but a few words, but they were to the point; and he had the satisfaction to perceive, as they grasped their cutlasses, that if their numbers were few and their frames exhausted, their spirit was as unsubdued as ever.

The corvette had in the meantime run ahead on a wind about a mile, when she wore round, and was now standing right on to the *Windsor Castle,* and had neared to within three cables' lengths. A few minutes were to decide the point. Her courses were again hauled up, and discovered her lee fore-rigging, bowsprit, catheads, and forecastle crowded with men ready for the dash on board as soon as the vessels should come in contact. Newton stood on one of the forecastle guns, surrounded by his men; not a word was spoken on board of the *Windsor Castle* as they watched their advancing enemy. They were within a cable's length of each other, and Newton could plainly distinguish the features of the gallant Surcœuf, who was in advance on the knight-heads, when a puff of wind, which at any other time would not have occasioned the starting of a royal sheet, took the sails of the corvette; and her wounded foremast, laden with men in the lee-rigging, unable to bear the pressure, fell over the side, carrying with it the main-top-mast, and most of the crew who had been standing in the rigging, and leaving the corvette an encumbered wreck. A loud shout from the forecastle of the *Windsor Castle* announced that the English seamen were but too well aware of their desperate situation, and that they hailed the misfortune of the Frenchmen as their deliverance.

"Now, my lads, be smart," cried Newton, as he sprang aft to the wheel, and put up the helm; "man the flying jib-halyards (the jib was under the forefoot); let go the main-top bowling; square the main-yard. That will do; she's paying off. Man your guns; half-a-dozen broadsides, and it's all our own."

The sun had disappeared below the horizon, and the shades of evening had set in before this manœuvre had been accomplished. Several broadsides were poured into the corvette, which had the desired effect of crippling her still more, and her encumbered condition prevented any return. At last the night hid both vessels from each other; and the breeze freshening fast, it was necessary that the remaining masts of the *Windsor Castle* should be properly secured. The guns were therefore abandoned; and during the time the seamen were employed in knotting the rigging and bending the spare sails, Newton consulted with his brother officers, who were unanimous in agreeing that all had been done that could be expected, and that to wait till the ensuing day, when the corvette would have repaired her damages, would be attended with a risk of capture, which the valuable property entrusted to their charge would never authorise. It was not until past midnight that the *Windsor Castle* was in a condition to make sail; but long before this Newton had contrived to leave the deck for a few minutes to communicate with Isabel. With most of the particulars, and with the death of Captain Oughton, she had already been made acquainted; and if there could be any reward to Newton for his gallantry and his prudence more coveted than another, it was the affectionate greeting with which he was welcomed and congratulated by Isabel, her eyes beaming with tears of delight as they glanced from his face and were shrouded on the deck.

Love and murder make a pretty mixture, although as antithetical as the sweet and acid in punch—a composition which meets the approbation of all sensible discriminating people. But I shall leave the reader to imagine all he pleases, and finish the chapter by informing him that when the sun again made his appearance the corvette was not to be discovered from the mast-head. The guns were therefore properly secured; the decks washed; a jury mizzen-mast stuck up abaft; Captain Oughton, and the gallant fellows who had fallen in the combat, committed to the deep with the usual ceremonies; the wounded made as comfortable as possible in their hammocks; the carpenters busied with the necessary repairs; and the *Windsor Castle*, commanded by Newton Forster, running before a spanking breeze at the rate of eight knots per hour.

CHAPTER XLVIII

" Ships are but boards, sailors but men ;
There be land rats, and water rats, water thieves,
And land thieves ; I mean pirates."
—SHAKSPEARE.

MOST prophetical was the remark made by Newton Forster to Isabel previous to the action, to wit, that it would make or mar him. The death of Captain Oughton, and the spirited defence of the *Windsor Castle*, were the making of Newton Forster. As a subordinate officer, he might have been obliged to toil many years before he could have ascended to the summit of the ladder of promotion ; and during the time which he remained in that situation, what chance had he of making an independence, and proposing for the hand of Isabel Revel ? But now that, by a chain of circumstances peculiarly fortuitous, he was in command of the East India-man, returning home after having beat off a vessel of equal if not superior force, and preserved a cargo of immense value, he felt confident that he not only would be confirmed to the rank which he was now called upon to assume, but that he had every prospect of being employed. As a captain of an Indiaman, he was aware that reception into society, wealth, and consideration awaited him; and what made his heart to swell with gratitude and exultation, was the feeling that soon he would be enabled to aspire to the hand of one to whom he had so long been ardently attached.

As the *Windsor Castle* plunged through the roaring and
complaining seas, with all the impetus of weight in motion,
Newton's eyes were radiant with hope, although his demeanour towards Isabel was, from the peculiar circumstances
attending their situation, more delicately reserved than before.

When the *Windsor Castle* touched at St. Helena, Newton
had the good fortune to obtain a supply of able seamen more
than sufficient for the remanning of his ship. They had been
sent there in an empty brig by a French privateer, who had
captured many vessels, and had been embarrassed with the
number of her prisoners. Having obtained the stores which
were required, Newton lost no time in prosecuting his voyage
to England.

It was about a fortnight after they had quitted St. Helena
that a strange sail was reported on the starboard bow; and
as they neared her, it was evident that her foremast was
gone, and that she was otherwise in a disabled state. When
the Indiaman was within a mile, the stranger threw out
neutral colours, and hoisted a whiff, half-mast down, as a
signal that she was in distress. Newton ordered the ship
to be kept away, and when alongside of the vessel lowered
down a boat, and sent the third mate to ascertain what
assistance could be afforded. With sailors, thank God! distress is sufficient to obtain assistance, and the nation or country
are at once merged in that feeling of sympathy for those
misfortunes which may perhaps but the next hour befall ourselves. The boat returned; and the officer informed Newton
that the vessel was from the island of Bourbon, bound to
Hamburg; that she had been dismasted and severely injured
in a gale off the Cape of Good Hope; and that when her
mast went over the side, one-half of her crew, who were up
at the time on the fore-yard, had been cast overboard and
drowned; that from the want of men and material they had
been unable to rig an effective jury-mast, and had in consequence been so long on their passage that their provisions
and water were nearly expended. The officer concluded by
stating that there were a French lady and two gentlemen,
with their attendants, who had taken their passage home in
the vessel. Newton immediately went down the side, and
pulled on board of the vessel to ascertain what assistance
could be afforded. When he arrived on board, he was met

328

by the Flemish captain, who commenced a statement of his misfortunes and his difficulties, when the French lady, who, unobserved by Newton, had come up the companion-ladder, screamed out as she ran into his arms—

"Ah ! mon Dieu !—c'est Monsieur Nu-tong !"

Newton looked at the lady, who had burst into tears, as her face lay upon his shoulder, and immediately recognised his former kind and affectionate friend, Madame de Fontanges ; close to him, with his hand extended, was her generous husband. The meeting was joyful, and Newton was delighted that circumstances had enabled him to render assistance to those who had been so kind to him in his former distress.

"Oh ! Monsieur Nu-tong, nous avons tant soufferts ? Ah ! mon Dieu !—point de l'eau—rien à manger," cried Madame de Fontanges; then smiling through her tears, "mais ce rencontre est charmant ;—n'est ce pas, mon ami ? " continued the lady, appealing to her husband.

"You do not remember Monsieur le Marquis ? " said M. de Fontanges to Newton. Newton turned his head, and recognised the governor of Guadaloupe, who had expressed such sympathy at his shipwreck, and had sent him away in the cartel instead of detaining him as a prisoner.

The vessel was indeed in a deplorable condition; and had she not received the timely assistance now afforded, would in all probability have soon been a scene of horror and of suffering. They had not more than three days' water remaining on board, and provisions barely sufficing for three days. Newton hastened to send back the boat with orders for an immediate and ample supply of these necessaries, in case of bad weather coming on and preventing further communication. Satisfied that their immediate wants were relieved, Newton took leave of his friends for the present, and returned on board his own ship, despatching his carpenters and part of his crew to the immediate refit of the vessel ; and then selecting a part of everything that the *Windsor Castle* contained in her store-rooms or on her decks, which he thought would administer to the comfort or the luxury of the passengers on board of the neutral.

In two hours they who were in a state bordering upon famine found themselves revelling in plenty. Before night the English seamen had a jury-mast up, and the sails set.

The Hollanders on board would have given their assistance, but they were told to remain on deck and make up for lost time, which they acquiesced in very readily, eating and drinking as if they were determined to lay in a stock for the remainder of the voyage. Newton, who had returned on board of the neutral to superintend the repairs and enjoy the society of his old friends, received from them a long account of what had occurred since their separation. At nightfall he took his leave, promising to continue under easy sail and remain with them for a day or two, until they were satisfied that all was right, and that they no longer required his assistance.

The narrative obtained by Newton may be thus condensed for the information of the reader. The Marquis de Fontanges had been appointed from the government of Guadaloupe to that of the island of Bourbon, which was considered of more importance. Monsieur and Madame de Fontanges accompanied him to his new command; and they had remained there for two years, when the ruling powers, without any ground, except that the marquis had received his appointment from the former government, thought proper to supersede him. Frigates were not so plentiful as to spare one for the return of an ex-governor; and the marquis, being permitted to find his way home how he could, had taken advantage of the sailing of the Hamburger to return to Europe or to France, or as he might find it advisable.

For two days, during which the weather was so fine that Madame de Fontanges and the gentlemen went on board of the *Windsor Castle*, and were introduced to the ladies, Newton continued under easy sail, each day despatching to the neutral everything which his gratitude could suggest; but as Newton was most anxious to proceed on his voyage, it was agreed that the next morning they should part company. At the close of the evening a strange sail was observed on the weather-beam; but as she carried no foretop-gallant sail, and appeared to be steering the same course as the *Windsor Castle*, she excited but a momentary observation, supposing that she was some homeward-bound neutral, or a merchant vessel which had separated from her convoy. During the night, which was dark, the moon being in her first quarter, the officer of the middle watch lost sight of their protégé; but this was to be expected, as she

330

did not carry a light. Before morning the wind fell, and when the sun arose it was a perfect calm. The officer of the watch, as the day dawned, went on the poop, surveying the horizon for their companion, and discovered her six or seven miles astern, lying alongside of the strange vessel which they had seen the day before. Both vessels, as well as the *Windsor Castle*, were becalmed. He immediately went down to Newton, acquainting him with the circumstance, which bore a very suspicious appearance. Newton hastened on deck; with his glass he could plainly distinguish that the stranger was a vessel of a low, raking description, evidently no merchantman, but built for sailing fast, and in all probability a privateer. The man at the mast-head reported that boats were constantly passing between the two vessels. Newton, who felt very anxious for the safety of his friends, accepted the offer of the second mate to take the gig and ascertain what was going on. In little more than an hour the gig was seen from the mast-head to arrive within half a mile of the vessels, and shortly afterwards the smoke from a gun, followed by a distant report. The gig then winded and pulled back towards the *Windsor Castle*. It was in a state of great excitement that Newton waited for her return, when the second mate informed him that on his approach he discovered that she was a flush vessel, pierced for fourteen guns, painted black, and apparently well manned; that she evidently, to use a nautical term, was "gutting the neutral;" and that, as they had witnessed, on their boat coming within range, the vessel had fired a round of grape, which fortunately fell short of them. She had shown no colours; and from her appearance and behaviour (as all privateers respect neutrals), he had no doubt that she was the pirate vessel stated, when they were at St. Helena, to be cruising in these latitudes. Newton was of the same opinion, and it was with a heavy heart that he returned to the cabin to communicate the unpleasant intelligence to Mrs. Enderby and Isabel.

There is nothing more annoying in this world than the will without the power. At any time a vessel becalmed is considered a very sufficing reason for swearing by those who are on board of her. What then must have been the feelings of Newton, lying on the water in a state of compelled inaction, while his friends were being plundered, and perhaps murdered by a gang of miscreants before his eyes! How eagerly and repeatedly did he scan the horizon for the coming breeze! How did Hope raise her head at the slightest cat's-paw that ruffled the surface of the glassy waters! Three successive gales of wind are bad enough; but three gales blowing hard enough to blow the devil's horns off are infinitely preferable to one idle, stagnant, motionless, confounded calm, oppressing you with the blue-devils and maddening you with the fidgets at one and the same time.

At last, as the sun descended, the breeze sprang up, first playing along the waters in capricious and tantalising airs, as if uncertain and indifferent in its infancy to which quarter of the compass it should direct its course. The ship again answered her helm; her head was put the right way, and the sails were trimmed to every shift which it made, to woo its utmost power. In a quarter of an hour it settled, blowing from a quarter which placed them to windward of, and they carried it down with them to within two miles of, the stranger and the neutral, who still remained becalmed. But as the wind freshened, it passed ahead of them, sweeping along the surface, and darkening the colours of the water, until it reached the vessels to leeward; one of which—the one that Newton was so anxious to get alongside of—immediately took advantage of it, and spreading all her canvas, soon increased her distance. When the *Windsor Castle* arrived abreast of the neutral, the stranger was more than two miles to leeward. A little delay was then necessary to ascertain what had occurred. Newton, who perceived M. de Fontanges on the deck, shouting to them and wringing his hands, rounded to, lowered down a boat, and pulled on board of the neutral. The intelligence communicated was distressing. The strange vessel was a pirate, who had plundered them of everything, had taken away Madame de Fontanges, Mimi and Charlotte, her two female attendants. The captain of the pirates had wounded and severely beaten M. de Fontanges, who had resisted the "*enlevèment*" of his wife; and after having cut away all the standing rigging, and nearly chopped through the masts with axes, they had finished their work by boring holes in the counter of the vessel; so that had not Newton been able to come up with her, they must all have perished during the night.

There was no time to be lost; the Marquis de Fontanges, M. de Fontanges, and the crew were hurried on board of the *Windsor Castle* (the pirate had taken care that they should not be delayed in packing up their baggage), and Newton, as soon as he returned on board, and hoisted up his boat, crowded every stitch of canvas in pursuit of the pirate, who was now more than four miles distant. But although the wind gradually increased, and was thus far in their favour, as they first benefited by it, yet as the sun went down, so did their hopes descend. At nightfall the pirate had increased her distance to seven miles. Newton pursued, watching her with a night-glass until she could no longer be distinguished. Still their anxiety was so great that no one went to bed on board of the *Windsor Castle*. When the day broke, the pirate was not to be discovered in any quarter of the horizon from the mast-head of the *Windsor Castle*.

CHAPTER XLIX

" She stood a moment as a Pythoness
    Stands on her tripod, agonised and full
Of inspiration gathered from distress,
    When all the heart-strings, like wild horses, pull
The heart asunder ; then, as more or less
    Their speed abated or their strength grew dull,
She sunk down on her seat by slow degrees,
And bowed her throbbing head o'er trembling knees."
—BYRON.

IT was with deep regret that Newton gave directions for the ship's head to be again directed on her course to England; but the property under his charge was of too great value to warrant risking it by cruising after the pirates, the superior sailing of whose vessel afforded no hopes of success. The melancholy situation of Madame de Fontanges threw a gloom over the party, which was communicated even to the seamen; while the anguish of M. de Fontanges, expressed with all the theatrical violence characteristic of his nation, was a source of continual reminiscence and regret. They had been four days on their voyage, making little progress with the light and

baffling winds, when they were shrouded in one of those thick
fogs which prevail in the latitude of the Cape de Verdes, and
which was rendered more disagreeable by a mizzling rain.

On the sixth day, about twelve o'clock, the horizon cleared
to the northward, and the fog in that quarter was rolled away
by a strong breeze which rippled along the water. Newton,
who was on deck, observed the direction of the wind to be
precisely the reverse of the little breeze to which their sails
had been trimmed ; and the yards of the *Windsor Castle* were
braced round to meet it. The gust was strong, and the ship,
laden as she was, careened over to the sudden force of it, as
the top-gallant sheets and halyards were let fly by the directions of the officer of the watch. The fog, which had still
continued thick to leeward, now began to clear away ; and
as the bank dispersed, the Marquis de Fontanges, who was
standing on the poop by the side of Newton, cried out,
"*Voilà un bâtiment !*" Newton looked in the direction pointed
out, and discovered the hull of a vessel looming through the
fog, about a quarter of a mile to leeward of the *Windsor Castle*.
One minute's scrutiny convinced him that it was the pirate,
who, not having been expeditious in trimming his sails, "laid
in irons," as seamen term it, heeling over to the blast. The
Windsor Castle was then running free, at the rate of four
miles an hour.

"Starboard the helm—all hands to board—steady so. Be
smart, my lads—it's the pirate—port a little. Hurrah ! my
lads—be quick, and she's all our own. Quartermaster, my
sword —quick !"

The crew, who were all on deck, snatched their cutlasses
from the capstern-head, in which they were inserted, and
before three minutes elapsed, during which the pirate had
not time to extricate himself from his difficulty, were all
ready for the service. They were joined by the Flemish
sailors belonging to the neutral vessel, who very deliberately
put their hands in their breeches-pockets and pulled out
their knives, about as long as a carpenter's two-foot rule,
preferring this weapon to anything else.

Monsieur de Fontanges, bursting with impatience, stood
with Newton at the head of the men. When the collision
of the two vessels took place, the *Windsor Castle*, conned so
as not to run down the pirate, but to sheer alongside, stove

in the bulwarks of the other, and carried away her topmasts, which, drawn to windward by the pressure on the backstays, fell over towards the *Windsor Castle*, and entangling with her rigging, prevented the separation of the two vessels.

" No quarter, my friends ! " cried Monsieur de Fontanges, who darted on board of the pirate vessel at the head of some men near the main-rigging, while Newton and the remainder, equally active, poured down upon his quarter.

Such had been the rapidity of the junction, and such the impetuosity of the attack, that most of the pirates had not had time to arm themselves, which, considering the superiority of their numbers, rendered the contest more equal. A desperate struggle was the result ; the attacked party neither expecting, demanding, nor receiving quarter. It was blow for blow. wound for wound, death to one or both. Every inch of the deck was disputed, and not an inch obtained until it reeked with blood. The voices of Newton and Monsieur de Fontanges, encouraging their men, were answered by another voice—that of the captain of the pirates—which had its due effect upon the other party, which rallied at its sound. Newton, even in the hurry and excitement of battle, could not help thinking to himself that he had heard that voice before. The English seamen gained but little ground, so obstinate was the resistance. The pirates fell ; but as they lay on the deck they either raised their exhausted arms to strike one last blow of vengeance before their life's blood had been poured out, or seized upon their antagonists with their teeth in their expiring agonies. But a party who, from the sedateness of their carriage, had hitherto been almost neutral, now forced their way into the conflict. These were the Flemish seamen, with their long snick-a-snee knives, which they used with as much imperturbability as a butcher professionally employed. They had gained the main-rigging of the vessel, and, ascending it, had passed over by the cat-harpins, and descended, with all the deliberation of bears, on the other side, by which tranquil manœuvre the pirates were taken in flank ; and huddled as they were together, the knives of the Flemings proved much more effective than the weapons opposed to them. The assistance of the Flemings was hailed with a shout from the English seamen, who rallied and increased their efforts, Newton's sword had just been passed through the body of a tall, powerful man, who had remained uninjured in the front of the opposing party since the commencement of the action, when his fall discovered to Newton's view the captain of the vessel, whose voice had been so often heard, but who had hitherto been concealed from his sight by the athletic form which had just fallen by his hand. What was his astonishment and his indignation when he found himself confronted by one whom he had long imagined to have been summoned to answer for his crimes —his former inveterate enemy, Jackson!

Jackson appeared to be no less astonished at the recognition of Newton, whom he had supposed to have perished on the sand-bank. Both mechanically called each other by name, and both sprang forward. The blow of Newton's sword was warded off by the miscreant; but at the same moment that of Monsieur de Fontanges was passed through his body to the hilt. Newton had just time to witness the fall of Jackson, when a tomahawk descended on his head; his senses failed him, and he lay among the dead upon the deck.

There was a shriek, a piercing shriek, heard when Newton fell. It passed the lips of one who had watched, with an anxiety too intense to be portrayed, the issue of the conflict; it was from Isabel, who had quitted the cabin at the crash occasioned by the collision of the two vessels, and had remained upon the poop " spectatress of the fight." There were no firearms used; no time for preparation had been allowed. There had been no smoke to conceal—all had been fairly presented to her aching sight. Yes! there she had remained, her eye fixed upon Newton Forster, as at the head of his men he slowly gained the deck of the contested vessel. Not one word did she utter; but with her lips wide apart from intensity of feeling, she watched his progress through the strife, her eye fixed—immovably fixed upon the spot where his form was to be seen; hope buoyant, as she saw his arm raised and his victims fall; heart sinking, as the pirate sword aimed at a life so dear. There she stood like a statue—as white, as beautiful —as motionless as if, indeed, she had been chiselled from the Parian marble; and had it not been for her bosom heaving with the agony of tumultuous feeling, you might have imagined that all was as cold within. Newton fell—all her hopes were wrecked—she uttered one wild shriek, and felt no more.

After the fall of Jackson the pirates were disheartened, and their resistance became more feeble. M. de Fontanges carved his way to the taffrail, and then turned round to kill again. In a few minutes the most feeble-hearted escaped below, leaving the few remaining brave to be hacked to pieces, and the deck of the pirate vessel was in possession of the British crew. Not waiting to recover his breath, M. de Fontanges rushed below to secure his wife. The cabin-door was locked, but yielded to his efforts; and he found her in the arms of her attendants in a state of insensibility. A scream of horror at the sight of his bloody sword, and another of joy at the recognition of their master, was followed up with the assurance that Madame had only fainted. M. de Fontanges took his wife in his arms and carried her on deck, where, with the assistance of the seamen, he removed her on board of the *Windsor Castle*, and in a short time had the pleasure to witness her recovery. The first endearments over, there was an awkward question to put to a wife. After responding to her caresses, M. de Fontanges inquired with an air of anxiety very remarkable in a Frenchman, how she had been treated. " Il n'y a pas de mal, mon ami," replied Madame de Fontanges. This was a Jesuitical sort of answer, and M. de Fontanges required further particulars. " Elle avait temporisée " with the ruffian, with the faint hope of that assistance which had so opportunely and unexpectedly arrived. M. de Fontanges was satisfied with his wife's explanation, and such being the case, what passed between Jackson and Madame de Fontanges can be no concern of the reader's. As for Mimi and Charlotte, they made no such assertion; but when questioned the poor girls burst into tears, and calling the captain and first lieutenant of the pirate barbarians, and every epithet they could think of, complained bitterly of the usage which they had received.

We left Newton floored (as Captain Oughton would have said) on the deck of the pirate vessel, and Isabel in a swoon on the poop of the *Windsor Castle*. They were both taken up, and then taken down, and recovered according to the usual custom in romances and real life. Isabel was the first to come to, because, I presume, a blow on the heart is not quite so serious as a blow on the head. Fortunately for Newton, the tomahawk had only glanced along the temple, not injuring the skull, although it stunned him and detached a very decent portion of his scalp, which had to be replaced. A lancet brought him to his senses, and the surgeon pronounced his wound not to be dangerous, provided that he remained quiet.

At first Newton acquiesced with the medical adviser, but an hour or two afterwards a circumstance occurred which had such a resuscitating effect, that weak as he was with the loss of blood, he would not resign the command of the ship, but gave his orders relative to the captured vessel and the securing of the prisoners as if nothing had occurred. What had contributed so much to the recovery of Newton was simply this, that somehow or another Mrs. Enderby left him for a few minutes *tête-à tête* with Isabel Revel; and during those few minutes, somehow or another, a very interesting scene occurred, which I have no time just now to describe. It ended, however, somehow or another, in the parties plighting their troth. As I said before, love and murder are very good friends; and a chop from a tomahawk was but a prelude for the descent of Love, with " healing on his wings."

The *Windsor Castle* lost five men killed and eleven wounded in this hard contest. Three of the Flemings were also wounded. The pirate had suffered more severely. Out of a crew of seventy-five men, as no quarter had been given, there remained but twenty-six, who had escaped and secreted themselves below in the hold of the vessel. These were put in irons under the half-deck of the *Windsor Castle*, to be tried upon their arrival in England. As I may as well dispose of them at once, they were all sentenced to death by Sir William Scott, who made a very impressive speech upon the occasion ; and most of them were hanged on the bank of the Thames. The polite valet of the Marquis de Fontanges hired a wherry, and escorted Mademoiselles Mimi and Charlotte to witness the *barbares* dangling in their chains ; and the sooty young ladies returned much gratified with their interesting excursion.

It will be necessary to account for the reappearance of Jackson. The reader may recollect that he made sail in the boat, leaving Newton on the island which they had gained after the brig had been run on shore and wrecked. When the boat came floating down with the tide bottom up, Newton made sure that Jackson had been upset and drowned ; instead of which he had been picked up by a

Providence schooner, and the boat having been allowed to go adrift with the main-sheet belayed to the pin, had been upset by a squall, and had floated down with the current to the sand-bank where Newton was standing in the water. Jackson did not return to England, but had entered on board of a Portuguese slave-vessel, and continued some time employed in this notorious traffic, which tends so much to demoralise and harden the heart. After several voyages he headed a mutiny, murdered the captain and those who were not a party to the scheme, and commenced a career of piracy, which had been very successful from the superior sailing of the vessel and the courage of the hardened villains he had collected under his command.

CHAPTER L

" Hope, of all passions, most befriends us here ;
Joy has her tears, and transport has her death.
Hope, like a cordial, innocent, though strong,
Man's heart at once inspirits and serenes ;
Nor makes him pay his wisdom for his joys.
'Tis all our present state can safely bear :
Health to the frame and vigour to the mind,
And to the modest eye chastised delight,
Like the fair summer evening, mild and sweet,
'Tis man's full cup—his paradise below."
—YOUNG.

WITH what feelings of delight did Newton Forster walk the deck of the *Windsor Castle*, as she scudded before a fine breeze across the Bay of Biscay ! His happiness in anticipation was so great, that at times he trembled lest the cup should be dashed from his lips ; and at the same time that he thanked God for blessings received, he offered up his prayer that his prospects might not be blighted by disappointment. How happy did he feel when he escorted Isabel on deck, and walked with her during the fine summer evenings, communicating those hopes and fears, recurring to the past, or anticipating the future, till midnight warned them of the rapidity with which time had flown away ! The pirate vessel,

339

which had been manned by the crew of the neutral and part of the ship's company of the *Windsor Castle* under charge of the fourth mate, sailed round and round them, until at last the Channel was entered, and favoured with a westerly breeze, the *Windsor Castle* and her prize anchored in the Downs. Here Mrs. Enderby and Isabel quitted the ship, and Newton received orders to proceed round to the river. Before the *Windsor Castle* had anchored, the newspapers were put into his hands containing a report of the two actions; and he had the gratification of acknowledging that his countrymen were not niggardly in the encomiums upon his meritorious conduct.

Newton presented himself to the Court of Directors, who confirmed his rank, and promised him the command of the first ship which was brought forward, with flattering commendation for his gallantry in protecting property of so much value. Newton took his leave of the august Leadenhall board, and hastened to his uncle's house. The door was opened by a servant who did not know him. Newton passed him and ran up to the drawing-room, where he found Amber in company with William Aveleyn, who was reading to her the despatch containing the account of the action with Surcœuf.

Amber sprang into his arms. She had grown into a tall girl of nearly fifteen, budding into womanhood and beauty—promising perfection, although not yet attained to it. William Aveleyn was also nearly half a foot taller ; and a blush which suffused his handsome face at being surprised alone with Amber, intimated that the feelings of a man were superseding those of boyhood.

"Where is my mother?" inquired Newton.

"She is not at home, dear Newton," replied Amber; "she walked out with your father. They are both well."

"And my uncle?"

"Quite well, and most anxious to see you. He talks of nobody but you, and of nothing but your actions, which we were just reading about when you came in. Pray, *Captain* Newton, may I inquire after your French friends? What has become of them?"

"They are at Sablonniere's hotel, Miss Amber; they have obtained their parole at the Alien Office."

The conversation was interrupted by the return of Newton's

father and mother, and shortly afterwards Mr. John Forster made his appearance. After the first greetings and congratulations were over—

"Well, Newton," observed Nicholas, "so you beat off a pirate, I hear."

"No, my dear father, we boarded one."

"Ah! very true; I recollect—and you killed Surcœuf."

"No, father, only beat him off."

"So it was; I recollect now. Brother John, isn't it almost dinner time?"

"Yes, brother Nicholas, it is; and I'm not sorry for it. Mr. William Aveleyn, perhaps you'd like to wash your hands? A lad's paws are never the worse for a little clean water."

William Aveleyn blushed: his dignity was hurt; but he had lately been very intimate at Mr. Forster's, and he therefore walked out to comply with the recommendation.

"Well, brother Nicholas, what have you been doing all day?"

"Doing all day, brother? really, I don't exactly know. My dear," said Nicholas, turning to his wife, "what have I been doing all day?"

"To the best of my recollection," replied Mrs. Forster, smiling, "you have been asking when dinner would be ready."

"Uncle Nicholas," said Amber, "you promised to buy me a skein of blue silk."

"Did I, my dear? Well, so I did, I declare. I'm very sorry—dear me, I forgot, I did buy it. I passed by a shop where the windows were full of it, and it brought it to my mind, and I did buy it. It cost—what was it it cost?"

"Oh! I know what it cost," replied Amber. "I gave you threepence to pay for it. Where is it?"

"If I recollect, it cost seven shillings and sixpence," replied Nicholas, pulling out, not a skein of blue silk, but a yard of blue sarsenet.

"Now, papa, do look here! Uncle Nicholas, I never will give you a commission again. Is it not provoking? I have seven shillings and sixpence to pay for a yard of blue sarsenet which I do not want. Uncle Nicholas, you really are very stupid."

"Well, my dear, I suppose I am. I heard William Aveleyn say the same when I came into the room this morning, because—let me see——"

341

"You heard him say nothing, uncle," interrupted Amber, colouring.

"Yes, I recollect now—how stupid I was to come in when I was not wanted!"

"Humph!" said John Forster; and dinner was announced.

Since the recognition of Mrs. Forster by her husband, she had presided at her brother-in-law's table. The dinner provided was excellent, and was done ample justice to by all parties, especially Nicholas, whose appetite appeared to increase from idleness. Since Newton had left England he had remained a pensioner upon his brother; and by dint of constant exertion on the part of Mrs. Forster, had been drilled out of his propensity of interfering with either the watch or the spectacles. This was all that was required by Mr. John Forster; and Nicholas walked up and down the house like a tame cat, minding nobody, and nobody paying any attention to him.

After dinner the ladies retired, and shortly afterwards William Aveleyn quitted the room.

Newton thought this to be a good opportunity to acquaint his uncle with his attachment to Miss Revel, and the favourable result. Mr. John Forster heard him without interruption.

"Very nice girl, I dare say, nephew, but you are too young to marry. You can't marry and go to sea. Follow your profession, Newton; speculate in opium—I'll find the means."

"I trust, sir, that I should never speculate in marrying; but had I acted on that plan, this would prove the best speculation of the two. Miss Revel has a very large fortune."

"So much the worse; a man should never be indebted to his wife for his money—they never forget it. I'd rather you had fallen in love with a girl without a shilling."

"Well, sir, when I first fell in love she had not a sixpence."

"Humph! Well, nephew, that may be very true; but, as I said before, follow your profession."

"Marriage will not prevent my so doing, uncle. Most captains of Indiamen are married men."

"More fools they! leaving their wives at home to be flattered and fooled by the Lord knows who. A wife, nephew—is a woman."

342

"'I hope that mine will be one, sir," replied Newton, laughing.

"Nephew, once for all, I don't approve of your marrying now—that's understood. It's my wish that you follow your profession. I'll be candid with you; I have left you the heir to most of my fortune, but—I can alter my will. If you marry this girl I shall do so."

"Alter your will, brother?" said Nicholas, who had been attentive to the conversation. "Why, who have you to leave your money to except to Newton?"

"To hospitals—to pay off the National Debt—to anything. Perhaps I may leave it all to that little girl, who already has come in for a slice."

"But, brother," replied Nicholas, "will that be just, to leave all your money away from the family?"

"Just! yes, brother Nicholas, quite just. A man's will is *his will*. If he makes it so as to satisfy the wishes or expectations of others, it is no longer his will, but theirs. Nephew, as I said before, if you marry against my consent I shall alter my will."

"I am sorry, sir, very sorry that you should be displeased with me; but I am affianced to this lady, and no worldly consideration will induce me not to fulfil an engagement upon which, indeed, my future happiness depends. I have no claim upon you, sir; on the contrary, I have incurred a large debt of gratitude from your kind protection. Anything else you would require of me——"

"Humph! that's always the case; anything else except what is requested. Brother Nicholas, do me the favour to go upstairs; I wish to speak with my nephew alone."

"Well, brother John, certainly if you wish it—if you and Newton have secrets;" and Nicholas rose from his chair.

"Surely, sir," observed Newton, not pleased at the abrupt dismissal of his father, "we can have no secrets to which my father may not be a party."

"Yes, but I have, nephew. Your father is my brother, and I take the liberty with my brother, if you like that better, not with your father."

In the meantime Nicholas had stalked out of the room.

"Nephew," continued Mr. John Forster, as the door closed, "I have stated to you my wish that you should not marry this young woman, and I will now explain my reasons. The girl left in my charge by my brother Edward has become the same to me as a daughter. I intend that you shall make three or four voyages as captain of an India-man ; then you shall marry her, and become the heir to my whole fortune. Now you understand me. May I ask what are your objections ? "

" None, sir, but what I have already stated—my attach-ment and engagement to another person."

" Is that all ? "

" Is it not enough ? "

" It appears that this young woman has entered into an engagement on board ship, without consulting her friends."

" She has no father, sir. She is of age, and independent."

" You have done the same."

" I grant it, sir ; but even were I inclined, could I, in honour or honesty, retract ? "

" Humph ! "

" Perhaps, sir, if you were acquainted with the young lady you might not be averse to the match."

" Perhaps, if I saw with your eyes, I might not ; but that is not likely to be the case. Old men are a little blind and a little obstinate. After toiling through life to amass a fortune, they wish to have their own way in disposing of it. It is the only return they can receive for their labour. How-ever, nephew, you will act as you please. As I said before, if you marry against my consent I shall alter my will. Now, empty the bottle and we'll go upstairs."

CHAPTER LI

" And, Betty, give this cheek a little red."
—POPE.

THE departure of Isabel in the *Windsor Castle* so immedi-ately after the death of Colonel Revel, prevented her com-municating to her mother the alteration which had taken place in her circumstances, and her intended return to England. The first intimation received by Mrs. Revel was from a hurried note sent on shore by a pilot-boat off Falmouth, stating Isabel's arrival in the Channel, and her anticipation of soon embracing her mother. Isabel did not enter into any particulars, as she neither had time, nor did she feel assured that the letter would ever reach its destination.

The letter did, however, come to hand two days before Isabel and Mrs. Enderby arrived in the metropolis, much to the chagrin of Mrs. Revel, who imagined that her daughter had returned penniless, to be a sharer of her limited income. She complained to Mr. Heaviside, who as usual stepped in, not so much from any regard for Mrs. Revel, but to while away the time of a *far niente* old bachelor.

"Only think, Mr. Heaviside," said the lady, who was stretched on a sofa, supported on pillows, "Isabel has returned from India. Here is a letter I have just received, signed with her maiden name! Her sisters so well married, too! Surely she might have stayed out with one of them! I wonder how she got the money to pay her passage home! Dear me, what shall I do with her?"

"If I may be allowed to see the letter, Mrs. Revel," said the old gentleman.

"Oh, certainly, it's nothing but a note."

Mr. Heaviside read the contents.

"There is very little in it, indeed, Mrs. Revel; not a word about the colonel, or why she left India. Perhaps the colonel may be dead."

"Then she might have gone to live with one of her sisters, Mr. Heaviside!"

"But perhaps he may have left her some property."

"And do you, a sensible man, think that if such was the case my daughter would not have mentioned it in her note? Impossible, Mr. Heaviside!"

"She may intend to surprise you, Mrs. Revel."

"She has surprised me," replied the lady, falling back upon the pillows.

"Well, Mrs. Revel, you will soon ascertain the facts. I wish you a good morning, and will pay my devoirs in a day or two to inquire after your health, and hear what has taken place."

To defray the expenses attending the "consignment" of the three Miss Revels to India, Mrs. Revel had consented to borrow money, insuring her life as a security to the parties who provided it. Her unprincipled husband took this opportunity of obtaining a sum which amounted to more than half her marriage settlement, as Mrs. Revel signed the papers laid before her without examining their purport. When her dividends were become due, this treachery was discovered ; and Mrs. Revel found herself reduced to a very narrow income, and wholly deserted by her husband, who knew that he had no chance of obtaining further means of carrying on his profligate career. His death in a duel, which we have before mentioned, took place a few months after the transaction, and Mrs. Revel was attacked with that painful disease, a cancer, so deeply seated as to be incurable. Still she was the same frivolous, heartless being; still she sighed for pleasure, and to move in those circles in which she had been received at the time of her marriage. But as her income diminished, so did her acquaintances fall off; and at the period of Isabel's return, with the exception of Mr. Heaviside and one or two others, she was suffered to pine away in seclusion.

Isabel was greeted with querulous indifference until the explanation of the first ten minutes ; then as an heiress, with the means as well as the desire of contributing to her mother's comforts, all was joy and congratulation. Her incurable disease was for the time forgotten ; and although pain would occasionally draw down the muscles of her face, as soon as the pang was over so was the remembrance of her precarious situation. Wan and wasted as a spectre, she indulged in anticipation of again mixing with the fashionable world, and talked of chaperoning Isabel to private parties and public amusements, when she was standing on the brink of eternity. Isabel sighed as she listened to her mother, and observed her attenuated frame. Occasionally she would refer to her mother's state of health, and attempt to bring her to that serious state of mind which her awful situation demanded ; but in vain. Mrs. Revel would evade the subject. Before a week had passed she had set up an equipage, and called upon many of her quondam friends to announce the important intelligence of her daughter's wealth. Most of them had long before given orders not to be "at home to Mrs. Revel." The few to whom, from the remissness of their porters, she

obtained admittance, were satisfied at their servants' negli-
gence when they heard the intelligence which Mrs. Revel had
to communicate. "They were so delighted; Isabel was
always such a sweet girl; hoped that Mrs. Revel would not
be such a recluse as she had been, and that they should
prevail upon her to come to their parties!" An heiress is
of no little consequence when there are so many younger
brothers to provide for; and before a short month had flown
away, Mrs. Revel, to her delight, found that the cards and
invitations of no inconsiderable portion of the *beau monde*
covered the table of her confined drawing-room. To Isabel,
who perceived that her mother was sinking every day under
the exertion she went through, all this was a source of deep
regret. It occurred to her that to state her engagement
with Newton Forster would have some effect in preventing
this indirect suicide. She took an opportunity of confiding it
to her mother, who listened to her with astonishment.

"Isabel! what do I hear? What! that young man who
calls here so often! You, that can command a title, rank,
and fashion, engage yourself to a captain of an Indiaman!
Recollect, Isabel, that now your poor father is dead, I am
your legal protector; and without my permission I trust you
have too much sense of filial duty to think of marrying.
How you could venture to form an engagement without
consulting me is quite astonishing! Depend upon it, I shall
not give my consent; therefore, think no more about it."

How often do we thus see people, who make no scruples
of neglecting their duties, as eagerly assert their responsibility when it suits their convenience.

Isabel might have retorted, but she did not. In few
words she gave her mother to understand that she was decided, and then retired to dress for a splendid ball, at which,
more to please her mother than herself, she had consented
to be present.

It was the first party of any consequence to which Mrs.
Revel had been invited. She considered it as her re-*entrée*
into the fashionable world, and the presentation of her
daughter; she would not have missed it for any consideration. That morning she had felt more pain than usual, and
had been obliged to have recourse to restoratives; but once
more to join the gay and fashionable throng—the very idea

braced her nerves, rendered her callous to suffering, and indifferent to disease.

"I think," said Mrs. Revel to her maid—"I think," said she, panting, "you may lace me a little closer, Martyn."

"Indeed, madam, the holes nearly meet; it will hurt your side."

"No, no; I feel no pain this evening—there, that will do."

The lady's-maid finished her task, and left the room. Mrs. Revel rouged her wan cheeks, and, exhausted with fatigue and pain; tottered to an easy-chair, that she might recover herself a little before she went downstairs.

In a quarter of an hour, Isabel, who had waited for the services of Martyn, entered her mother's room to announce that she was ready. Her mother, who was sitting in the chair, leaning backwards, answered her not. Isabel went up to her, and looked her in the face—she was dead!

CHAPTER LII

" My dearest wife was like this maid,
And such my daughter might have been."
—SHAKSPEARE.

THE reader may be surprised at the positive and dictatorial language of Mr. John Forster relative to Newton's marriage, as detailed in a former chapter; but as Mr. John Forster truly observed, all the recompense which he had to expect for a life of exertion was to dispose of the fruits of his labour according to his own will. This he felt; and he considered it unreasonable that what he supposed a boyish attachment on the part of Newton was to overthrow all his preconcerted arrangements. Had Mr. Forster been able to duly appreciate the feelings of his nephew, he probably would not have been so decided; but Love had never been able to establish himself as an inmate of his breast. His life had been a life of toil. Love associates with idleness and ease. Mr. Forster was kind and cordial to his nephew as before, and the subject was not again renewed; nevertheless, he had made up his mind, and having stated that he would

348

alter his will, such was his intention, provided that his nephew did not upon mature reflection accede to his wishes. Newton once more enjoyed the society of Isabel, to whom he imparted all that had occurred. "I do not wish to play the prude," answered Isabel, "by denying that I am distressed at your uncle's decision; to say that I will never enter into his family without having received his consent, is saying more than my feelings will bear out; but I must and will say that I shall be most unwilling so to do. We must, therefore, as Madame de Fontanges did with the pirate captain, temporise, and I trust we shall be as successful." Newton, more rational than most young men in love, agreed with Isabel on the propriety of the measure, and satisfied with each other's attachment, they were by no means in a hurry to precipitate their marriage.

It may be recollected that Newton Forster felt convinced that the contents of the trunk which he picked up at sea, when mate of the coasting vessel, was the property of the Marquis de Fontanges. During their passage home in the *Windsor Castle* he had renewed the subject to M. de Fontanges, and from the description which he gave from memory, the latter appeared to be of the same opinion. The conversation had not been revived until some time after their arrival in England, when Newton, anxious to restore the articles, desired M. de Fontanges to communicate with the marquis, and request that he would appoint a day upon which he would call at his uncle's and identify the property. The marquis, who had never been informed by M. de Fontanges that the supposed relics of his lost wife remained, sighed at the memory of his buried happiness — buried in the vast grave, which defrauds the earth of its inherent rights—and consented to call upon the ensuing day. When the marquis arrived, accompanied by M. and Madame de Fontanges, he was received in the drawing-room by Mr. John Forster, who had brought from his chambers the packet in question, which had remained locked up in the iron safe ever since Newton had first committed it to his charge. After their introduction to each other, the marquis observed in English—

"I am giving you a great deal of trouble, unavailing indeed; for allowing that the articles should prove to be mine, the sight of them must be a source of renewed misery."

"Sir," replied Mr. John Forster, "the property does not belong to my nephew, and he has very properly reserved it until he could find out the legal owner. If the property is yours, we are bound to deliver it into your hands. There is an inventory attached to it," continued the old lawyer, putting on his spectacles, and reading, "one diamond ring—but perhaps it would be better that I should open the packet."

"Will you permit me to look at the diamond ring, sir?" observed M. de Fontanges. "The sight of that will identify the whole."

"There it is, sir," replied Mr. John Forster.

"It is, indeed, that of my poor sister-in-law!" said M. de Fontanges, taking it up to the marquis. "My brother, it is Louise's ring!"

"It is," cried the marquis passionately, "the ring that I placed in the centre of her *corbeille de mariage*. Alas! where is the hand which graced it!" and the marquis retreated to the sofa and covered his face.

"We have no occasion then to proceed further," observed Mr. John Forster, with emotion. "The other articles you, of course, recognise?"

"I do," replied Monsieur de Fontanges. "My brother had taken his passage in the same vessel, but was countermanded. Before he had time to select all his own baggage, which was mixed with that of his wife, the ship was blown out to sea, and proceeded on her voyage. These orders of merit were left with her jewels."

"I observe," said the old lawyer, "which I did not when Newton entrusted the packet to my charge, that the linen has not all the same marks; that of the adult is marked L. de M., while that which belonged to the child is marked J. de F. Was it the marquis's child?"

"It was; the linen of the mother was some belonging to her previous to her marriage. The maiden name was Louise de Montmorenci; that of the child has the initials of its name, Julie de Fontanges."

"Humph! I have my reasons for asking that question," replied the old lawyer. "Newton, do me the favour to step to my chambers and open the safe. You will find in it, on the right-hand side, another small bundle of linen ; bring it here. Stop, Newton, blow the dust out of the pipe of the key before you put it in, and be careful it is well inserted before you turn it, or you may strain the wards. In all other points, you may be as quick as you please. My Lord Marquis, will you allow me to offer you some refreshment ?—a glass of wine will be of service. Brother Nicholas, do me the favour to call Amber." Newton and Nicholas—both departed on their respective missions. Amber made her appearance.

"Papa," said Amber, "do you want me ?"

"Yes, my dear," said Mr. Forster, handing her the keys ; "go down to the cellaret and bring up some wine. I do not wish the servants to come in just now."

Amber reappeared with a small tray. She first handed it to the marquis, who was roused at her voice.

"Papa requests that you will take some wine, sir. It will be of service to you."

The marquis, who had looked earnestly in her face when she had spoken, took the wine, and drinking it off, bowed as he replaced the glass. He then sunk back on the sofa.

When the rap at the door announced the return of Newton, Mr. John Forster requested M. de Fontanges, in a low voice, to follow him, and directing Newton, whom they met on the stairs, to return, they proceeded to the dining-parlour.

"I have requested you to come down, sir," said Mr. John Forster, "that I might not, without being certain, raise hopes in your brother the marquis, which if not realised would create bitter feelings of disappointment ; but I remarked the initials on the linen of the child, and if my memory, which is not very bad, fails me not, we shall find corresponding ones in the packet now before us ; " and the old lawyer opened the bundle and displayed the contents, which proved to be marked as he had surmised.

"Most true," replied Monsieur de Fontanges. "They are the same, and of course part of the property which was picked up."

"Yes; but not picked up at the same time, or at the same spot, or by the same person. Those above-stairs were, as you know, picked up by my nephew, these by a brother, who is since dead ; and in these clothes an infant was also washed upon the beach."

" His child ! " exclaimed Monsieur de Fontanges. " Where was it buried ? "

" The child was restored to life, and is still living."

" If it is," replied Monsieur de Fontanges, " it can be no other than the young lady who just now called you father. The likeness to Madame la Marquise is most astonishing."

" It is as you suppose, sir," replied Mr. John Forster. " At my brother's death he bequeathed the little girl to my protection ; and I trust I have done justice to the deposit. Indeed, although an alien by blood, she is as dear to me as if she were my own daughter ; and," continued the old lawyer, hesitating a little, " although I have the satisfaction of restoring her to her father's arms, it will be a heavy blow to part with her ! When my brother spoke to me on the subject, I told him it was trouble and expense enough to bring up a child of one's own begetting. I little thought at the time how much more I should be vexed at parting with one of another's. However, with the bundle, she must be returned to the lawful owner. I have one more remark to make, sir. Do me the favour to look at that drawing of my poor brother's which hangs over the sideboard. Do you recognise the portrait ? "

" Triton ! " cried Monsieur de Fontanges ; " the dog which I gave my poor sister-in-law ! "

" You are indebted to that dog for the life of your niece. He brought her on shore, and laid her at my brother's feet ; but I have all the documents, which I will send for your perusal. The facts I consider so well established as to warrant a verdict in any court of justice ; and now, sir, I must leave you to make the communication as soon, and, at the same time, as cautiously, as you please. Newton, send Amber down to me."

We will pass over the scenes which followed in the dining-parlour and drawing-room. The Marquis de Fontanges discovered that he was blest with a daughter, at the same time that Amber learned her own history. In a few minutes Amber was led upstairs to the arms of her father, whose tears of sorrow at the loss of his wife were now mingled with those of delight, as he clasped his daughter to his heart.

" What obligations do I owe to your whole family, my dear friend ! " said the marquis to Newton.

"I will not deny it, sir," replied Newton; "but allow me to observe, that for the recovery of your daughter you are equally indebted to the generosity of your own relatives and your own feeling disposition. Had not Monsieur and Madame de Fontanges protected and assisted me in my distress; had not you, instead of throwing me into prison, set me at liberty, you never would have known where your daughter was to be found. Had not one of my uncles hastened to the relief of the vessel in distress, and the other protected your little girl after his death, she would not have been now in existence. My gratitude for your kindness induced me to remain by your ship, and subsequently to rescue you from the pirate, or you would not have now been a prisoner in this country—an evil which, under divine Providence, has been changed to a blessing, by restoring to you your daughter. We have all, I trust, done our duty, and this happy issue is our full reward."

"Humph!" observed the old lawyer.

CHAPTER LIII

"Thus far our chronicle—and now we pause,
Though not for want of matter, but 'tis time."
—BYRON.

AMBER, or Julie de Fontanges as we must now call her, quitted the abode of her kind protector in such distress, that it was evident she regretted the discovery which had been made. She was too young to be aware of the advantages of high birth, and her removal was for some time a source of unfeigned regret. It appeared to her that nothing could compensate for the separation from her supposed father, who doted on her, from Mrs. Forster, who had watched over her, from Nicholas, who amused her, and from Newton, whom she loved as a brother. But the idea of going to a foreign country, and never seeing them or William Aveleyn again, and though last, not least, to find that she was not an Englishwoman, and in future must not rejoice at their victories over her own nation, occasioned many a burst of tears when left alone to her own meditations. It was long before the devotion of her father, and the fascinating attentions of M. and Madame de Fontanges, could induce her to be resigned to her new condition. Mr. John Forster felt his bereavement more deeply than could have been supposed. For many days after the departure of Julie he seldom spoke, never made his appearance except at dinnertime, and as soon as the meal was finished hastened to his chambers, where he remained very late. Intense application was the remedy which he had selected to dispel his care, and fill up the vacuum created by the absence of his darling child.

" Newton," said he one evening, as they discussed a bottle of port, " have you considered what I proposed? I confess to you that I am more than ever anxious for the match; I cannot part with that dear child, and you can bring her back to me."

"I have reflected, sir; but the case must be viewed in a very different light. You might affiance your adopted daughter at her early age, but the Marquis de Fontanges may not be so inclined; nay, further, sir, it is not impossible that he may dislike the proposed match. He is of a very noble family."

"I have thought on that subject," replied Mr. John Forster; "but our family is as well descended, and quite well enough for any Frenchman, let him be a marquis or even a duke. Is that the only obstacle you intend to raise —or if this is removed will you again plead your attachment to another?"

" It is the only one which I mean to raise at present, sir. I acknowledge Julie de Fontanges to be a sweet girl, and as a relation I have long been much attached to her."

" Humph!" replied the old lawyer; " I always thought you a sensible lad—we shall see."

Now, be it observed that there was a certain degree of the Jesuitical on the part of our friend Newton on this occasion —excusable only from his wish that the mortification of his uncle at the disappointment of his hopes should not be occasioned by any further resistance on his part.

To M. de Fontanges, who was aware of Newton's attachment to Isabel, he had, previous to the discovery which had taken place, communicated the obstacle to his union, raised

354

by the pertinacity of his uncle. After the removal of Julie, M. de Fontanges acquainted his brother with the wishes of Mr. John Forster, and explained to him how much they were at.variance with those of Newton.

The first time that Newton called upon the marquis, the latter, shaking him warmly by the hand, said, " I have been informed, my dear Newton, by my brother, of the awkward predicament in which you are placed by the wish of your uncle, that you should marry my Julie when she grows up. Believe me when I say it, there is no man to whom I would sooner confide the happiness of my daughter, and that no consideration would induce me to refuse you, if you really sought her hand; but I know your wishes, and your attachment to Miss ,Revel, therefore be quite easy on the subject. Your uncle made his proposition when Julie had no father to be consulted. The case is now different ; and for your sake I intend for a time to injure myself in the opinion of your good relation. I shall assume, I trust, what, if ever I had it, would be immediately sacrificed to gratitude—I mean, high aristocratical pride ; and should your uncle make the proposal, refuse it.upon the grounds that you are not noble by descent. No one will deny your nobility on any other point. Do you understand me, Newton ? and will my so doing be conformable to your wishes ? "

" It will, Monsieur le Marquis, and I thank you most sincerely."

" Then make no objection when he proposes the match a second time ; leave all the obloquy on my shoulders," said the marquis, smiling.

This arrangement having been made, it was not surprising that Newton heard his uncle's renewal of the proposition with such calmness and apparent acquiescence.

" We dine with the marquis to-morrow, Newton," observed Mr. John Forster ; " I shall take an opportunity after dinner of requesting a few minutes' interview,.when I shall put the question to him."

" Certainly, sir, if you think right," replied Newton.

: " Well, I'm glad the dear girl has changed that foolish name of Amber. What could possess my brother ? Julie is very fine, nevertheless ; but then she was christened by French people."

The next day the parties met at dinner. Isabel Revel had been asked; and having heard from Madame de Fontanges of the plan agreed upon, and anxious to see the old lawyer, she had consented to join the party. The dinner passed off as most dinners do when the viands and wines are good, and everybody is inclined to be happy. Isabel was placed next to Mr. Forster, who, without knowing who she was, felt much pleased with the deference and attention of so beautiful a young woman.

"Newton," said his uncle, when the ladies retired and the gentlemen packed up their chairs, "who was that young lady who sat next to me?"

"The young lady, my dear uncle, whom I did wish to introduce to you as my intended wife — Miss Isabel Revel."

"Humph!—why, you never spoke to her before dinner, or paid her any common civility!"

"You forget, sir, your injunctions, and——"

"That's no reason, nephew, why you should forget common civility. I requested that you would not marry the young lady; but I never desired you to commit an act of rudeness. She is a very nice young person; and politeness is but a trifle, although marriage is a very serious thing."

In pursuance of his plans, when the gentlemen rose, Mr. John Forster requested a few minutes' conversation with the marquis, who, bowing politely, showed the way to a small study on the same floor.

Mr. Forster immediately stated his wish that an engagement should be formed between his nephew and Julie de Fontanges.

"Mr. Forster," replied the marquis, drawing up proudly, "the obligations I am under to your family are so great, that there are but few points in which I could refuse you; and I therefore am quite distressed that, of this proposal, I am obliged to decline the honour. You may be ignorant, Mr. Forster, that the family of the De Fontanges is one of the oldest in France; and with every respect for you and your nephew, and all gratitude for your kindness, I cannot permit my daughter to form a *mésalliance.*"

"A *mésalliance!*—humph! I presume, sir, in plain English it means marrying beneath her rank in life?"

THE MERCHANT SERVICE

The marquis bowed.

"I beg to observe, sir, said Mr. John Forster, "that our family is a very old one. I can show you our pedigree. It has lain for some years by the side of your daughter's bundle in the iron safe."

"I have no doubt of the excellence of your family, Mr. Forster. I can only express my deep regret that it is not noble. Excuse me, Mr. Forster; except you can prove that——"

"Why, I could prove it by purchasing a dozen marquisates, if I thought proper!"

"Granted, Mr. Forster. In our country they are to be purchased; but we make a great difference between the parvenus of the present day and the *ancienne noblesse.*"

"Well, Mr. Marquis, just as you please; but I consider myself quite as good as a French marquis," replied Mr. Forster, in a tone of irritation.

"Better than many, I have no doubt; but still we draw the line. Noble blood, Mr. Forster."

"Noble fiddlestick! Monsieur le Marquis, in this country, and the inhabitants are not fools, we allow money to weigh against rank. It purchases that, as it does everything else, except heaven. Now, Monsieur le Marquis——"

"Excuse me, sir; no money will purchase the hand of Julie de Fontanges," replied the marquis.

"Well then, Monsieur le Marquis, I should think that the obligations you are under in restoring your daughter to your arms——"

"Warrants your asking for her back again, Mr. Forster?" replied the marquis haughtily. "A labourer might find this diamond solitaire that's now upon my finger. Does it therefore follow that I am to make him a present of it?"

"Humph!" ejaculated Mr. Forster, much affronted with the comparison.

"In short, my dear sir, anything which you or your family can think of, which it is in our power to grant, will make us most happy; but to sully the blood of the most ancient——"

John Forster would hear no more; he quitted the room and walked upstairs before the marquis had completed his speech. When he entered the drawing-room, his countenance plainly expressed his disappointment. Like all men who have toiled for riches, he had formed plans in which he considered his wealth was to command success, and had overlooked every obstacle which might present itself against the completion of his wishes.

"Newton," said he, as they stood apart near the window, "you have been a good lad in not persisting to thwart my views, but that French marquis, with his folly and his *ancienne noblesse,* has overthrown all my plans. Now, I shall not interfere with yours. Introduce me to Miss what's her name; she is a very fine girl, and from what I saw of her during dinner, I like her very much."

Isabel exerted herself to please, and succeeded. Satisfied with his nephew's choice, flattered by his previous apparent submission, and disgusted with the marquis, Mr. John Forster thought no more of Mademoiselle de Fontanges. His consent was voluntary, and in a short time Isabel Revel changed her name.

It was about five months after Newton's marriage that he received a letter from the Board, appointing him to the command of a ship. Newton handed the letter over to Mr. Forster.

"I presume, sir, it is your wish that I should accept the offer?"

"What offer?" said the old lawyer, who was reading through a case for counsel's opinion. "*Melville*—for Madras and China. Why, Newton, I really do not see any occasion for your going afloat again. There is an old proverb: 'The pitcher that goes often to the well is broken at last.' You're not tired of your wife already?"

"I hope not, sir; but I thought it might be your wish."

"It's my wish that you should stay at home. A poor man may go to sea, because he stands a chance to come home rich; but a man who has money in hand and in prospect, if he goes to sea he is a fool. Follow your profession as long as you require it, but no longer."

"Why, then, do you work so hard, my dear sir," said Isabel, leaning over the old gentleman, and kissing him in gratitude for his decision, "Surely you can afford to relax a little now?"

"Why do I work so hard, Isabel?" replied Mr. Forster, looking up at her through his spectacles. "Why, you expect to have a family, do you not?"

Isabel blushed; the expectation was undeniable.

"Well then, I presume the children will have no objection to find a few thousands more to be divided among them by-and-by—will they, daughter?"

The conversation was interrupted by the entry of a servant with a letter; Mr. Forster broke the seal and looked at the signature.

"Humph! from the proud old marquis. 'Very sorry, for a short period, to have fallen in your good opinion—should have rejoiced to have called Newton my son-in-law!' Humph! 'Family pride all assumed—Newton's happiness at stake—trust the deceit will be pardoned, and a renewal of former intimacy.' Why, Newton, is all this true?"

"Ask Isabel, sir," replied Newton, smiling.

"Well then, Isabel, is all this true?"

"Ask Newton, sir," replied Isabel, kissing him. "The fact is, my dear sir, I could not afford to part with Newton even to please you, so we made up a little plot."

"Humph!—made up a little plot—well—I sha'n't alter my will, nevertheless;" and Mr. Forster recommenced the reading of his brief.

Such is the history of Newton Forster, which, like most novels or plays, has been wound up with marriage. The last time that I appeared before my readers, they were dissatisfied with the termination of my story; they considered I had deprived them of "a happy marriage," to which, as an undoubted right, they were entitled, after wading through three tedious volumes. As I am anxious to keep on good terms with the public, I hasten to repair the injury which it has sustained by stating that about three years after the marriage of Newton Forster, the following paragraph appeared in the several papers of the metropolis :—

"Yesterday, by special license, the Right Honourable William Lord Aveleyn to Mademoiselle Julie de Fontanges, only daughter of the Marquis de Fontanges, late Governor of the Island of Bourbon. The marriage was to have been

solemnised in December last, but was postponed in consequence of the death of the late Lord Aveleyn. After the
ceremony, the happy couple," &c. &c. &c.

.   .   .   .   .   .

And now, most arbitrary public, I consider that I have
made the *amende honorable,* and that we are quits; for if you
were minus a happy marriage in the last work, you have a
couple to indemnify you in the present.

THE END